THE STONES OF NAPLES

THE STONES OF NAPLES

Church Building in Angevin Italy

1266–1343

CAROLINE BRUZELIUS

YALE UNIVERSITY PRESS

NEW HAVEN AND LONDON

Designed by Gillian Malpass

Printed in China

Library of Congress Cataloging-in-Publication Data

Bruzelius, Caroline Astrid.
The stones of Naples : church building in Angevin Italy,
1266–1343 / by Caroline Bruzelius.– 1st ed.
p. cm.
Includes bibliographical references and index.
ISBN 0-300-10039-6 (cl : alk. paper)
1. Church architecture–Italy--Naples. 2. Architecture,
Gothic–Italy–Naples. 3. Church architecture–France–Influence.
4.Anjou, House of–Art patronage. 5. Naples (Kingdom)–Civilization.
I. Title.
NA5621.N2B78 2004
726.5'0945'730904–dc22

2003018954

A catalogue record for this book is available from
The British Library

Frontispiece
Naples, San Lorenzo Maggiore, interior from the west (author)

Contents

Preface

There can be no better example of the limitations imposed by stylistic definitions than those presented by the term "Italian Gothic," which for more than a century has been diagnosed as strangely intractable, unreceptive, and stubbornly resistant to the style that dominated the High Middle Ages in Europe. The buildings of the Kingdom of Naples under the French kings (the "Angevins") in the thirteenth and fourteenth centuries, from the conquest of Charles of Anjou in 1266 to the death of his grandson, Robert the Wise, in 1343, have been seen as a solution to this anomaly: here were French rulers in a Francocentric court who introduced, above all under Charles of Anjou, French architecture executed by French architects and builders. This has been the cliché or the topos, and there has been little consideration of whether it really works (I will in this book suggest something quite different: that the colonial culture of the French in Italy led to a kind of conservatism, even ossification, of artistic form). In any event, the subject is left out of most books on Gothic architecture and is even absent from many studies of medieval architecture in Italy. The Gothic churches of the Kingdom of Naples are a minor footnote, one in which their "Frenchness" is assumed and emphasized at the expense of other issues and concerns.

This volume is a small step towards enlarging the vision of the "Gothic" world to include southern Italy, although this term as a definition of the style of these monuments is nothing if not problematic. Indeed, for that reason, the use of the term "Gothic" will be mostly avoided as essentially meaningless in the context of the particular solutions found in the design and erection of the churches of this part of Europe. I shall also avoid describing the buildings of this period as "Angevin," for this adjective also creates confusion, given the enormous variety and eclecticism of the material production of the kingdom and court of Naples. "Angevin" as a description tends to suggest that the monuments were exclusively the result of royal patronage, whereas, as will be

seen, both clerical and lay individuals were often the primary movers: thus "Angevin" can only usefully describe a phase of south Italian history and its kings, not its monuments. And both terms are particularly inappropriate in view of the powerful revival of Italian building traditions in the 1290s and afterwards.

My study concerns the monuments of three rulers, their wives, administrators, and courtiers. But in the vast and diverse terrain that was the Kingdom of Naples, it would of course be impossible to produce a comprehensive study, and I make no pretense of doing so. My focus is primarily on a series of Neapolitan churches, with some discussion of other large-scale monuments elsewhere in the kingdom where they illuminate certain types of issues. I have left out of my study, or treated only in passing, broad areas of stylistically coherent local building, such as the remarkable churches of the Abruzzo (L'Aquila, Atri, Larino, and elsewhere) or those of the Principality of Taranto. Instead of a comprehensive and exhaustive overview of the entire kingdom, my concern has been to provide an analysis of some significant monuments, especially those of Naples; to examine some themes in the architectural production of southern Italy in these years; and to produce something along the lines of a social history of architecture, one that attempts to solve certain issues of chronology and style, of course, but which is primarily concerned with placing the monuments of Naples in the broader context of the courts and capitals of medieval Europe. I would like to be able to see buildings as part of a dimly discernible social process, not only in terms of their meaning and function, but also in terms of their conception and production. So it is issues such as the shift towards mendicant spirituality, for example, that interest me, a process that takes place in large part as what Paul Binski has so charmingly described as the "feminine surge" in the early fourteenth century. As a tool for readers I have added at the conclusion of the narrative a checklist of monuments in the Kingdom of Naples, again with no

1 *(facing page)*   Santa Maria di Realvalle, south flank of south aisle (author)

pretense of providing a comprehensive discussion or bibliography.

The Angevin court of Naples was intimately tied not only to the courts of the north (in particular that of France), but also to the papacy in Rome and then Avignon, of which its king was a vassal. The city was furthermore in the center of a sea that had been dominated for centuries by Byzantium and Islam, and where the conclusive failure (1291) of the Latin kingdoms of the Holy Land may have brought particular intensity to the experience of French colonialization in southern Italy. Although there is little evidence that the Angevins had the interest and receptivity to other cultures that had existed in the courts of Roger II or Frederick II, the Mediterranean exposure of the kingdom meant that it was always at the crossroads of trade, ideas, and travel east to west and north to south; the Mediterranean was the "highway" to the East and the Holy Land, and Naples was one of the central stations en route. So the issue of receptivity on the part of the rulers themselves is perhaps irrelevant: if northern courts have been described as "social entrepôts" of diversity and heterogeneous cultures, it cannot be sufficiently emphasized how much this was also the case in southern Italy because of its heterogeneous populations, languages, religious practices, and cultures. It will be seen that one of the primary issues confronting the second Angevin ruler, Charles II, was precisely the creation of some sense of national identity and unity through architectural projects.

We are thus concerned here with issues that have to do with court cultures as well as colonial environments. With regard to the latter, the issues were in many ways similar to those of the Crusading kingdoms in the Holy Land. In each, the need to maintain a permanent and stable population of settlers required a series of strategies, and as part of these the foundation of churches and monasteries, the cultivation of the mendicants and the other religious orders, and the construction of tombs and dynastic monuments, all played a vital part.

Another web spun across the surface of this study is that of the religious cultures of the period, and in particular the importance of the Kingdom of Naples as both a bastion of orthodoxy (especially under Charles II) and a refuge later for religious dissidence (with the notorious support of Queen Sancia of Mallorca and her brother Philip). Fringe religious movements had a long history in southern Italy, but perhaps no monument embodies these tendencies more than the majestic Neapolitan convent of Santa Chiara, which played an especially important role in the protection of Spiritual Franciscans in the troubled decades of the 1320s and 1330s.

This study has been structured in relation to the reigns of the first three generations of Angevin rulers of Naples, for the divergent interests, policies, origins, and ambitions of each ruling couple determined the cultural and material life of the kingdom during their reigns. But in no way is this organizational structure intended to ignore or diminish the vital contributions of the ecclesiastical, administrative, courtly, and mercantile elites of the realm, for, as will be seen, private individuals and charitable associations were of fundamental importance in shaping the spiritual and material culture of the kingdom. Individuals such as the Archbishop of Naples, Filippo Minutolo, his contemporary the great Bartolomeo da Capua, and others closely tied both to the court and to their native cities were as important as the royal family in creating the architectural fabric of southern Italy. Until the recent work of the past few years, and in particular that of Giovanni Vitolo and his students, the historical tradition had largely ignored lay patronage, and it is part of the purpose of this narrative to reinsert it. It is equally important to integrate into the story the role of a number of royal and noble women: although the patronage of the dowager queen Margaret of Tonnerre (Charles of Anjou's second wife) occurred in France, and therefore falls outside of the scope of this study, that of her successors, Mary of Hungary and Sancia of Mallorca, as well as other women of the court and the cities, forms an important part of this volume and provides rich topics for further study.

It is difficult, however, to construct a coherent and continuous narrative on the architecture of southern Italy in any period. Wars, earthquakes, and – at times as devastating as the former two combined – changes in style and taste (especially redecorations in the Baroque period) have destroyed or transformed the buildings. Much of the archival material has been lost, most particularly the Angevin Registers, burned in 1943, until then perhaps the most important single medieval archive to survive into the twentieth century.

The bombs and fires of the Second World War are only among the most recent of 700 years of misfortunes and disasters that stretch from the outbreak of the War of the Vespers in 1282 (only sixteen years after the arrival of the new French regime) to the earthquake of 1980. The invasion of Calabria, Apulia, Basilicata, and much of Campania by Sicilian and Spanish troops in the war of 1282 meant that much in the path of the invaders was obliterated, and many towns were abandoned and inaccessible until the peace treaty of 1302. The monuments erected by the Angevins before the war would have been mostly damaged or destroyed. Tragic though all this is, by far the greatest source of devastation in southern Italy has been earthquakes, and for the buildings in this study especially those of 1349 and 1456. The consequences of these disasters, in the form of the repairs and rebuildings of many of the buildings under consideration, will form an important part of the narrative.

No "whole cloth" can be created from this tattered fabric: our narrative must be pieced together like a patchwork quilt, with the knowledge that there are innumerable *lacunae* that might have filled gaps and answered questions. I have attempted here a series of glimpses, insights, and hypotheses into the architecture produced during the eight decades of rapidly changing circumstances between about 1270 and 1350 in the Kingdom of Naples. Sometimes the focus will be tight on a certain monument, at other times opened broad and large. There are certain periods when a cultural policy in architecture emerges clear and strong, as after 1294, when Charles II definitively returned to Naples, but this type of consistency is the exception rather than the rule. Local traditions, regional building methods, the need to adapt extraneous ideas to local materials and workmanship, and the influence of Roman models and "provincial" styles, were persistent countercurrents to royal attempts to systematize or impose an architectural style related either to French or to broader European tendencies. The issues were sometimes the result of personal taste or ideological preference; at other times decisions seem to have been made in relation to the types of construction expertise available. Within the kingdom, and even within the royal family, there was a broad range of artistic taste, and strong preferences for different religious orders. This is especially evident in matters of burial.

The narrative of this book, fractured and incomplete though it may be, is placed against the grid of the intellectual structures that have organized our knowledge of the art and architecture of the past into categories and compartments. But as southern Italy, and perhaps Italian Gothic architecture in general, does not readily conform to the system, so it has usually seemed necessary to explain the anomalies as the deficiency of the period and place in question, and wrestle with the intractability of the evidence rather than redefine the categories. As noted above, Italian Gothic has been seen as obtusely resistant to the powerful visual and structural advances of the Gothic style that prevailed elsewhere in Europe, and the first three generations of French control in Naples are seen as a period when this difficulty was at least briefly rectified by close and immediate contact with patrons, architects, and masons from the north. The rulers of Naples have thus been seen as second only to the Cistercians as importers of Gothic forms to Italy –

a second moment when artistic developments in the Italian peninsula and those of the north were (at last) synchronized. I shall suggest in this volume that there were other and often more active architectonic values at work, and that although some of the Angevin patrons might indeed have desired artistic forms that recalled their homeland, or provided the aura of ultramontane sophistication (as at Santa Maria della Consolazione in Altomonte), the production of these foreign forms usually presented technical difficulties. The reason why, in the end, there is little here that "looks French" is not only because the materials were different, the labor force often either scarce or possessing other kinds of expertise, the patrons interested in other issues, and the king himself frequently insolvent, but also because the issue of "Frenchness" itself was a complicated and highly charged concept. There are only a few surviving works of architecture or sculpture that attest to French workmanship (the tomb of Isabelle of Aragon in Cosenza cathedral, parts of the church of Sant'Eligio al Mercato in Naples); far more common are examples of monuments where a certain aura of "Frenchness" is achieved through the use of Gothic signifiers (pointed arches, window tracery, stained glass, and crocket capitals). The cathedral of Naples, as we shall see, is an interesting example of this kind of "bilingualism." At the same time, the roles of the Franciscans and the papal curia (filled with French clergy) in the process of the transmission of northern architectural ideas to Italy, have generally been underestimated. Most common, however, are monuments in which there is a clear return to local architectonic values, especially the use of ancient columns, wooden truss ceilings, high transepts, and flat wall surfaces. What is unique about the architecture of the Angevins in the Kingdom of Naples is not so much its "Frenchness" as its ability to incorporate certain French ideas within an architectural framework that reflected, and sometimes reinvented, the traditional structural language of southern Italy.

Why this is so is the story of this book.

★　★　★

For a book that has taken so long to write the list of people to thank is endless, as is the list of institutions that have in various ways assisted my research and the creation of the photographic archive that this study required. I started the project with simultaneous fellowships from the American Academy in Rome and the Fulbright Commission in Italy, and continued it with regular support from Duke University (including Women's Studies at Duke), a grant from the Center for

Advanced Study in the Visual Arts in 1988, as well as generous support from the Rockefeller Foundation at Bellagio, the Guggenheim Foundation, and the great snowy peace of the Clark Art Institute for the final revisions. The Getty Photographic Archive, the Samuel H. Kress Foundation, and the Graham Foundation supported the photographic campaigns that were indispensable to the project. Some of my happiest memories of long treks through remote parts of southern Italy were in the company of the photographers who worked with me, in particular the late Barbara Bini, Chester Brummel, Massimo Velo, and Giovanni Genova.

Many prelates and local historians were generously assisted me to gain access to the monuments. At the American Academy in Rome, Marina Lella made countless telephone calls to superintendencies to provide access to sites and clear the path for photographic work. I would especially like to thank the Soprintendenza ai Beni Ambientali ed Architettonici of Naples, as well as the superintendencies of Bari, L'Aquila, Caserta and Potenza for their generous assistance.

Nothing could have been done without libraries and librarians and their staffs, and I warmly thank Christina Huemer and Antonella Bucci of the American Academy in Rome, as well as the late Leonard Boyle of the Biblioteca Apostolica Vaticana, the Hertziana, the Biblioteca Nazionale in Naples, the Istituto Italiano per gli Studi Storici and its director, Stefano Palmieri, and the library of Duke University.

It was a pleasant surprise when I first started working in Italy to find such a generous welcome among medievalists and architectural historians, beginning with that of the late Richard Krautheimer. Peter Fergusson and Serena Romano both bravely slogged through early versions of this manuscript. I thank also, and most warmly, Julian Gardner, Valentino Pace, Roberto Rusconi, André Vauchez, Mary Stroll, Reginald Foster, Antonio Cadei, Jürgen Krüger, Hank Millon, Giovanni Vitolo, Francesco Aceto, Alessandra Perriccioli Saggese, Marina Righetti Tosti-Croce, Rosario Villari, Pina Belli d'Elia, Mario Agrimi, Robert Suckale, Christian Freigang, Michael Davis, Stephen Murray, Rosalba di Meglio, Francis Newton, Anne Scott, Mario Gaglione, Ronald Witt, Christian Brebbia, Willibald Sauerländer. Pierluigi Leone de Castris, Ronald Musto, Ferdinano Bologna, Attilio Spanò, Peter Kurmann, Brigitte Kurmann-Schwarz, Jill Caskey, and Angelo Ambrosi, all of whom were generous in their comments, questions, corrections, and assistance.

In Naples Dott.ssa Filomena Sardella, Direttore del Museo e del Palazzo Reale di Napoli, was invariably helpful, and I also particularly thank architects Guido Gullo and Cosimo Tarì of the Soprintendenza ai Beni Ambientali ed Architettonici di Napoli e Provincia. In the cathedral of Naples Don Domenico Felleca and his staff facilitated access to all parts of the buildings, and at San Lorenzo Maggiore Don Bernardino was also willing to open all doors and spend hours with me up on the roof.

Above all, I owe a deep debt of gratitude to Gillian Malpass, who has worked with me on this book with infinite grace and goodwill.

I dedicate this book to my son, Anders Wallace, who began at the same time.

Note on Nomenclature and Terminology

The Kingdom of Sicily has gone by several titles from its unification by the Normans to its absorption into the modern state of Italy. Because the outbreak of the War of the Vespers in 1282 effectively separated the island of Sicily from the rest of southern Italy, Sicily and Sicilian monuments do not enter into this study; they have their own history under Spanish rule and influence. It has therefore seemed more appropriate in this context to adopt consistently the title of the Kingdom of Naples, even though Charles of Anjou in 1266 became King of Sicily. When I refer to France and things French it is to the geographical parameters of the France of Louis IX.

The names of the individuals in this study are known to us through medieval texts that provide a wide range of spellings in both Latin and French. I have usually chosen to use the language of the nationality of the individual (thus Pierre d'Angicourt or Pierre de Chaules and Giovanni Pipino da Barletta or Bartolomeo da Capua), except in those rare instances when an English equivalent is current and well known (Charles of Anjou, Robert the Wise). The kingdom remained perennially multilingual, and so is this book.

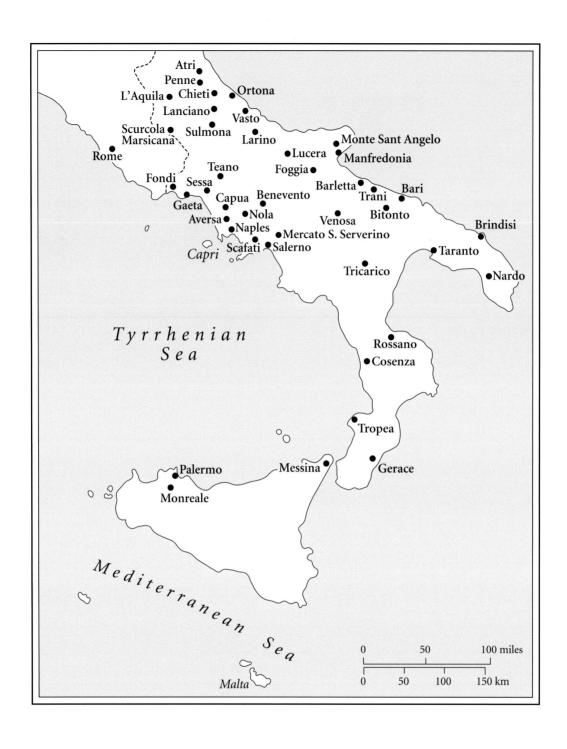

Atri
Penne
L'Aquila Chieti Ortona
Lanciano
Vasto
Scurcola Sulmona
Marsicana Larino Monte Sant Angelo
Rome Lucera Manfredonia
Teano Foggia
Fondi Sessa Barletta
Gaeta Capua Benevento Trani Bari
Aversa Nola Bitonto
Naples Venosa Brindisi
Scafati Mercato S. Serverino
Capri Salerno Tricarico Taranto
Nardo

Tyrrhenian Sea

Rossano
Cosenza

Tropea

Palermo Messina Gerace
Monreale

Mediterranean Sea

Malta

0   50   100 miles

0   50   100   150 km

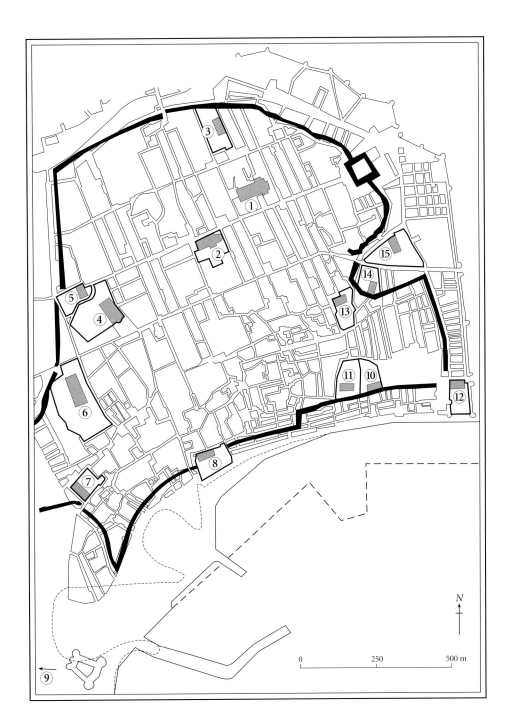

Plan of Naples in 1343 (after Krüger)

1 Cathedral
2 San Lorenzo Maggiore (Franciscan)
3 Santa Maria Donnaregina (Clarissan)
4 San Domenico (Dominican)
5 San Pietro a Maiella (Celestinian)
6 Santa Chiara (Franciscan and Clarissan)
7 Santa Maria la Nuova (Franciscan)
8 San Pietro Martire (Dominican)

9 Santa Croce e Trinita (Franciscan)
10 Sant'Eligio
11 San Giovanni a Mare
12 Santa Maria del Carmine (Carmelite)
13 Sant'Agostino (Augustinian)
14 Santa Maria Egiziaca (Augustinian)
15 Annunziata

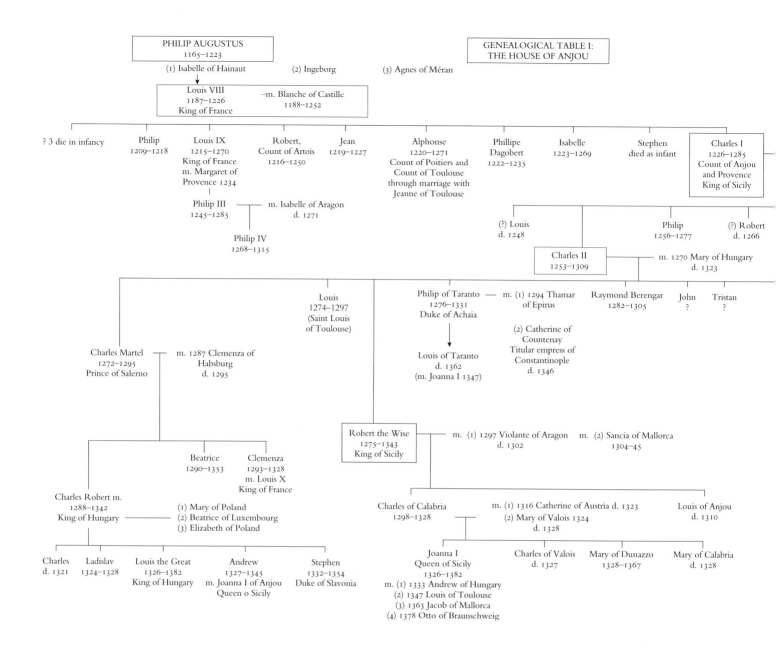

PHILIP AUGUSTUS
1165–1223

GENEALOGICAL TABLE I:
THE HOUSE OF ANJOU

(1) Isabelle of Hainaut   (2) Ingeborg   (3) Agnes of Méran

Louis VIII
1187–1226   —m. Blanche of Castille
King of France   1188–1252

? 3 die in infancy | Philip 1209–1218 | Louis IX 1215–1270 King of France m. Margaret of Provence 1234 | Robert, Count of Artois 1216–1250 | Jean 1219–1227 | Alphonse 1220–1271 Count of Poitiers and Count of Toulouse through marriage with Jeanne of Toulouse | Phillipe Dagobert 1222–1235 | Isabelle 1223–1269 | Stephen died as infant | Charles I 1226–1285 Count of Anjou and Provence King of Sicily

Philip III
1245–1285   — m. Isabelle of Aragon
                        d. 1271

Philip IV
1268–1315

(?) Louis d. 1248   Philip 1256–1277   (?) Robert d. 1266

Charles II
1253–1309   — m. 1270 Mary of Hungary
                        d. 1323

Louis 1274–1297 (Saint Louis of Toulouse) | Philip of Taranto 1276–1331 Duke of Achaia | — m. (1) 1294 Thamar of Epirus | Raymond Berengar 1282–1305 | John ? | Tristan ?

(2) Catherine of Countenay
Titular empress of
Constantinople
d. 1346

Louis of Taranto
d. 1362
(m. Joanna I 1347)

Charles Martel
1272–1295   — m. 1287 Clemenza of
Prince of Salerno   Habsburg
                              d. 1295

Robert the Wise
1275–1343   — m. (1) 1297 Violante of Aragon   m. (2) Sancia of Mallorca
King of Sicily   d. 1302   1304–45

Beatrice 1290–1353 | Clemenza 1293–1328 m. Louis X King of France

Charles Robert m.
1288–1342   (1) Mary of Poland
King of Hungary   (2) Beatrice of Luxembourg
                        (3) Elizabeth of Poland

Charles of Calabria
1298–1328   m. (1) 1316 Catherine of Austria d. 1323   Louis of Anjou
                        (2) Mary of Valois 1324   d. 1310
                        d. 1328

Charles d. 1321 | Ladislav 1324–1328 | Louis the Great 1326–1382 King of Hungary | Andrew 1327–1345 m. Joanna I of Anjou Queen o Sicily | Stephen 1332–1354 Duke of Slavonia

Joanna I
Queen of Sicily
1326–1382
m. (1) 1333 Andrew of Hungary
(2) 1347 Louis of Toulouse
(3) 1363 Jacob of Mallorca
(4) 1378 Otto of Braunschweig

Charles of Valois d. 1327 | Mary of Dunazzo 1328–1367 | Mary of Calabria d. 1328

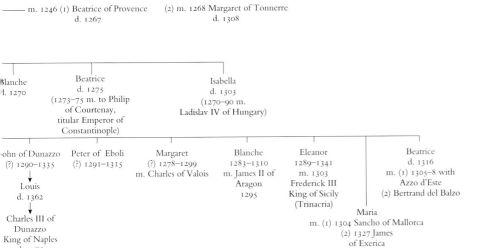

m. 1246 (1) Beatrice of Provence   (2) m. 1268 Margaret of Tonnerre
           d. 1267   d. 1308

Blanche
d. 1270

Beatrice
d. 1275
(1273–75 m. to Philip
of Courtenay,
titular Emperor of
Constantinople)

Isabella
d. 1303
(1270–90 m.
Ladislav IV of Hungary)

John of Dunazzo
(?) 1290–1335

Peter of Eboli
(?) 1291–1315

Margaret
(?) 1278–1299
m. Charles of Valois

Blanche
1283–1310
m. James II of
Aragon
1295

Eleanor
1289–1341
m. 1303
Frederick III
King of Sicily
(Trinacria)

Beatrice
d. 1316
m. (1) 1305–8 with
Azzo d'Este
(2) Bertrand del Balzo

Louis
d. 1362

Charles III of
Dunazzo
King of Naples
d. 1386

Maria
m. (1) 1304 Sancho of Mallorca
(2) 1327 James
of Exerica

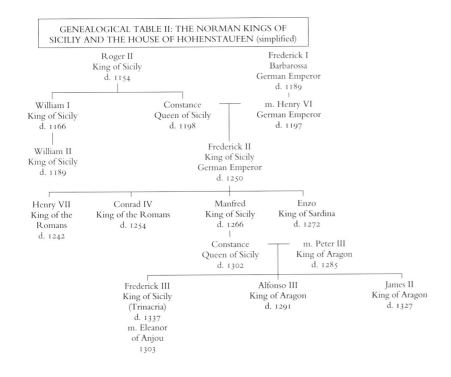

GENEALOGICAL TABLE II: THE NORMAN KINGS OF
SICILIY AND THE HOUSE OF HOHENSTAUFEN (simplified)

Roger II
King of Sicily
d. 1154

Frederick I
Barbarossa
German Emperor
d. 1189

William I
King of Sicily
d. 1166

Constance
Queen of Sicily
d. 1198

m. Henry VI
German Emperor
d. 1197

William II
King of Sicily
d. 1189

Frederick II
King of Sicily
German Emperor
d. 1250

Henry VII
King of the
Romans
d. 1242

Conrad IV
King of the Romans
d. 1254

Manfred
King of Sicily
d. 1266

Enzo
King of Sardina
d. 1272

Constance
Queen of Sicily
d. 1302

m. Peter III
King of Aragon
d. 1285

Frederick III
King of Sicily
(Trinacria)
d. 1337
m. Eleanor
of Anjou
1303

Alfonso III
King of Aragon
d. 1291

James II
King of Aragon
d. 1327

Introduction

In Italy, where Dante is second only to mother's milk, the tale of the conquest by Charles of Anjou, the defeats of Manfred and Conradin, and the reputations of the French rulers of Naples are almost as familiar as life itself. But the connection of this history to the material remains of the past is remote even to those suckled at the breast of the poet, and to the rest of the world the story of Charles and his successors, and the history of their buildings, is barely known. Although medieval southern Italy is familiar for its Norman and Swabian buildings, the architecture of the Angevins, which dominates Naples and many other south Italian cities, has rarely been considered outside the local context.

The character and design of the churches reflect the political tendencies of each reign, from the heavy-handed colonialism of Charles I (1266–85), to the search for integration under his son Charles II (1289–1309), and finally to the refined and sophisticated court of Robert (1309-1343) and Sancia – a court culture to which, however, a radical fringe of Spiritual Franciscanism closely allied to the queen added a strange and brooding touch. Under Charles II and Robert new sources of influence, including those from Spain (especially Catalonia), Hungary, and Tuscany, came to dominate the scene. For painting, much of this story has been told with great brilliance by Ferdinando Bologna in his monumental study of the Angevin court of Naples. But the architecture, especially that of religious buildings, has been only sporadically explored, and that exploration has tended to oversimplify the character and extent of the importation of ultramontane forms and techniques of building to the Kingdom of Naples.[1]

How did it happen that a Frenchman, the brother of the Capetian king Louis IX of France, became king of Sicily? This is a long and complex story, one that in one way or another involved all the major courts of Europe, and only the broad outlines of the main events can be sketched in here. It began with the death of the childless Norman king William II in 1189, which initiated a long period of turmoil in the Kingdom of Sicily. The succession passed to his aunt Constance, daughter of the first Norman king, Roger II, and wife of the future German emperor, Henry VI Hohenstaufen. The prospect of submersion into the German empire elicited great resistance among the south Italian barons, who proposed Tancred, Count of Lecce, a descendant of Roger II through his father. At the same time, in Rome it raised the specter of the German empire, united with the Kingdom of Sicily, to the north and south of the papal domains. But Tancred died in 1194, as Henry VI was making his way south through the kingdom to lay claim to his wife's inheritance. Henry was crowned in Palermo on Christmas day 1194, while Constance remained in Apulia to give birth to their son, the future and formidable Frederick II.

The government of Henry VI was bitter and short, for after surviving several plots on his life the king died of dysentery (though many said poison) in Messina in 1197. The widowed Constance, advised by Innocent III, took control, but, in ill health and anxious for the fate of her son, she established in 1198 a regency council to administer the kingdom, and placed young Frederick under the guardianship of the pope. Frederick (at three and a half) was crowned king at Palermo in May 1198, and six months later Constance was dead.

The minority of Frederick was dominated by factional and self-serving interests on the parts of the German and Norman barons. In 1208, the fourteen-year old Frederick reached his majority. Brought up in Palermo, the island of Sicily was the apple of his eye, and in time he was able to restore to it an orderly government. His inheritance of the empire, however, led to dramatic tensions: crowned Emperor of Germany in 1220, these expanded domains meant that he no longer had time to spend on the island, and the affairs of the kingdom took second place to those of the empire. The coronation of Frederick as emperor meant above all that the union of Sicily with the empire so feared by the

2 *(facing page)*   Lucera, exterior of the castle (author)

papacy was embodied in his person and though he promised to pass the kingdom to his infant son and go on Crusade, he made no haste to do either.

By the 1240s the popes were looking for a champion to unseat Frederick, and they approached the courts of England and France for suitable candidates. Richard of Cornwall refused the overture, and although Charles of Anjou, the youngest brother of Louis IX, was also initially approached, he deferred to his elder brother's reservations. But Frederick died in 1251, and his legitimate heir, Conrad, in 1254. This left the kingdom in the hands of Frederick's illegitimate son Manfred, regarded by King Louis of France as a godless interloper and usurper of the rights of Conrad's son, Conradin. In the meantime, however, Henry III of England had agreed that his son, Edmund, aged only eight, should stand in to resolve "the Sicilian business."

The English plan, however, entailed the payment of vast sums to the papacy, sums well beyond Henry's means. The issue became part of the wider struggle between the baronage and monarchy of England, and negotiations were eventually called off by Pope Alexander IV in 1258, leaving the papacy, richer by about 60,000 English marks and Henry much debilitated both politically and financially.

With the accession of Urban IV to the papacy in 1260, the matter of the Sicilian champion was resolved in favor of France. Louis IX had substantial concerns about the rights of the young Hohenstaufen heir, Conradin, whose position had been usurped by his half-brother Manfred. In 1263 Louis agreed that Charles of Anjou might resume negotiations with the papacy, and by late July of that year he was the accepted and official champion of the church.

The conditions of the initial treaty were strenuous for the French and greatly to the advantage of the papacy (and it will be seen in the course of this study that the financial strains and political limitations imposed on Charles of Anjou were to weigh heavily on him and his heirs). He was not only to pay the remainder of the enormous English debt to the papacy contracted during the negotiations with Henry III, but was also required to provide the Pope with three hundred knights or ships whenever they were required, and his annual tribute to the papacy of 8,000 ounces of gold and a white horse was far more than the Norman annual tribute. Charles and his heirs could no longer operate as apostolic degelegates in the kingdom, and had no voice in ecclesiastical jurisdiction or appointments. The clergy could not be taxed, and neither could the king enjoy the revenues of vacant bishoprics. His right to levy taxes in general was restricted, and he was sworn to assure the rights and

privileges of the administration of "Good King William." In the earlier version of the treaty, the Pope retained the right to depose Charles, in which case the king could not claim the allegiance of his vassals.

In return, Charles and his heirs were to receive apostolic protection and a three-year crusading tithe levied on the ecclesiastical revenues of France, Provence, and the Kingdom of Arles. The Pope pledged to preach the Crusade against Manfred and promised to prohibit the election to the empire of any claimant to the throne of Italy. The three-year crusading tithe levied on the churches of France, as well as the declaration of the invasion as a crusade (but one against fellow Christians), were to cause great comment and trouble. In part to counter the dubiousness of the enterprise, and as part of the papal propaganda campaign, Manfred was accused of close association with the Muslim communities in his kingdom.

Urban IV died in 1264, and Clement IV, a Frenchman closely linked to the royal house of France, replaced him in February 1265. The new Pope urged Charles to make haste to Rome, where he arrived in May to the jubilation of the city, which offered him the position of senator, and he was invested with the kingdom on 28 June. On 6 January 1266 he and Beatrice were crowned King and Queen of Sicily in Saint Peter's. When the army arrived in Rome in February, Charles initiated his campaign: he met Manfred's forces in the plain outside the papal city of Benevento on 26 February and by the end of the day, Charles was victor, Manfred was dead, and the kingdom to the south was open to the French conqueror and his troops. To the horror of the Pope, the French went on to pillage the city of Benevento and slaughter its inhabitants. Charles entered Naples triumphantly on 7 March 1266. The victory was complete, and one by one Manfred's supporters made their submission or were offered amnesty.

Although the initial victory was swift, control of the kingdom was to prove difficult. There were Hohenstaufen heirs: chief among them was Conradin, who in 1268 came to claim his inheritance, was defeated in a great battle on the plain of Tagliacozzo in the Abruzzo and was later decapitated in the market square of Naples. The arrival of Conradin had brought out many of the barons still sympathetic to the Hohenstaufen cause, and those who were not captured fled to join resistance movements elsewhere. Manfred's eldest daughter, Constance, had been married in 1262 to Peter of Aragon, and twenty years later, with the rebellion of the Sicilian Vespers, was to lay claim to Sicily as the legitimate heir to the Hohenstaufen line. Manfred's three young sons by his second wife, Helena, conveniently forgotten by all parties, languished in prison (first at Castel del Monte, then in the Castel dell'Ovo of Naples) until their deaths many decades later.

★   ★   ★

The history of the Angevin monuments is bound up with the ambitions of the monarchs and the vicissitudes of their reigns. When Charles of Anjou rode into Naples in the late winter of 1266, it is said that crowds greeted him with jubilation and the keys to the city.[2] Exalted by the papacy as "pugil et athleta Christi," and lauded by poets as the embodiment of knightly valor, the king seemed to fulfill the prophecy of the arrival of a new Charles to succor the Church of Rome and relieve the Kingdom of Sicily from the impiety of Frederick II and his sons.[3] The very name of the new conqueror awakened a memory of Charlemagne's defense of the papacy centuries before.[4] Although by the time of the conquest in 1266 the papal crusade against the Hohenstaufen had been in the making for decades, and papal champions of various nationalities had been considered, Charles's swift triumph over Manfred was also seen as a particularly French achievement, the apogee of the international prestige of France and its court, the reflection of the long relationship of mutual support between the French crown and the papacy.[5]

Yet if the inhabitants of the kingdom had hoped that the advent of a "new Charles" would introduce an era of peace, justice, and well being – including a release from wars and the heavy taxation imposed by Frederick and his sons – they were soon to discard that hope. The infamous Battle of Benevento that won the kingdom for Charles of Anjou was a harbinger of the disaffection and rebellion that were rapidly to follow.[6] After the defeat of Manfred and his troops, the Angevin soldiers rampaged through the papal city of Benevento, with murder and pillage on a scale that made an impression even in times inured to savagery.[7] As noted by Barbero and others, the supporters of the French conquest soon had good reason for second thoughts about the conqueror and his officials.[8] Many of the voices that had predicted victory and exalted Charles in 1266 turned with disappointment against him (see for example the shift in the tone of the chronicle of Salimbene).[9] There were riots in Orvieto in 1281 fostered by calls for death to the French.[10] Resistance and rebellion were thus not only that of the well-known revolt of Sicily in 1282; from 1268 onwards, and broadly distributed through southern Italy, disaffection and resistance were widespread.[11] Even the recent literature presents a wide range of views, including the positive re-evaluation of Charles I (1998) in Jean Dunbabin's biography, which seeks to redeem him from his reputation as a "chilly thug."[12]

So, from the beginning, few individuals have been more enmeshed in controversy and in nationalistic feeling than Charles of Anjou.[13] After the Battle of Benevento even Clement IV, an old family friend, and one of the king's original champions, described his protégé and vassal as "nec visibilis, nec adibilis, nec affabilis, nec amabilis."[14] The frequent revolts, the regular episodes of insurgence and disruption, and finally the War of the Vespers, all attest to the difficult legacy of Charles's conquest and the tension generated by the social and economic consequences of his ambitions. His successors, Charles II and Robert, although they managed to integrate the French court into the cultural landscape of Italy, nevertheless continued to struggle with some of these negative aspects of their inheritance, especially the excesses of the conquest and the execution of Conradin.[15] Even the brilliant circle of artists, poets, and intellectuals gathered at the court of Naples by Robert could not entirely dispel the cloud, as Dante and his contemporaries remind us. If crimes of a sanguinary nature could not be laid at the door of Charles of Anjou's successors, then they could be accused of the peculiar defect of lameness, excessive piety, and "selling" their children in marriage (Charles II) or the venal sin of avariciousness (Robert).

Thus the initial promise of Charles's conquest, and the hopes of the papacy for a ductile, profitable, and peaceable kingdom, did not come to fruition. Indeed, the forceful assertion of French power in Italy and the king's repeated attempts at the expansion of French control throughout the eastern Mediterranean began to seem reminiscent of the ambitions of the Hohenstaufen and the Normans, a development regarded by the papacy with an alarm that might have been tinged with irony, for these were among the very offences perpetrated by Charles's predecessors.[16]

In this general atmosphere of dismay, one is tempted to wonder whether even Charles might not himself have been occasionally disillusioned by the sometimes harsh realities of his new kingdom, as well as by the notorious fickleness of its subjects. Abulafia has recently observed that southern Italy's reputation for wealth was based primarily on trade and taxation rather than upon natural resources and general economic well-being: the perpetual state of economic crisis of the Angevin court may relate not only to the vast expense of the initial conquest, the plans and preparations for expansion to the east, and the numerous rebellions, but perhaps also to the fact that the financial resources of the kingdom had been overestimated from the outset.[17] And although warned of the unreliability of his subjects, Charles does not seem to have been prepared for the widespread defection of the local barons in 1268 when Frederick's grandson Conradin descended into Italy to claim his inheritance.[18] As noted above, revolts occurred with regularity throughout Charles's reign, culminating in the final and irremediable insurrection of 1282, the War of the Sicilian Vespers.[19]

The consequences of this insurrection can hardly be overestimated; for our purposes perhaps the most important aspect was the profound shift in the attention of the Angevin dynasty away from the creation of an Angevin "lake" in the eastern Mediterranean to a focus on central and northern Italy and Europe.[20] And, as a result of the War of the Vespers, Naples in the 1290s became the firmly established capital, one closer to Rome, Marseilles, and the western Mediterranean.[21] The city replaced Palermo as the primary seat of royal authority and thus earns a prominent place in this narrative.

In the years after the conquest of 1266, Charles had sought to expand his dominions towards the eastern Mediterranean by attempting to conquer Constantinople and the Holy Land.[22] He also purchased the right to the throne of Jerusalem and designated himself its ruler in all royal documents: the Kingdom of Naples was thus above all a staging point, both strategic and economic, as well as a source of manpower and materials, for further conquest aimed at the creation of a Mediterranean empire extending from Marseilles to Jerusalem. But each time his ships were ready to sail, the plan was thwarted: in 1268, as Charles began to put into place his first project for the conquest of the East, revolts erupted in response to the descent of Conradin, into Italy.[23] The king had to abandon his attempt to quell the most alarming of these revolts, that of the Muslim community at Lucera in Apulia, to march his army towards Rome to meet Conradin, the last of the viable Hohenstaufen claimants, defeating him at Tagliacozzo in August 1268. In 1269–70 renewed plans for the East were interrupted by Louis IX's crusade to Tunis. Later, a fleet for the East was diverted from its original destination to combat the revolt of Sicily of 1282.

Like the crusaders in the Holy Land before him, Charles became aware that he needed a permanent, stable, and faithful base of French settlers in his new kingdom.[24] After the revolts of 1268, edicts were issued that threatened to revoke the Italian fiefdoms of French knights absent from Italy for more than a year; official court documents were frequently issued in French as well as Latin; and royal offices were increasingly assigned to French (hence trustworthy) administrators.[25] In 1268

calls went out for settlers from France, Provence, and Forcalquier to settle disaffected areas such as Lucera in order to provide a stable base of faithful French colonists. The broadsides requested settlers with specific skills, among them carpentry and construction.[26] The decision to found the Cistercian abbeys of Realvalle and Vittoria, although stimulated by and tied to negotiations with the Cistercians over the payment of the crusading tithe, seems also to have been in part an attempt to use monastic communities to assist in the process of stabilizing the French colonialization. One might note that the need for French settlers continued to be a concern in the fourteenth century; in 1315, for example, Robert encouraged French settlers by reaffirming their exemption from taxation for themselves, their families, and their descendants.[27]

Another effect of the rebellions and the War of the Vespers was the desertification of the regions of the kingdom under siege (Calabria, Basilicata, and parts of Campania), or those permanently lost (in Sicily nothing survives from the short period of Angevin control between 1266 and 1282).[28] The eradication of the Muslim community of Lucera in August 1300 was in part conceived to provide a new home for the dislocated and displaced Calabrians. Little, if any, construction would have taken place in those regions between the outbreak of the war in 1282 and the peace of Caltabellota in 1302.[29]

The churches of southern Italy during the reign of Charles I were thus erected in an environment in which the king was not infrequently on the defensive within his own lands and on the offensive elsewhere. The evidence suggests that it may have taken some time for Charles to understand the tensions and complexities of ruling multilingual, multi-religious, and multicultural southern Italy. The arrogance and corruption of some of his French officials and retainers seem to have exacerbated regional and ethnic discord, a difficulty that emerged, for example, in the troops amassed for battle at Tagliacozzo.[30] Even the French retainers, among whom Charles might have hoped to find stable supporters and loyal citizens, were often unreliable and dominated by self-interest.[31] Yet if little natural unity existed among the peoples of the kingdom, a certain unanimity does seem to emerge in their dislike of the oppressions and exactions of the French regime.[32] As will be seen, Charles of Anjou's building sites were a microcosm of the state of tension that existed in many parts of his kingdom.

The disruption caused by opposition to French rule interfered with military expansion and with numerous other projects, especially buildings.[33] Funds intended for construction were funneled elsewhere; masons and builders were transformed into soldiers; and the technical experts (carpenters, engineers, and architects) were sent off to direct siege operations or construct the machinery for such operations.[34] Apart from the diversion of funds and manpower, the rebellions led to the partial destruction of many of the fortifications of the kingdom, which then required renewed Angevin repairs. Endemic unrest was repeatedly to affect the progress of building projects; one can for example imagine that after the outbreak of the war in 1282 many of the new churches of Naples (Sant'Eligio al Mercato, San Lorenzo Maggiore) remained unfinished and under scaffolding for more than a decade.

Charles of Anjou would obviously have been aware of the powerful cultural and artistic legacies of his predecessors, not only those of Frederick II and his son Manfred, but also those of the Norman conquerors a century before.[35] The character of certain royal proposals or projects suggests an awareness of Norman and Swabian precedent. So there was a second battlefield and a second battle to be won, not of military victories but of image, prestige, and representation. And there were at least a few moments during Charles's reign when the king seems to have felt that the particularly French triumph of 1266 needed to find expression in a visibly French cultural legacy.[36] This is attested above all in the foundation documents for the two Cistercian abbeys of Realvalle and Vittoria but also in the choice of French clergy in various royal chapels.[37] In the second generation during the reign of Charles II, issues of dynastic prestige and representation were played out particularly in royal burial chapels, tomb monuments, and demonstrations of lineage and authority, as have been examined recently in the studies of royal tombs and burial practice by Enderlein and Michalsky.[38]

A narrative that has to do with architecture is intimately connected with the issues of the various types of resources: stone, wood, workmen, and, perhaps above all, money. Our story here is largely one of indebtedness, often of monumental proportions. There were, first of all, the moral debts to the Church and to the monastic orders for support during the conquest (Charles had specifically evoked the prayers of the churches and monasteries of the kingdom before Benevento).[39] Insofar as he was a patron of religious architecture, the king seems to have approached the matter of the foundation of churches as part of a system or economy of exchange; numerous documents express the idea that his support for the Church was in thanks to God for the successful conquest of the kingdom.[40] As will be seen in detail in the next chapter, his foundation of the Cistercian abbeys of Realvalle and Vittoria in 1274

was explicitly in gratitude for victory and in memory of the Capetian line.

But the other debt, the financial debt, is a far more significant part of the narrative. The Kingdom of Naples was born deeply encumbered by immense loans from Florentine and Roman bankers.[41] As vassals of the papacy, the Angevin kings owed the Holy See an annual tribute of 8,000 *once d'oro* and a white horse. Even before the Battle of Benevento in 1266 Charles was deeply in debt,[42] and by 1276 he was so in need of funds that he pawned the regalia. Repayments on the debt were almost always in arrears, and by the reigns of Charles II and Robert had accumulated to staggering sums. The five-year crusading tithes that had been imposed upon France by the papacy to support Charles's venture were deeply resented and sometimes vigorously resisted by the churches and orders obliged to pay them, and futhermore they would not have sufficed to cover the vast expense of the conquest and the daily costs of the court.[43] In the Kingdom of Naples the imposition of almost annual levies also caused deep resentment.[44] Indeed, as Percy has noted, the total income from taxes imposed by Charles of Anjou was two to three times greater than that acquired by his brother Louis IX, ruler of a more densely populated and far wealthier kingdom.[45]

The debts were exacerbated by the expenses caused by Charles of Anjou's plans for further conquest and by the revolts that erupted in Charles's dominions from 1268 onwards. The accumulation and compounding of debt continued to harry Charles II, Robert, and their descendants with ever more deeply damaging consequences to the kingdom.[46] It is indeed astonishing that, after 1294, Charles II, the greatest Angevin patron of religious architecture, and perhaps one of the most conspicuous church-building kings of the Middle Ages, was able to assist in sponsoring so many monuments in spite of tax reforms and an income considerably reduced from the years between 1266 and 1285 under Charles I.[47] Is it possible that the style and structure of these monuments reflect this climate of financial exigency?

The problem of funds is closely related to issues that have to do with the labor force. The Angevin Registers are one of the main surviving sources of information about the organization of royal building workshops in medieval Europe, and the story is not a cheerful one.[48] Skilled labor was hard to find; masons were brought long distances to various royal projects, often against their will. In many instances manual labor was conscripted. Wages were systematized throughout the kingdom, and were low (equivalent to the sustenance of a prisoner).[49] There were few French workmen in rela-

5

tion to the total size of the workforce and the foreigners seem for the most part to have been individuals with special expertise: architects, engineers, master carpenters, and skilled sculptors or masons who, as "high-level" workers (and therefore at times listed by name in the documents), were often paid either by a regular salary or by the piece instead of with daily wages. There are, on the whole, few surviving examples of monuments erected with great architectural structural complexity or workmanship of outstanding quality; for the most part the character of construction conformed to the limited skills of a largely untrained labor force and the exigencies of local materials (sometimes brick or soft volcanic stone). I shall suggest that when Charles of Anjou insisted in the documents that certain elements, such as windows or roof tiles, be produced "ad modum franciae," he did so precisely because this type of "French" work was so difficult to achieve in his kingdom.[50] Even the meager remains of the lavishly sponsored abbey of Realvalle attest to a process of accommodation to local materials and craftsmanship, as the crude rubble walls show. At the two Cistercian abbeys the difficulties were often the result of an inconstant and inadequately trained workforce, difficulties at times compounded, at least at Realvalle, by a shortage of high-quality stone.[51] One long-term consequence of the practical difficulties presented by the untrained and disaffected labor force may have been defects in both structure and construction (especially important in matters such as the mixing of mortar). Later in the fourteenth century, when sculptors came from Tuscany to execute tombs and carve the portal of San Domenico Maggiore in Naples, their arrival may have been a matter not only of taste, but also of necessity, for there is little surviving evidence of sculptors skilled in marble work and inlay in medieval Naples.

The Angevin architectural legacy, at least during the reign of Charles I and the first years of the reign of Charles II before 1294, was therefore sporadic and in some ways fragile, even ephemeral.[52] The documents that concern building projects in the Angevin Registers (these concern primarily the buildings of Charles I) suggest that Charles I's ambitious goals were compromised by the realities of debt and the types of labor and the materials available. The story here – at least until 1294 – is thus one of difficulty and struggle, at times played out with physical violence at the sites. Several projects were abandoned shortly after, or even before inception, such as the construction of an abbey at the battle site of Benevento in commemoration of Charles's victory of 1266, or the plan to remodel the cathedral of Acerenza. We should probably recognize in Charles I a patron pressed and distracted by other interests and larger ambi-

tions; religious foundations took second place to the practical needs of defense and fortification and ambitions of eastern conquest. Virtually all documented building projects suffered from financial and labor conditions that seem to have been far from satisfactory.[53] The contrast with the famously energetic builder kings of the thirteenth century, Louis IX of France and Henry III of England, could not be more striking.

Yet buildings and especially churches are not simply the function of money, masons, and materials. The churches of the Angevin kings and their court, though often fragmentary and often reconstructed, were infused with pious aspirations and profound religious sentiment. If these monuments with their original interior decoration (wall paintings, liturgical furnishings, tomb monuments, etc.) were still intact, the new tone and the spiritual component introduced by the French conquerors after 1266 would have been far more striking than they are today. (Documents for Realvalle, for example, write of colored glass, and fragments of such glass have been found at San Lorenzo Maggiore.[54]) The Angevin kings and their court (as well as the lay public) also founded numerous hospitals and hospices; these pious foundations were established not only for the indigent and for prostitutes, but also for those wounded and maimed in battle. Other charitable foundations, such as Sant'Eligio al Mercato in Naples, were founded with the express purpose of attending to the care and burial of *forestieri* – the French and Provençal soldiers and their attendants who had come without family to Italy.

The Angevin kings also had an important role in the development of the cult of saints in southern Italy. Leaving aside the canonization of one of their own as Saint Louis of Toulouse in 1317, the "discovery" of the relics of the Magdalen by Charles II stimulated the rapid development of her cult and numerous churches and chapels were founded in her honor (although many have lost their original dedications and taken on the name of the founder of the order, as at San Domenico in Naples and San Domenico in L'Aquila). The cult of the Magdalen led to the proliferation of fresco cycles that emphasized penitence, an important aspect of late medieval spirituality that had particular relevance for the Kingdom of Naples because the cult was energetically promoted by Charles II.[55] The Angevin kings were also devoted to Saint Nicholas of Bari, to the shrine of the Archangel Michael at Monte Sant'Angelo, and to San Gennaro in Naples, and in each of these sites donated reliquaries or contributed to large-scale construction projects to enhance and promote the cult of the saint.

Unfortunately, although many of the churches discussed in this volume were part of larger monastic com-

3 (*facing page*)   Naples, San Domenico, main portal, detail of right jamb (author)

plexes erected at the same time, almost none of the monastic buildings survives. Urban renewal has been particularly inimical to monastic complexes in the cities: in Naples the cloisters at Santa Maria Donnaregina and Sant'Agostino alla Zecca were demolished by the late nineteenth-century *risanamento* (urban renewal). Even where a complex has survived it is almost always in a modernized form rebuilt in the sixteenth century or later. The churches thus often seem strangely detached from the original monastic or urban environments in which they were erected, with the exception of the cloister of Santa Chiara in Naples, a rare example of a conventual complex that remains essentially intact. The discussion of churches separate from the monastery or convent is a sad necessity in this volume, the result of the paucity of surviving evidence. Historical circumstances thus again constrain the discussion to the surviving and visible "tip of the iceberg" of monasteries.

Restorations have led also to the restructuring of interior spaces. In Naples modern restoration began in the early twentieth century with the work of Gino Chierici, who over three decades stripped much of the Baroque decoration from the interior of San Lorenzo Maggiore and reconstructed much of Santa Maria Donnaregina. In 1943, in Naples as in many other Italian cities, the devastation of Allied bombardments reduced many of the most important monuments to rubble or to a fractured shell (Santa Chiara). The post-war restorations, informed by modern aesthetics, have tended to be a form of spoliation of their own, leaving us vast and barren spaces sometimes redolent of a 1950s and 1960s' aesthetic.

A history of damage and misfortune has a number of obvious consequences for the study of architecture. Because of the reconstructions in Naples in particular, the creation of a construction chronology based on the study of the fabric of the walls and structural details is rarely possible. Moldings, bases, and capitals, if not chipped away for Baroque redecoration, have often been replaced in the buildings that were bombarded and restored. Only rarely can one read in the fabric of the structure the history of its construction, and rarely does the student have full confidence in the details that permit the re-creation of the construction process or the identification of an architect, master mason, or sculptor. This is all the more regrettable because the documents often provide the names of individuals whose work one is tempted to search for in the masonry.

Yet ironically the tragic bombardments of 1943 also made some parts of this study possible. The shaking down of the Baroque in the bombing of Naples revealed the medieval shells beneath, and for a variety of reasons the restorations returned the churches to a version of their medieval appearance. The post-war restorations provide us with a version, or interpretation, of medieval Naples that for centuries had not been visible. Although one might question many aspects of the restorations, which are almost without exception undocumented, they are as it were, the only surviving "filter" through which we can observe the buildings.

There is far less architectural sculpture in the churches of the kingdom than we tend to associate with medieval architecture in general. Only in Apulia are external decorative programs and elaborately sculpted portals common (Altamura and Bisceglie, for example). Where exterior ornament does occur, it was produced by local schools of craftsmen and mostly existed in regional isolation, as in the decorative portals of the Abruzzo (Atri, L'Aquila, Penne, Larino, Ortona) or of Apulia (Altamura, Bitetto). This paucity of architectural ornament also means that decorative detailing, often among the important criteria for dating, is rare.

Yet it may be that the austerity of the monuments derives from an aesthetic that sets a plain exterior against a richly ornamented interior. In this it would have adhered to an Italian tradition of church decoration that focused on the interiors rather than the exteriors. Unfortunately, it is not clear to what extent the interiors of the thirteenth- and fourteenth-century churches were designed in relation to fresco painting in particular, since too little survives of these decorative programs. Special attention was reserved in interiors for programs of liturgical decoration or tomb monuments.

Finally, this study must also be framed in terms of two broader issues particular to the Kingdom of Naples. A style at least in part imported from elsewhere means that the natural evolution of forms is stopped in its tracks: architectural concepts are frozen in the time of their introduction into the new terrain, and do not go through the natural process of development, change, or evolution that occurs in the home environment. This is visible not only in the successive Cistercian and Franciscan importations of French elements, but also in the introduction of Rayonnant design via the papal and Angevin courts.

At the same time, a strong element of continuity found in the Italian masonry tradition rooted in local (and family) practices of carving and construction favored continuity over change. There is a particular tendency in southern Italy towards a static quality in both local and imported styles that seems to stand in opposition to the rapid pace of architectural development elsewhere. Over and over again in this study the artistic environment of southern Italy seems to have been based on premises profoundly different from those of Europe north of the Alps, and especially those of thirteenth- and fourteenth-century France.[56] When we are concerned with elements of importation, the templates often seem to have been established twenty, thirty, or forty years previously and become part of a workshop tradition that favored continuity rather than change. Indeed, in the cathedral of Naples, some of the surviving bases are either antique or medieval imitations of the antique. Beginning in the 1290s a taste for *spolia*, especially important in the reign of Charles II between 1295 and 1309, adds additional complication to the scene: ancient materials, used either as building blocks (the churches in Lucera) or as decorative elements (the columns inserted in the piers of the cathedral of Naples), dominate the character of the medieval fabric; at times the monument seems to have been conceived and designed more in response to architectural fragments from antiquity than the "up-to-date" models of the present. By 1295, at the latest, modernism (in the sense of the Gothic style ubiquitous north of the Alps) was rejected in favor of tradition, and this preference for a well-established native architectural language, one suspects, applied not only to the large-scale concepts in architecture but also to the handling of details (the cathedral of Naples, again). Here the practical concerns of workmen and materials are combined with the larger role of architecture as presentation and ideological statement. An especially complex monument in this regard is the captivating church of San Lorenzo Maggiore in Naples.

The literature on the Gothic architecture of southern Italy has usually tended to lose sight of the importance of other sources for the importation of northern forms, particularly the papal court and the Franciscan order. The Franciscan churches of Campania (Teano, Aversa, Eboli, Nocera Inferiore, and Nola, among others) attest to a highly consistent and systematized approach to building and decoration that is far more logically placed within the context of the order than the court architecture of the Angevins. The repetition of molding types and rib profiles from one building to another would suggest that we are in the presence of Franciscan architectural expertise that is independent of that of the Angevin court. And yet, as will be seen in the chapter on San Lorenzo Maggiore in Naples, the "unraveling" of the distinct threads of the religious order, the Francocentric environment of the court, and the strong presence of local and indigenous taste is difficult indeed. Monastic taste is in itself conservative and self-referential. Thus "Frenchness" arrived in Naples and the kingdom in many forms and with many "degrees of separation," both structural and symbolic. The sources also were varied: there is not only the architecture of the Parisian court and Provence, but also that of the monastic orders, self-consciously distinct and with their own clear identity.

The ideological aspect of Angevin church architecture has other ramifications and this means that we are in effect concerned with more than two forms of conservatism. Apart from the issues of ancient materials and the evocation of the antique, and also apart from issues of monastic architectural reticence, in "colonial" cultures, where prestige is associated with the extraneous ruling force, the impulse towards conservatism is strong and becomes a means of affiliation with the regime. This is particularly true of a court culture where aristocratic values, such as noble lineage and association with the ruling family, would have been of primary importance. In this environment, historical associations, exalted lineage, tradition, and continuity were far more valued qualities than innovation and change. So forms that were perhaps new and innovative at their first introduction (for example, the capitals and clusters of shafts in the portal of Sant'Eligio al Mercato of the 1270s) become standarized and do not evolve. So to a certain degree, if "Frenchifying" details had a long life in the Kingdom of Naples, it was as a set of *ossified* forms: by the last decade of the thirteenth century these exist in monotonous and conservative repetition, as visible in the capitals of the Neapolitan churches of the period around 1300 (the cathedral, San Lorenzo Maggiore). After about 1270 Angevin architecture thus consists of long periods of conservative repetition tied to the rigidity of colonial court culture, intermingled in the 1320s and 1330s with brief interludes of new influences (France again, Catalonia, Siena), which in turn were integrated into a stable formula that persisted for decade after decade.

There were also periods in which architectural design was highly unified throughout the kingdom, as when castles were erected by Charles I under the direction of Pierre d'Angicourt and other architects both French and Italian. This is particularly noticeable in the churches built during the reign of Charles II. In the 1290s the concern for homogeneity (although one would not, I think, attribute these similar monuments to the same master mason or workshop) seems especially significant, and it is tempting to suppose that Charles II wished to use architectural forms as a means to unite the kingdom with the common stamp of his churches and abbeys.

The reader may be irritated by the many issues of dating left open in this study. There can be no question here of a tidily unified chronology or of a resolved sequence of buildings. Asking questions is a first step to finding answers, but with material as fragmentary and as frequently reconfigured as that in this study, the answers may be long in coming.

Chapter 1

CHURCH BUILDING
DURING THE REIGN OF CHARLES I

> For after a prince has had a triumph, he sits. Therefore after the triumph of Christ it is
> concluded, in the last chapter of Mark [16:19] Jesus sits at the right hand of God. And in that
> way King Charles I sits; after many victories he sits on the throne of the Kingdom, so that one
> may apply to him the text of Revelation [3:21]: To him that will overcome, I will give to sit
> on my throne. There are three things here – Firstly, the glory of the one who triumphs . . .
> Secondly, the rights of the one who holds possession . . . because the kingdom was given to
> him by the church . . . Thirdly, the excellence of the one who sits in authority . . . Hebrews
> [1:8] his throne is forever and ever.[1]

Charles of Anjou was interested in architecture. He provided instructions on design, specifying details such as dimensions of rooms and wall widths to his master masons, keeping a sharp eye on the many projects underway, and insisting that work be completed on time.[2] On occasion he took on the role of architect, as when he designed a harbor tower at Brindisi, which to his outrage collapsed shortly after completion.[3] Beginning in 1277 he attended to the construction of the two Cistercian abbeys of Realvalle and Vittoria with a degree of interest striking in a man who had other pressing concerns.

But this was not a king especially interested in building churches, nor did he have either the concentration or the means to do so. Most of the religious projects associated with Charles of Anjou were stimulated by external requests and petitions, and, in the instance of the Cistercian abbeys, even by what one might call "moral blackmail." In Naples one of the primary promoters of religious buildings was the Burgundian archbishop Ayglerius (1269–1282), who functioned as an intermediary between certain pious confraternities and religious orders and the king, following in the footsteps of some of his distinguished predecessors in the episcopal see of Naples.[4] In spite of a historical tradition to the contrary, Charles was on the whole a passive, incidental, or even "accidental" patron of church building, usually providing land, or the rights to the use of forests or quarries, in response to specific requests. Yet in these matters

strict categorization is often not possible, for in the instance of the abbeys of Realvalle and Vittoria, initially stimulated by what Buczek has called the "tortuous struggle" over tithes with the Cistercian order, by 1277 the king was deeply engaged in their construction.[5] Furthermore, assessment of his patronage is complicated by the ruined state of almost all the monuments connected with him and the loss of many documents. Ironically, it may be that Sant'Eligio al Mercato in Naples, a church with a somewhat tangential connection to the king, may reflect his tastes in architectural matters more closely than any other surviving building in southern Italy, for its style accords with that of the church that he rebuilt in Aix-en-Provence for the burial of his first wife, Beatrice of Provence, as well as with the spirit of his written instructions concerning his lost palace chapels.[6]

It may well be that two projects, one at the beginning of his reign and one at the end, reveal the episodic and inconstant nature of this king's religious patronage. In the first instance, in July 1269, during the siege of Lucera, Charles instructed the Giustiziere of Benevento to provide the materials necessary for the construction of a church outside Benevento where Manfred had been defeated. At the same time he named Alberico de Catalano, his clerk and familiar, as superintendent of the new works and ordered that the stones necessary for construction be transported to the site.[7] Although the order was renewed two days later, the project seems to have been abandoned, for no evidence survives of the construction of a church and there are no further documents.[8] One is tempted to conclude that other concerns and expenses, such as the ongoing siege, took precedence.[9] Charles was afterwards distracted by the urgent and extensive repairs required at many of the castles, and indeed the widespread rebellion in favor of Conradin in 1278 itself would have reminded him of the necessity of keeping all fortifications in optimal condition. So the king's attention shifted rapidly from the spiritual to the practical, and indeed his subsequent itinerary from September 1269 included many of the fortifications that urgently needed repairs.[10] In those intensely busy eighteen months, plans for a new church on the battlefield of Benevento were abandoned or forgotten, never to appear again.

In a second instance much later in his reign, just before the loss of Sicily in 1282, Charles explored the possibility of reconstructing the cathedral of Acerenza in its exact dimensions at another site.[11] But here also no work was accomplished, and no further documents attest to the project. We may think that these episodes were fairly typical of the king's attention span for pious enterprises, episodes with noble intentions but of short duration, the king always pressed between his own political ambitions and practical concerns.

If discussions of taste and aesthetic preference are fluctuating and approximate at the best of times, in the Kingdom of Naples the fragmentary nature of the evidence makes this type of analysis especially precarious. What the king preferred in 1266 may not have been what he found to be appropriate ten to fourteen years later. In the case of tomb monuments and royal commemoration, for example, there may have been several phases of royal taste.[12] The splendid royal tomb of Isabelle of Aragon, the first wife of Phillip III of France who died returning from the Crusade of 1270 and was buried in Cosenza cathedral (pls. 5 and 6) is a monument in a pure French style, but later commissions for tombs involved instead the use of ancient marbles. This change was perhaps the result of a developing taste for the materials traditionally associated in Italy with power and authority, but it could also have reflected the status or preferences of the deceased. Since the marble tombs are lost, we cannot be sure. And during the course of Charles's reign, the character of architectural projects may also have come to reflect not only a range of practical experience obtained from projects in progress, but also a growing contact with the wide variety of cultures present in the kingdom. An interesting sidelight in this regard is the king's interest in Arab medicine: in 1277, for example, he ordered Matteo Scillato of Salerno to give Latin lessons to a Master Musa of Palermo so that

5 Cosenza, cathedral, tomb of Isabelle of Aragon (author)

the latter could translate Arab medical texts.[13] We also find unskilled Muslim labor at work at some construction projects, although never any evidence of an Islamic style in the royal buildings themselves.[14] To the difficulties of identifying a clear sense of royal taste one might add to the evolving mixture the influence of the court, his two wives, the papacy, and the religious orders. Yet because so little is left, there can be no certainty in any of this.

This chapter deals with the churches associated with Charles I and their stylistic affinities in roughly chronological order. Issues of workshops and the organization of labor, derived mostly from the documents that concern construction at the Cistercian abbeys of Realvalle and Vittoria, can be found in Appendix 1, although some aspects of a more general nature are also treated here. To this king have also been attributed two of the most important medieval churches of Naples, the cathedral and San Lorenzo Maggiore. The former should have been dismissed (and this long ago!) as the result of the scholarship of Biagio Cantèra and others, while the king's purported connection to the latter, the most traditionally "Gothic" of the monuments of Naples, still persists tenaciously, above all because of the "Frenchness" of the choir. The Angevin Registers, however, which, in spite of losses attest with considerable detail and completeness to Charles of Anjou's architectural projects and pious donations, make no mention of his support for San

Lorenzo. I shall propose in the next chapter that the tradition of his association with this church was mostly a sixteenth-century fiction created as part of an anti-Aragonese political movement.[15]

Although the churches traditionally associated with Charles I are mostly in Naples (which was not yet capital of the kingdom), the most important and secure examples of his patronage are elsewhere: the Cistercian abbeys of Santa Maria di Realvalle (near Pompeii in Campania), Santa Maria della Vittoria (Abruzzo), and, in France, Saint-Jean-de-Malte in Aix-en-Provence and parts of Saint-Urbain at Troyes. In a few cases there are also monuments for which no documents are known, such as the apse of Sant'Agrippino a Forcella, whose dating may be contemporaneous with the reign of Charles I, but which may also be later (the ravaged state of the ruin prevents any firm conclusions). Elsewhere, Baroque decoration still covers some churches of central importance, such as Sant'Agostino alla Zecca and Santa Maria del Carmine in Naples, the medieval walls of which, insofar as they still exist, we may never see.

Although the vexed question of Charles of Anjou's character may have implications for the depth of his piety and his activity as a church builder, this is not an issue that can be satisfactorily addressed here. It can, however, be said that the king recognized the importance of monastic foundations and religious institutions, and clearly depended upon them as sources of spiritual and political strength.[16] Prior to conquest, in December 1265, he invoked the prayers of the monasteries and churches of the kingdom, and promised his thanks in tangible form for their support.[17] He also wrote to the bishops of Bari, Reggio, Sorrento, Amalfi, Naples, Palermo, Salerno, Brindisi, Otranto, Siponto, Taranto, and Messina, although many were in fact absent because the papal interdict against the Hohenstaufen rulers was still in effect. Charles thus exerted himself to ensure the support of important episcopal seats and monastic institutions, and in time came to guarantee their fidelity by ensuring that loyal retainers were appointed to the bishoprics and abbatial seats.

It is almost certainly not a coincidence that the two first religious foundations in Naples associated with the early patronage of Charles of Anjou were established on either side of the Piazza del Mercato (the Campo Moricino), within two years of the execution of Conradin in 1268.[18] The creation of the two churches

6   Cosenza, cathedral, detail of the tomb of Isabelle of Aragon (Chester Brummel)

flanking the piazza can be seen, if not as expiation, then at least as a purification of a place of terrible notoriety.

The new market was also the heart of the first Angevin expansion of the city away from the densely packed and ancient center.[19] Here was open land conveniently accessible to the port. Merchandise and refuse need no longer pass through the narrow grid plan of the Greco-Roman city. In moving the market close to the port, it might be noted that Charles of Anjou followed the example of his grandfather, Philip Augustus, in the urban works of Paris some sixty years previously, and this forms part of several projects that suggest that Charles looked to the works of his grandfather with special admiration. The royal donations of land to the Carmelites and to the confraternity of Sant'Eligio affirmed and, as it were, "anchored," this new part of Naples.

On 2 July 1270, in response to a request from three Frenchmen, Joannes Dottun (Jean d'Autun), Guillelmus Burgundio (Guillaume de Borgogne), and Joannes Lions (Jean de Lyon), Charles donated a piece of land for the construction of the hospital and church of Sant'Eligio (pls. 7–9).[20] These individuals have recently been identified by Giovanni Vitolo as members of the French merchant community and not nobles, as had been thought since the seventeenth century. The project thus emerges as an early and conspicuous example of lay patronage on the part of one of the foreign merchant communities in the city.[21]

The hospital was dedicated to three important French saints: Denis, Martin, and Eloi.[22] By 1279, when Charles made a further donation of land to expand the church and the hospital, the complex was, however, referred

7 Naples, Sant'Eligio, view of nave from the west (Massimo Velo)

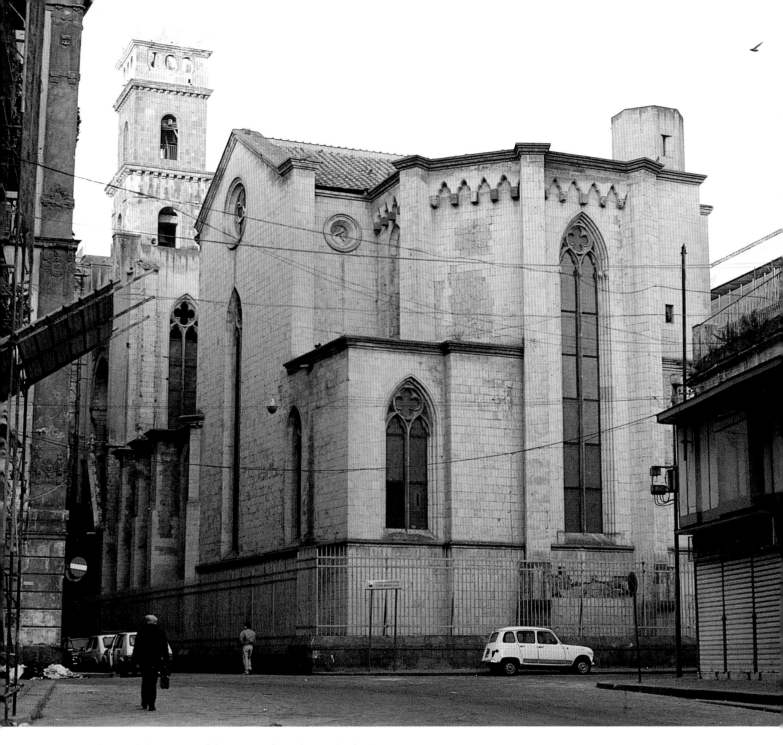

8　Naples, Sant'Eligio, view of the exterior from the east (author)

to simply as Sant'Eligio (Saint Eloi).[23] The confraternity also had the important function of burying those foreigners who had no family or residence in Naples, probably mostly French and Provençal nationals who had come to Italy as merchants, soldiers, or camp followers.[24]

As both hospital and cemetery, it was appropriate that the new foundation be placed outside the walls of the city. It was to become an important part of Neapolitan religious culture that extended beyond the French community and later received support and donations from the Aragonese court.[25] Sant'Eligio was built close to the older hospital of San Giovanni a Mare, located slightly to the west and owned by the knights of Saint John of Jerusalem; as will be seen, there are some interesting connections between the two sites (pl. 10).[26]

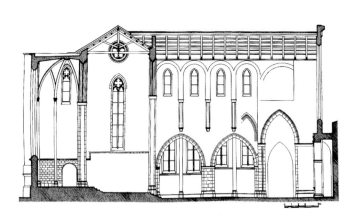
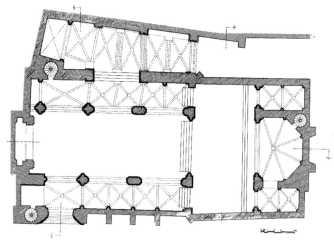

9 Naples, Sant'Eligio, longitudinal section and plan (after Venditti 1969)

The foundation of Sant'Eligio was avidly promoted by Archbishop Ayglerius, the first Frenchman appointed by Charles of Anjou to the Neapolitan see, himself Burgundian like the three founders. Chioccarello mentions that the archbishop's arms were placed on the exterior of the apse, although they have not survived.[27] The vaulted bays of the outer aisle on the north, added perhaps around 1300 to expand the church, contain keystones that bear the fleur-de-lys and the images of two bishops, although it is not clear which bishops are represented (pl. 11). This part of the hospital complex of the first decade of the fourteenth century still retains some of its fresco decoration, and can perhaps be associated with the donations of Charles II in 1302 and 1304.[28] Repeated donations of land suggest that the hospital grew rapidly and was soon in need of more space.

Although Sant'Eligio has usually been cited as one of the purest examples of French Gothic in Naples, it is a severely mutilated and restored monument (pls. 7–9). The plan and elevation were modified several times during construction in the late thirteenth and fourteenth centuries, perhaps first because of a protracted interruption of construction caused by the outbreak of the war of 1282. The church underwent further reconstruction in the fourteenth and fifteenth centuries, either to repair flaws in its stability or to repair damage from the earthquakes of 1349 and 1456. This is attested by the piers in a harder gray stone (*pietrarsa*, frequently in use after *circa* 1350) that replaced the more rapid scansion of the original supports in the church of 1270 (pls. 9 and 12).[29] The church was bombed on 3 August 1943, and the subsequent restoration removed what remained of the nineteenth-century incrustations that had concealed the

medieval structure.[30] Unfortunately, no documentation of that restoration has survived, although Venditti mentions some of the discoveries made at the time, such as the foundations of the first apse, underneath the present transept and the original position of the first set of nave piers.

10 Naples, the area of Sant'Eligio from the plan of Naples of 1775 by G. Carafa Duca di Noia

On the plan: 8. the Campo Moricino, or Piazza del Mercato,
14. Sant'Eligio
15. San Giovanni a Mare
166. Sant'Agostino alla Zecca

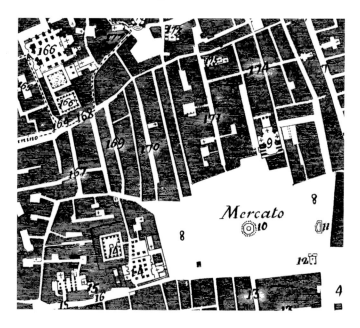

16

The second royal donation of land in 1279 provided a long and narrow strip of the Campo Moricino to enlarge the hospital, cemetery, and the church by 3 canne in width and 41 canne in length, to be measured from the stone cross located near the hospital (a modern copy of the thirteenth-century cross still survives in what may – or may not – be the original location to the east of the apse; the original is in the west bay of the nave).[31] A detail of a map of Naples of 1775 (pl. 10) suggests that a long narrow north–south strip was taken from the Piazza del Mercato (the Campo Moricino) for the enlargement of the church and hospital. The church as first built (phase A: pls. 12 and 13) terminated at the east with a polygonal apse located underneath the area that is now the transept.[32] A later donation of land in 1279 permitted the insertion of a transept and reconstruction of the apse in the area of the marketplace (phase C: pls. 13 and 16). The important change in style and structure between the vestiges of the nave, probably built rapidly sometime after 1270, and the transept, erected well after 1279, suggests that work on the reconstruction and expansion of the east end was probably delayed; I shall suggest below that the delay extended until the 1290s.

The earliest part of the church to survive is thus the nave (phase A: pl. 13). Several features of the original elevation were unusual. The bays are only 3.7 meters wide, and thus extremely narrow (see the hypothetical reconstruction of the first program, pl. 14).[33] The triple shafts still extant in the upper wall would have descended to the ground to form compound piers consisting of clustered shafts around a square core. As a result of the narrowness of the bays, the arcade arches were sharply pointed (pl. 15). On the aisle walls, each bay is separated by a single large half-column flanked by slight rounded shafts. The shafts of the nave, which survive only in the central part of the wall between the rebuilt piers and the clerestory windows, indicate that the nave was designed to be rib-vaulted, like the aisles below. The upper vaults were to be supported by flyers erected above the strongly projecting buttress walls of the nave exterior (pl. 17).

During the 1270s the four-bay nave was expanded to the west (phase B: pl. 13) by a much deeper bay, 7.07 meters wide, which would have joined the nave to a west façade, fragments of which can be seen embedded in the adjacent buildings. The western extension of a wider bay and façade seems to have been initiated while work was still underway on the nave to the east, for the piers are identical and there is no evidence that the vaults had yet been erected in the narrower bays to the east (nor are there any indications that they ever were). Half of another similarly large bay lies buried in the west wall, presumably part of a façade and tower structure that is

11 Naples, Sant'Eligio, a keystone in the northernmost aisle (Massimo Velo)

12 Naples, Sant'Eligio, hypothetical reconstruction of the original plan (Mark Hoffman)

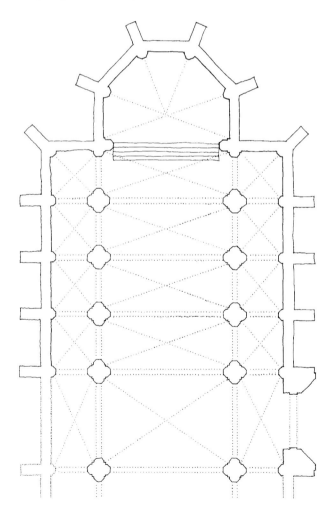

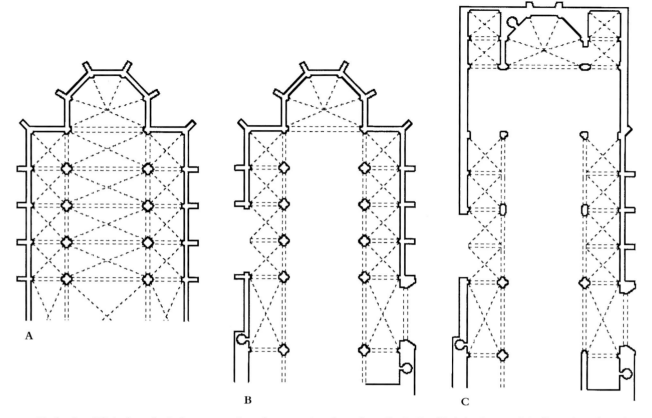

A   B   C

13   Naples, Sant'Eligio, hypothetical reconstruction of construction chronology (Irwin Sentilles). A: plan as originally projected; B: plan as expanded in the late 1270s; C: final plan (?after 1294) with transept and reworked east end.

now destroyed or absorbed into the apartment building to the west. The western expansion of the church forms part of a second phase of construction after the setting out of the first four tightly spaced central bays.

Do the wider western bays reflect the acquisition of further land to the west that permitted the expansion of the church and the enlargement of the bay dimensions? Or do they simply represent a "correction" to the original cramped design? Only one thing is clear: the stylistic consistency between the larger western bays and those to the east suggests that this work took place without a significant interruption, and it is therefore possible to date these parts of the building, as well as the portal, to before 1282 (for this portal, see below and pls. 4, 19, and 20).

What is important is that the elevation and structure of Sant'Eligio in its original design would have been entirely new in southern Italy. Rib vaults, though well known by the 1270s, were mostly based on conservative models, such as those of the twelfth-century churches of the Cistercians, and were characterized by a strong contrast between the heavy transverse arch and lighter ribs. The pier types that supported such vaults, moreover,

were massive in section, quite different from the lighter, thinner, and more delicate forms that once would have existed at Sant'Eligio. Furthermore, if my suppositions about the character of the design of the vaults originally planned are correct, the transverse arches and ribs would all have been of equal weight and diameter, like the shafts that support them below, so that the articulation of the wall and the vaults would have had an overall unity of similar elements. Bay divisions would have been expressed by the vertical rise of the slender clusters of triple shafts (pl. 14).

However, by the time of the reconstruction of the present plan with the addition of a transept and triple apses (phase C: pl. 13), erected on the land given in 1279, the plan to vault the nave had been abandoned. The new transept was never intended to be vaulted (pls. 9 and 16). Slightly trapezoidal in shape (it is almost one meter wider on its southern side than on the north: 9.27 vs. 8.34 m.), it is taller than the nave, and may have been among the first of the tall "boxy" transepts that came to characterize the major Neapolitan buildings (the cathedral, San Lorenzo Maggiore, and San Domenico) in the decades after 1294.

sion and thrust inherent in a rib-vaulted system, even those of a narrow span like that of the nave of Sant' Eligio (8.78 m.).[34] Since it appears that the decision to change the character of the covering was made during the process of construction, it is worth recalling that Sant'Eligio was founded shortly after the conquest and is therefore the earliest documented religious building under French rule. The master mason (certainly also French) would therefore have had little time to develop experience with the local materials and their properties. The construction of the aisle vaults may have been a "test" case of the capacity of local stone to resist stress and compression. Indeed, the later reworking of the lower nave supports *en sous-oeuvre* in about 1350 or later in gray stone (*pietrarsa*), rather than tuff, may be an oblique confirmation of the weakness of the latter.

The rejection of rib vaults may also have resulted from other considerations. As will be seen in the discussion of the abbey church of Realvalle, masons skilled in the complex carving of ribs were in short supply and their wages were high. The original decision to adopt a "French" architectural language at Sant'Eligio perhaps involved the confraternity in levels of expense that they could ill afford, especially in view of special collects to support the war effort and the plan to expand the church with the second donation of land. As noted above, the outbreak of the war in 1282 probably led to

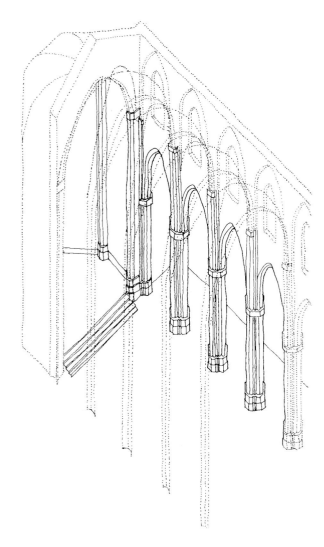

14 Naples, Sant'Eligio, hypothetical reconstruction of the original apse and vaults (Mark Hoffman)

At Sant'Eligio there was thus an important shift in character from the nave to the new transept and apses. This is confirmed not only in the different conception of volume, space, and wall surfaces, but also in the details, such as moldings and base profiles. The changes in these details, along with the transformation of the premises of the structure, suggest quite clearly that a substantial break took place between the initial construction of the nave and the later expansion to the east of the transept. Although the land to the east was acquired in 1279, probably a decade or more passed before the insertion of the transept and the reconstruction of the apses.

Why were vaults abandoned in the nave? There were probably several reasons. One may have been the recognition that the static properties of the local yellow tuff were not sufficiently resistant to the effects of compres-

15 Naples, Sant'Eligio, detail of the recovered arcade arches of the thirteenth century (Massimo Velo)

16   Naples, Sant'Eligio, view of the south transept and nave from the east (Massimo Velo)

an interruption of almost all construction in Naples; when work was renewed, presumably in the mid-1290s, the aesthetic parameters were different.

It seems likely that the plan to vault the main vessel was probably abandoned by the time that work had reached the base of the clerestory walls; there is no evidence that flyers were ever constructed above the exterior wall buttresses (pl. 17). As a result, the horizontal profile of the strongly projecting wall buttresses came to dominate the exterior of the south flank of the church.

The original elevation of Sant'Eligio (phase A) thus consisted of two stories with slender triple shafts that rose through the compound piers to the vault departures (pl. 14). In spite of the compacted character of the bays, there is a strong resemblance to the church of Saint-Jean-

de-Malte in Aix-en-Provence, a church rebuilt with the patronage of Charles in the 1270s to contain the tomb of Beatrice of Provence and the tombs of her father and grandfather (pl. 18).[35] The first documents for the reconstruction of Saint-Jean in Aix date from 1272, and the church was completed in 1277.[36]

In both structures there is a strong predilection for flat wall surfaces, although at Sant'Eligio the existence of aisles created a two-story elevation (Saint-Jean-de-Malte was originally without aisles, and the arched openings along its nave are of later date). In each monument, the plain nave walls are interrupted only by the slender and continuous shafts, creating an austere version of the Rayonnant sensibility for multiple small-scale elements. This austerity might not be surprising in a hospital church,

17 (facing page)   Naples, Sant'Eligio, buttresses on the south flank (Massimo Velo)

but it is significant at Aix, a royal monument commissioned by the king as a burial church for his wife and her forebears. Although Saint-Jean is two years later than the foundation documents of Sant'Eligio, it is probable that the hospital structures were built first, before the church, in order to attend to the infirm.

The lean and austere architectural vocabulary of Sant'Eligio and Saint-Jean in Aix has its origins in the Paris basin. The thin uninterrupted shafts on a flat wall

18 Aix-en-Provence, Saint-Jean-de-Malte, view of the interior from the west (author)

surface are reminiscent of those in the nave of the collegiate church of Larchant, and ultimately derive from the nave of Notre-Dame in Paris.[37] This restrained and austere architectural vocabulary recalls ideas that would have dominated the Parisian scene in the decades between about 1190 and 1220.

There may also have been some relationship to the monastic churches built by Louis IX after his return from Crusade in 1254. Although these are all destroyed, the evidence suggests that they may have been severe in style.[38] The 1270s in particular saw the construction of a number of monuments with a similar aesthetic in Provence, such as the Templar chapel at Avignon, constructed probably between 1273 and 1281, and the cathedral of Aix, both of which share some of the same types of visual and spatial effects of Sant'Eligio and Saint-Jean-de-Malte.[39]

There are also some interesting connections between Sant'Eligio and the neighboring church and hospital of San Giovanni a Mare (pl. 10, no. 15), which, like Saint-Jean-de-Malte in Aix, belonged to the Knights Hospitaler. Both Neapolitan churches are accessible through portals along their south flank. Although mostly built in the twelfth century, San Giovanni a Mare was expanded towards the east with a flat-ended chevet in the late thirteenth or early fourteenth century, and the nave, like that of Sant'Eligio, consists of four short bays, in this instance supported by reused ancient columns. As one of only three foundations of the Knights in southern Italy, San Giovanni a Mare was an important site for the order and would clearly have benefited from the new political regime with its renewed ties to Provence.

The similarities of Sant'Eligio to Charles of Anjou's church in Aix permit the suggestion that the nave of the Neapolitan church might reflect aspects of the king's tastes in the 1270s, and that these may ultimately have been derived from the Parisian milieu of earlier in the century – indeed, from the Paris that Charles would have known in his youth. Although there is no record of the name of the architect or master builder at Sant'Eligio, it is highly probable that he was French and possibly from the northeast, for the style of Saint-Jean- de-Malte seems as new to Provence as that of Sant'Eligio is to Naples.

The spare and utilitarian vocabulary of these monuments corresponds to Charles's instructions for the interior volumes in the palace chapel of Bari, in turn modeled on the royal chapel at the castle of San Lorenzo near Foggia.[40] The taste suggested by these monuments is certainly distinct from that of Louis IX in Paris and its environs, which, at least prior to the Crusade of 1248–54, are among the most ornate productions of the Gothic style (Saint-Denis, the Sainte-Chapelle, Saint-Germain-en-Laye).[41] Nor does this style relate to the brittle and refined architecture of late thirteenth-century Burgundy (for example, Saint-Thibaut-en-Auxois), or the western bays of the nave of Saint-Urbain at Troyes, which Charles himself helped to complete in the 1270s with donations of wood and stone.[42]

Yet if there is a reference to Parisian architecture at Sant'Eligio, it takes the form of a "recollection" of the austerity of the buildings associated with Philip Augustus, the lean and limpid style that characterized the churches of 1180–1220 in Paris and its region. In that sense, one might even view the aesthetic of these buildings as strangely anachronistic, perhaps as a result of the personal tastes of the king, who, as we saw, expressed his preferences for simple and austere wall surfaces in other projects (now lost) to his architects.

Although fragmentary remains of a façade lie buried in the wall of the apartment house to the west of Sant'Eligio, the scale of the large portal on the south flank of the church indicates that it was always intended for its present location as an entrance from the market to the east (pl. 4). The quality of the execution of the clustered shafts, the finely modeled leaves and crockets of the archivolts, the small-scale and delicate execution of the bases (App. 5, fig. 1), and the delicate tracery of the gable indicate that this was the work of a French sculptor familiar with northern French prototypes (pl. 20). Recent cleaning has revealed, however, an additional element to the design: the archivolts are carved of two types of stone, gray *pietrarsa* flanking a torus of creamy white limestone, so that an element of color was integrated into the conception of the architectural forms. The handling of the bases, crockets, and the head of Christ at the apex of the gable suggest a high-level Parisian workshop, analogous to the chapels on the flanks of Notre-Dame in Paris, the chapel of Navarre of the Collegiate church of Mantes, and other central monuments of Parisian sculptural design of the last quarter of the thirteenth century (pl. 21).[43] The "lumpy" capitals are also similar to those on the tomb of Isabelle of Aragon at Cosenza (pl. 6).

A stairway to the west of the south portal contains remains of a tower and provides access to a narrow passage behind the gable of the portal. In the Aragonese period this structure was expanded to become the clock tower over the street along the south flank of the church (pl. 17).[44]

The other new church established in the new market quarter of the city was that of the Carmelites, reconstructed over the site of an earlier foundation famous for a much-venerated image of the Virgin.[45] In 1270 the

19 Naples, Sant'Eligio, detail of the south portal (author)

king gave 30 square cannae (79.380 square meters) for the construction of a church and monastery in memory of his parents, Louis VIII and Blanche of Castile.[46] Charles may have come to know the order when he was in the Holy Land during the crusade of 1248, and Louis IX had founded a chapel for them in Paris in 1260.[47] Tradition reports a donation from Charles's second wife, Margaret of Tonnerre, of 1,000 ducats, and an equal sum provided by Elizabeth of Bavaria, the mother of Conradin.[48] In 1301 Charles II made further donations of land "pro fieri faciendo Oratorio fratribus predicte Ecclesie . . ."[49]

20   Naples, Sant'Eligio, detail of the south portal (Massimo Velo)

The Carmelites were a relatively new order of obscure origins that seems to have emerged from the eremitic communities on Mount Carmel in the Holy Land.[50] They made an impression on the crusaders of 1248–54, a number of whom began to support their migration to Europe as the Muslim reconquest began to threaten the communities. The order flourished in the urban environments of Europe and received considerable support in the last years of the thirteenth century from Boniface VIII. In Naples itself, the miraculous image

21   Saint-Denis, France, triforium capitals in western bays, south flank of the nave (author)

of the Virgin ("La Bruna") became and is still the object of special veneration, and this image no doubt accounts for much of the wealth and importance of the foundation.[51]

The medieval church was damaged in an earthquake in 1731, and the church was elaborately and beautifully restored between 1755 and 1766 by Nicola Tagliacozzi Canale (pl. 22). The present façade is the work of Giovanni del Gaizo and the tower of Giovanni Giacomo di Conforto.[52]

In the case of the Carmine, the lavish Baroque decoration was preserved after the bombardment of 1943. The only visible remains of the older church are the rib vaults encased in Baroque plaster visible at the east end. A plan of 1662 preserved in the Archivo de Simancas indicates a simple cross-shaped plan with seven lateral chapels on either side of an aisleless nave, a type of plan fairly standard for mendicant foundations of the thirteenth century (pl. 23).

The third urban project in Naples that can be associated with Charles of Anjou and his son Charles II is the grand Augustinian monastery of Sant'Agostino alla Zecca. Originally a Basilian convent dedicated to Saint Vincent, the property was given to the Augustinian friars in 1259.[53] The site was expanded with the gift of a cemetery outside the walls on the east side of the city by Archbishop Ayglerius in 1270, and at that point the new monastic complex was begun.[54] In 1279 Charles of Anjou donated more land outside the walls near the Porta Nuova for the completion of the conventual buildings: "pro faciendo claustro, domibus, et horto necessariis pro dictis fratribus."[55] In May 1300 Charles II gave further funds of 89 once for the construction of the church, and in December 1301 he provided 60 more "in subsidium constructionis operis fabrice loci et Ecclesie, quam nos ipsi fundavimus," stipulating that the church be dedicated to the Magdalen.[56] Construction nevertheless extended well into the fourteenth century.[57] During the tenure of Giacomo da Viterbo, a noted Augustinian scholar, as Archbishop of Naples (1302–8), the monastery rose to even greater prominence and prestige, becoming one of the most important of the

22   Naples, Santa Maria del Carmine, interior from the west (Archivi Alinari, Florence)

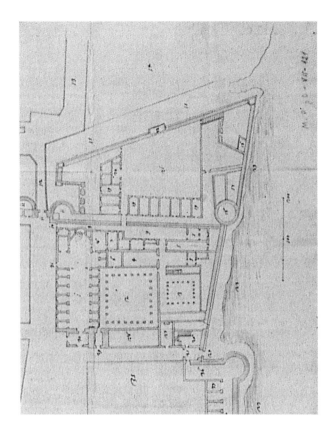

23 Naples, Santa Maria del Camine, plan from the Archivio General di Simancas, 1662 (Ministerio de Educacíon, cultura y Deporte, MPD. VII-121)

Augustinian *studia*. A donation by Bartolomeo da Capua assisted in the completion of the apse; De Lellis noted that the arch over the chancel carried the arms of the Da Capua and Loria families.[58]

By 1287 Sant'Agostino had become a *studium generalium* of the Augustinian order, and in 1300 the site of a General Chapter. On that occasion Charles II gave the friars a relic of the head of Saint Luke in a silver reliquary and promised an income of 30 once a year for the *studium*.[59] The continued wealth and importance of Sant'Agostino are attested not only by the splendor of the Baroque decoration, executed between 1641 and 1697 by Bartolomeo Picchiatti, but also by its considerable income, which in the sixteenth century is recorded as 6,000 ducats to support a community of sixty friars.[60]

The monastic complex, like the medieval church, was vast in scale. There were two cloisters, one large and one small, eight small dormitories, a library, archive, and other practical structures that served the needs of the community, the faculty, and the students.

But today almost nothing remains of all this. Rebuilt many times, starting after the earthquake of 1456, what remained of the medieval complex was effectively obliterated by the nineteenth-century urban renewal of Naples. The restoration of the splendid Baroque church is only now being completed (2003), while the medieval structure lies hidden within the walls.[61] The approximate plan published by Alisio reveals a wide church, consisting of a nave flanked by narrow aisles and shallow lateral chapels along the outer walls (pl. 24).[62] In the lateral chapels some rib vaults are visible under the stucco, which confirms that the plan of the present building is that of the medieval church.

Only the chapter house at Sant'Agostino survives as a medieval structure. In 1903 this building excited Emile Bertaux's interest because he thought that the two central capitals were Swabian.[63] I believe, however, that all the pieces of the chapter house supports (bases, columns, and capitals) are reused antique elements, some with later recutting, as is visible from the reversed Doric capital used as a base, the columns, and the capitals (pl. 25). The keystones and portal carry the arms of the Galeota family (pl. 26), and the style of the portal, framed as a series of slender moldings in colored marble, is characteristic of a variety of Neapolitan portals of the 1330s and later. The chapter house is thus a late addition to the

24 Naples, Sant'Agostino alla Zecca, plan (Alisio 1980)

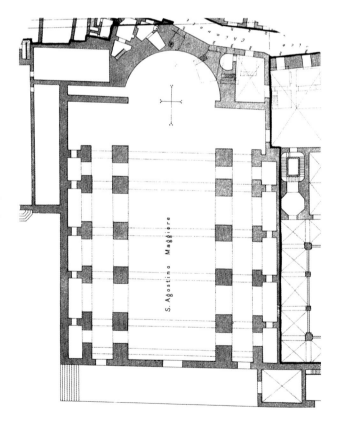

25 Naples, Sant'Agostino alla Zecca, capital of the chapter house (Giovanni Genova)

26 Naples, Sant'Agostino alla Zecca, Galeota arms at entrance portal to chapter house (Giovanni Genova)

original complex and clearly fourteenth century – perhaps even mid-fourteenth century, in date.

In 1279 Charles initiated work on the Castel Nuovo by the sea, at a site slightly to the west of the city. In doing so, he displaced a Franciscan community established in the ruins of a Roman villa,[64] for which an older church dedicated to the Virgin provided the name of Santa Maria di Palazzo. In their adoption of an (abandoned?) church and in their detachment from the city, this first Franciscan settlement of Naples reflected the early character of the order.[65] When Charles requisitioned the site for the construction of the new royal residence in 1279, he gave the Franciscans a new location closer to the city in exchange.[66] The new Franciscan foundation was called Santa Maria la Nova and was later heavily patronized by the Aragonese nobility.

The church and monastic complex now date entirely from the fifteenth century and later, without any visible remains of the medieval structures.[67] However, the plan of the church – a large rectangular hall with flanking lateral chapels and a square chancel – is no doubt that of the medieval monument and corresponds in type to the similar plans at the Carmine and Sant' Agostino.

When the king initiated the reconstruction of the new monastery in 1279 he guaranteed masons and materials for the work. Nevertheless, construction proceeded slowly, in spite of an indulgence of 2 December 1290 for those who visited the church.[68]

In the "religious politics" of Naples a further note might be added on Santa Maria la Nova. Although its fame is now eclipsed by that of the Franciscan houses of San Lorenzo and Santa Chiara, both favored by the Angevin nobility and the court, Santa Maria la Nova remained an important Franciscan center, and was closely associated with the Strict Observance. It was one of the few houses to adhere to a tradition of poverty and austerity: in 1585, when the community consisted of 150 friars, it accepted no external income, as was also the case with the friars in the communities of Santa Chiara and Santa Croce.[69]

The battered remains of the small apse of the parish church of Sant'Agrippino a Forcella (pl. 27), originally also a Basilian foundation, cannot be dated with any certainty, but would in a general sense seem to be the product of the Francocentric interests in Naples.[70]

The two religious foundations that we can associate most specifically with Charles of Anjou, however, are two rural projects: the Cistercian abbeys founded in 1274 to commemorate his victories at Benevento in 1266 and Tagliacozzo in 1268 (pls. 28–30).[71] Now reduced to fragments of walls and piles of rubble, these two monuments were once the most prominent examples of Charles of Anjou's religious patronage in Italy, and by 1277, at least, were envisioned to function as centers of French culture and spirituality.[72] After 1277, in particular, Charles closely followed the progress of construction and associated the monasteries with his parents as well with his two great military victories. Yet the story of these foundations, their construction and subsequent decay, is intimately tied to the vicissitudes of French rule in the kingdom; the particularly unhappy history of the abbey of Santa Maria

27 Naples, Sant'Agrippino a Forcella, apse (Massimo Velo)

because of his family's long and close ties to the order,[76] but above all because he was in desperate need of their contribution. In his testy letters to Clement IV, Charles blamed his failure to pay his debts on this and the other recalcitrant orders,[77] and it was only after nine years of litigation and the mediation of the papacy that a compromise was reached. In late 1272 the Cistercians sent four of their most powerful abbots to Rome. From there they traveled to Naples in the first days of January 1273 to finalize a compromise solution with Charles, ultimately settling on a payment of 30,000 pounds, a fraction of the original total, but a significant sum nonetheless.[78]

It must have been on this occasion, and as a *quid pro quo*, that the king agreed to found the two abbeys, for his first instructions on the founding of the new houses appear only after the Cistercian General Chapter of September 1273. The statutes of the chapter state that two monks from the abbey of Loroux and two monks from the abbey of Royaumont were to travel to Naples to establish a pair of monasteries in accordance with the strictures of the order.[79]

Irrespective of the combination of circumstances and motivations that may have led to these foundations, what is striking is Charles's engagement in the projects after 1277. Did the construction of the abbeys simply bring

28 Santa Maria della Vittoria, plan from excavations of 1898 (Fiocca 1903)

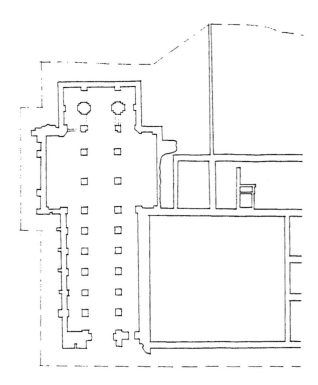

della Vittoria attests with pungency to the fact that the nationalistic and politicized role with which they were invested was not lost on contemporaries.

Although Charles of Anjou was perhaps no more than a conventionally active patron of religious projects, he nonetheless became actively and deeply involved in the construction of these two sites. His interest in detail (the style of roof tiles, pavements, materials for wall construction and window frames, for example) and his impatience with delay are recorded in hundreds of documents and are similar in his obsessive attention to detail in the documents that concern the construction of the royal palaces, especially that of Bari.[73]

The foundation of the abbeys in 1274 was stimulated by the resolution of litigation with the Cistercian order over the payment of the special crusading tithe declared in France to support Charles's conquest. The agreement between Charles of Anjou and Urban IV for the conquest of Sicily had from the outset identified the enterprise as a crusade, an important designation because it thus entitled Charles as papal champion to the proceeds of the tithe declared for three years (1264–67).[74] Several orders, among them the Templars and the Cistercians, resisted these taxes on the grounds of their traditional immunity.[75] The obstinate refusal of the Cistercians seems to have especially rankled with Charles, perhaps

29　Santa Maria della Vittoria, view of ruins in the early twentieth century (Rome: Istituto Centrale per il Catalogo e la Documentazione)

out the king's passion for architecture? Was he worried about the state of his soul, or determined to do these foundations "right"? Was his interest and absorption in the abbeys the result of his own piety and the strong Capetian family alliance with the Cistercian order? I tend to think not, and would instead suggest that the degree of royal engagement after 1277 suggests a level of personal interest that far exceeded his need to be a good host to the Cistercian guests, especially when he had been rather cross with the order as a whole.

There may also have been an element of personal interest in the construction of Realvalle and Vittoria that stemmed perhaps from Charles's youth in Paris. The Cistercian abbey of Royaumont, intimately associated with Louis IX, was the site of Charles of Anjou's earliest recorded "architectural" experience. According to Guil-

laume de Saint-Pathus, Louis IX not only worked alongside the monks carrying stones for the construction of the abbey, but also obliged his younger brothers to participate. The chronicles suggest that the younger siblings were not entirely enthusiastic about this enterprise, and Charles (perhaps then aged about six?) attempted to stop and play. They were reproved by their elder brother, who urged them to emulate the untiring work of the monks.[80] In the south Italian Cistercian venture, not long after Louis IX's death at Tunis in 1270 and the initial preparations for his canonization, the episodes recounted by Guillaume de Saint-Pathus may have taken on greater significance, especially if they formed part of the verbal tradition that surrounded the recently deceased king. Both Charles and the Cistercians would have had a common interest in promoting a Capetian saint, espe-

30 Santa Maria di Realvalle, flank of south aisle (Barbara Bini)

probably made in 1282, in which he emphasized that his mother, Blanche, at her death as a Cistercian nun, was the *sancta radix* who gave birth to the holy "branch" of Louis IX.[81]

But there are other considerations as well: the abbeys were in strategically important sites. Vittoria is on the northern borders of the kingdom, not far from the main road that gave access through the Abruzzi mountains to the south, while Realvalle, located by the main route from Naples to Calabria, is in a region described as volatile and in need of tighter royal control and greater security.[82] Many of Charles's most intense building projects were on the edges of the kingdom, in areas that were later to be the sites of new towns founded by Charles's successors for precisely the same reasons.[83]

It may also be that Charles realized that the abbeys could serve the needs of the new French colonists and help him to settle the kingdom. It was hard to persuade the settlers, whether noble or common, to stay in Italy, and the king was forced to enact measures to prevent those enfeoffed with large domains from returning to France. The foundation documents of 1277 for Realvalle and Vittoria suggest that he was hoping that the abbeys would become centers of French piety, and that they would be used for family burial. They also reveal the king's thinking about their function: founded in gratitude to God and the Virgin for his victories, and in memory of his parents, they were also to honor the Frenchmen who "cum multis sudoribus, et laboribus, cum multa insuper effusione sanguinis" had liberated the kingdom from the hands of its Swabian persecutors.[84] Only men from France, Provence, and Forcalquier were allowed to become monks, so that they would pray more diligently for the souls of French nationals and their descendants in the kingdom.[85] In a lengthy and detailed recital of his thinking, Charles further stated that a mixture of nationalities within the abbeys would lead to dissent and discord, an observation perhaps based on his experience with the tensions in his multi-national army. It was thus necessary that all members of the monastic communities speak the same language to preserve harmony and the quality of religious life, whereas discord would damage the reputation of the abbeys, impeding their role as the object of veneration and support from the French community.[86] In the event that these strictures were abrogated, the properties would revert to the crown.[87] Charles thus viewed the abbeys as cultural centers, sanctuaries that would become magnets for French piety and points of reference for the settlers. This emphasis upon the abbeys as uniquely French strongholds was in keeping with a speech that the king is said to have given on the eve of the Battle of Taglia-

cially in view of currents in the papacy and papal curia that were contrary to French interests. And the Cistercian abbots who came to Naples to reach a settlement on the tithe may well not have hesitated to remind Charles of his family's long allegiance to the order and his own early experiences in return for their financial contribution towards his conquest. That there was some royal interest in the long-term benefits of a close association with the Cistercians emerges, for example, in Charles's depositions for the canonization of Louis IX, cozzo, in which he emphasized that it was the French who fought on behalf of the Lord's work;[88] we might also note that the documents on the burial chapel of his son at Trani cathedral also insisted on French clergy.[89]

The documents pertaining to Vittoria were studied by Pietro Egidi shortly before the First World War, a study exemplary for the thoroughness and care with which the evidence for the foundation and construction of the abbey is considered.[90] The site has been excavated twice, in the years 1899–1902 and again in 1985–86.[91] In contrast, Realvalle, located outside the town of Scafati near Pompeii, is better preserved but has never been excavated. The recent (1989–90) construction of a house directly over what would have been the area of the crossing and apse has now rendered excavation impossible; at the time of the construction of this house, however, the bases of the crossing piers were visible.[92]

The founding documents date only from 1277, when the monastic communities were called to the site from France. By then construction had been underway for three years, presumably to provide housing for the monks. As has been observed on many occasions, the name of Santa Maria della Vittoria recalled Notre-Dame-de-la-Victoire, a monastery outside Senlis founded by Philip Augustus after the Battle of Bouvines in 1214.[93] Yet Charles gave precedence to Realvalle because it commemorated his first and greatest victory in Italy, the Battle of Benevento when the kingdom was won.[94]

The first document issued by the royal chancery concerning the abbeys was a letter of 1 January 1274 to the abbot of Casanova in the Abruzzo requesting hospitality for the two Cistercian monks recently arrived from France, Peter and John, who were to prepare for the construction of Santa Maria della Vittoria.[95] He sent to the Abruzzo his royal representatives, Simon of Angart and Pietro de Carrellis, along with a certain friar Giacomo and Pierre de Chaules, to join the abbot of Casanova and the two new Cistercian monks to identify the site and estimate what would be necessary in labor and materials for the construction of the monastery.[96]

The two monks from France were from the abbey of Loroux (or Oratorio) in Anjou.[97] By February Charles had named the supervisors of the project: the judge Angelo da Foggia in collaboration with the monk Peter of Oratorio.[98] The two were identified as the accountants, or *expensores operis*, while Pierre de Chaules supervised construction as a general manager "que pecunia recepta, ad constructionem dicti operis cum notitia et consilio dicti clerici."[99] Pierre de Chaules, cleric and trusted familiar of the king, presided over many major work sites between 1274 and 1283, even though he never

received the title *prothomagister*.[100] In May 1274 he was instructed to take on also the supervision of the new work at Santa Maria di Realvalle, and to spend alternate months at each site.[101] By that time, the two monks from the abbey of Royaumont had also arrived in Italy, and were sent to the site of Scafati along with a *prothomagister*, Gauthier d'Asson, and the *expensores operis*, *Petro de Burgna, gallico*, and *Iacobo Pullino de Scala*.[102]

The two monks sent to found Realvalle, Nicholas and Robert, were from the French royal abbey of Royaumont. They arrived in May 1274, and Charles sent them, with his agents, to the site of Scafati, near Pompeii.[103] An architect is mentioned from the start as present in the project, although he is not at first named in the documents and Pierre de Chaules was still supervising this project and the ongoing work at Vittoria.[104] Each abbey was to have three account books, that of Pierre de Chaules, that of the Cistercians, and that of the king's agent (the *magister rationalibus*).[105]

The architect at Realvalle was named in August 1274, when several documents were issued that concerned the salary of Gauthier d'Asson. He was, however, to follow the instructions of Pierre de Chaules.[106] In April 1278 Gauthier was replaced by Thibaud de Saumur, *prothomagister* from that day until the completion of the work.[107]

Although the documents are scanty for the first three years, work seems to have proceeded at both sites in spite of changes in personnel. In July 1277 Charles wrote to the abbots of Royaumont, Loroux, and Cîteaux to send abbots, twenty monks, and ten *conversi* (lay brothers) to settle each of the two new monasteries. At the same time, he sent instructions for the acquisition of liturgical books for each community.[108] With the arrival of the monks in late 1277, management of the projects passed to the hands of the new abbots, whose names subsequently appear in the documents of the abbeys.

The church of Vittoria was consecrated during a visit by Charles on 12 May 1278, although it is unlikely that more than the presbytery and perhaps the transept were completed by that time.[109] The king's visit precipitated new urgency in construction, for it was followed by a series of rapidly issued orders for masons and other laborers.[110] Charles gave specific instructions on the type of construction to be accomplished, ordering that "all the work in the church be executed with formwork except for the quoins, windows, the ribs of the vaults and the pillars which should be made of cut stone."[111]

At both sites shortages of funds and labor, recalcitrant workers, and other difficulties hindered progress. The king was adamant that work should continue at a rapid pace, and his supervisors strained to fulfill these demands.[112] And in spite of the difficulties in finding an adequate workforce, work proceeded apace: in 1280 at Vittoria a request was made for the beams for the centering of the vaults and metal for the completion of the doors and windows.[113] In 1281 it was announced that the monks' dormitory was almost complete.[114] In March and April 1281 orders for roof tiles and more wood for roofs and centering suggest that work was rapidly reaching completion.[115] In April and May 1282 several documents concern glass for the refectory, dormitory, and church. It is probably safe to assume that, by 1282 or 1283, the major buildings of the monasteries were covered and put into use, for the texts include mention of items such as the choir stalls for the monks.[116]

The documents concerning Realvalle and Vittoria thus provide an exceptional record of the progress of construction of a Cistercian abbey. When funds were in hand, construction was fast, as would normally have been the case with any well-funded Cistercian foundation. It is striking that much was built in spite of the extraordinary expenses of Charles's other projects, above all the repairs to castles and fortifications but also the construction and equipping of galleys for the projected campaigns in the East.

Almost nothing remains at either site. Already in 1313 the forces of the emperor Henry VII threatened to destroy Vittoria in retribution for the death of Conradin.[117] By the sixteenth century the abbey lay in ruins. Several of its portals were inserted into churches in Scurcola Marsicana (pl. 33). Charles's stipulations on the nationality of the monks may itself have caused some of the difficulties: the monastic population seems always to have been small, so that the maintenance of farm properties and the buildings were probably always assigned to lay workers. Both were repeatedly damaged by earthquakes, and Realvalle, already partially abandoned, was affected by the eruption of Vesuvius in 1631. Early in the sixteenth century Vittoria was abandoned, while Realvalle, swampy and snake-filled as described by Summonte, survived until the early nineteenth century.[118] It is interesting also to note that in the various records of aristocratic patronage in Naples, neither abbey seems ever to have received significant support from noble or lay patrons, or to have been the object of special attention outside the royal family.

The plan of Vittoria (pl. 28) is roughly based on that of the rebuilt east end of the mother house of the Cistercian order, Cîteaux in Burgundy, reconstructed between about 1190 and 1200.[119] This type of extended rectangular chevet was adopted to provide a large number of eastern chapels while at the same time preserving the flat-ended chevet characteristic of the order.

The plan type is found in the choir of the ruined church of Fontainejean near Bourges (Loiret), which has been dated to the fourth decade of the thirteenth century. Indeed, the dimensions of Fontainejean are similar to those of Vittoria: the nave and aisles were roughly 20.5 meters wide inside the walls, and the transept was about 40 meters long, thus projecting about 10 meters on either side of the crossing.[120] Cistercian practice would tend to suggest that the aisles would have been a quarter of the total width of the nave (about 5.15 m.) and the nave approximately 10.30 meters wide.[121] If Cistercian rules of proportion were adhered to here, the total height of the nave of Vittoria would have equaled its total width, placing the vaults (if they were completed) at about 20.5 meters above ground level. This would have been about the height of the nave of Sant'Eligio, which was, however, about 2 meters narrower. On the basis of analogy with other Cistercian elevations, it can be proposed that the elevation of both Vittoria and Realvalle would have been two-storied, consisting of a nave and a clerestory.

What else can be said about a missing building? Fragments of wall indeed attest that the lower walls of the church at Vittoria were built in ashlar masonry (pl. 31), while the upper surfaces seem to have been of rubble. A base discovered in a doorway not far from the southeast corner of the church where it abuts the cloister attests to French templates (pl. 32). This is also true of the jamb profiles of the doorways taken from Santa Maria della Vittoria and set into the church of Sant' Antonio in Scurcola Marsicana (pl. 33). The few architectural details that survive suggest that the construction was executed by masons well trained in French detailing and using French templates.

We can also suppose that the Cistercian monks brought with them the plan. This may have been as schematic as those drawn by Villard de Honnecourt much earlier in the thirteenth century (pls. 28 and 34) or a more developed drawing. The apparent absence of an architect at Vittoria until several years into construction may suggest that the monk Peter, documented at the site until the arrival of an architect in the late 1270s, might have had that role. John, the other Cistercian at Vittoria, disappeared almost immediately from the records, however. Did he die, or, like so many Frenchmen, return home? Peter of Oratorio may have had some level of architectural expertise, but he seems to have been the only member of the Cistercian order at these two sites who did: all other workers seem to have been hired or conscripted.

At Realvalle there is different but equally exiguous evidence on the character of the church. Five bays of the

31 Santa Maria della Vittoria, detail of ashlar masonry of wall structure (author)

32 Santa Maria della Vittoria, detail of base from east range of cloister (Marina Righetti Tosti-Croce)

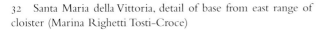

33 Scurcola Marsicana, portal of Sant'Antonio (Barbara Bini)

south flank of the nave, part of the cloister, and several conventual buildings survive (pl. 30), though much modified since construction. There has been no excavation.

The construction of the walls is less refined at Realvalle. Whereas there was an abundant supply of limestone near Vittoria, some of it purportedly from the ruins of the Roman town of Alba Fucens, high-quality materials were scarce near Realvalle. The walls are therefore built of roughly shaped rubble held together with a large amount of mortar. The work was organized into horizontal beds that correspond to the coursing of the

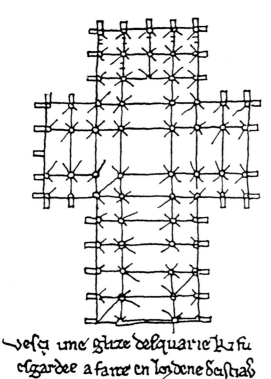

Ueſa une gliƷe deſquarie ki fu
eſgardee a faire en loidene baſtiaƷ

34 Villard de Honnecourt, "Voici une église . . ." (after Dimier 1949)

best sculpture in northern French workshops (compare that of the triforium of Saint-Denis of the 1270s, for example: pls. 21 and 36).

The meager remains at each site permit only limited interpretations of the evidence. Whether in the end ambitious claims can be made for them as important sources for the importation of French workmanship and architectural ideas is uncertain.[122] That the plan of Realvalle later inspired that of San Lorenzo Maggiore cannot be demonstrated without excavation and seems improbable.[123] Evidence of a Cistercian presence in the design and construction process is minimal; only the monk Peter of Oratorio may have had distinct architectural competence, although this is not in fact specified in any of the documents that concern Vittoria. Peter may have transmitted the Cîteaux plan (and elevation?) to Italy, for Vittoria is the first and only (surviving) example in the peninsula of the expanded rectangular presbytery associated with that filiation. He may also have had a role in determining other features of the monastic buildings and the elevation of the church. But no other Cistercians active in the design or labor force are identified, and in general the documents on the construction of both

35 Santa Maria di Realvalle, base (author)

single half-columns of the aisle bays carved out of gray tuff. As the walls rose, the rubble masonry became less tidy, perhaps because Charles kept urging greater speed to the work. The walls would presumably have been covered with plaster and whitewash and painted with false jointing, so that the rough surfaces would have been concealed. Lancet windows are inserted in the upper aisle walls above a horizontal cornice.

The aisle columns are 6.25 meters apart. If we can assume again that the bays were square and that the same rules of proportion applied here as in other Cistercian churches, the nave would have been about 12.50 meters wide and the total width of the nave including the aisles about 25 meters. The church may thus have been larger than Santa Maria della Vittoria, and the height, at roughly 25 meters also, would have been roughly comparable to structures such as Longpont in France.

At Realvalle the workforce was divided into several segments: French masons paid by the piece worked alongside Italian counterparts. Stonecutters from Naples were employed to carve the columns, bases, and plinths (pls. 30 and 35), but the French sculptors executed most of the capitals, at least if we can judge from the surviving examples. In spite of weathering, the variety and delicacy of the carving of the capitals are reminiscent of the

36   Santa Maria di Realvalle, capital of south aisle (Barbara Bini)

abbeys demonstrate the frequent and acute shortages of skilled workmen at both sites, a situation that would not have been likely if a significant number of Cistercian masons had been present.[124]

Nor can it be said that the two abbeys reflected the tastes of the court in Paris. The plan of Vittoria, and the physical remains at Realvalle, suggest a continuity of the strongly formed Cistercian models developed in the thirteenth century with an updating of details such as capitals and portal moldings. There is no surviving evidence of the elegance of Paris, Parisian Rayonnant, or "court style" prototypes at Realvalle or Vittoria. Instead, the evidence suggests a typically utilitarian and Cistercian approach to the conventual buildings and the church, the kind of sensible and austere Gothic that may well have coincided with Charles of Anjou's own taste in buildings.

The documentation of the construction of the two abbeys, however, is a remarkable source of information about the character of a royal construction project. Although the registers on the construction of Realvalle and Vittoria start after a three-year period of silence in 1274, there is in 1277 a sudden profusion of documents. The lacuna suggests at least two possibilities: either work in the first three years after the inception of the abbeys proceeded smoothly and uneventfully (although there

seem to be fairly regular payments for part of that period at Vittoria, smooth progress would have been unusual in the Kingdom of Naples), or the king was less engaged than he was to become later in the construction process. After 1277 the number of texts is striking, and reflects a shift in Charles's level of interest and involvement: a cynical view, as suggested above, might attribute this to a political agenda related to the canonization of Louis IX. It would appear that a site visit to Santa Maria della Vittoria in anticipation of the arrival of the monastic community later that year stimulated a flurry of activity: the essential buildings were clearly far from ready, and the king was perhaps in danger of encountering public embarrassment and loss of Cistercian support for the canonization procedures.[125] So, although letters were written to France in July 1277 requesting the arrival of monks for both abbeys, the rash of documents generated after this visit indicates that much remained to be done to house the new communities.[126]

There were large numbers of workmen at the sites, ranging from almost 300 at Realvalle to more than 500 at Vittoria, but here, as in Charles's other construction projects, the sites were plagued by absenteeism and desertion. In 1279 and 1280 local authorities were constantly exhorted to return fleeing workers, in chains if necessary, and those found were to be fed bread and water.[127] New workers were to be obtained at any cost, and transported to the building sites in chains if necessary.[128] The problem was especially acute in 1278 and continued until the completion of the works in the early 1280s.[129] Since the administrators were mostly Frenchmen, one can well imagine that there were also misunderstandings and hostility between the Italian labor force (who must have spoken a variety of dialects) and their French supervisors. Gualtiero, the supervisor at Vittoria, tried to improve conditions by increasing the stipend, for which he was bitterly reproached by the crown and ordered to pay the difference out of his own funds.[130]

The king was impatient with the progress at the building sites. In his view the workers were lazy and incompetent.[131] At Vittoria in June 1278 he imposed an armed guard to enforce a full day's work on the laborers and to place in chains any who attempted to flee or were uncooperative or slow.

Much of the workforce was conscripted.[132] The supervisors at the building sites (and this is true for all of Charles's construction projects) sent requests to the king for the workmen they needed (both skilled and manual labor) and the king ordered his regional administrators to obtain the requisite number of workers for building sites in their jurisdiction. If a certain region could not provide an adequate number of laborers, neighboring regions were required to fulfill the quotas.[133] As Egidi notes, the justiciar of the Abruzzo was regularly required to fulfill requests for workmen, but when these could not be found, laborers were requisitioned from the regions of Campania, Basilicata, and Molise.

Estimates of the population of the kingdom vary widely, from Pirenne's roughly 1.2 million inhabitants to estimates of between 3 and 4 million.[134] In the late 1270s Charles of Anjou had as many as ten or fifteen major construction projects underway simultaneously, at times with 300–500 workers apiece. If this figure is roughly correct, then as many as 5,000–7,000 men may have been employed in construction, a number that comprised a significant proportion of the male population. When the war of 1282 broke out, many of these would have been sent off to fight, leaving the buildings in a state of suspension and robbing the kingdom of the labor trained in construction between 1268 and 1282.

The difficulties of the labor situation may explain to some extent why the architectural legacy of the first generation of the Angevin conquest was so ephemeral. Skilled masons were hard to find, and much of the workforce was conscripted, working for minimal wages, and often far from home. Under these circumstances the quality of work produced was probably poor. This would have been particularly problematic if supervision were not adequate during the mixing of mortar. The rubble masonry, as at Realvalle, would have been particularly vulnerable if mortar was poor (one colleague has described the situation as like that of a cardboard box filled with wet pebbles); even in ashlar masonry, exposure to water can rapidly damage the adhesion of the wall surfaces. In the case of the two Cistercian abbeys, maintenance of the monastic complex in the perennially under-populated sites must always have presented difficulties.

The documents for Vittoria also provide indications of the social context into which Charles's abbeys were inserted, and here in particular the local French community enfeoffed with properties.[135] The behavior of some of these individuals suggests that we are sometimes in the presence of full-blown feudal anarchy. On 28 January 1278, only a few months after the monastic community had arrived at the site, Charles had to ask his bailiff to take action against Eudes de Toucy, the king's "consaguineo carissimo," for having stolen carved stones intended for the construction of the abbey. In 1279 the lands of Vittoria were invaded by three French noblemen, perhaps brothers, from Saint-Gilles. Also in 1279, Milon de Calathas stole 400 sheep and 4 bulls from the monks. Again, in 1280, the king's "dearest cousin," Eudes de Toucy, prevented the monks from exercising their fishing rights in the Fucine lake. Eudes on this occasion seems to have gathered together a group of local barons to impede the monks' access to the water. Litigation on this matter continued through the reigns of Charles II and Robert. Thus, rather than becoming the locus of French piety and burial, as Charles had intended and even specified in the foundation documents, the abbey of Vittoria, at least, was a maelstrom of dissent and litigation, and, as noted elsewhere, there seems to have been a notable absence of pious donations to these houses from either the native or the French population.

Nor were things much better within the walls. In December 1279, only two years after the arrival of the French monastic community, the abbot asked the king for assistance in suppressing and punishing a disruptive faction of the community who were in contempt of religion, who disrupted monastic discipline, and who "vagabonded" outside the walls of the monastery. Had the mother house sent off its most troublesome faction to this new terrain?[136] If so, this would have been typical of many (later) colonial cultures.

The isolation of the two monasteries meant that their artistic impact on local building traditions was restrained. Cistercian monasteries, in any event, were not open as a rule to the general public, and we have seen that the workforce, brought in from elsewhere, would naturally have gravitated towards home again. There are a few portals that reflect Santa Maria della Vittoria in the Marsicano, as at Magliano de' Marsi (pls. 208 and 209), and it may be that there were elements (now lost) of architectural design that had an impact on nearby monuments in towns like Sulmona. But the state of the evidence suggests that there was no profound impact of the two abbeys on their local areas. And it may well be that in the difficult circumstances of their conception, gestation, and delivery, the two Cistercian abbeys were to remain sterile elements in the artistic landscape of southern Italy.

Charles also expressed devotion towards several local cults and holy sites in Puglia, among them the grotto of the Archangel Michael at Monte Sant'Angelo and the shrine to Saint Nicholas at Bari. In November 1276 he donated the bell from Manfredonia to the shrine of Saint Nicholas, which he declared a royal monument in gratitude for the cure of his son Philip.[137] Devotion to this saint was continued by Charles II, who provided a variety of reliquaries and helped to fund repairs to the towers, and this saint's popularity is attested in the wall paintings of the Cappella Minutolo and the Cappella Tocco in the cathedral of Naples.

The other important shrine for southern Italy was the grotto of the Archangel at Monte Sant'Angelo on the Gargano. The shrine has its origins deep in the obscurities of the Lombard past and was associated with the arrival of the Normans in southern Italy; there are testaments to both phases of the cult in the first staircase below the grotto in what is now the museum and in the vaults of the narthex to the grotto itself.[138]

The king was at Manfredonia and visited Monte Sant'Angelo in March 1267 and again in 1271, 1272, and 1273. In the visit of 1272 he accompanied Gregory X to the site.[139] He issued in 1271 an order to repair the road from Manfredonia to Monte Sant'Angelo in order to assist the visits of pilgrims.[140] Probably in connection with this work Charles created a new entrance to the grotto from the piazza, with a new staircase descending from this location.

The entrance porch was entirely rebuilt in the eighteenth century and no original traces of the medieval structure survive (pl. 38). The stairs that descend to the grotto behind the entrance porch retain, however, their pointed vaults and are flanked on the sides by burial niches, none of which preserves its inscription (pl. 39).

37 (*right*)   Monte Sant'Angelo, view of the tower (Barbara Bini)

38 (*below*)   Engraved view of the entrance to the sanctuary of Monte Sant'Angelo, Monte Sant'Angelo (Bibliotheca Hertziana)

39 Monte Sant'Angelo, view of the Angevin stairway to the grotto (Barbara Bini)

The most striking survival of Charles's contributions to the site is the octagonal tower (pls. 37 and 40), which still bears an inscription recording his support:

TEMPORE QUO CHRISTI CARNEM DE VIRGINE SUMPSIT
ANNO DOMINI MCCLXXIIII SUB PONTIFICATU GREGORII X
PROSPERE REGNANTE DOMINO CAROLO SICILIE ARCHIDI-
ACONO SUADENTE FELICE COEPTUM HOC OPUS PRO-
TOMAGISTRO IORDANO E MARANDO FRATE EIUS ENTE
XXVII MARCI HORA PRIMA SOLIS SECUNDE INDICTIONIS[141]

Yet in spite of what would appear to be the certainty of the date, the Angevin Registers record in 1278 that the chapter of the Monte Sant'Angelo requested assistance for the tower, which was threatening to collapse.[142] Had it been left incomplete? Was it poorly constructed?

Giordano and Marando of Monte Sant'Angelo were local masons well documented in the Angevin Registers for their work on the walls of Manfredonia. In 1278 Giordano is described as *prothomagister* at Manfredonia, a site where Marando was also present.[143]

The octagonal tower is decorated with an assortment of double and single windows. Some of the masonry appears to be reused Roman blocks (pl. 40). The architectural design and detailing, as was noted by Calò Mariani and others, is fully consistent with the Apulian

40 *(facing page)* Monte Sant'Angelo, base of the tower (Barbara Bini)

41   Bitonto, San Francesco, chancel arch and rib vault in altar area (Chester Brummel)

workshops active in the time of Frederick II, and there are, for example, strong affinities with the architecture of Castel del Monte, whose octagonal form it seems to imitate.[144]

In 1283 Charles also supported with a donation of land the reconstruction of the church of San Francesco at Bitonto (pls. 41–47).[145] This church, eclipsed by the beauty and importance of the cathedral of Bitonto, has been closed for decades and in 1999 underwent an important restoration.[146] As is typical of Franciscan architecture (Eboli, Lucera, etc.), the structure is a simple rectangular hall church with a square rib-vaulted chancel.

The patron of the work was Sergio Bove, a figure of considerable importance in the area of Bitonto. Originally from Ravello, he was part of the enterprising group from the Amalfi coast that spread its administrative and financial tentacles to Apulia. Bove was buried in the apse of the church in a large tomb, now unfortunately lost. Charles of Anjou had stipulated that the new church should be dedicated to the Magdalen. But it is not certain how much work was initially accomplished, for

there is another donation in 1291 "pro fabrica Ecclesiae et officianarum loci dictorum fratrum, quae in civitate Botontin construebatur."[147]

I believe that the east end of the church can be associated with the donation of Charles of Anjou in the 1280s. The chancel area has rich decorative detailing and the entrance arch, as well as the capricious consoles that support the rib vault of the apse, are particularly noteworthy and charming (pls. 41 and 42). Although Castellano has stated that these were new in Apulia and are therefore examples of Northern importation, no possible Northern source comes to mind.[148] Only the pointed profile of the rib suggests an updating of the local architectural vocabulary.

Although probably later in date, the same can be said of the west portal and of the cloister portal (pls. 44 and 47), which are among the most lively and beautiful examples of the flourishing sculptural workshops based in Apulia. The sculpture is related to portals at Sant' Agostino and San Francesco in Andria, constructed during the reigns of Charles II and Robert.[149] The hand-

43 Bitonto, San Francesco, interior from west (Chester Brummel)

42 (*right*) Bitonto, San Francesco, console of the chancel area (Chester Brummel)

some triple lancet window of the west façade is a nice example of imported French styles executed by local craftsmen (pl. 46).

How close is any of this to the tastes or preferences of Charles of Anjou or to the immediate circles of the court? The evidence suggests that we are, above all, in the presence of a delightful and eccentric local tradition characterized by the inventiveness of regional craftsmen,

a type of building that will later find more elegant and subdued expression in the east end of Santa Maria Maggiore in Barletta and in the portals of the mendicant churches of Andria. There is nothing to reveal a relationship with the sculptural workshops of any of the sites discussed above, such as Sant'Eligio and Realvalle.

In conclusion it may be said that perhaps the most fundamental contribution that Charles of Anjou made to southern Italy was not a legacy of religious building, but rather the construction of castles and fortifications and the urban reconfiguration of Naples. The latter was achieved by two centrally important urban works: the construction of the Castel Nuovo, which moved the center of political activity from the swampy, malodorous, and vulnerable area of the Castel Capuano to the sea in the southwest, and the construction of the Campo Moricino, or new market, by the port. In both cases Naples expanded towards the sea, leaving the insalubrious center behind.[150] Congestion was relieved by the

41

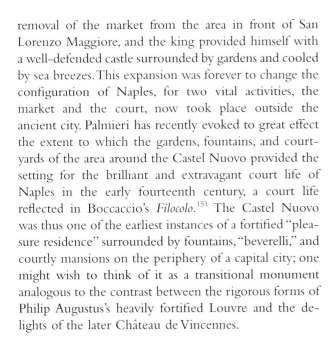

45   Bitonto, San Francesco, west façade (author)

46   Bitonto, San Francesco, triple lancet window of west façade (Barbara Bini)

removal of the market from the area in front of San Lorenzo Maggiore, and the king provided himself with a well-defended castle surrounded by gardens and cooled by sea breezes. This expansion was forever to change the configuration of Naples, for two vital activities, the market and the court, now took place outside the ancient city. Palmieri has recently evoked to great effect the extent to which the gardens, fountains, and court-yards of the area around the Castel Nuovo provided the setting for the brilliant and extravagant court life of Naples in the early fourteenth century, a court life reflected in Boccaccio's *Filocolo*.[151] The Castel Nuovo was thus one of the earliest instances of a fortified "plea-sure residence" surrounded by fountains, "beverelli," and courtly mansions on the periphery of a capital city; one might wish to think of it as a transitional monument analogous to the contrast between the rigorous forms of Philip Augustus's heavily fortified Louvre and the de-lights of the later Château de Vincennes.

Although little remains of the religious projects of Charles of Anjou, and although, more importantly, he was not a king inclined to spend either time or money on church building, it is nonetheless possible to draw some inferences about his taste in architectural matters. He clearly had a preference for austere and rather simple structures, as at Saint-Jean-de-Malte in Aix and as is confirmed by his instructions for the construction of chapels, such as that at the castle of Bari.[152] In Naples, the hospital church of Sant'Eligio, for all its irregu-larities and anomalies, would seem to reflect this royal taste.

The Cistercian style of the abbey churches of Realvalle and Vittoria would thus seem to have coin-cided with the tastes of the king himself – a match of the predilections of the patron with those of the recip-ients of his attention. Although the ruined condition of these sites precludes detailed conclusions about the char-acter of the elevations, one can suppose that they would

44 (*facing page*)   Bitonto, San Francesco, west portal (Barbara Bini)

47 Bitonto, San Francesco, base and decoration of west portal (author)

have adhered to certain proportional systems characteristic of the order and that they conformed to the general austerity still present in Cistercian architecture in the thirteenth century.

On the other hand, and especially in Apulia, Charles was associated with projects that entirely reflected local architectural expertise and styles. Although French masters, such as Pierre d'Angicourt, were present in the area, they were assigned to the work on fortifications. The reconstruction of the stairs to the grotto and the tower at Monte Sant'Angelo, and San Francesco at Bitonto, were executed in a local style.

The emphasis on "Frenchness" that emerges in the documents on Realvalle and Vittoria refers above all to the two abbeys and reflects their special function in relation to the settling of a French population in the kingdom. As noted above, when Charles specified that elements should be executed "in the French manner" he may have done so precisely because this was so difficult an effect to achieve.

Although the surviving churches and chapels that can be associated with Charles of Anjou suggest connections to architecture in Provence and the Ile-de-France, there is no attempt to imitate the buildings of Louis IX in Paris. With the exception of the portal of Sant'Eligio and the tomb of Isabelle of Aragon in Cosenza, the simple and lean forms of the surviving buildings in southern Italy could not be more different from the chapels and churches of Paris and its environs between 1235 and 1280. The rejection of the ornate and delicate architectural language of the Rayonnant style is all the more striking because it was precisely this architectural language that was exported to much of Europe as *opus francigenum*, and that can be seen, for example, in the overt and ostentatious Frenchness conspicuously produced in the newly conquered French domains of the Midi, as at Carcassonne and Narbonne, as well as in such far-flung spots as Famagusta in Cyprus.[153]

But it would be incorrect, I think, to attribute this to an opposition to the style associated with Charles's pious and church-building brother Louis IX. Instead, it may be possible to see in the character of Charles's buildings a more positive type of choice, one that vaguely recalls work associated with the time of his grandfather, Philip Augustus, and monuments far more austere than those erected in the first decades of rule under Louis IX. If so, then Charles of Anjou's aesthetic choice was one that could be associated, whether consciously or not, with a recent era of great distinction, rather than the style currently in fashion in Paris. This more austere architectural language was well suited to the circumstances in which Charles found himself in southern Italy – a time when perhaps a style of rigorous and austere mural force, perhaps a type of "muscular simplicity," was preferable to elaborate elegance and refinement.

Chapter 2

SAN LORENZO MAGGIORE IN NAPLES

The graceful turning arches and slender clerestory windows in the apse of San Lorenzo, framed in the vast arch of the transept, have become symbols of French influence in southern Italy (pl. 48).[1] The attribution of the church to Charles of Anjou and the French architects in his wake has seemed confirmed by the plan with ambulatory and radiating chapels, bar tracery, and rib vaults supported by external flyers: this "grazioso e bel tempio" (as it was described by Boccaccio in the *Filocolo*) is understood to exemplify an intensely French moment between 1266 and 1282.

The church and monastic complex of San Lorenzo, perhaps more than any other in Naples, are also linked to the literary and political history of the city, for it was here in 1334 that Boccaccio was stricken by the *coup de foudre* for Maria d'Aquino, immortalized as Fiammetta, and here also Petrarch, residing in the monastery, trembled and quaked through the devastating tempest of 1343.[2] Because of its intimate association with the three tribunals of city government, San Lorenzo was also in the front line during many of its major political struggles, and in 1510, 1547, and 1647 it was at the center of the revolts, in part because it was conveniently adjacent to the canon foundry and an armory, which until 1649 were located next to the western range of the cloister.[3] Although at times the friars were participants in these revolts against the Aragonese and the Inquisition, the propinquity of civic authority to the monastic community seems on the whole to have been cause for constant tension and struggle over space.[4]

The political role of the monastery has to a large extent conditioned and skewed historical interpretations, for the site has been associated with anti-Aragonese political theory that exalted by contrast certain aspects of Angevin rule.[5] The close involvement of San Lorenzo in issues of Neapolitan identity and autonomy meant that beginning in the sixteenth century the Franciscan church was described as "French" or "Angevin" for reasons that had as much to do with

opposition to Spain as with historical evidence of Angevin patronage. Two French kings (Charles II and Robert) were, of course, involved in some phases of construction of San Lorenzo, but at the end of this chapter I shall suggest that a large part of the building that we see today — a church in many ways profoundly different in appearance from that of about 1300 — was created in collaboration with civic patrons and especially the members of the Seggio di Montagna, who managed the finances of the Franciscan house. There was one conspicuously important individual whose role in the entire reconstruction of the nave and transept has either been suppressed or forgotten.

Although construction of San Lorenzo bridged the reigns of Charles I, Charles II and Robert, it seems probable that work began earlier and lasted longer, and above all that work preceded royal support. Construction was episodic and intermittent, driven by the need for subsidiary altars for the Franciscan community and later by the creation of private commemorative chapels for local donors. So the seductive aura of "Frenchness" notwithstanding, the church appears to be more the work of the Franciscans and the civic aristocracy of Naples than of royal patrons. Perhaps more than any other building in Naples, we are in the presence of a monument that has an almost amoeba-like quality to its growth and change (all of which eventually enclosed in a Baroque carapace which has now been mostly removed), and I propose that this characteristic of the site consists not only of repeated additions to the church, but also of a single grand and glorious "subtraction" that created the spaces we see today. This is, as a result, a difficult narrative, and the sequence of construction involves foundations underneath the transept pavement (elements that cannot be photographed), the destruction of parts of the Early Christian mosaics, and a sequence of deductions derived from the documents and the visible remains.

No part of San Lorenzo has remained untouched. Although the subject of our discussion here are the addi-

49 Naples, San Lorenzo Maggiore, view of the nave and apse prior to restoration (Soprintendenza per i Beni Architettonici ed Ambientali di Napoli e Provincia)

tions to the ancient basilica that began in the third quarter of the thirteenth century, the building has continued to be modified, improved, repaired, embellished, restored, and un-restored ever since. In these circumstances conclusions on construction must of course remain hypothetical.

In spite of its historical importance for Naples, San Lorenzo has suffered long periods of neglect. In the sixteenth century the ambulatory and radiating chapels were closed off from the apse and abandoned for more than 300 years until about 1882.[6] In 1654 De Lellis described the church in its Baroque restoration as rising like a phoenix from the ashes (pl. 49),[7] but the terrible earthquake of 1688 imposed a whole series of new repairs and reconstructions.[8] The church has always had grave problems of stability, in part the result of the design of the nave and the materials used there[9] and its construction over the "honeycomb" of the ancient city market beneath, but also because of frequent and devastating earthquakes. A restoration over several decades at the start of the twentieth century was undertaken by Gino Chierici, who removed much of the (splendid) Baroque decoration, revealing the medieval structure and fragments of frescoes underneath.[10] The walls exposed by Chierici also brought to light a series of late medieval and Renaissance repairs and reconstructions, some of which probably were necessitated by the earthquakes of 1349 and 1456. His work also consisted of a series of erasures and corrections to anomalies in the medieval walls, and these add to the difficulties of interpretation.

Although San Lorenzo is considered the "most Gothic" church of Naples, every part of the church, from the gracious choir in the east to the vast and barn-like nave of some decades later, took as its point of departure the Early Christian basilica that once occupied the site. The plan of the old church was discovered in 1954.[11] Recent excavation of the Roman market underneath the church and cloister has added important new information about the site not available to scholars working even as late as the mid-1980s (pl. 50).[12] There had, of course, been many hints of the ancient riches to be found under the present pavement, for in 1594 Summonte had already mentioned ancient marbles discovered on the occasion of the insertion of new tombs, and new burials or work on the foundations must often have penetrated the older remains.[13] But an understanding of the relationship of the thirteenth-century church to the basilica beneath has only been possible since the discovery of the plan of the latter and the recent conclusion of the excavations of the street and market underneath it, the so-called *scavi* of San Lorenzo.[14] These revealed the continuation of the Greco-Roman street deep under the transept, the foundations of a *macellum* under the cloister, and a string of lower shops of Roman date in the lower story of the market, all probably destroyed or half buried by a mud slide in the late fifth century.[15] The Roman market was itself built over Greek remains of much greater antiquity, some fragments of which can also be seen in the *scavi* below the cloister.

The Early Christian basilica was erected during the tenure of Bishop John II ("the Mediocre") sometime between 517 and 537 over the market in the forum (pl. 51).[16] Described as a striking example of the influence of North African and Near Eastern forms on the Early Christian architecture of Naples,[17] it consisted of a wide nave separated from the side aisles by reused ancient columns with an apse flanked by a *prothesis* and a *diaconicon*. The church was preceded by a deep narthex at the west end of the building which probably had a lean-to roof against the west façade wall, perhaps something like the arrangement that can still be seen at the church of San Vitale on the Via Nazionale in Rome. The excavations exposed partially preserved mosaics of outstanding beauty in the pavements of both of the lateral chapels alongside the apse: as will be seen below, the partial

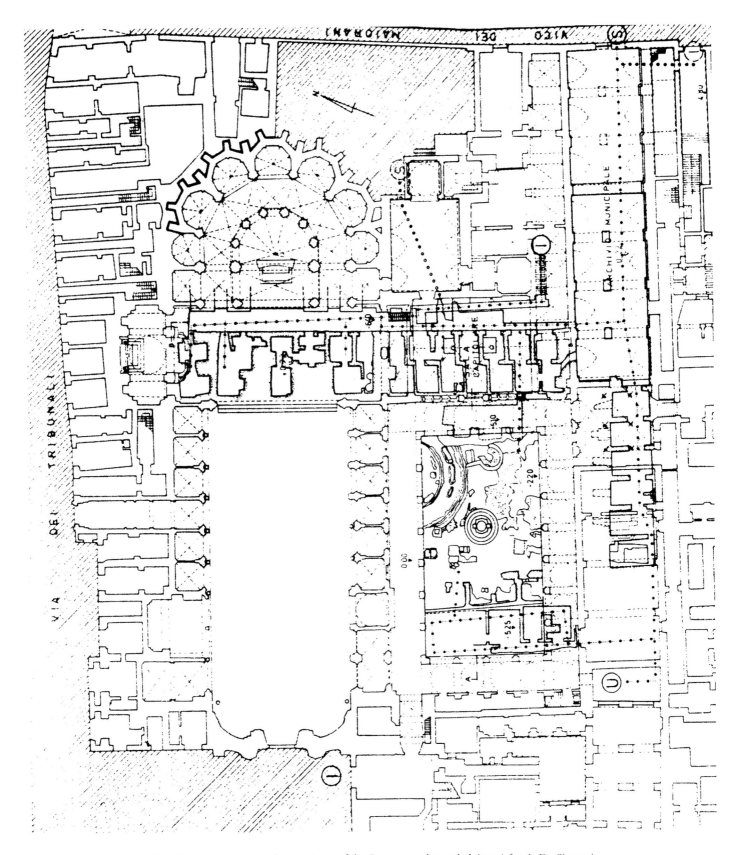

50   Naples, San. Lorenzo Maggiore, ground plan and excavations of the Roman market and cloister (after A. De Simone)

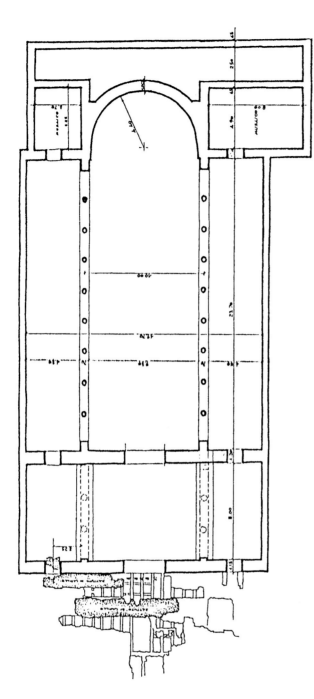

51 Naples, San Lorenzo Maggiore, ground plan of the Early Christian church (from Rusconi 1965)

destruction of these pavements is an important clue in the reconstruction of the ground plan of the thirteenth-century church. In the fourteenth-century rebuilding of the nave most of the ancient columns that separated the nave from the aisles in the old basilica were relocated between the pre-existing lateral chapels (pl. 68); a few others, possibly from the deep narthex, can be seen in old photographs of the excavations at the west end of

the present church. In order to unravel the complicated and intricate relationship of the thirteenth- and fourteenth-century church and conventual complex, and to understand the various phases of its construction, the discussion here must also concern the monastery as a Franciscan *studium*.

The Franciscan Studium at San Lorenzo Maggiore in Naples

In 1234 the sixth-century basilica of San Lorenzo was given to the Franciscans.[18] The foundation of this second Franciscan house in Naples (it had been preceded by Santa Maria di Palazzo some years before) reflected a fundamental change of the order from a lay to a clerical community. We have seen in chapter one that the earlier Franciscan house of Naples, Santa Maria, had been established around 1216 outside the city at the site later to be occupied by the Castel Nuovo.[19] This first Franciscan community, founded in the early years of the movement, reflected the eremitic tendency of the order, as it was placed in an isolated location removed from the city.[20] The friars could thus venture forth to preach and perform good works by day, but retire to the seclusion of their refuge for prayer and contemplation modeled on the life of Saint Francis.

Although Francis was himself opposed to the possession of buildings and to study, even within his lifetime circumstances within the order were changing rapidly. By 1230 the bull *Quo elongati* dispensed with the authority of Francis's testament and permitted the acquisition of property. The founder's opposition to learning was also rapidly overturned.[21] *Quo elongati* permitted the acquisition of books, which in turn made possible the development of and need for libraries and teaching. As early as 1228 a lecturer was appointed for the friars in Germany, followed rapidly by study centers in Oxford, Bologna, Padua, and Paris.[22] Frate Elia, Minister General from 1232 until 1239, actively encouraged theological study, although he was himself a lay member of the order.

By the 1230s, therefore, the character of the Franciscans was undergoing profound change.[23] Attendance at General Chapters became limited to Ministers General and Guardians, all of whom after about 1230 were clerics in accordance with the strictures of the *Regula bullata*.[24] Preaching was also limited to clerics. After 1239 lay brothers were formally excluded from holding office in the order, and their future recruitment was strictly reduced — as Knowles noted, "the simple solitary brethren of the hermitages . . . became a regional survival of aching memory."[25] Lay brothers continued in the order as servants or often as specialized laborers.[26] The Franciscans to whom we shall have cause to refer as architects and building supervisors may well have been lay members of the order and were perhaps admitted precisely because of their practical skills and expertise in the construction and decoration of churches and conventual buildings.[27]

The process of clericalization had profound implications not only for the nature of the order, but also for its architecture. Clericalization meant education and training, and the major houses from the 1230s onwards acquired books and libraries.[28] The presence of priests meant that increasingly the churches in the larger cities had to be expanded to include private chapels for the daily masses of the ordained friars, now in the majority. Certain Franciscan houses were created as, or developed into, study centers or *studia* for the advanced training of preachers and teachers, as at the Cordeliers in Paris, San Francesco in Bologna, and San Lorenzo Maggiore in Naples.[29] The location of the new Franciscan house in Naples at the site of the market and the intersection of the *decumanus maior* and the Via Augustale thus placed this convent in the heart of the city.[30]

As Recupido noted, the acquisition of San Lorenzo by the Franciscans in 1234 coincided with the reopening of the *universitas studiorum* of Naples founded by Frederick II a decade before.[31] The Franciscan *studium* attracted students not only from within the kingdom, but also from abroad – Salimbene, for example, noted that an English student, Frater Gualterius (Walter the Englishman), studied there with John of Parma, which must have been in the early 1240s.[32]

Archbishop Peter of Sorrento (1217–1246), a figure of great importance in the city in the second quarter of the thirteenth century, promoted the new settlements of the Dominicans and the Franciscans in the center of Naples in the 1230s.[33] The second Franciscan community thus reflected the new character and interests of the order (for which the old and isolated site of Santa Maria di Palazzo was neither useful nor appropriate) and a deliberate attempt to place these friars near the other seats of study between the cathedral and the recently founded Dominican house.[34] Although there are no precise documents on the date of the foundation of the Franciscan *studium* of Naples, we know that John of Parma (1208–1289), one of the most noted teachers of the order and papal legate in 1239 to the court of Louis IX, taught there before his appointment as Minister General in 1247.[35] In the early 1250s the Franciscan *studium* may have been further encouraged by Innocent IV during the months that he spent in Naples before his death there

in 1254, and it is noteworthy that the pope was devoted not only to the cult of Saint Lawrence but also to the Franciscans. That Innocent saw the need to reform Naples is indicated by his creation of a *studium generale* of law and theology within his palace in the months before his death.[36]

If San Lorenzo was a *studium*, if not from the start then from early on in its Franciscan life (that is to say, by around 1240 or the early 1240s at the latest), there would have been an obvious need for appropriate spaces for a community that would have consisted of lay brothers, clerics, masters of theology, and students (and therefore dormitories, a refectory, storage and service rooms). Indeed, the conventual complex of San Lorenzo, although almost entirely rebuilt in the Baroque period, still testifies to several large-scale and architecturally significant spaces dating from the middle third of the thirteenth century as well as a series of cloisters.[37] The earliest of these visible seem to be the small cloister south of the atrium and the refectory. The latter, though covered on the interior, still preserves some medieval windows on the exterior; and equally important are the two windows (but not the portal) of the chapter house (pl. 52).

The use of ancient columns and capitals in the small cloister and the atrium (where they support groin vaults) is fully consistent with the taste for antique materials common in the architecture in the kingdom in the 1230s and 1240s.[38] The refectory is entirely frescoed on the interior, but its scale is vast: 10 by 45 meters. The windows, pairs of rectangular openings with chamfered edges, are typical of mid-thirteenth-century utilitarian Gothic found frequently in the south and remarkably persistent; similar forms can be seen as late as the 1320s in the monastic structures of Santa Chiara.

The most interesting (and difficult) of the conventual structures is the chapter house, which has had at least three separate phases of construction, the first about 1260–70, the second as a rebuild or repair around or after the middle of the fourteenth century, and the third in the early seventeenth century. It is placed above the early medieval *seggio*, historically and politically the most important site at the Franciscan complex (pl. 53). *Seggi* were the meeting places of local aristocratic assemblies established in the early Middle Ages as part of the governance of Naples.[39] That of San Lorenzo was particularly significant because it was located next to the forum and market. This political role was to continue at the tower now to the south of the west façade, as noted by D'Andrea and others.[40] The coincidence of spiritual and political functions at San Lorenzo had a long life, and in the thirteenth century this type of association may have made the site particularly attractive to the Franciscans.[41]

52 Naples, San Lorenzo Maggiore, exterior of the Chapter House (Giovanni Genova)

53 Naples, San Lorenzo Maggiore, interior of the Chapter House (Giovanni Genova)

The pair of large four-lancet windows in bar tracery on the exterior of the chapter house can be stylistically associated with various monuments of the 1260s, among them the papal palace of Viterbo.[42] The particular form of the pattern at San Lorenzo, with heavy rounded arches, would seem, however, to descend from a more general Rayonnant diaspora rather than the specific example of Viterbo itself, because the pattern was a common one.[43] A particularly striking example is the Angel Choir of Lincoln Cathedral, begun around 1245, although at San Lorenzo neither the angels nor the voluptuous use of crockets appear. The ponderous and rounded moldings of the chapter house windows have little of the subtle play of light across fillets and cavets that is usually found at this date in northern examples,

and the windows contrast strongly with the slender and attenuated moldings of the later entrance portal. The modifications to the chapter house may have occurred as a result of the earthquake of 1349, when substantial work was also carried out in the transept. At this time, a new entrance doorway from the cloister was inserted and the lunette above was painted.[44]

The interior of the chapter house, entirely covered by later frescoed decoration, may also have been reconstructed after the earthquake of 1349, as is suggested by the curious stilting of the arches above the central supports (pl. 53).[45] But since the interior has been covered with stucco and paint an analysis of the structure is impossible. Perhaps the four-lancet windows into the chapter house formed part of a first cloister outside the

Early Christian basilica and its first lateral chapels, and gave access to the ancient *seggio*, which, like the old basilica, might have been kept intact for some time? The Vico Gigante, one of the narrow north–south streets of the Greek grid, could have continued to provide access from the north to the *seggio* and, before the erection of the new transept and choir, to the conventual complex as a whole (pl. 50).

These suggestive remains reflect the construction of a large monastic complex at San Lorenzo in the middle third of the thirteenth century. Some texts, such as a donation of funds in a will of February 1261 for the construction of an infirmary, attest to specific buildings.[46] Other less precise transactions reflect the rapid growth of the convent, which expanded primarily to the south, but also to the west and east of the old basilica with acquisitions and exchanges of property that continued into the fourteenth and fifteenth centuries.[47] The length of the refectory, as long as the nave of the old basilica, indicates that it was intended to seat a community of considerable size (pl. 50). And although there is little precise evidence on the number of friars, various scholars suppose that in the thirteenth century they numbered between seventy and ninety; in the sixteenth century 110 friars were recorded at the site.[48] In the context of a *studium*, it is also likely that there were separate and different dormitories for clerics, lay brothers, and students or novices, for example, and that by the mid- to late thirteenth century the masters might well have had private rooms.

Although relations between Frederick II and the papacy were increasingly difficult after Frederick's excommunication in 1227, until 1239 the emperor seems to have remained reasonably well disposed towards the mendicant friars in his kingdom.[49] In 1236, for example, he asked to be remembered by the Franciscans in their prayers and participated in the translation of Saint Elizabeth of Thuringia. After 1239, however, Frederick came to see the mendicants as the "angeli mali," and expelled all who were not his subjects from the kingdom. Although the orders maintained their houses in the kingdom in the difficult decade of the 1240s, the communities must have experienced considerable struggles, difficulties no doubt aggravated by Innocent IV's deposition of Frederick in 1245.[50] It was nevertheless precisely in this period, variously stated as between 1240 and 1245, or at least sometime before 1247, that John of Parma taught in Naples, so that some element of continuity of the community and its educational function can be assumed. Archbishop Peter of Sorrento's encouragement of both the Dominicans and Franciscans in Naples must have played a part in supporting theological studies as an antidote to heresy.[51] Theology in Italy was usually taught by the friars, and the Dominicans had been present and teaching in Naples since early in the thirteenth century.[52] In addition, Charles of Anjou's letter of 1272 advertising the charms and attractions of the revived university of Naples, though it makes no mention of the Franciscan *studium*, specifically refers to the teaching of theology.[53]

The Historical Tradition

Because the Gothic reconstruction of San Lorenzo coincided with the early decades of Angevin rule, the church has always been seen as a symbol of French artistic domination.[54] In recent historiography, the style of the chevet in particular is perceived as "proof" of the legacy of the French masters and masons brought to Italy by Charles of Anjou.[55] Already in the sixteenth century, before the invention of architectural history as a discipline, histories and guidebooks of Naples attributed the construction of San Lorenzo to Charles I, at times going so far as to link his patronage with his purported vow to Saint Lawrence on the eve of the Battle of Benevento.[56] Renate Wagner-Rieger, the first architectural historian to study the monument in detail, affirmed this traditional association of the choir with the first French king and linked it stylistically to his (mostly destroyed) Cistercian abbey of Realvalle. Krüger's monograph of 1986 and the work of Berger-Dittscheid four years later contributed many new fundamental observations on the church, the most important of which is perhaps the latter's perception that the concordance of the chevet's dimensions with those of the old Early Christian nave indicate that the Gothic east end was not begun as the first stage of an entirely new church that would replace and supplant the Early Christian basilica, but was rather an extension of this old building. The chevet was thus simply an addition that greatly expanded the apse and the altar area and added numerous radiating chapels. Berger-Dittscheid's observations on the relation of the new chevet to the old basilica give new significance to the terms "pro complenda" and "reparationis" mentioned in the documents of 1284 (see Appendix 3).

The literature on San Lorenzo considers the nave to be the result of the patronage of Charles II in a project begun in the mid- to late 1290s (pl. 68). It is viewed as a radical change in design from the original "French" project of the chevet into an "Italian" single-cell nave, presumably the work of an Italian master mason employed by Charles II. As a result, San Lorenzo has been seen as a metaphor for the rapid integration of the French regime into the Italian cultural landscape, and as such it has been understood to have a dual personality, pulled between its Gothic chevet and the sharply different volumes of its Italian nave. Little or no thought has been given to the transept that joins the two.

The literature diverges, however, on several other fundamental points that concern the church and the few documents that concern its construction. This includes the amount of the fine imposed in 1284 on Matteo Rufolo of Ravello (400 versus 40 once), the function of the monastic complex and church (Franciscan *studium* as opposed to royal burial church), and the chronology of construction. Although Krüger, Cadei, and Schenkluhn made the vital association of San Lorenzo with the major Franciscan *studia* of Paris, Bologna, and Padua, their studies were focused on the plan of the chevet and did not concern the entire monastic complex and the way in which this conditioned construction of the church.[57] As regards royal burial, evidence from the reign of Charles II (see the next chapter) indicates that during his reign tombs were placed in the cathedral. The two royal tombs of the early fourteenth century at San Lorenzo were for princes, not rulers, and these in any event coincided with the construction of – and hence the inaccessibility of – the royal burial chapel at the cathedral.[58]

The only two documents that concern the rebuilding of the church before the 1290s pertain to the permutation of a fine imposed upon the Rufolo family in 1284 (see Appendix 3). They occur precisely when Charles I was absent from the realm (January 1283–June 1284) raising funds and troops for the war in Sicily, and are related to the Prince of Salerno's attempts to punish corruption in the kingdom. Given the elder Charles's comportment upon his return (he hanged the judge who had pronounced the sentence on the Rufolo family), there can be little doubt that the events that precipitated the donation to the Franciscans would not have occurred had the king been present in Naples. The amount of the donation of 1284 specified for construction at the church ("uncias auri quadragentas", "quadrigentas," or "quatrigintas") has been resolved as 400 once, which might well have covered much of the cost of the chevet.[59]

San Lorenzo and the Angevin Rulers of Naples

The church has been so closely identified with the French royal family that it takes some effort to recall that the documents of 1284 were the result of the reforms instigated by Charles II (as Prince of Salerno) while serving as regent for his father absent in France. The prince attempted to address some of the practices that

gave rise to the revolt, which resulted in the establishment of the reforms of the Plain of San Martino, and the legal proceedings against a number of corrupt royal officials, including members of two prominent families of the Amalfi coast, the Rufolo and the della Marra. Both families were famously wealthy (cf. the colorful version of this conspicuous wealth in Boccaccio's *Decameron*, Day 2, novella 4) and well integrated with the royal court: they had provided loans to Charles I as well as to Frederick II before him, and various members of both families had served as important officials (*magistri portulani et procuratores*, *procurator Apuliae*, and *magistri rationalis* among others) in various provinces of the kingdom.[60] Apart from their properties in Ravello and Scala, they also came to acquire large holdings (as well as political and economic power) in Apulia, a base that enhanced their private trading relationship with the ports in the east and in North Africa.

Matteo Rufolo and his son Lorenzo had both held the offices of *secretus, magister portulanus et procurator Apulie*,[61] and made loans not only to Charles I, but also to the Prince of Salerno, the latter concluding a loan agreement with them less than a month before the decree for their arrest issued on 26 May 1283.[62] It has been suggested for this reason that the arrests and the subsequent trials and executions were at least in part cynical attempts to obtain urgently needed funds for the royal coffers that had been severely strained by the costs of the war. But it is also likely that the prince wished to be seen to be punishing the corrupt,[63] although, as Percy has observed, the war of 1282 had precipitated a new level of financial crisis, and a sharp increase in taxation was imposed in 1282 and 1283.[64]

On 22 June 1283 the court issued orders for the arrests of Angelo, Ruggiero, Lorenzo, and Galgano della Marra, as well as Matteo and Lorenzo Rufolo, all accused of extortion and other crimes in the areas of their jurisdiction.[65] Their goods, lands, and possessions were confiscated.[66] Lorenzo Rufolo and two members of the della Marra family were hanged.[67] Their families were imprisoned and subjected to severe penalties.[68]

The families made desperate attempts to raise funds from their remaining resources to pay the fines and to free the surviving members of the family.[69] A month into his incarceration at the castle of Mesiano in Calabria, Matteo Rufolo was granted permission to receive a visit from two Franciscans, Abbot John Rufolo and friar Abamotus.[70] (In the genealogy of the Rufolo family published by Schulz and von Quast, a Iohannes is listed as a grandson of Matteo Rufolo, although there is no way to confirm whether the Abbot John in question was this particular relation.[71]) The two clerics appear to have intervened effectively on Matteo's behalf, for his wife and children, and Lorenzo's family, were freed from jail and allowed to return home.[72] Five days after the visit of the Franciscans to Matteo, the crown agreed to impose the fine of 2,000 gold once upon him, and the same day a letter was sent from the king to the guardian of the Franciscan order requesting the delivery of these funds from San Francesco in Assisi, where they had been deposited by Matteo for safe keeping (we are at some distance here from the poverty of Saint Francis).[73] Angelo della Marra's family had also deposited money at the mother house of the order.[74] These deposits would seem to attest to considerable financial relationships between the two families and the Franciscans, and perhaps represent their attempt to keep part of their wealth outside the kingdom in something that might today resemble a Swiss bank account – but in Assisi.[75] The documents also attest a complex three-way negotiation between the Franciscans, the Rufolo/della Marras, and the royal representatives.

Upon conclusion of the settlement, Matteo was freed from prison and reinstated in the documents as *devotus noster*.[76] Later texts of April and May 1284 detail his attempts to raise funds from other sources to cover his fine.[77] The last of these involved the assistance of his father, Nicola Rufolo, famous for his commission of the pulpit in Ravello cathedral.

Sthamer has suggested that the legal proceedings against the Rufolo and della Marra families may have been drawn up by Bartolomeo da Capua, who less than a decade later was to become the great *protonotaro* of the kingdom and legal advisor to both Charles II and Robert the Wise, but this has recently been dismissed by François Widemann.[78] Much later Bartolomeo da Capua was also to play an interesting and important role in the reconstruction of the nave of San Lorenzo, and this connection is also interesting if elusive. As a member of the local nobility, it is in any event likely that da Capua knew the Rufolo and della Marra families well.[79]

Much remains that is murky here, but several aspects of this narrative are significant for San Lorenzo: there was a strong Rufolo and della Marra connection to the Franciscans, and the families deposited their money at the mother church of the Franciscans at Assisi; two Franciscans, one of whom seems to have been a member of the Rufolo family, were permitted to visit Matteo Rufolo in prison, and their intervention significantly improved the circumstances of the disgraced family. Furthermore, the increase in December 1283 or January 1284 of Matteo's penalty by 400 once to include a donation for the "completion" or "repair" of the church of San Lorenzo in Naples occurred only after the death of

Matteo's eponymous son, Lorenzo. Fragmentary though these glimpses are, it seems clear that there was a connection between the 400 once designated for the church of San Lorenzo, the recovery of all or part of the 2,000 once deposited with the Franciscans at Assisi, and the death of Lorenzo Rufolo.

Where does this leave the traditional attribution of the chevet to Charles I of Anjou? He was absent from 12 January 1283 until 18 June 1284, leaving his son and heir as vicar general of the realm for the duration of his absence, and so was not connected with this document.[80] The texts that pertain to the construction of the choir were negotiated between the Franciscans, the Prince of Salerno, and Matteo Rufolo. The proceedings against the Rufolo and della Marra families, instituted and concluded during his absence, indicate that the king was unaware of the actions taken against the two families who had served him for more than a decade as administrators and bankers. And indeed, on his return to Naples, already infuriated by the capture of the Prince of Salerno in a sea battle in the bay of Naples only a few days before, Charles I repudiated the reforms of the San Martino and hanged the judge, Tommaso da Brindisi, who had pronounced the sentences against the Rufolo and della Marra clans.[81]

Indeed, with this as background, we can imagine that Charles of Anjou on his return to Naples shortly after his son's capture could have been further enraged that work on the church of San Lorenzo, financed in part with Rufolo money, would have represented not only filial error but also funds that found their way to the wrong pockets.

The Rufolo Documents on San Lorenzo

The two letters concerning the Rufolo fine, issued in concert with the friars minor of San Lorenzo, specify that 400 once will be provided for the completion or repairs to the church in addition to the total fine owed to the crown by Matteo Rufolo. In the second document, of 6 May 1283, the Prince of Salerno appropriated the gift for the remission of his and his predecessors' sins.

The documents were composed in relation to an external event, the fine imposed upon the Rufolo family (only a small part of which was to concern San Lorenzo). They were produced to mark neither the beginning nor the end of work on the Franciscan church, and are above all the product of the ties between the order and the Rufolo family. The terms used are "completion" and "repair," and here we do well to recall Berger-

Dittscheid's suggestion that the chevet was erected as an extension of the old basilica:[82] as she noted, not only do the horizontal dimensions correspond with those of the basilica, but presumably also the height of the chevet vault would have corresponded to that of the wooden truss ceiling of the old church.

These observations are important for the meaning of certain terms in the documents. Although Recupido observed in 1961 that the excavations of 1955 revealed severe lesions in the masonry of the old apse that may have required its reconstruction, the term "pro complenda" in the document of 15 January suggests that in 1283 the project of the chevet was already well underway and proceeding towards the connection with the older church "ibi constructa."[83] It is, although, also possible that the term could refer either to the subsidiary chapels and secondary altars in the chevet or to those in the nave, chapels essential for the private masses of the Franciscan clergy, or that the "repairs" mentioned could have been just and only that (here it is worth recalling the earthquakes of 1267, 1274, and 1284).[84] The important sum of 400 once suggests a large-scale project, however.

Could Charles I have been responsible for the inception of the work on San Lorenzo at some unknown date but obviously before the outbreak of war in 1282? There are several reasons why this seems unlikely. This king was not, as seen in the previous chapter, an energetic patron of church building. The Angevin Registers do not suggest special favor shown to the Franciscans at any site, and, in fact, to the contrary, make numerous calls for the arrest of vagrant or itinerant friars. Although he was an extraordinarily thorough administrator, and although the documents confirm the almost obsessive interest that Charles had in architectural projects – for Realvalle and Vittoria there were well over 600 texts in the archive before it was burnt in 1943 – there are no traces in the Registers of a particular connection between Charles of Anjou and San Lorenzo.[85] It is true, of course, that documents have been lost, but even in the sixteenth century when the legend of royal patronage was (somewhat miraculously) part of an important local myth about Charles's "democratic instincts," no sources are referred to. And nowhere do the letters issued on behalf of the Franciscan house by Charles II in the 1290s suggest that San Lorenzo was founded or patronized by his father, unlike documents that refer to construction elsewhere, as at Santa Maria la Nova.[86] In the rich context of documentation for Charles of Anjou's building, here the silence is deafening.

It has also often been stated that San Lorenzo was intended as a royal necropolis.[87] But there is strong evidence to contradict such conclusions. After the death in 1270 of Louis IX (as a martyr) on the Tunisian crusade, Charles was able to keep only his brother's entrails (though he wanted more), and these he buried with great pomp at Monreale, not in Naples.[88] Charles's first wife, Beatrice of Provence, was temporarily buried in the cathedral of Naples at her death in September 1267 until her remains were transferred to Aix-en-Provence. At that point, as noted above, Charles specified that her tomb in the cathedral be kept intact and continue to contain her "dust." The king's son Philip (d. 1277) was buried in Trani cathedral. At his own death Charles joined his wife in the cathedral of Naples, while his heart went to the Dominicans in Paris and his entrails were interred at the cathedral of Foggia. As noted, the first royal burial at San Lorenzo, that of Raymond Berengar, the brother of Louis of Toulouse and Robert the Wise, occurred only in 1305, when the new royal burial chapel at the cathedral was under construction.

If Charles I can be detached from a funerary association with San Lorenzo, what of the involvement of his son, the Prince of Salerno and the future Charles II? This king's connection to San Lorenzo dates from 1296–7, well after the first intense wave of religious projects undertaken on his return to Naples. At that date the adoption of a Franciscan project may reflect the new attachment to the Franciscan order in the royal family generated by Prince Louis of Toulouse, who along with his two younger brothers had recently returned from prison where they had been placed as substitute hostages for Charles II. Louis emerged as a Franciscan and renounced the throne for the religious life.[89] It is also true in a general sense that both Charles I and Charles II seem to have favored the Dominicans over the Franciscans.[90] Although the Franciscans played a role in the preparation for the conquest of the kingdom in 1266, their efforts were never singled out for special gratitude by Charles I, and the hearts of both kings were buried in Dominican houses, while neither left any part of his body to the Franciscans.[91]

So it may be that the family involvement with the Franciscans and royal participation in the works at San Lorenzo are owed to the young Louis of Toulouse, who returned briefly to Naples in 1295.[92] After his death, his mother, Mary of Hungary, supported the reconstruction of the Clarissan convent of Santa Maria Donnaregina, where she chose to be buried, and it was Mary, more than either Charles I or Charles II, who was the first conspicuous royal patron of the Franciscans in the Angevin family. Louis of Toulouse himself had no role in the project of San Lorenzo: he departed soon for his episcopal seat in southern France and died young and far from home. Louis's sympathies were in any event with the Spiritual rather than the Conventual branch of the Franciscan order, whereas San Lorenzo was a center for the training and intellectual formation of clericalized Franciscanism.[93] Insofar as he was allied with the Spiritual Franciscans, construction projects to Louis might even have been anathema. Was royal sponsorship of Franciscan projects after the young prince's death an attempt to reclaim his errant and marginal spirituality within the hierarchy of the order?[94]

The Chevet

The choir of San Lorenzo is among the most handsome examples of "French" architectural thinking to be found anywhere in Italy, a building whose beauty has given it special prominence in all considerations of south Italian Gothic (pls. 48 and 54). At some point after the donation of the basilica to the Franciscans in 1234, a series of lateral chapels was also added to the nave, and although it has usually been assumed that the chevet was built before these, I shall suggest the reverse.[95]

The ground plan has often been associated with that of major French monuments of the thirteenth century, and in particular that of the Cistercian abbey of Royaumont near Paris (pl. 55).[96] This prompted Wagner-Rieger's suggestion that the Franciscan church was inspired by Charles of Anjou's foundation of Realvalle and designed by the Cistercian monks from the nearby abbey, a proposition that would have explained how the complex structures of French Gothic, combined with the certain monastic austerity of the two-story elevation, came to be produced in Naples.[97] She saw the plan and elevation of the chevet as confirmation of the importation of French architectural and spatial concepts to southern Italy by the Angevin kings and as proof of the continued vitality of the Cistercian order as the promoters and disseminators of the Gothic style in Italy.[98]

Yet many aspects of the chevet, such as the massive hemicycle piers, are archaic, and structural details have little relationship to contemporary elements in either French or Cistercian architecture. Although these anomalies have been explained as the result of the conservative nature of Cistercian design,[99] the contrast with the modernity of the surviving details at Realvalle is striking. In the Ile-de-France and Provence slender hemicycle supports are always used, rather than the ponderous trapezoidal forms of the hemicycle piers, and there is simply no evidence for supports of this type at any Cistercian abbey.[100] Compared to the scant remains of Real-

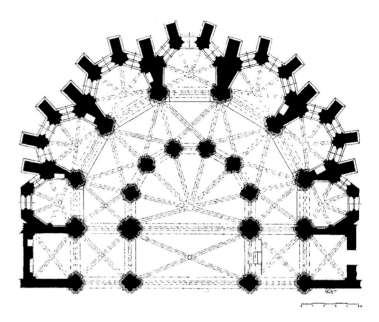

54   Naples, San Lorenzo Maggiore, plan of chevet (after Venditti 1969)

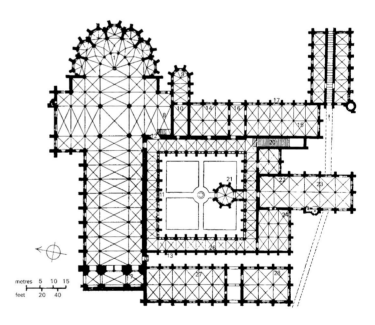

55   The Cistercian abbey of Royaumont, plan

valle and Vittoria, San Lorenzo seems conspicuously less pure in its use of French prototypes. The capitals have none of the rich sculptural inventiveness of those at Realvalle: the crockets at San Lorenzo, though distantly based on French models (pl. 56), derive from forms that were decades old and seriously out of date by the 1270s. Nowhere at San Lorenzo is there the variety and refinement still evident in the battered and weathered capitals at Realvalle (pl. 36).[101]

Cistercian apses with an ambulatory have columns around the hemicycle. The documents from Realvalle confirm the existence of simple cylindrical supports there. The heavy hemicycle piers with four substantial shafts at San Lorenzo (pl. 58) are a highly unusual design for apse supports, which diverges dramatically in its aesthetic from counterparts in thirteenth-century France, where such elements are cylindrical, sometimes with attached shafts, as at Ourscamp (pl. 57). The ponderous hemicycle piers of the Franciscan church indeed contradict the logic of spatial fluidity and luminosity that had been central to French Gothic design since the time of Abbot Suger at Saint-Denis; they represent instead a clumsy translation of the traditional cruciform pier with shafts to a radial arrangement. One might consider this unusual design a sort of "signature" element that divorces the conception of this chevet from direct French workmanship.

Other details are also unusual, such as the heavy "traveling" molding that descends from the plinth to become

56 (*left*) Naples, San Lorenzo Maggiore, detail of capital in hemicycle (author)

57 (*below*) Ourscamp, view of the chevet from the west (author)

58   Naples, San Lorenzo Maggiore, piers of the hemicycle (author)

the step into each chapel (pl. 59). Here too there is no counterpart in French monuments. The simple profiles of the bases are unlike contemporary French models, and the capitals, as noted, are repetitive versions of the crocket formula with some leafy capitals that have no counterpart in the repertory of elements north of the Alps.

Thus San Lorenzo, for all its immediate and seductive aura of "Frenchness," is a monument in which the Gothic style is strangely anachronistic and labored. The piers in particular are ponderous and massive, but there is a striking resemblance between them and the supports of the Franciscan church of San Francesco in Bologna, built between about 1236 and 1263 (pl. 60). Here the supports, though constructed in alternating layers of light and dark stone, are also based on a trapezoidal core, and there is also a two-story elevation with rib vaults on the interior supported by flying buttresses on the exterior, features also found in San Lorenzo but otherwise rare in medieval Italy.[102]

In 1985 Schenkluhn observed that plans with ambulatories and radiating chapels appear consistently in Franciscan *studia,* and it has been thought that the model was probably the now-destroyed Cordeliers, the Franciscan church in Paris and center of Franciscan studies (pl. 61).[103] The plan type was adopted at Padua and Bologna. Schenkluhn supposed that the order had selected a design and style that conveyed some elements of "French" feeling. That "Frenchness" on some level may have been part of the order's architectural consciousness is reflected also in various details of the decoration and structure of San Francesco at Assisi.

Curiously, although a great deal of scholarly attention has been expended in the direction of Cistercian expertise in architecture and construction, the obvious and important participation of Franciscan builders in the erection of their churches and conventual buildings has received almost no attention whatsoever. I noted in the last chapter that a Fra Giacomo, perhaps a Franciscan,

59 Naples, San Lorenzo Maggiore, detail of the ambulatory plinths (Jill Caskey)

assisted the initial phase of the setting out of one of Charles's Cistercian abbeys, and it is also well known that Franciscan friars were mosaicists (Fra Jabobo Torriti in Rome) and architects (Filippo de Campello at Assisi).[104]

60 Bologna, San Francesco, hemicycle piers (Bildarchiv Foto Marburg)

The final chapter of this book will consider this issue in relation to the startling consistency of moldings in the smaller Franciscan churches of Campania, a consistency that can be most sensibly explained as the work of itinerant Franciscan architectural builders. It is likely that they were lay members of the order and were presumably admitted precisely because they had this type of expertise. But the builder friars remain for the most part nameless.

It seems likely that instead of being the result of Cistercian influence, or a copy of Realvalle (or any other Cistercian site), the chevet of San Lorenzo is the product of Franciscan expertise and is based on models used elsewhere within the order, such as San Francesco in Bologna. Although there are references in this architec-

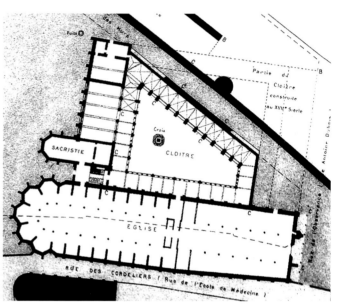

61 Paris, Ste Madeleine (the Cordeliers), plan

ture to French models, there is also a quite notable deviation from them – this is what might be called "second-hand" Frenchness, one dominated by a monastic aesthetic.

The chevet probably remained incomplete for some time, until work was picked up again in the mid-1290s with the support of Charles II. Although work on the new choir may have started in the 1270s, it was probably disrupted by the outbreak of the war of 1282 and the heavy taxes raised to support the Angevin effort to regain the island of Sicily and the invaded areas of southern Italy.

But was the choir the first Gothic addition to the old basilica? Although the generic quality of the Gothic

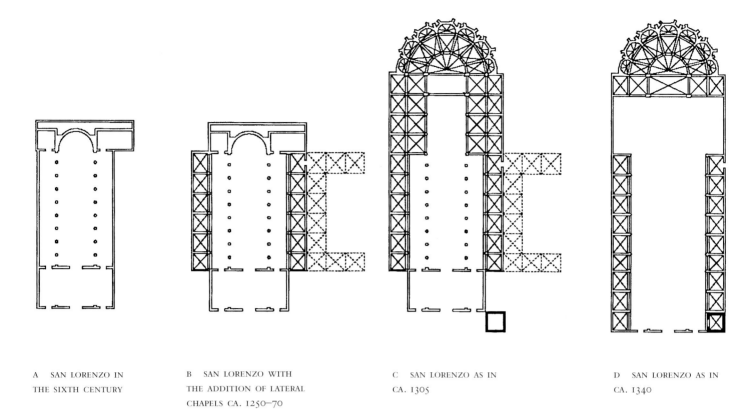

A SAN LORENZO IN
THE SIXTH CENTURY

B SAN LORENZO WITH
THE ADDITION OF LATERAL
CHAPELS CA. 1250–70

C SAN LORENZO AS IN
CA. 1305

D SAN LORENZO AS IN
CA. 1340

62   Naples, San Lorenzo Maggiore, schematic plan of construction phases (Irwin Sentilles)

detailing does not permit precise dating, it is likely that at least the three eastern chapels and entrance from the cloister on the south flank of the nave were added before the chevet.[105] This work could be dated as early as the 1260s, and thus have formed part of the adaptation of the site to Franciscan use (pl. 62B), in particular, to its use as a *studium*. The three easternmost chapels on the north side of the nave and the entrance from Via Tribunale also seem close to the south chapels in date, and may thus antedate the choir as well.

Work on the chapels must, of course, have been related to the construction of a monastic complex that reflected the rapid growth of the community and the need for spaces suitable for its teaching function. The ground plan of the entire complex (pl. 50) indicates that the chapels on the south flank of the church lay between what appears to have been the older medieval tower at the southwest corner of the basilica (later converted into the westernmost side chapel on the south flank of the church) and the south chapel flanking the sixth-century apse.[106] The plan of the cloister was integrally related to this range of chapels on the south. Although nothing of this early cloister survives, its construction would have been tied to the addition of the chapels on the south

flank of the church, chapels required by the liturgical needs of the ordained friars in the *studium* of San Lorenzo. Berger-Dittscheid's suggestion that these may have been added to the old basilica while the aisles were still in place is indeed "confirmed" by a consideration of the internal logic of the entire monastic complex. It was only later, with the suppression of the old nave and aisles of the basilica, that the ancient columns were moved to the side walls between the chapels and an outer row of arches added above their original arched openings to thicken and strengthen the wall.[107].

The type of Gothic detailing found in the chapels is of a generic type that occurs at any number of sites after about 1250; there is nothing here that necessarily places them at the end rather than towards the middle of the thirteenth century. By 1230 and after, window patterns of double lancets and rosettes were standard features of Gothic design. While some of the capitals are close to those at the cathedrals of Lucera and Naples (both *circa* 1294–1300), others can be dated to the third quarter of the thirteenth century. As noted elsewhere, there is reason to think that the Franciscan architectural vocabulary had a certain repertoire of standard elements that were repeated from site to site.

61

The eastern nave chapels, at least those on the south side, were therefore probably added while the cloister was being reconfigured in the decades around the middle of the thirteenth century, a process that took place as the community began to grow and as its role as a study center was affirmed (pl. 62B). As San Lorenzo grew in size and importance, though, it would quickly have become clear that the number of secondary altars was still too small: more chapels were added elsewhere in the nave and plans were initiated for a new choir with an ambulatory and additional chapels. All this would have required extensive negotiations for additional land in the crowded city center.

The precedence of the nave chapels over the addition of the Gothic chevet is confirmed by the alignment of the latter with the outer walls of the former (pls. 50 and 62C). The easternmost opening on the south side was a door to the cloister and adjacent buildings and was presumably aligned with the friars' liturgical choir (no trace of which survives and which in any event was moved between 1563 and 1580 to a site behind the main altar in the apse).[108]

To summarize: the new chevet was aligned with the basilica, its outer walls corresponding to the lateral chapels added to the nave. The work on the chapels may have begun in the 1260s, and the addition of the choir began perhaps in the next decade; there is no reason to associate either the beginning or completion of the work with the documents of 1283. The new chevet was attached to an older nave to which its proportions were coordinated. It is possible to think of other examples of such arrangements in the twelfth and thirteenth centuries: Abbot Suger's east end at Saint-Denis, for example, was designed "ad formam priori et posterioris operas conjugendi," and Gothic chevets that expanded older naves can be seen not only in the context of monastic architecture (Pontigny, Ourscamp, pl. 57) but also in cathedrals, as at Le Mans. Apart from solving issues of space, the arrangement can also suggest a certain respect for, or even veneration of, the older monument and the antiquity of the site. It would also have been at least partially in keeping with Saint Francis's idea that instead of building new churches, old ones should be repaired and renewed.

The adaptation of the old basilica at San Lorenzo was probably episodic and organic: the church grew in relation to the growth of the Franciscan community and the donation of funds from private patrons and donors. Construction of the thirteenth-century church may be seen as an ad hoc process attested by the variation in the heights of the chapel openings and in the dimensions of plinths and types of base profiles (App. 5, fig. 2).

The recent research of Rosalba di Meglio has discovered evidence for donations to private chapels in the thirteenth and early fourteenth centuries.[109] As elsewhere in this period, although chapels were initially required for liturgical reasons, the friars quickly accommodated them to the lay desire for private burial chapels that "overlapped" the liturgical use of these spaces. Although Durandus, for example, referred to prohibitions on lay burials in churches in the 1290s, it is evident from other sources and other sites that such burial was already becoming common practice and that the mendicant orders in particular depended on this type of patronage as a source of revenues.[110]

Schenkluhn also observed that this type of Gothic architecture was in keeping with the intellectual and academic pretensions of the Franciscan order.[111] Louis IX of France, as formal protector of the Franciscans, played a vital role in the order's success as a teaching and intellectual institution, and under his protection and influence the first and principal Franciscan *studium*, where Bonaventure and other distinguished members of the order studied and taught, was established in Paris.[112] An aura of "Frenchness" was not only a salient characteristic of many of the more important Franciscan buildings in Italy, including San Francesco at Assisi, but was also a quality particularly cultivated as a distinctive feature of the churches connected with *studia*, as Cadei and Schenkluhn have demonstrated.[113]

It seems likely that after an initial phase of direct French influence in the 1250s, forms were transmitted from one Italian monastery to another, independent of contemporary developments in France. This sort of "second-hand," or associative, "Frenchness," motivated by ambitions and associations within the order, would seem to be fundamental to the design of the church in Naples and explains the strangely antiquated handling of elements far better than an association with the architects and builders brought to Naples by Charles of Anjou.

Reinserted into a Franciscan context, the chevet of San Lorenzo is part of the urbane and self-consciously scholarly character of the order as it evolved in the middle of the thirteenth century. The Franciscans were now members of a well-established religious community, well-educated and well-trained preachers and teachers respected by the public. Bonaventure himself favored larger and more solidly constructed houses. In its new form as a clerical order, a new type of architecture was developed for the prestigious and especially important Franciscan establishments, one ultimately indebted to French sources and models (mostly monastic, as Schenkluhn points out). In late thirteenth-century

Naples this would of course have had particular resonance; indeed, for the Franciscans the *studium* was in the center of the new political and intellectual capital of the kingdom and the choice of an architecture of prestige was essential.

In hindsight one might observe that the mingled motivations and sources behind the concept of the chevet of San Lorenzo were so clearly articulated by its Franciscan builders that they became, as it were, a self-fulfilling prophecy: the aspiration to Frenchness was expressed with such clarity that the church could easily be adopted as a site for royal patronage and burial and as a legend of Charles of Anjou's patronage.[114] The tombs within the church, and the suggestiveness of the language of the architecture, led later generations with their own aspirations (and especially those of late fifteenth- and early sixteenth-century Naples) to conclude that the church was – and could only ever have been – a royal foundation.

63   Naples, San Lorenzo Maggiore, apse and south transept arm, east side (Giovanni Genova)

The "Ghost Church at San Lorenzo": The Transept and Nave

The tall and uninterrupted transept visible today at San Lorenzo represents a dramatic transformation of the space that once connected the Gothic chevet to the sixth-century nave (pl. 48). The barely visible vault departures at the corners of the south transept arm (pl. 65), the remains of plinths (one of which is now visible in the area adjacent to the sixth-century mosaic pavement in the south transept arm), and the deliberate destruction of the sixth-century pavement in alignment with the nave walls indicate that double aisles continued from the chevet across what is now the transept to join the older basilica to the west. There was therefore no transept in the original configuration of the church. This observation can be confirmed in the foundations of the *scavi* underneath, where above the remains of the Roman shops that line the *vicolo* adjacent to the market, foundation walls of *tufo giallo* (yellow tuff) have been added above the brick walls of the Roman buildings. Some foundation walls for the transept piers, removed in the restoration of the Roman market, were also constructed across the Roman street and can be seen in photographs of the 1950s when the initial excavations were made underneath the transept area.

The chevet thus continued across what is now the transept as three bays of double aisles (pl. 62c). This would have connected the ambulatory to the friars' entrance and the aisles to the west. The connecting bays, supported by compound piers that were squared versions of the hemicycle supports, carried rib vaults over the aisles and the pointed arches of the arcade. Fragments of the rib vaults of the double aisles, rising to the height of the chevet arcade, can still be seen against the present transept walls (pls. 64 and 65). As there were no vaults over the main volume there was no need for a shaft facing the nave on the piers.

The nave of the old basilica would have connected without interruption to the double aisles of the new construction to the east, a plan similar to that of the church of the Cordeliers in Paris (pl. 61).

If it can be assumed that the work on the chevet was underway in the 1270s or by the early 1280s, and was either greatly slowed (or interrupted altogether) by the war of 1282,[115] its completion almost certainly took place as the result of the donations made to San Lorenzo in 1296–7 and 1299 by Charles II. The document recording these gifts suggests work was underway "in subsidium operis," and the second implies imminent completion: "in subsidium perfectionis operis." The work was presumably finished by 1305, when the first of the royal tombs was installed, and the two tombs in turn may be related to, or indeed explain, the two anomalous fragments of frescoes discovered by Chierici on the east and west walls of the south transept arm. Attributed by Bologna to Montano d'Arezzo, these can be dated to the first decade of the fourteenth century, when Montano was active in Naples and Montevergine. They represent the *Nativity* on the west wall and on the east the *Dormition of the Virgin* (pls. 64 and 65).[116] The fresco frag-

64 Naples, San Lorenzo Maggiore, south transept arm, west side (Giovanni Genova)

65 Naples, San Lorenzo Maggiore, south transept arm, east side (Giovanni Genova)

ments, and a few traces of destroyed baldachins, may be what remains of the tombs or burial chapels of Prince Raymond Berengar (d. 1305), brother of Robert and Louis of Toulouse, and Prince Louis (d. 1310), son of Robert and his first wife, Violante. The document of 1305 that concerns the tomb of Raymond Berengar speaks of 50 once given by Charles II to San Lorenzo "for the construction of a chapel in the church where his son is buried and the erection of an altar and the painting of the chapel...".[117] D'Engenio described the tomb of Louis in the east wall of the south transept (therefore near or beneath the scene of the *Dormition*, as well as near the tomb of Catherine of Austria). The tombs of the two princes, mentioned briefly by D'Engenio in 1624, were destroyed in the remodeling of the church a few decades later. By Summonte's time they no longer existed, although the author states that they used to be found to the right of the main altar and "appresso la cappella maggiore."[118]

If this proposition is acceptable, one can, I think, imagine a pair of tombs that combined paintings, altars, and baldachins along the lines of the fifteenth-century tomb of Cardinal d'Alençon at Santa Maria in Trastevere, Rome (pl. 66). The latter has been for the most part destroyed, but it was recorded by Seroux D'Agincourt as a baldachin over an effigy and fresco panel.[119]

It may therefore be possible to suggest that the double aisles on the south had become a royal burial chapel by about 1305–10. As noted by Bologna and Leone de Castris, Montano d'Arezzo was intimately connected with the court, carrying out commissions for various members of the royal family at sites in Naples and nearby.[120] South transepts were often privileged places of burial (at Palermo the imperial tombs were in the south transept arm), and in monasteries these would have been adjacent to the monastic community and therefore physically close to the population that prayed for the souls of the deceased.

64

The supposition of an Angevin family chapel in this part of the church is perhaps confirmed by the later burial of Catherine of Austria, the first wife of Charles of Calabria, in 1323.[121] The peculiar position of the tomb in its present location (first bay on the south side of chevet) and its strangely contracted state are highly significant, for as we shall see its recomposition forms part of the tale of the extraordinary reconstruction of the church in the 1320s. Francesco Aceto made the important observation that the tomb of Catherine presents a series of anomalies and modifications that indicate that it was originally carved for a larger space and as a conventional wall tomb. And of course the much later tombs

66 Seroux d'Agincourt, tomb of the Cardinal d'Alençon in Santa Maria in Trastevere, Rome (Biblioteca Apostolica Vaticana)

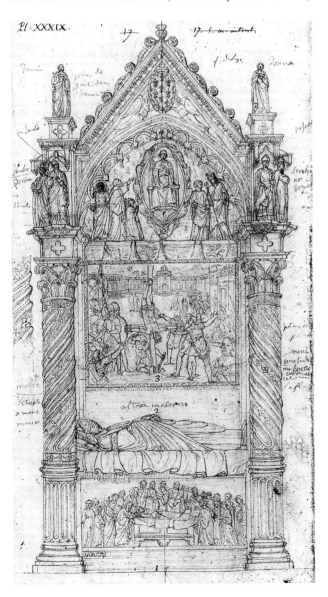

of the Durazzo in the north transept arm would have been a complement to this ensemble.

The transept and nave in their present state represent several phases of reconstruction and repair, some of which (the transept terminations, the western crossing arch) date from the second half of the fourteenth and the fifteenth centuries. The most profound moment of transformation at San Lorenzo, however, came with the decision to dismantle the Early Christian basilica and create one vast space out of what had formerly been the nave and aisles of the old building. It would also have been at this moment that the vast new transept was created, for the transition from the large single volume of the new nave (the space comprised by the entire Early Christian basilica, nave and side aisles) to the much narrower dimensions of the chevet required a transitional space between the two parts of the building (pls. 48, 62D and 67).

It seems probable that the radical transformation of this church took place at the end of a pivotal year for the history of San Lorenzo, 1323. At her death in February of that year, Catherine of Austria left a large bequest to the church that included a donation for the construction of a chapel dedicated to Louis of Toulouse. As Aceto noted, the modification of her tomb by Tino da Camaino himself must therefore have occurred between 1323 and the sculptor's death in 1332.

Much later that year, in December, Giovanni, the eldest son of the great protonotary of the kingdom, Bartolomeo da Capua, also died, and was buried at San Lorenzo. The death of Giovanni seems to have precipitated the creation of the group of the triple Da Capua family chapels at the west end of the south side of the nave, noted in guidebooks and descriptions until the sixteenth century.[122] (The tombs were subsequently dismantled and moved to the opposite side of the nave.)

The Da Capua chapels, however, were located outside and to the west of the Early Christian nave, partially adjacent to the narthex of the old basilica and partially inserted within the older southwest tower (pls. 50, 62D, and 67C). The narthex, approximately 8 meters deep, was presumably a lean-to structure against the west façade of the old church and not a volume formally integrated with the nave, so that the plan to construct the Da Capua chapels would have meant that the entire west end of the building needed to be rethought. The creation of these chapels entailed a decision to lengthen the church and to reconfigure it entirely by lengthening the nave to absorb the deep narthex and west tower and by widening it to erase the old nave and aisles of the basilica, in effect creating the space that we see today. This was a fundamental reconstruction that would have preserved

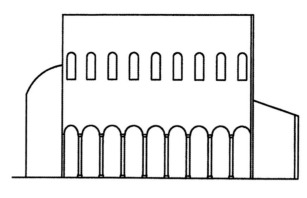

A   THE SIXTH–CENTURY BASILICA

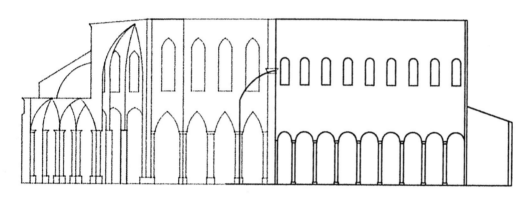

B   THE SIXTH–CENTURY BASILICA EXTENDED TO THE EAST WITH THE GOTHIC CHEVET
AND LINKING BAYS

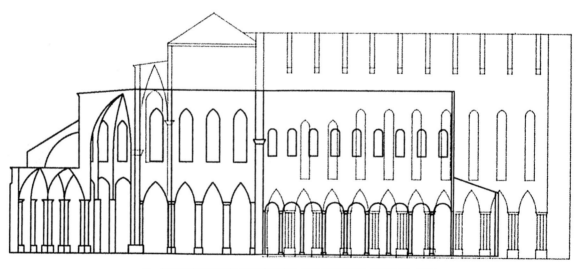

C   RECONSTRUCTION OF THE NAVE AND TRANSEPT AFTER CA. 1324

67   Naples, San Lorenzo Maggiore, schematic reconstruction of building phases (Irwin Sentilles)

68   Naples, San Lorenzo Maggiore, view of the north side of the nave from the east (author)

only the exterior walls of the side aisles, which had already been penetrated by lateral chapels. At this point the columns of the aisles were moved between the chapel entrances and used to support an outer arch that thickened the wall above the chapels that sustains the weight of the much taller elevation and new, much wider, truss ceiling (pls. 62D, 67, 68, and 69).

In this process the church would have been lengthened by almost a third beyond the Early Christian basilica, permitting the construction not only of three additional chapels on each side, but of course also requiring the construction of an entirely new west façade. Sixteenth-century sources speak of the entire façade as the work of Bartolomeo da Capua, and, indeed, in spite of its Baroque reconstruction, this is confirmed by the Da Capua arms on the west portal and the upper level of the southwest tower (pls. 71 and 73).[123] The portal itself will be addressed in the discussion of Da Capua's patronage in the last chapter of this book, but it may be noted

for now that the great elegance and sophistication of the pink marbles and delicate moldings that decorate this structure represent one of the masterpieces of Neapolitan design in the fourteenth century (pls. 72, 73, and 158).

The transept would have been reconfigured during this process, one that left the chevet as the only remaining part of the Gothic extension to the old basilica. The piers and double aisles connecting the basilica to the east end were dismantled, and tall walls were erected over the remaining enclosing shell to create the high transept typical of Neapolitan monuments after about 1295. Oculi were inserted in the tall flat eastern wall of the transept, and the first quadripartite vault of the chevet was reconstructed at a higher level than that of the hemicycle to accord with the level of the new and higher nave roof (pl. 48). The entire structure of the upper walls of the nave, the transept arms, and the first straight bay of the chevet are constructed in continuously bonded coursed masonry (pl. 75).

67

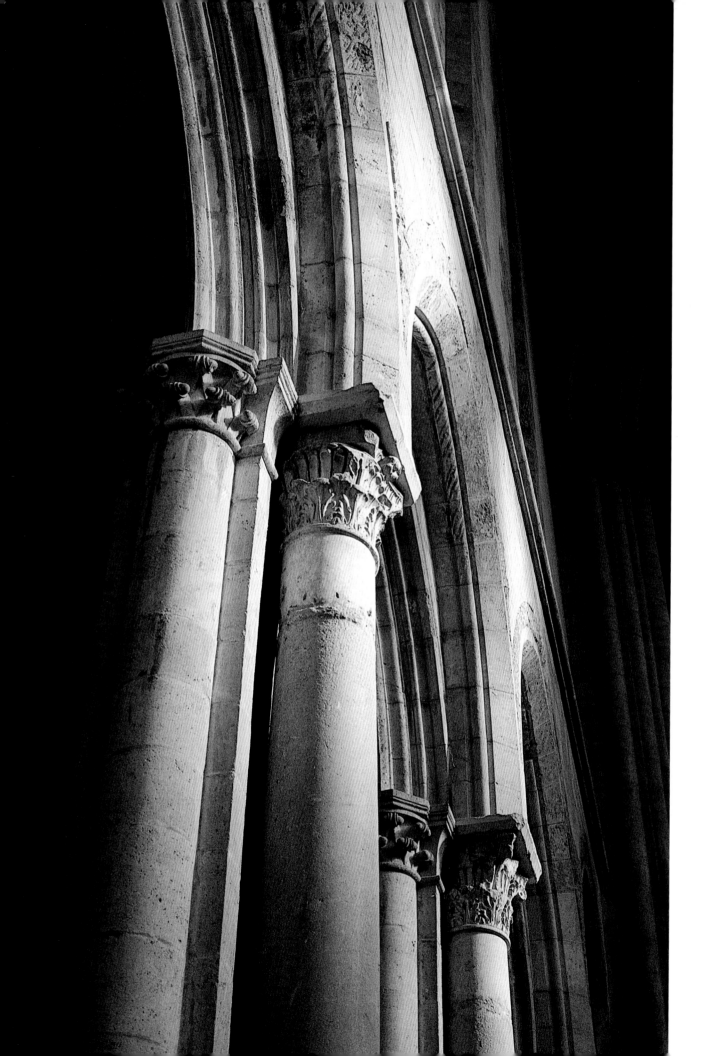

70   Naples, San Lorenzo Maggiore, vaults of the chevet (author)

It can probably be assumed that during this process the tombs of the two royal princes in the south transept arm and their sculptural and painted decoration would have been preserved in place. But the tomb of Catherine of Austria, which was in the process of construction, was reconfigured to become a freestanding monument that gave passage from the altar to the sacristy. It may be that some tracery elements were dismantled and reused. The lancet windows in the north and south walls of the transept arms, as well as the shorter lancets at the east end of the nave, were perhaps part of the three original connecting bays between the chevet and the Early Christian basilica and were reintegrated into the reconstructed church.

The expansion towards the west starting in early 1324 is confirmed by the purchase of a small garden and some houses adjacent to the church owned by Andreas Cannutus de Neapoli in order to "perficere" the church.[124] Furthermore, in May 1324 Pope John XXII issued an indulgence for those who visited the chapel of the

Virgin "in honorem beatissimae virginis construendam."[125] And although in her will of 1323 Catherine of Austria had left funds for the execution of a chapel to be dedicated to Saint Louis, as we have seen, this chapel was not completed until 1343, when a payment was made to Nicola Caracciolo for the execution of the work.[126] Above all, D'Engenio Caracciolo noted that the arms of Bartolomeo da Capua could be seen throughout the church, a decoration that was presumably painted and lost in either the Baroque redecoration or the twentieth-century restoration.[127] The only part of the Da Capua heraldry that survives today is that on the west portal (pls. 71 and 73) and the upper parts of the tower at the southwest corner of the church.

The transept has been modified again since its reconstruction begun in 1324, however. Both arms were subsequently lengthened at ground level: that on the north is now entirely covered with sumptuous Baroque marbles, while the south arm, also deepened, seems to date from after the earthquake of 1349. The form of the

69 (facing page)   Naples, San Lorenzo Maggiore, detail of the arcade arches, north side of nave (author)

71 Naples, San Lorenzo Maggiore, tower of the southwest corner, upper level: the De Capua family arms (author)

72 Naples, San Lorenzo Maggiore, detail of marbles, west portal (Giovanni Genova)

piers in the far wall of the south transept arm, which are polygonal in shape with molded capitals, is akin to those rebuilt in the nave arcade at Sant'Eligio, and those of the nave of the Incoronata, dated to the reign of Joanna I, in about or after 1357. All in turn relate to forms that developed in the mid-fourteenth century, such as those of the great abbey of La Chaise Dieu in the Auvergne.

One last observation may be made: if it is correct that the nave of San Lorenzo was reconstructed beginning in 1324, the monument might well have been a "response" to the ongoing construction of the other great Franciscan foundation of Naples, Santa Chiara, begun in 1310 (and the focus of a later chapter). The dominant feature of Santa Chiara is a vast wide nave without aisles flanked by lateral chapels, a program that is in some ways reflected in the reconfigured nave of San Lorenzo. Furthermore, if it is legitimate to think of Santa Chiara as representing the poverty-minded branch of the Franciscans, and San Lorenzo as representing the Conventuals, then the restructuring of San Lorenzo may even have been a competitive response to the massive project begun by Queen Sancia for the "poor" Franciscans on the other side of town.

This new interpretation of the dating and raison d'être of the nave may be startling to those readers who are familiar with the church of San Lorenzo and the historiographical tradition associated with the monument. But of course, sooner or later, the Early Christian basilica *was* dismantled, and it makes sense for many reasons to think of that process as intimately connected with the lengthening of the church and the construction of a new façade patronized by Bartolomeo da Capua, begun after the death of his son and underway before his own death in 1328.

If this new reading of San Lorenzo has merit, it resides not so much in the different proposal for the plan of the transept that connects chevet to nave, or in the new date proposed for the reconstruction of the nave itself, but rather in the suggestion that the church as it appears today is the result of the multiple and overlapping exigencies of the Franciscan community in collaboration with the patronage of the urban aristocracy, especially that of the local insula and *seggio*, and above all that of Bartolomeo da Capua. We can thus propose a reading of this building not so much as an "Angevin" monument but rather as the expression of the confluence of the liturgical requirements of the friars in an order now mostly clerical, and the desires of private patrons for commemorative chapels within the church. Of course several Angevin kings did have a role in this building, especially after the death of Louis of Toulouse when Charles II took on its completion, but their role should

73 (*facing page*) Naples, San Lorenzo Maggiore, west portal (Giovanni Genova)

75   Naples, San Lorenzo Maggiore, exterior of the south side of nave and transept arm (author)

be seen as part of the larger process of renewal and reconstruction that was rooted in monastic and civic concerns. In effect, royal patronage attached itself to a church that was already expanding and flourishing in the center of the city.

The powerful tradition that has associated the church of San Lorenzo with Charles of Anjou, and that has considered it a dynastic monument and royal foundation, is primarily dependent on a sixteenth- and seventeenth-century tradition carved in stone in an inscription of 1763 over the west portal.[128] Because it was adjacent to the Tribunals of Naples, San Lorenzo became linked with a phase of Neapolitan history that was considered

"democratic" – a moment when the Angevins, in contrast to their Aragonese successors after 1456, respected the rights of local government and the people of Naples. This historical reading performed two miracles: Charles of Anjou became a patron of pious projects as well as a ruler who respected and defended Neapolitan self-government.

Perhaps it was indeed thus, but in the absence of documents or any other tradition to this effect it seems far more plausible that the first of the French rulers was co-opted *a posteriori* for reasons unique to the troubled history of fifteenth- and sixteenth-century Naples.

74 (*facing page*)   Naples, San Lorenzo Maggiore, exterior of the chevet (author)

Chapter 3

RELIGIOUS ARCHITECTURE DURING THE REIGN OF CHARLES II AND MARY OF HUNGARY

"we can prove the love of God lying hidden in the inner side of the mind of Charles through the twofold action of charity open to view on the outside. He undoubtedly continued to give many and generous alms right up to the end of his life, and to show active kindness to the poor for the sake of God. He also greatly loved and expanded the liturgical worship of God, and it was a source of delight to him, so that in his household and chapel the worship of God flourished much and continuously . . . and in his lands he founded, constructed, and endowed many churches and religious places . . .[1]

Charles I died in January 1285. His eldest son, Charles, Prince of Salerno, had been taken prisoner in June 1284 by the famous admiral Roger of Lauria, who had defected to support the Hohenstaufen claim through Constance, wife of Peter of Aragon. The captive prince had been taken first to Sicily, and then to Spain, and after Charles I's death the Kingdom of Sicily was under a regency government patched together under Robert II, Count of Artois, and the Cardinal-legate, Gerard of Parma. In 1288, Charles II was set free by the terms of the treaty of Canfranc in return for a payment of 50,000 silver marks and for sending three of his sons as hostages in his place. (The three boys, Robert, Louis, and Raymond Berengar, were to remain in Aragonese captivity until the peace treaty brokered by Boniface VIII in June 1295).

In November 1288 Charles II was liberated from prison and traveled to Naples across southern Europe, passing through France and Tuscany and interrupting progress south for his coronation in Rieti.[2] But with the peace treaty in question and the promises to his captors in Aragon unresolved, he was not yet at liberty to focus his energies on either the kingdom or its capital, and his Neapolitan sojourn in 1289 was brief: he remained in the city only from 4 July to 10 August, and again from 1 to 15 September.[3] Not until five years later, in April 1294, when a resolution of the peace treaty that would bring the liberation of his three sons held hostage in Cat-

alonia was imminent, could Charles II return definitively to the Regno and make Naples once again his home. It had been almost ten years since his capture in 1284, and Naples for that decade was without a king in residence.

With his return in April 1294 the city took on new life: there was an intense spurt of activity, as though projects and repairs incubating in the minds of the king, his advisors, and the religious authorities suddenly burst into life. Within two or three months of his arrival, Charles II was involved in a series of urban works and construction projects that were to change forever the character of the city. Perhaps these were the result of the king's oft-expressed affection for Naples (a sentiment all the more striking because his ignominious defeat and capture ten years earlier had occurred in the Bay of Naples in full view of the city and had precipitated a bloody revolt against the French),[4] but they also reflected two other things. The first was the need to affirm the role of Naples as the new capital of the kingdom after the loss of Palermo and to assert the city as the political and administrative center in the realpolitik of a regime mutilated by the loss of Sicily. The other was the simple fact that, since the third or fourth decade of the thirteenth century, there had been little by way of major construction projects, especially church building, in the kingdom in general and Naples in particular.

The new projects were oriented towards the quality of civic and religious life; the health of the citizens was to be enhanced by paving the streets, draining the swamps, repairing the aqueducts, and reconstructing the harbor, as well as protection and defense (city walls and arsenals). The priorities of Charles I, who had maintained, repaired, and expanded the internal system of fortifications (Lagopesole, Lucera, Melfi, for example), as well as the defensive system of the castles down the eastern coast of Apulia (Manfredonia, Barletta, Bari, Mola di Bari), were put aside in favor of projects on the west coast and the northern borders in an effort to affirm the boundaries with the Papal States and the North, now the central focus of royal interest and concern. Charles I's ambitions towards the East were by now long gone, and royal attention shifted emphatically towards central Italy and southern France: the focus was now Europe and the western Mediterranean. Charles II's building projects were thus in direct contrast to those of his father before him, and this was reflected in the character and style of these architectural enterprises, now based on Roman and indigenous Campanian models. The king's fervent involvement in church building was part of a larger process of regeneration and reform.

Although the civic and defensive structures have been destroyed and their nature is therefore hard to judge, it may be permissible to extrapolate from the character of the religious architecture, in which case we might imagine that they were for the most part severe and utilitarian. It is striking that so many projects were undertaken in spite of the ongoing and crushing debt to the Holy See and to various (mostly Tuscan) bankers.

It will be recalled that, until 1282, Palermo, in name at least, was still the capital of the kingdom. But if Charles II maintained any hope of regaining the city, with its monumental palaces and churches and the remains of his uncle Louis IX in Monreale, this does not seem to have been a factor, for Naples by 1294 was taking its place as capital.[5] Surely ease of travel by road to Rome and the good harbor with access to Marseilles were important factors. But even before the war of 1282 the Angevin rulers had spent little time in Sicily, out of the sphere of interest for Charles I's projects for eastern expansion. Under Charles II foreign policy required a location nearer to France (and especially Provence), Tuscany, and the papacy. Furthermore, Naples, with its community of distinguished jurists and scholars, its great physical beauty, and its distinguished past history, was a logical, obvious, and splendid choice.[6]

Although Charles II focused his energies on the new capital, a few other sites, especially those of strategic or commercial importance, were also the recipients of special royal favor. These included cities that had been faithful in times of trouble, such as Barletta, one of the

few towns in Apulia that remained allied with the Angevins when the rest of the region revolted in 1282. The cause of Barletta was probably promoted by one of its most distinguished citizens, Giovanni Pipino, who by the mid-1290s was one of Charles II's most trusted associates; Pipino's interests were also favored by Robert of Artois and Clement V.[7] Cities along the northern borders of the kingdom, such as L'Aquila and Sulmona, were also important recipients of special royal attention, and here new towns were founded to consolidate the mountainous border areas. Throughout the kingdom, the mendicant orders, especially the Dominicans, were encouraged, and given Charles II's ardent patronage of the order it would be reasonable to suppose that they played a special role in his policies of consolidation.

Although the urban and civic projects of Charles II are destroyed, the many churches that survive are a testament to his energetic activity as a builder and as a promoter of religious projects. This chapter will identify and describe the character, design, and construction of the churches and abbeys in a style that was unique to southern Italy and that had a strong mendicant flavor. There are frequent references to indigenous Italian building traditions and specifically, I believe, not only to Naples's Early Christian past, but also to the basilicas of Rome. Although Charles II had often spent long periods in Paris, both as Prince of Salerno and as king, and although he was surrounded by a court in many ways still strongly flavored by French culture, he and his closest advisors (who appear to have been mostly Italian) made little more than perfunctory reference to architectural tastes and trends in France, or, for that matter, Provence.[8] In a public context, at least, the monuments erected during his reign represent a neutralization of the French character of the court, and this is especially striking if one reflects on the architecture of Paris in the second half of the thirteenth century that would have been known to Charles II, such as the recently completed church of Saint-Denis (where the king stayed on at least one occasion), the transepts and eastern chapels of Notre-Dame in Paris, and the royal palace on the Ile-de-la-Cité. There is nothing in the surviving Angevin monuments of Naples to suggest any attempt to reflect these familiar models:[9] no evidence of interest in the increasingly elaborate patterns of Parisian tracery, in slender and delicate clusters of shafts, or yet of the elegance and refinement associated with the courts of Philip III and Philip IV in Paris and its environs.[10] To the contrary, what survives in Naples and elsewhere in the kingdom suggests a desire to promote the visual preferences of indigenous building traditions combined with a general taste for austerity and a sense of

78 Saint-Maximin-la-Sainte-Baume, Provence, view of the interior (Centre des monuments nationaux/MONUM.)

imitation of classical acanthus-leaf capitals suggest a deliberate evocation of antiquity and of a local building tradition.

The interiors are austere, with an emphasis on flat walls and wooden truss ceilings over nave and transepts. Was this austerity to have been covered with frescoes? With the exception of the royal palace chapels at the Castel Nuovo, the nuns' choirs at Santa Chiara and Santa Maria Donnaregina, and various private chapels in the churches of the city, no evidence in the documents or the monuments survives of painting in the interiors of the churches. Had they been intended to include fresco programs, one might imagine a symbiosis between structure and painting that in some way informed and enhanced the architectural frame, something along the lines of the painted decoration in the triforium of the transept arms of Assisi.[11] The state of the evidence prohibits any extended discussion of this issue, and we may only suppose that if the walls had been intended as surfaces for painting, this too would have constituted a dramatic departure from French precedents and a continuation of earlier indigenous traditions of decoration. If frescoes were once planned or existed, we then might wonder also if these would have formed a "partnership" with the development of preaching and sermonizing that played an important role in the spiritual life of the kingdom.[12]

There is therefore little in the Kingdom of Naples erected during the reign of Charles II that attempts to reproduce French models, and the strong contrast between the architecture erected by this king in his Provençal and his Italian domains is also striking. This is particularly compelling in the case of Saint-Maximin-la-Sainte-Baume (pl. 78), Charles II's most important project in Provence, in comparison with the cathedral of Naples (pl. 79).

Naples, 1294–1309

THE CATHEDRAL

Of the many religious monuments associated with Charles II in Naples, only the cathedral, the royal chapel at the Castel Nuovo, and the outer structure of San Domenico remain reasonably intact (pls. 79, 97, and 105).[13] A monument of singular grandeur and harmony, the cathedral has been ignored in most studies of Italian Gothic architecture, perhaps because it has been rebuilt and redecorated many times with the result that its exterior and interior have been largely transformed.[14] Yet the essential structure remains powerfully present under-

local history and context. This shift reflects the realities of local labor and materials. Although echoes of French design are sometimes found in the rib vaults of apses and aisles and in altar niches and the bar tracery of windows, the models tend to be those of a previous generation (and seem to have been produced in a standardized manner, perhaps by the piece in local workshops). To judge from the one intact façade of about 1310, that of the cathedral of Lucera, discrete episodes of Gothic detailing were combined with (and adjusted to conform to) *spolia* elements as well as to traditional Italian thinking about design (pl. 77): there is, between the sharp forms of the gable and the ancient columns that support it, a sort of lean and austere rendition of certain Rayonnant ideas, such as the very slender shafts. But there is nothing in this mix that could be mistaken for French work of the decades between about 1290 and 1310 – on the contrary, the use of classical materials and the

79   Naples, cathedral, view of the nave arcade, north side, from the west (Massimo Velo)

neath later incrustations and repairs, and this building emerges as a profoundly original and majestic monument that fuses local tradition in construction techniques and materials with discreet elements of northern Gothic design.[15]

Initiated by Archbishop Filippo Minutolo at the time of Charles II's definitive return to Naples in April 1294, the cathedral became the centerpiece of the urban renewal of Naples, part of the larger project to confirm the city's status as the new capital of the truncated kingdom.[16] With an expression of dedication to its archbishop "dilecto consiliario familiari e fideli nostri," and with special reverence, "specialem habentes in domino caritatis affectum," Charles II issued a document on 16 June 1294 that supported the project for the reconstruction.[17] The next day he gave Minutolo the right to sell grain without payment of tithe; in years of grain shortage the king promised the archbishop an annual

income of 100 once for the fabric of the church.[18] In other, later, documents Charles II described himself as the founder.

The project for the new church was intended from the outset to incorporate a chapel for the tomb of Charles I, the monument of his first wife, Beatrice of Provence (empty after 1277), and other members of the royal family; in that sense the rebuilding of the cathedral should be considered one of the first definitive (but short-lived) steps towards the creation of an Angevin royal necropolis.[19] The royal tombs were to be adjacent to the transept, a zone reserved for the commemoration of the bishop-saints of Naples, many of whose remains had been translated to a series of *arcosoliae* with portraits within the second of the two Early Christian basilicas at the site, the Stefania.[20] Once the east end of the new cathedral was complete, the remains of these bishops were translated again to new altars in the three eastern

80 Naples, cathedral, tomb of Filippo Minutolo (Giovanni Genova)

apses dedicated in their honor. Since both kings and bishops (but especially bishops) were to be celebrated in the new church, it was fitting that both royal and episcopal authority were joined together in its construction. As we shall see, however, there can be no doubt that the reconstruction of the church was above all the bishop's initiative. His primary purpose was to celebrate the long tradition of episcopal authority in Naples.[21]

Filippo Minutolo, elected to the episcopacy of Naples in 1288, had close ties with the royal family (pl. 80).[22] He was a canon of the cathedral as early as 1269, and from 1271 onwards was *chierico palatino* and royal counselor.[23] He represented Charles I in Lombardy and in 1271 assisted him in Viterbo in negotiations with the Holy See on the immense royal debt.[24] Before his election to the see of Naples, he had been Archbishop of Salerno. In 1295 Charles II suggested to his son, Carlo Martello, that Filippo Minutolo should be the first and foremost of his counselors in his new role as heir to the throne of Hungary.[25]

Given the weight of tradition and history, the decision to rebuild the cathedral was a serious one. Perhaps the (supposed) earthquake of 1293, said to have destroyed

the nearby Clarissan church of Santa Maria Donnaregina just to the north, provided the impetus for the rebuilding, although earthquake damage is not mentioned in the documents that concern the reconstruction of the cathedral.[26] In any event, the burden of tradition must have been onerous and accounts for many aspects of the siting and dimensions of the new church (pls. 81 and 82). For example, according to tradition the chapel of Santa Maria del Principio off the left aisle of Santa Restituta represented the location of the first Early Christian church or chapel at the site.[27] Santa Restituta itself has been legendarily associated with Constantine, and is, if not Constantinian, nonetheless certainly a fourth-century monument (pl. 82[A]).[28] In the following centuries two baptisteries, a second basilica (the Stefania, pl. 82[B]), and numerous other churches, chapels, service quarters, the episcopal residence, courtyards, and towers were added to the original core, forming what must have been a large complex of elaborate structures, many richly decorated with sculpture, mosaics, and painting. The site thus consisted of two large basilicas parallel to each other with their apses in the north and their entrances, perhaps preceded by atria, to the south. Between the two ran one of the narrow streets of the Greco-Roman grid plan, which also ran north–south. The new cathedral was placed at right angles to the two older buildings: its transept covered the location of most of the basilica of the Stefania, and its nave replaced part of Santa Restituta. Part of Santa Restituta was preserved, however, and is still present in the form of a large truncated basilica off the north aisle of the present cathedral.

The new Angevin cathedral was situated in such a way as to permit the partial preservation of some of these monuments and to "remember," in the dedications or some aspects of the reconfiguration of the spaces, others. The relationship between old and new and the sensitivity of the new design to the history of the site will form a large part of this chapter. The emphasis on the ancient traditions suggests that the primary function of the new cathedral was to affirm the historical – indeed, apostolic – roots of the church of Naples and its natural role as the new capital of the kingdom.[29]

As noted above, the initiative for the rebuilding in the late thirteenth century came from the archbishop, who proposed the reconstruction to Charles II almost immediately after his return in 1294. Although the king did not have much in the way of funds – he was himself in debt to the archbishop for a personal loan of 100 once – he was in a position to assist the project in other important ways.[30] On 24 November 1296 he assigned an

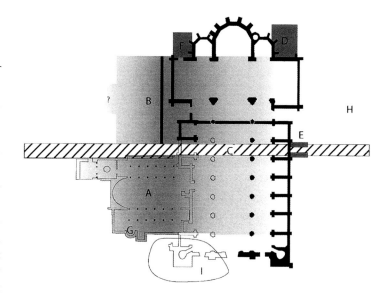

82   Schematic plan of the cathedral of Naples with the locations of the earlier structures (Irwin Sentilles)

A   Basilica of Santa Restituta
B   Basilica of the Stefania
C   Roman road
D   Cappella Minutolo/Cappella San Pietro
E   The tower of 1233
F   Cappella di San Lorenzo/Cappella San Paolo
G   Chapel of Santa Maria del Principio
H   Piazza Riario Sforza
I   ?Area of property acquisition in 1311

81   Naples, cathedral, plan (from De Stefano 1974)

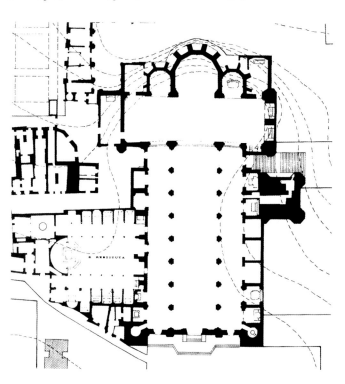

annual rent to the cathedral, associating the contribution with the burial of his parents' remains, the construction of a memorial chapel and the saying of memorial masses.[31] On 29 August 1299 he ordered every family in Naples to contribute 1 grano each week for a duration of two years "in subsidium expensarum fabrice maioris Neapolitanae Matris Ecclesie quam in honorem B. Marie Virginis nos ipsi de novo fundavimus."[32] The collection of this tithe presented difficulties, as indicated by documents of 1303 and 1304.[33] Later on, when the finances of the kingdom were more secure, royal donations were given towards the progress of the work: in September 1308, for example, Charles II donated 50 once "in subsidium fabrice maioris ecclesie Neapolitanae."[34] Other royal concessions of tithes occurred in 1308 and 1309.[35]

It may well be that the cathedral itself was wealthy, or at least that it was recovering its wealth after the dispersal of its properties and revenues in the first half of the thirteenth century.[36] Filippo Minutolo's predecessors, especially Archbishop Ayglerius, who served during the reign of Charles I, had begun to restore the properties and incomes of the cathedral usurped under Hohenstaufen rule.[37] According to Summonte, Charles I bequeathed to the cathedral the tithe of Scanaggio.[38] The recovery or new acquisition of income-bearing properties was continued by Filippo Minutolo and, after his death, by Giacomo da Viterbo, elected 12 December 1302.[39] In 1303 the new archbishop obtained the restitution of the cathedral tithes that had reverted to the crown during the vacancy of the episcopal see, and throughout his term he was consistently energetic in asserting the rights of the cathedral's patrimony.[40]

Minutolo, as the loan to Charles II attests, was himself a man of considerable means.[41] Although we have no documentation of his personal contributions to the overall project apart from his burial chapel (pl. 84), the plan and concept of the transept and eastern apses as the locus of the commemoration and exaltation of the bishops and bishop-saints of Naples, central to the entire program of the cathedral, must have been devised by

83   Naples, cathedral, western bays of the nave in the north aisle (Massimo Velo)

Minutolo and his circle. The exaltation of the distinguished Early Christian past was emphasized in many other aspects of the new building, among them the fresco decoration of the Minutolo chapel. His social prominence may also have assisted in obtaining financial contributions from the patrician families of Naples in return for the dedications of the private family chapels that flanked each side of the nave, which seem to have been part of the original conception of the church.[42]

If the supposed earthquake of 1293 damaged the old cathedrals and instigated (or provided the excuse for) the rebuilding, it may be that the greater damage occurred in the Stefania (pl. 82[B]).[43] Although its location has been much debated, it is now generally agreed that the Stefania, many times repaired and restored over the centuries, lay on an axis parallel to that of the first basilica of Santa Restituta, on the other side of the Roman street that lay between the two monuments and underneath what is now the north transept. Its entrance, like that of Santa Restituta, must have been off the *decumanus* leading to the Porta Capuana.

The initial phase of the work probably consisted of dismantling the southern bays of the nave and atrium of the Stefania in order to create the foundation for the new transept (pl. 82[B]). If the pavement found in the excavation outside the north transept was that of the much-repaired presbytery and side aisles of the Stefania, this church would have extended considerably to the north of the present transept.[44]

It is likely therefore that Charles II's commission for the new head reliquary of San Gennaro in 1304 is an indication that, after ten years of work, the new apse and transept were soon to be ready for use and the translation of the sacred relics from the remains of the old Stefania.[45] As if to confirm the urgency of the progress of the work and ensure its funding, the king renewed in 1305–06 his insistence on the payment of the tithes by the citizens of Naples for the construction of the church.[46]

The first ten years would thus have consisted of the rapid construction of the new cathedral starting in the east and extending almost its entire length. The donation of the Filomarino chapel on the south side of the nave in 1298 (now under the present San Gennaro chapel) and a burial in the Piscicello chapel in 1301 may be indications of more rapid progress on the south than on the north.[47] The possibility that the north aisle may have lagged slightly behind the south is also suggested by indications of a possible shortage of granite columns on the north in the bays adjacent to the façade (pl. 83), and the presence of lancet windows in each bay (all later suppressed) into the nave of Santa Restituta, which sug-

84 (*facing page*)   Naples, cathedral, Cappella Minutolo (Giovanni Genova)

85   Santa Restituta, view of the interior from the west (Pedicini)

gests, of course, that the latter was not originally intended to abut the present nave.[48] A document of 24 July
1313 refers to the need to acquire a house and a garden
adjacent to the cathedral in order to complete the
church, which might account for the slight delay on the
north side, and although the location of this property is
not specified, it is possible that it was located west of
Santa Restituta.[49] Above all, the blocked lancet windows
along the entire length of the north aisle (now concealed
by nineteenth-century stucco on the interior of the
cathedral and the organ loft in Santa Restituta) indicate
clearly that the fourth-century basilica was to be either
demolished or reduced still more in size and be entirely
detached from the cathedral.[50]

   The preservation of most of the basilica of Santa
Restituta is therefore a change in plan made during construction and it can perhaps be related to two incidents
of interest. In 1310 the Beato Nicolò, a Lombard pilgrim
who lived as a hermit with a reputation for great sanc-
tity on Pizzofalcone, was murdered by a Provençal

courtier of Queen Mary of Hungary.[51] His body was
buried in Santa Restituta and soon translated to a chapel
to the left of the apse of Santa Maria del Principio in
the left aisle.[52] Queen Mary was particularly devoted to
the hermit, which may in part account for the decision
to bury him in Santa Restituta and maintain its connection to the new cathedral. In 1313, according to
Zigarelli, the canons obtained exclusive rights to this
basilica.[53] If, as the windows along the north wall of the
nave suggest, Santa Restituta was originally intended to
be reduced further in size, or completely destroyed, this
plan seems to have been abandoned by the time of the
burial of the Beato Nicolò in 1310, and the old basilica
under the canons then obtained renewed importance.
Santa Restituta was subsequently restored with pointed
arches above the columns (part of a Gothic capital and
an arch survive in an area concealed under the organ
loft), lancet windows, and also probably the conversion
of the outer aisles into lateral chapels (pl. 85). If this
chronology is correct, the north aisle of the cathedral

would have been mostly complete by 1310 or shortly before. As a result of the decision to preserve the old church there may have been, however, a shortage of granite columns for the completion of the western bays on the north side.

In 1305 Charles II requested beams from the forests of Calabria to be brought to Naples for the cathedral. But when they arrived in 1307 they were found to be rotten and could not be used.[54] Later documents issued by Robert as Prince of Salerno beginning in May 1309 provided the solution: sixty-three massive beams intended for the palace of Quisisana and the chapel of the Castel Nuovo were to be taken for the cathedral instead.[55] These suggest that work was reaching the upper walls, at least in the eastern parts of the cathedral, by *circa* 1305, slightly over ten years after the initiation of construction.[56]

The texts suggest that construction proceeded with great rapidity, and there is no reason to think that this was not so. The church was consecrated in 1314 and a new liturgy instituted in 1317, both under the direction of Archbishop Umberto d'Ormont.[57]

In contrast to the texts on the roof beams, there are, however, no documents on the transportation of ancient columns, large numbers of which were incorporated into the design of the cathedral. These are inserted in sets of three into concavities on the lower level of each rectangular pier (pls. 83 and 86). A second group of substantially taller and heavier columns flank the transept piers and the entrances to the absidial chapels, and a third group of smaller and more precious marble columns are placed in the three polygonal apses of the east end (pl. 76). There are thus three distinct groups of reused columns, each with its own dimensions.

86 Sketch of pier structure in the cathedral, Naples (Irwin Sentilles)

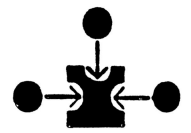

In the nave piers and the chapels, the continued projection of shafts above the horizontal molding is created out of ashlar masonry carved to appear as a second upper columnar shaft. The nave supports therefore consist of ancient columns embedded into concavities in the lower part of the pier, the projections of which are continued above by shafts bonded with the pier structure. All this is now covered with painted plaster, but the original disposition can be seen in the bay restored by De Stefano at the west end of the north aisle.

The number of ancient columns is striking: there are a total of about forty-six smaller granite and marble columns attached to the nave piers, twelve larger columns at the crossing supports and at the entrance to the three central eastern apses, and, originally at least, twenty-four smaller and more precious marble columns in the angles between the polygonal sides of the three apses of the hemicycle (of which the sixteen in the side chapels survive).

The differentiation of the columns is especially interesting because various historical reconstructions have concluded (on the basis of the evidence of the number of wall hangings installed in the ninth century) that the old basilica of the Stefania had twelve columns.[58] The hypothesis of twelve large columns in the Stefania (pl. 82[B]) would seem to be confirmed by the number of larger reused columns that survive in the cathedral transept and openings to the central and lateral apses, in the area that roughly corresponded to the location of the Stefania.[59] The forty-six smaller granite columns incorporated into the nave piers were probably taken from the dismantled bays of Santa Restituta and the atrium or atria of the two basilicas.[60]

In the context of the reuse of ancient materials, it is interesting to note that both Chierici and Venditti, who saw the cathedral during its various phases of restoration, refer to wall surfaces covered with *opus reticulatum* decoration above the spandrels of the arcade arches.[61] As can be seen in the wall between Santa Restituta and the cathedral, the new church was also partially built in *opus mixtum*. The cathedral was thus at least partially constructed in revived classical building techniques, which correspond with the classicism evident in the choice to reuse the ancient columns in the cathedral.

If the twelve larger and forty-six smaller columns can be associated with the two older basilicas and their atria, where did the precious marble columns of the absidial chapels come from? There are some remains of fine quality marble columns in the excavations underneath the *curia vescovile*, perhaps part of an iconostasis or bema in the earlier churches, in which case they might have been used for some time as part of elaborate pulpits, like

87   Naples, cathedral, detail of south wall, Cappella Tocco (Massimo Velo)

88   Naples, cathedral, coffered vault of Peter of Sorrento's tower of 1233 (author)

those of Salerno, each of which has twelve precious columns.[62] It is worth noting that at various moments during Angevin rule precious marbles were brought to Naples: one of the earliest of these importations took place in 1265–66, when 4 once and 16 tarì were spent on the transportation of marbles from Aversa to Naples, and in the early fourteenth century Charles II gave permission for the search for ancient materials at Baia.[63]

To the south of the two older basilicas, possibly as a termination of one of the atria and in alignment with the Roman road to the north (pl. 82[C]), there remains part of a tower built by Archbishop Peter of Sorrento in 1233, the interior of which still survives encased in massive fifteenth-century masonry (pl. 82[E]).[64] This tower now flanks the portal on the south side of the nave that gives access to the Piazza Riario Sforza, a portal that was perhaps the most important mode of access to the cathedral in the fourteenth century. De Stefano noted that the coffered pointed barrel vault (pl. 88), now encased within the Aragonese exterior masonry, is identical to the vault of the cathedral tower at Caserta Vecchia (pl. 89).[65] The latter is identified by an inscription as the work of Bishop Andrea of Capua in 1234, a year after the tower of Naples.[66] The two identical coffered vaults are testaments to the classical tastes of the Kingdom of Sicily in the first half of the thirteenth century, important evidence of strong classical currents in Campanian ecclesiastical circles.[67]

At Caserta Vecchia the upper structure has been identified as produced by the so-called Siculo-Campanian school of masons. It was strongly based on Islamic sources (and perhaps craftsmanship) for its design, and constructed in part with *spolia* materials.[68] In the fourteenth-century repairs of the Neapolitan tower con-

ducted by Cardinal Filomarino, some ancient marbles and columns were found under its foundations, elements that might have formed part of interlaced window openings or arches like those at Caserta Vecchia.[69]

The alignment of the barrel-vaulted opening in the tower of 1233 coincides with the Greco-Roman road that still exists on the north between Santa Restituta and the *curia vescovile* (pl. 82[C]). The Neapolitan tower therefore served as a passage-tower over a road between the two basilicas of Santa Restituta and the Stefania, giving access to the baptistery of San Giovanni in Fonte on the north and to the core of the episcopal complex.

This is important because the portal and tower on the south flank of the cathedral functioned as the primary entrance to the church from the main *decumanus* of the city that passed from the Porta Capuana to the old market. The present configuration of Naples after the nineteenth-century "sanitization" (in which the grand

89   Caserta Vecchia, cathedral, tower (Chester Brummel)

90   Naples, cathedral, view from the south (from the Baratta plan, 1629)

Via del Duomo was inserted in place of the narrow north–south vicolo that had preceded it; an imposing neo-Gothic façade was then erected), has completely obscured the original importance of the traditional entrance from the south. The south portal is now closed off and abandoned (pl. 91). This portal thus "remembered" the historic entrances to the cathedral from the south and was used as the most important entrance for decades after the completion of the new church.

The bell tower of Peter of Sorrento marked the road between the two ancient basilicas, as we have seen. The nave of the new cathedral of 1294 was designed to come to the edge of the tower, which, intact until the earthquake of 1456, continued to give special prominence to this entrance to the cathedral on the south flank (pl. 90). Its importance is perhaps attested by the date of 1302 for the first of the two bells installed in the tower, which suggests that this south entrance on the flank of the new cathedral was to continue as a major means of access to the building.[70] The present portal, perhaps replaced after the earthquake of 1349, could also have served originally as temporary access to the eastern parts of the new cathedral while work proceeded on the completion of the nave and the façade. The historical importance of this portal and the piazza in front of it is confirmed by the colossal scale of the foundations of the new tower begun by Cardinal Raynaldus Piscicello after the earthquake of 1456, which also caused severe damage in the south transept arm and along the south aisle of the nave.[71] The new bell tower project initiated by Piscicello, whose arms mark the unfinished structure as it now stands, was abandoned when it reached the level of the aisle arcade windows. The cathedral portal on to what is

now Piazza Riario Sforza opened on to the Via dei Tribunali and continued to serve as a major entrance to the cathedral. Until 1322 a monumental bronze horse, which was held to have miraculous healing properties for horses, presided over this piazza; in that year it was melted down to make the second of the two bells.[72]

On the eastern side of the south transept arm there is perhaps the "memory" of another historic tower and chapel in the form of the Cappella Minutolo (pl. 82[D]). Dedicated to Saint Peter, like its predecessor constructed in the late eighth century by Bishop Stephen II (see below), the chapel was founded by Archbishop Filippo Minutolo, who was buried there in 1301 (pls. 80 and 84) It is one of the few parts of the cathedral to survive with some of its complement of paintings and tomb sculpture partially intact.

The chapel was added to the new cathedral shortly after the lower walls of the eastern apses had been completed, for the buttresses of the Cappella Tocco are incorporated into its interior. The chapel was therefore erected about 1298–1300 at the earliest. It is situated above heavy groin-vaulted spaces described by De Stefano as an "ipogeo," but which bear no traces of earlier masonry structures and must therefore be coeval with the new chapel above.[73]

The Cappella Minutolo may have been erected on the site of a tower and chapel dedicated to Saint Peter built five centuries before by Bishop Stephen II (767–800), whose additions to the cathedral complex consisted of two towers and a church or chapel dedicated to Saints Peter and Anastasia. The chapel was adjacent to one of the towers and located somewhere in the vicinity of the south transept arm, probably on the east side of the atrium of the Stefania, where the Cappella Minutolo is now located (pl. 82[D]).[74] The previous tower at the site of the Cappella Minutolo may thus have been a pair with Peter of Sorrento's tower of 1233, located to the west and flanking the entrance or atrium of the Stefania on the opposite side. The Cappella Minutolo, with Peter prominently displayed in its cycle of frescoes, perhaps represented a deliberate attempt to preserve or re-evoke historical memories associated with that part of the cathedral complex.[75]

As noted recently by Romano, the Petrine theme in the frescoes not only recalled the old chapel and tower at the site, but also accorded with the theme of "sacred episcopacy" which, as we shall see, dominates the entire area of the transept and also informed its design.[76] The absidial chapel that adjoins the Cappella Minutolo (the Cappella Tocco) held the remains of Saint Aspren; the main apse beyond was dedicated to San Gennaro and also contained the relics of Saints Agrippino, Euticeto,

91   Naples, cathedral, entrance adjacent to the south transept (Chester Brummel)

and Acuzio; and the right chapel (the Cappella Galeota) held the remains of Saint Attanasio as well as those of Giuliano, Lorenzo, and Stefano. When Archbishop d'Ormont later built the Saint Paul chapel on the far north side of the transept arm as the burial chapel for himself and his Burgundian predecessor Ayglerius, he confirmed and expanded this iconographic program embedded in the east end of the new cathedral as a shrine for apostles and bishops, but also added a French connection. Summonte states that this last chapel was built over the "vecchio sacello dedicato a San Lorenzo,"[77] but no evidence survives of this older structure, which was excavated in the nineteenth century to create a vaulted burial area for the bishops. However, it might be noted that at his death in 1254 it is said that Pope Innocent IV was buried at the cathedral in a chapel dedicated to San Lorenzo. In this case, however, the dedication of the new chapel, rather than reflecting that of its predecessor, adopted a new name, that of Saint Paul, perhaps in order to emphasize the apostolic theme. This chapel (also known as the Cappella degli Illustrissimi) was the last of the three additional structures to be erected in the early fourteenth century around the transept and was probably begun upon the completion of the royal burial chapel (later dedicated to Saint Louis of Toulouse, now the sacristy), and therefore roughly about 1314–15, some five years after the completion of the burial chapel, and perhaps as early as 1310 and certainly by the time of the

92 Naples, cathedral, entrance to the royal chapel, now the sacristy (author)

consecration of the cathedral in 1314.[78] The (now lost) tomb of Ayglerius dated to 1315, and the fresco of the Tree of Jesse, attributed to Lello da Orvieto, are dated (by Bologna) to 1315.[79]

A consecration in 1314 and the institution of a new liturgy in 1317 by Bishop d'Ormont suggest that in those years much of the church was complete and in use.[80] As Francesco Aceto has noted, however, the remaining fragments of the west portals are the work of Tino da Camaino in the 1320s, and Mary of Hungary is known to have left a donation to the cathedral "ad opus" at her death in 1325.[81]

Other documents provide hints as to the progress of the work on a more detailed level. As noted, Charles II's commission in 1304 for the gold reliquary for the skull of San Gennaro suggests that preparations were being made to put the east end of the new cathedral into use. The transept would have been accessible through the portals at the east end of the nave on north and south. In the years between 1294 and 1305, when the east end of the new cathedral was under construction, the nearby basilica of San Giorgio may have been used for some of the larger state ceremonies, such as the declaration of the primogeniture of Robert in 1297.[82]

The commission for a new reliquary of San Gennaro thus probably forms part of the larger program of the preparation of the main altars of the new cathedral. This in turn suggests that what remained of the venerable church of the Stefania was to be dismantled to make way for the construction of the royal burial chapel outside the north transept arm, which from the wall surfaces was constructed after the transept that it abuts (pl. 92).

Although Charles II issued an annual rent in November 1296 for the construction of the burial chapel in memory of his parents, his son Carlo Martello, and Clemenza, his daughter-in-law, work would appear to have been delayed until about 1306, when Robert, as Prince of Salerno, cited an agreement between the king and the late Filippo Minutolo on its erection.[83] In 1308 the heir to the throne donated a tithe "de cappellis in maiori ecclesia faciendis . . . pro domina Regina matre ipsius Robertis."[84] On 30 June 1309 Charles of Calabria ordered the royal treasurer to pay the salary of a certain Master Theodoric of "Alemania" and Giletto his brother for commemorative paintings and a statue of Charles II in the chapel.[85] After the canonization of Louis of Toulouse in 1317 the chapel was dedicated in his honor; De Stefano has published the only known photographs of the fragmentary remains of fleur-de-lys decoration and a narrative cycle of frescoes commemorating the life of the saint found above the vaults of the seventeenth-century sacristy.[86] New tombs of Charles of Anjou,

Charles Martel, and Clemenza were commissioned in 1333 when Robert entrusted Sancia with the supervision of this project.[87]

The new cathedral was thus erected rapidly and for the most part during the lifetime of its chief patron, Charles II. Given the scale of the church this was a considerable achievement. The "Constantinian" basilica of Santa Restituta, rededicated to the use of the canons, was subsequently embellished with mosaics and painted decoration of great beauty, a process inspired or perhaps stimulated by the burial in the church of the Beato Nicolò (pl. 85). In 1320 Charles of Calabria, heir to the throne, made a donation to the altar of Santa Maria del Principio, which perhaps supported the renovation.[88] The completion of the mosaic by Lello da Orvieto in 1322 suggests that by this date the transformation of the outer aisles of the double-aisled basilica into lateral chapels was complete, and that Santa Restituta, remodeled with pointed arches over the arcades, new windows, and lateral chapels, was ready to be put into use.[89] The life and miracles of the Beato Nicolò refer to a translation of his relics that took place between 1310 and 1319, a translation associated with Archbishop d'Ormont and which therefore probably dates to before the archbishop's death in 1320.[90] A few battered fragments of frescoes of a late thirteenth-century or early fourteenth-century date were applied to the northeast corner (a *Last Judgment*) of the basilica and to the west wall abutting the Angevin nave.[91] The new liturgy was instituted by d'Ormont in 1317, and the reform of the clergy by Giovanni Orsini after 1328 consolidated the overall organization of the cathedral clergy.[92]

The integration of the old basilica of Santa Restituta into the overall program of the cathedral is also attested by the *Chronicon di Santa Maria del Principio*, a text of liturgical instructions for the canons at various sites in both the cathedral and Santa Restituta, dated by Monti to between 1311 and 1337,[93] a dating recently revised by Vitolo and Romano to between 1311 and 1317.[94] The *Chronicon*, which emphasizes the role of Saint Peter in the conversion of Saint Aspren, first Bishop of Naples, and the Constantinian origins of Santa Restituta, attests to the revitalization of the old church under the canons stimulated by the burial, cult, and miracles of Beato Nicolò, as well as by the renewed importance of the cult of Constantine under the guidance of Archbishop d'Ormont.[95] Vitolo noted that between 1311 and 1319 a life of the Beato was composed by Giacomo de Pisis, member of the court, suggesting that the renewed importance of Santa Restituta – and indeed the decision not to detach the old basilica further from the new cathedral – may have resulted from his burial and royal

involvement in his cult.[96] We may wish to recall that Charles of Calabria played a role in the new mosaic program for the apse of Santa Restituta, and, as noted above, Mary of Hungary left funds for the cathedral in her will.

A tentative chronology for the construction of the cathedral can therefore be proposed as follows:

- transept and eastern apses completed by *circa* 1304–05
- Minutolo chapel *circa* 1299–01
- Chapel of Saint Louis of Toulouse, or royal burial chapel, *circa* 1306–10
- d'Ormont (Saint Paul) chapel *circa* 1310–14
- remodeling of Santa Restituta decided in 1310, completed 1318–22
- west portal by Tino da Camaino after 1325.

The name of the architect of the cathedral is not known. Giorgio Vasari, writing in the sixteenth century, attributed it to a protégé sent by Nicola Pisano, a certain Maglione, who when in Naples also finished the church of San Lorenzo Maggiore. De Dominici's attribution to Masuccio I and Masuccio II has long been dismissed as an invention.[97] Far more plausible is Carabellese's suggestion that the architect was Riccardo Primario, who died sometime between 1310 and 1313 and who belonged to a family of Neapolitan builders.[98]

The plan of the cathedral is strikingly like that of other monuments erected by Charles II, San Domenico Maggiore in Naples, San Domenico in L'Aquila, and the cathedral of Lucera (these will be discussed below): a long nave with compound piers and a projecting transept with two polygonal chapels flanking a polygonal apse. Ancient columns are used in both of the cathedrals, although at Lucera there is nothing like the profusion found in the cathedral of Naples. The general plan type is based on Dominican models and has a strong typological resemblance to Santa Maria sopra Minerva in Rome and Santa Maria Novella in Florence. A Dominican source of inspiration, or an architect with experience in a Dominican context – or the presence of a Dominican architectural advisor or supervisor? – might also explain the strong similarity of plan, pier types (square or rectangular cores with attached shafts), and the restriction of vaulting to chapels and sometimes the aisles.[99]

The cathedral of Naples is one of the earliest examples of a cathedral planned from the outset with lateral chapels flanking both sides of the nave, a feature that also reflects the influence of mendicant planning.[100] In Naples San Domenico was designed with lateral chapels along the length of both sides of the nave, and

93 Naples, cathedral, reconstruction of the apse by F. Strazzullo, 1957

these were added to San Lorenzo Maggiore in a series of campaigns starting perhaps as early as the 1260s. Although by about 1292 lateral chapels also appear at the cathedral of Orvieto, it was still unusual in the late thirteenth century for cathedrals to be planned with this feature from the outset – although of course lateral chapels were frequently added to already-existing naves. At the cathedral the first private family chapels are the Filomarino chapel of 1298 and the Minutolo chapel of about 1298–1300, and as noted above they may have

formed an important part of the financial support for the erection of the new church.

The most striking aspect of the new cathedral, however, is the use of ancient columns in the piers, the projections of which are continued as coursed masonry to the departures of the arcade vaults (pls. 79 and 83). In the absidial chapels, the shafts that rise to the departures of the ribs are designed to accord with the reused marble columns below (pl. 93). The ancient columns are always reused whole and where necessary extended by additional pieces of granite; in the nave and crossing piers they are inserted into semicircular concavities on three sides of each support. These ancient materials were complemented with an incised pattern in imitation of *opus reticulatum* masonry in the spandrels (not visible at present) and the construction of at least some of the side walls in *opus mixtum*.

Although the deliberate evocation of ancient building techniques and the use of ancient materials are innovative in the context of the preceding two decades of Angevin architecture, in Campania this was common practice, and of long standing. Numerous monuments in the region around Naples, not only cathedrals (such as Salerno, where Minutolo had served as bishop before his appointment in Naples) but also monastic churches (the first and most conspicuous example is Montecassino) used ancient columns. Norman builders in particular paced them down naves singly or in pairs. But to my knowledge the only surviving churches where the columns are systematically inserted into semicircular indentations in piers and continued as coursed masonry shafts above are in Campania, as in the crossing piers of the cathedrals of Caserta Vecchia and Sessa Aurunca.[101]

The systematic integration of the ancient columns into the piers seems more than a local building tradition, however. The complexity of this task at the cathedral of Naples suggests that it was precisely the antiquity of these columns that was important: their presence was a vivid reminder of the antiquity of the site and its venerable Early Christian origins.

And Naples of course would have had good reason to be proud of its ancient heritage: according to local legend, the Apostle Peter, proceeding towards Rome from Cesarea, disembarked at Pozzuoli and stopped in Naples, where he converted Saint Aspren, first Bishop of Naples.[102] When Paul later disembarked in Pozzuoli in AD 61 he found a Christian community already established there. The tradition of the apostolic formation of the Church of Naples was kept alive in the images of the apostles preserved in the catacombs outside the city, where fragments of frescoes attest to the vitality of this

94 Naples, cathedral, view of the south flank from the roof of Sant'Agostino (Soprintendenza per i Beni Architettonici ed Ambientali di Napoli e Provincia)

legend and the cult of the apostles and the bishop-saints of Naples throughout the Middle Ages.

This tradition would have been important above all to the bishops and archbishops of the city, who could thus consider their seat of "apostolic" foundation, and indeed of slightly greater antiquity than that of Rome.[103] Although these types of apostolic foundation legends were common in the High Middle Ages, those of Naples had more legitimacy than most; that they were important to Minutolo and his successors is indicated by the emphasis on the lives of the apostles and that of Peter in particular in the Minutolo chapel, especially the scene in which Minutolo is presented to the Crucified Christ by Saints Peter and Gennaro. As Romano has noted, the decoration of the catacombs of San Gennaro, followed by that of the basilica of the Stefania, recorded the sequence of bishop-saints and bishops of Naples. The

transept of the Angevin cathedral, located over the remains of the Stefania, was reserved for bishops and organized to commemorate the bishop-saints of Naples in its main apses, with the slightly later addition of the Minutolo chapel to the south and the Saint Paul chapel for Ayglerius and d'Ormont on the north (pl. 82[F]). The transept was thus an episcopal program and served as a reminder of the antiquity of the Church of Naples and its apostolic origins. As a two-step afterthought, Minutolo and d'Ormont "elevated" themselves into this distinguished company by the addition of their respective chapels.

The use of ancient columns and Roman building techniques (*opus reticulatum* and *opus mixtum*) are also combined with a high transept that is a distinctly Roman feature (pls. 90 and 94), suggesting that the overall program was intended as much as possible to be *in more*

95   Naples, cathedral, Cappella Tocco, capitals and vaults (author)

romano. Indeed, d'Ormont's liturgy of 1317 organized the church "ad instar basilicarum patriarchalium Urbis."[104] If Summonte's description of representations of Constantine in the frescoes of the royal burial chapel is correct, then the theme of *romanitas* would have been evident in some of the painted decoration as well.[105] This detail is important, for the paintings, as we saw, were commissioned by the royal family for the burial chapel; one may therefore be tempted to conclude that the Angevins also participated in the attempt to evoke consciously the Antique and Early Christian past, as well as the legendary associations with the apostles and Constantine.

Yet the church would also have had a Gothic flavor, especially in its rib-vaulted eastern chapels and aisles, although this is less visible now than it would have been before the reconstruction of the main apse in 1581. The polygonal central apse and the side chapels were illuminated by long bar-tracery windows, and the ribs were supported by crocket capitals. The original disposition is visible still in the Cappella Tocco, where fragments of fourteenth-century frescoes, tombs, and altar niches also survive (pls. 87 and 95).

An examination of the architectural details in the Cappella Tocco may help us to understand the nature of the design and the origins of the designer. The bases (App. 5, fig. 3), with their high and sharply defined upper torus and deep cavet, are not related to base types in France in the second half of the thirteenth century, which tend instead towards an undulating and slouching profile (good examples of these can be seen in the tomb of Isabelle of Aragon at Cosenza and the portal of

Sant' Eligio). The crocket capitals (pl. 95), distantly derived from those of French monuments of about 1230–50, represent standardized forms with a repetitive, "workshop," regularity, examples of the rigidification of imported architectural detailing that occurs in the Kingdom of Naples. Here, as with other Gothic detailing in Naples in this period, we are witnessing a process in which imported forms have become rigid formulae with little or no natural evolution. The evidence suggests that these "Frenchifying" details were produced by local workshops in a "French manner," a phenomenon that can be noted in almost all the other monuments produced after the first decade of Angevin occupation. But we must not confuse these Gothic details with issues of spatial or structural conception, for the Gothic elements are adjusted – or, indeed, subjected – to the reused antique elements. The shafts and capitals in the eastern chapels rise from single marble columns, very unlike the clusters of delicate shafts that can be found in French (or Provençal) monuments of about 1290–1300. Ribs thus spring from a single support whose diameter is determined by the ancient column below. The result is a Gothic architectural idiom continuously and consciously adjusted to and integrated with the *spolia* elements that are the point of departure. The ultimate result is profoundly different in character from current monuments in France.

Is the architectural evidence at the cathedral of Naples sufficient to allow us to determine the origins of the architect? Is this a relevant question, especially since by this time there were numerous second-generation Frenchmen living in Naples and elsewhere in the kingdom? Precisely because the historiography of thirteenth-century Gothic architecture in southern Italy has usually been framed in terms of the national origins of the architects (usually assumed to be French), it is a question that must be addressed here, at least briefly. We shall concern ourselves with the primary architect at the inception of the work whose design, I believe, was followed throughout the construction of the new basilica.

The secondary literature on Neapolitan Gothic is permeated by the names of the French masons and master builders who came to southern Italy in the retinue of Charles of Anjou, among them individuals encountered in previous chapters such as Gauthier d'Asson, Baucelin de Linnais, and others. Of these the most famous was the military architect Pierre d'Angicourt, who directed the work at the castle of Lucera and was involved with the fortifications of Barletta and other sites.[106] If we can draw any conclusions from the fact that in 1304 the course of a street in Barletta was changed to allow him to enlarge his house, we can assume that until his death he continued to be highly valued. It has been asserted more than once that the cathedral of Naples is an example of Pierre d'Angicourt's work, although perhaps without much reflection on the character of the conception and detailing of the building in question. Are such assumptions supported by the surviving architectural evidence?

The best-preserved bases are those in the Cappella Tocco (App. 5, fig. 3). In France such bases appeared in monuments well over eighty years previously, as was noted above. The capitals and polygonal abaci, almost identical in their conception and carving to those in the choir of San Lorenzo, have little or no relation to contemporary types of capitals and architectural detailing in France or Provence. They are archaic even in relation to the triforium of San Francesco or the altar ciborium at Santa Chiara in Assisi, both far more closely related to French prototypes. By the 1290s bar tracery, rib vaults, and crocket capitals were common not only in the Kingdom of Naples but also in Franciscan monuments throughout Italy.

Given the integration of antique elements in a manner consistent with Campanian practice, the use of standardized and archaic Gothic elements, and architectural detailing (such as base profiles) that has no analogies with contemporary French models, it is logical to propose that this cathedral was designed by a local master brought up in a regional building tradition of carving and construction in *tufo* and *piperno*. He was familiar with the inheritance of Roman construction techniques and the incorporation of antique elements. Although such an individual could well have been employed by or partially trained in the workshops of Charles of Anjou, such as Realvalle, the main references in the cathedral itself are to Italian building traditions. A Campanian or Neapolitan architect of this caliber might be found, for example, in the De Vico family, some of whom are recorded as having worked at Realvalle, Santa Chiara, and San Martino.[107] Another important building family that emerged in the late thirteenth century was that of Riccardo Primario and his sons Attanasio and Galiardo, masons employed on various royal projects including the port of Naples, Santa Maria Donnaregina, Santa Chiara, the castle of Quisisana at Castellamare, and who collaborated with Tino da Camaino on the construction of Santa Maria di Donnaregina and San Martino.[108] An architect-builder trained in local traditions, and yet also aware of the new trends that came in with the Angevins and the mendicant orders, could have brought these elements together in the original and monumental design of the cathedral of Naples.[109] Thus, although Carabellese's attribution of the cathedral to Riccardo Pri-

mario cannot be proven, he was certainly right to propose an Italian, not a French, architect.

If the use of *spolia* elements in the cathedral of Naples evoke Norman-Campanian prototypes, we may enquire why this was so. Certainly the recollection of the last of the Norman kings, especially William II (the Good), may have suggested the positive aspects of foreign domination. Angevin law and Angevin rhetoric under Charles II often referred to the "time of good king William" as a prototype and precedent.[110] It might be imagined that the king's advisors, who included not only Bartolomeo da Capua but also Bishop Filippo Minutolo, may have counseled the king to support a design for the new cathedral that not only recalled the distinguished and glorious history of Naples itself, and specifically that of its ancient cathedral complex, but also made reference to the monuments of the Norman kings, monuments that were present as splendid evocations of an important moment of the *regno*. If this was the case, then the design of the new cathedral of Naples was not only a reference to the historical past of the site, but possibly also an ideological statement. Charles II later commissioned Bartolomeo da Capua and Filippo Minutolo to work together on the new constitutions of the kingdom, constitutions that recognized the previous customs and laws of the different populations of the *regno*, including, of course, Norman law.[111] At the death of Filippo Minutolo, Bartolomeo da Capua pronounced two sermons on the late archbishop, exalting his compatriot and collaborator and exhorting the chapter and canons to elect a new archbishop of Italian origins. The reassertion of Italian – Campanian – identity seems to have been an issue in this environment.

CHARLES II's DOMINICAN FOUNDATIONS
IN NAPLES

Long before he collaborated on the reconstruction of the cathedral, Charles II was a patron of the Dominican order. In January 1284, while still Prince of Salerno and vice-regent, he laid the first stone of the new Dominican church and *studium* of Naples, San Domenico Maggiore, in a location in the heart of the old city on one of the main *decumani* running east–west (now Via Benedetto Croce).[112] Squeezed within the Greco-Roman grid in the densely packed center of the city, the apse of the church is to the south, closing what is now a piazza named after the church on its north side, and the entrance is to the north within a large courtyard (pl. 96). Before the arrival of the Dominicans, the site consisted of a hospital and monastery, parts of which were reworked by the Dominicans and reconsecrated in

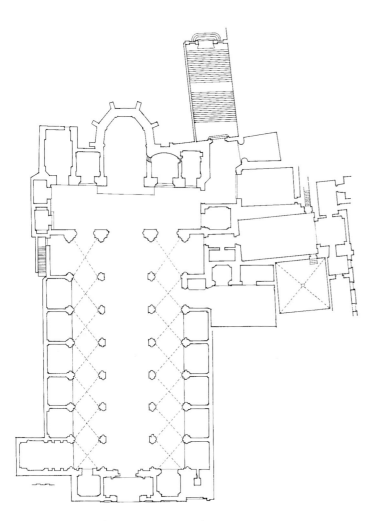

96   Naples, San Domenico, plan

and indeed the building conforms to the type of architecture introduced in the 1290s. It was completed in 1325 with assistance from Charles of Calabria, who gave 50 once to a master Pons to finish the work, and from Bartolomeo da Capua for the work on the main portal.[114]

San Domenico would appear for many reasons to be a crucial monument for the development of south Italian architecture in the late thirteenth century. It was among the first churches to introduce lateral chapels along the length of the nave as a systematic part of its design. In other respects also the plan may have been the model for those of the cathedrals of Naples and Lucera (pls. 81, 96, and 108), and perhaps that of San Domenico in L'Aquila (pl. 127). But San Domenico is particularly intractable to study: the interior was entirely covered with gold and stucco decoration after 1849 by Federico Travaglini (pl. 97). Bases and capitals were systematically obliterated in the process. Only the Brancaccio chapel (pl. 98), famous for its cycle of frescoes, gives any indication of the original medieval structure and its painted decoration, but here too the architectural details have been destroyed. One has the nagging sense that this is a central monument, but there is today little left to see.

Certain observations can nonetheless be made. The piers consist of a square core with three attached shafts on the sides and back. These are almost identical in form to the supports of the cathedral of Naples, as noted above, except that there is no evidence for the use of ancient columns. Like the cathedral, the apses, aisles, and lateral chapels are polygonal and rib-vaulted, and like the cathedral and Sant'Eligio al Mercato, the transept was a high, uninterrupted, and unvaulted volume. The central apse is deep, like that of the Dominican churches of Santa Maria sopra Minerva in Rome and Santa Maria Novella in Florence, and the chapels to either side of the main apse were rectangular. The relationship to the monuments in Florence suggests that the plan of the building may date from the 1280s, even if little was constructed in that decade, and it could therefore be that the design of San Domenico had an impact on the plans for other royal building projects through the presence of Dominicans (and their pupils, such as Bartolomeo da Capua) in royal circles. Strongly projecting chapels and side apses flanking the central apse are elements new to the kingdom, and the high transept would seem to form part of the *romanitas* seen in the cathedral.

On 29 April 1299 Charles II, in the presence of Archbishop Filippo Minutolo, laid the first stone of the Dominican church of San Pietro Martire (pls 99a and b). Founded in an area near the port known as the Calcaria because it was here that the lime-making furnaces were located, the site was once occupied in the

1254. A portion of these structures survives off the transept arm to the right of the main apse.[113]

January 1284, however, was not a good time to initiate a new construction project in Naples. Charles I was away in France raising money and troops for the war against Sicily, and the prince himself was taken captive only six months later in June. Legend has it that the prince's Dominican confessor, Fra Guglielmo Tonais, who had accompanied him in the naval engagement against Ruggiero Lauria, was also captured. Although it has often been stated that work on the church began again when Charles II was liberated in 1288, this seems unlikely, since he was required by the terms of his release to remain outside the kingdom, and there were far more pressing issues that would have distracted him, among other things the conclusion of the treaty that would bring about the liberation of his three sons. Insofar as the king was essential to the project, it is more probable that the church as we know it now was begun after 1294,

97 (facing page)   Naples, San Domenico, general view of the interior (Massimo Velo)

98   Naples, San Domenico, Brancaccio chapel (Giovanni Genova)

ninth century by the Muslim population brought in by Bishop Anastasius II.[115] Smaller in scale than San Domenico, and placed on a site that may well have presented fewer impediments than the earlier church, it seems to have been erected with considerable speed. In 1296 the king requested stone from the city of Pozzuoli as well as from the castellan of the Castrum Salvatoris (Castel dell'Ovo).[116] In March 1300 he arranged for the delivery of wood without the payment of tithe.[117] Up to

his death, the king acquired a series of surrounding properties to create the space necessary for the conventual buildings and the church.[118]

Although a first consecration took place between 19 and 25 August 1303,[119] some elements of the church or monastic complex remained unfinished until after 1343. In that year they were badly damaged by the flood (or tidal wave?) associated with the tempest of 1343, and the portal was reconstructed in 1347 as the gift of Giacomo

Capano, a noble and official of Robert's court.[120] Greatly favored by the Aragonese, and especially by Isabella di Chiaramonte, wife of Ferdinand I of Aragon, the monastery thrived and expanded and was later entirely rebuilt.[121] The church, reconstructed in the sixteenth century, was truncated by the insertion of the avenue Corso Umberto I (known as the "Retifilio") in the late nineteenth century; no evidence of the medieval structure remains.[122]

There is, however, one highly schematic view of the monastery church preserved in a notarial document in the Archivio di Stato of Naples (pls 99a and b).[123] Insofar as this is a reliable document, the church is represented as a large barn-like structure, apparently consisting of one central vessel, perhaps similar to (though smaller than) Sant'Agostino alla Zecca.

Nothing remains of the third Dominican house in Naples associated with royal support, the Dominican convent of San Pietro a Castello, constructed for Charles II's sister, Isabella, the widow of King Ladislaus of Hungary, who returned to Naples after her husband's assassination in 1290. In 1301, with the permission of Boniface VIII, the ancient monastery in the Castel dell'Ovo was transformed into a Dominican community.[124] Isabella died there in October 1303.[125] When the convent was destroyed in 1427 the nuns were moved to the convent of San Sebastiano, which thereafter was named San Sebastiano e San Pietro.[126]

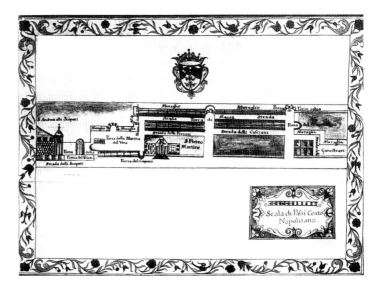

99a and b   Naples, San Pietro Martire (from Feniello 1998)

Mary of Hungary and the Convent of Santa Maria Donnaregina

The convent of Santa Maria Donnaregina is a much older Basilian foundation, located on the periphery of Naples. It became Benedictine and by 1237 had adopted the Clarissan rule.[127] It has been reported that in 1293 the convent was badly damaged by an earthquake, and at some point within the next five years Mary of Hungary, Charles II's queen, became engaged in the project to rebuild. In 1298 she provided funds for the reconstruction of the dormitory, and in 1307 she participated in a transaction to finance the reconstruction of the church through the sale of wine and produce.[128]

In 1314 Ubertino da Cremona, a Franciscan *praepositus*, was appointed to supervise the construction of the new church. By 1316, when John XXII issued indulgences on behalf of the convent, much of the structure must have been complete, and it was consecrated a few years later in 1320 (pls. 100–03).[129] There is every reason to think that with the queen's support it was erected with considerable dispatch, and the regulations governing enclosure would have provided every incentive to do so.

The ubiquitous presence of the arms of Hungary and Anjou in the vaults of the lower story marks this church as particularly Mary's own, and the queen was buried at her death in 1323 in a splendid tomb by Tino da Camaino behind the main altar, now located on the east flank (left side) of the nave.[130] The painted decoration refers repeatedly to the Angevin family, through the cycle of the life of Saint Elizabeth of Thuringia (the great-aunt of Mary), the sequences of Hungarian and Angevin saints depicted on the walls of the choir, and the iconography of the Last Judgment scene, which not only represents members of the two royal families, but as has been noted also refers to a special, and specifically datable, interpretation of the Beatific Vision, a theme unusual at the date of the cycle.[131] The arms of Hungary and Anjou are also joined in the vaults of the lower church.

Because of this fresco cycle, attributed variously to Pietro Cavallini or his school, Santa Maria Donnaregina is among the most published and studied monuments of

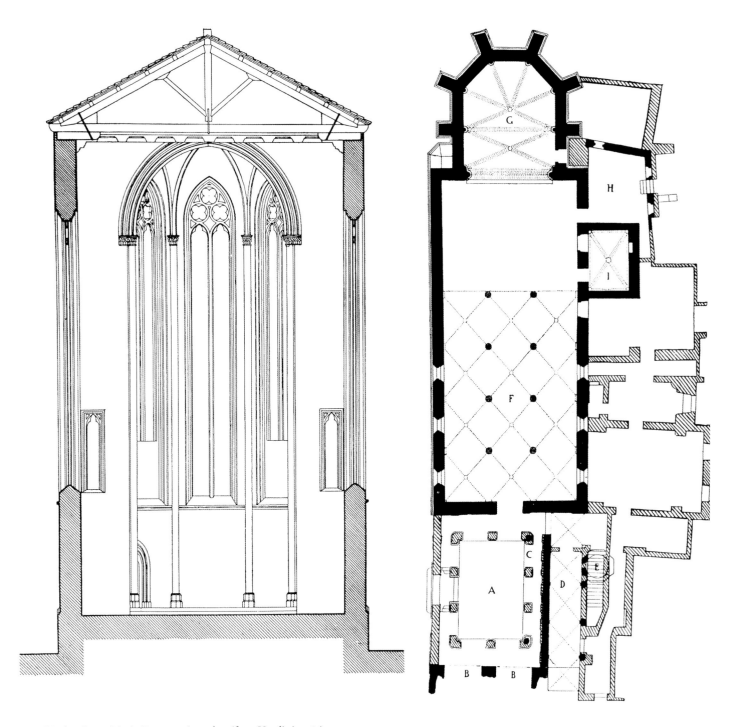

101   Naples, Santa Maria Donnaregina, plan (from Venditti 1969)

Angevin Naples.[132] Yet ironically little of this flow of ink has had to do with the architecture, as though the plan and structure were passive shells into which the painted decoration was placed. It has been frequently observed, however, that the church was enlarged during construction, for the nun's choir was extended one bay further towards the apse while work was still underway, trun-cating the first of the long lancet windows of the nave (pl. 102). This extension to the gallery may have coincided with the increase in 1318 of the number of friars associated with the convent from four to six; the document on this also refers to the construction as "de novo construi facit."[133] If the gallery was extended about 1318, and the church consecrated two years later, it could be that the fresco cycle of the nuns' choir (and perhaps the whole church) could sensibly have been painted in the intervening two years, but questions of the attribution and date of the paintings are outside the scope of this book. The modified church with the new window scheme is represented in the model of the church on the tomb of Mary, completed by 1326.[134]

The existence of tombs of 1319 and 1321 in the nave would also tend to confirm an early completion.[135] So construction and decoration took about thirteen years, although the initial document of 1307 may have more to do with preparations for financial support for the work, as well as the clearing of the site, than actual construction.

Santa Maria Donnaregina was intended from the start to be decorated with frescoes; we can therefore without question speak here of an architecture in dialogue with its painted decoration. The flat surfaces of the upper choir, which is an unarticulated architectural box (pl. 102), were planned to contain a series of large-scale narrative scenes. I have suggested elsewhere that the location and disposition of the choir were designed to guarantee strict enclosure, in keeping with Boniface VIII's recent strictures on enclosure, and that the fresco cycle was therefore especially important as the visual accompaniment for the mass performed below (the liturgy was in effect invisible from the stalls of the conventual community).[136] If the enclosed box of the nuns' choir can be taken as the point of departure for the entire program, the building can be understood in terms of consisting of four parts, each with its own community: the lay church under the nuns' gallery in the four bays of the nave near the entrance; the queen and her immediate circle (when present) in the zone adjacent to the apse flanked by the tall lancet widows (where Mary's tomb now permanently recalls her presence); the clergy in the apse, with access from two portals, one on the east and one on the west; and of course the nuns' choir above. As a prestigious royal convent constructed shortly after Boniface VIII's bull of 1298 on the enclosure of religious women, Donnaregina might be seen to exemplify acquiescence to the pope's wishes: the nuns in their choir would have had to stand at the edge of the balustrade to witness the priest at the altar – with a screen at the top of the balustrade, as would usually have been the case, the religious community would have been entirely invisible to laymen, nobility, and clergy alike.[137]

The nave underneath the nuns' choir is about one third of the height of the church and is covered with twelve groin-vaulted bays supported on octagonal pillars (pl. 100). Had this space remained only three bays deep, as originally intended, it would have occupied one half

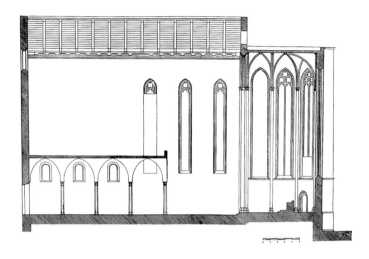

102   Naples, Santa Maria Donnaregina, section (from Venditti 1969)

of the total length of the nave. It is dimly lit by three round-headed lancets placed high in the left (east, because the altar is in the south) wall; the other side abuts the conventual buildings and was never opened to windows. The bases vary widely in their profiles and are not consistent with those of the apse (App. 5, fig. 3).

The nave is deliberately austere in comparison to the elegant polygonal choir dominated by tall double-lancet windows (pl. 100). After an initial rectangular straight bay, the chevet rotates as five parts of an octagon. Doorways in and out of this space suggest that the small community of friars (six) had separate access to the church and a small sacristy on the inner side (to the west of the nave), through which, presumably, confession and the Eucharist would have been offered in the course of the liturgical year (pl. 101). The sacristy is adjacent to the Loffredo chapel, probably added to the west flank of the church during construction *circa* 1315–20.[138] The conspicuous position of the chapel attests to the close ties between Francesco Loffredo (d. 1300), who offered the keys of Naples to Charles I when he arrived in the city in 1266, and the royal family.[139]

As one of the few Clarissan churches built *ex novo* and with ample funding in Italy, this is of course an exceptional monument. It would be interesting to know how the church relates to the larger context of religious architecture for women in the Franciscan order, and especially the elite convents founded by royal patrons. But this subject is difficult: in Italy, with the exception of Santa Chiara in Assisi, almost all churches of the Clares were adapted from older (often Benedictine) structures.[140] This was an architecture of improvisation, creating enclosed choirs in an ad hoc manner on a case by case basis, apparently without any systematized approach

103　Naples, Santa Maria Donnaregina, the nuns' choir (Massimo Velo)

except for the need for the separation of the religious community from lay public and clergy. For Donnaregina, it would be tempting to refer to earlier prestigious royal foundations of the order, such as the convent founded for Isabelle de France by Louis IX at Longchamp, but nothing remains of these monuments and no record survives of their original plans.[141] Perhaps the best evidence for convent architecture erected with royal patronage comes from Spain and Germany, as in the splendid royal convents of Pedralbes outside Barcelona and Königsfelden in the Aargau,[142] but both are slightly later than Donnaregina in date. There are examples of churches with suspended upper choirs over the entrance in German convents, and such an arrangement may also have existed in the now-destroyed convent of Princess Margaret of Hungary at Buda. But we are in the area of conjecture here, and until new material or excavations enrich the evidence at our disposal the sources for the design of the church of Donnaregina must remain a mystery.

However, one final point should be made. Although the polygonal chevet and tracery windows suggest an aura of "Frenchness," we should note again that, as at San Lorenzo, the details are distant from contemporary monuments in France or Provence. The shafts rising to the vaults in the apse are heavy and single, the bases archaic (insofar as they are original – and the restoration is substantial here), and the tracery consists of a fairly standardized pattern. This again seems to be an example of Franciscan "Frenchness" rather than an example of a directly imported architectural language.

THE CAPPELLA SANTA BARBARA IN THE CASTEL NUOVO

Memorial sermons pronounced upon the death of Charles II refer not only to his construction of churches and abbeys throughout the kingdom, but also to his fostering of religious worship in his own household.[143] And although the Castel Nuovo included two chapels

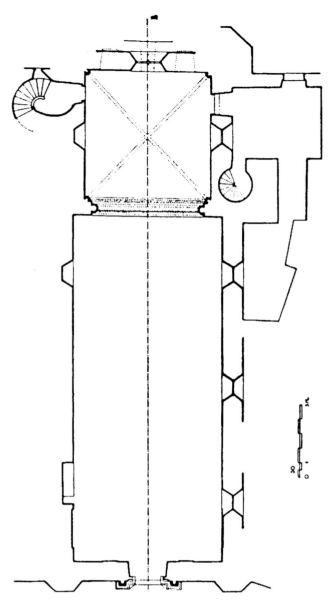

104 Naples, Castel Nuovo, the Palatine Chapel, plan (from Chierici 1934)

of 1456, some fragments can be seen in the window embrasures found during the restorations of Filangieri early in the twentieth century, and others were discovered in excavations that took place under the palace in 1998.[146]

The palatine chapel of Naples is a large rectangular hall covered with a flat wooden truss ceiling that concludes with a square rib-vaulted presbytery. There could be no greater contrast to the delicate and lavish architectural volumes of the palace chapels of France, such as that built by Philippe le Bel at Vincennes, for example; the austerity of Charles II's chapel seems (again) a deliberate choice in the direction of a large, simple, and austere interior volume. Since Charles had already commissioned painters such as Montano d'Arezzo to decorate the smaller chapels at the Castel Nuovo, it seems likely that the palatine chapel was intended from the outset to be painted, although work was delayed for some decades.[147] The conception of the palace chapel as a vast single hall, large enough to accommodate the royal household and court, is vivid confirmation of the king's encouragement of religious worship "especially in his own household," and its grandiose scale contrasts with that of the more restrained spaces of most other palace chapels.

Charles II's Religious Patronage outside Naples

Whereas Charles I fortified the east coast of Apulia, repaired castles throughout the central and eastern parts of the kingdom, and somewhat improbably planted two Cistercian abbeys near roads on the north–south axis, Charles II turned his attentions elsewhere. With his accession to the throne in 1288 he inaugurated shifts in policy and focus that were profoundly different in character from those of his father: he reinforced the northern borders, where he also established solid economic and administrative centers, and built many churches, all of them in the hearts of cities. In the urban works of the north this king was probably inspired by the development of new towns in the contrados of Tuscany, for the plans of the new settlements in the kingdom were clearly inspired by those of the Florentine new towns.[148] San Giovanni Valdarno and Castelfranco, both founded in 1299, are models for the plan of Cittaducale, for example, established probably in 1307 or 1308 (pl. 106).[149] On the northern borders of the kingdom, the restoration of the city of L'Aquila, destroyed by Manfred in 1259, was also part of this process. Here a series of smaller towns or villages were

erected by Charles of Anjou, Charles II initiated the construction of a third and much more monumental palatine chapel beginning in September 1307 (pls. 104 and 105).[144] This structure is now the only substantial part of the Angevin castle to remain intact, the rest having been reconstructed under the Aragonese. It was essentially finished by Charles II's death in May 1309, although the king's will asked Robert to complete the work. Two decades later Robert called Giotto to Naples to decorate the chapel with a cycle of scenes from the Old and New Testaments.[145] Although these were destroyed by Alfonso of Aragon after the damage of the earthquake

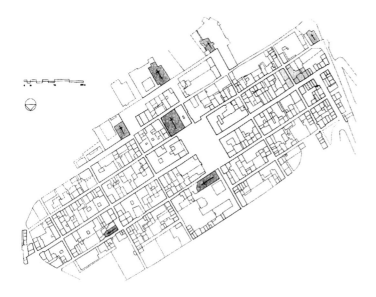

106   Cittaducale, city plan (from Friedman 1988)

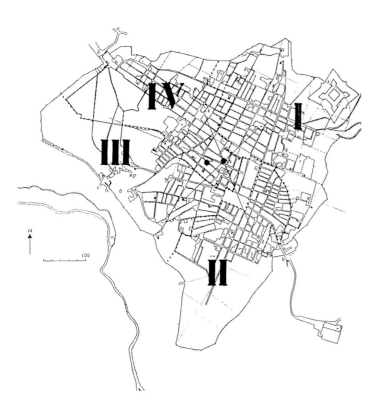

107   L'Aquila, city plan (from Clementi and Piroddi 1986)

moved into the larger city, but the identity of these communities was maintained through the creation of a series of *piazze* and churches that reproduced the dedications of the former village parishes (pl. 107).[150] Elsewhere, the construction or reconstruction of churches throughout the kingdom, and the king's repeated and generous support to monasteries and other religious foundations, was part of a long process of internal consolidation and reinforcement that used the Church, and especially the mendicant orders, as active agents, a process from which Robert was later to reap the benefits. Some of the work, like that of L'Aquila, was clearly designed to create stable population centers that would support trade and become regional strongholds; others, like Lucera, were resettled in order to accomplish not only a "purification" of the realm through the eradication of the Muslims, but also to settle populations displaced by the invasion of Basilicata and Calabria by Spanish and Sicilian troops after 1282. Without question, Charles II left the most profound impact on the material culture of his kingdom, but this culture was above all dominated by religious motivation.

LUCERA AND ITS CHURCHES

Few episodes in the reign of Charles II are more charged than the annihilation of the Muslim community of Lucera and the creation of a Christian town over the ruins of that once thriving city.[151] Roman Lucera had been destroyed and abandoned by Constans II in 663, reoccupied by the Lombards after 793, and returned to Byzantine hands in the late tenth century. In 1060 this remote spot was seized by the Normans. Between 1223 and 1246 Frederick II resettled the rebellious Muslim population of Sicily in the middle of the fertile plains of the Capitanata, thus isolating the Sicilian Muslims from possible contact with their supporters in North Africa. The new colonists were experienced farmers, and the cultivation of wheat in the rolling plains of the *tavoliere* around the city would have been important in feeding the kingdom.[152] Frederick II erected an elaborate and gracious *palacium* on the outskirts of the town on a site overlooking the Muslim center and the vast expanse of the plains below.[153] Thereafter the Muslims of Lucera became loyal supporters of Frederick and his sons, and Charles I struggled long to bring them to subjection after the conquest of the kingdom in 1266. Although the city surrendered in 1266, in February 1268 it rebelled in favor of Conradin and was defeated by Charles only after a protracted siege that lasted until August 1269. In punishment, the king demolished the walls that enclosed the city.[154]

In order to create a counter-bastion of Christian retainers at Lucera, from 1270 Charles I erected one of his most impressive and best-preserved fortifications to enclose Frederick II's *palacium* within a new Christian settlement that contained a small church.[155] After 1278 a moat was dug to separate this Christian fort from the Muslim town, over which a drawbridge was constructed in 1281.[156] In 1274 Charles sent out broadsides to encourage Christians from Provence, Forcalquier, and France to settle the new town within the fortification, promising houses, livestock, and land.[157] A total of 128 houses were built for the settlers, but in 1276 most remained still empty, and by 1278 many were in ruins. Charles subsequently instituted proceedings against the corrupt officials who had built the houses, who were condemned to rebuild them at their own expense. But by then the small Christian community had mostly disappeared, either because they had moved elsewhere, or died of malaria: of the 150 families who arrived between 1274 and 1278 only about twelve remained in 1280. It has been suggested that the survivors took refuge in the hill towns to the west where the climate was more salubrious: Egidi in 1911 reported the survival of communities in the mountains to the west where the population still spoke an archaic form of Provençal dialect.

Yet while the fortified Christian town struggled, the Muslim city beside it thrived. Its population has been estimated at about 35,000 to 40,000 souls.[158] In the general shortage of construction labor, Charles I at times resorted to workers from Lucera for various building projects: in May 1274, for example, he used 300 manual workers for his fortification wall around Frederick's *palacium*, and Muslims also served in the king's armies as archers.[159] A number of skilled trades were represented in the city, among them intarsia workers, carpenters, and weavers.[160] Amari noted that intarsia workers from Lucera were called to Melfi, Canosa, and Naples.[161]

In 1300 Charles II charged one of his most able and loyal advisors, Giovanni Pipino da Barletta, with the task of dismantling the Muslim city and taking its surviving population into captivity. Egidi summarizes the range of possible reasons for this action, which range from religious intolerance to financial expediency. The year 1300 was one of severe famine in the kingdom, and Muslims of Lucera were reputed to have the richest and fullest granaries in Apulia.[162] Charles II might have benefited not only from the much-needed grain, but might have hoped to refill his empty coffers with Muslim wealth. Early in 1300 royal officials imposed high taxes on Lucera, which the community protested.[163] In July royal officials wrote a palliative letter stating that the complaints would be examined, although Egidi observes that

this was apparently a ruse, for at the same time initial preparations were being made for the attack on the city.[164]

Pipino entered the city on 15 August 1300, apparently without opposition and perhaps under the pretext of resolving the dispute over taxation. It was only after he and his soldiers were ensconced in the main strategic points that members of the most important families were arrested and taken out of town, eventually to prison in Naples. By the time that the Muslims became aware of the threat, it was too late for effective armed protest; Pipino then proceeded to seize the remaining Muslims by force, constraining them to leave the city with only the possessions they could carry. They were held for some time under armed guard and then sold into slavery.[165] The entire operation lasted from Assumption Day (15 August) to Saint Bartholomew's day (24 August).

The destruction of Muslim Lucera was described as a purification of the realm for the first Jubilee in 1300.[166] The king's pious declarations sanctioned the massacres of groups of Muslim captives by local populations as they were taken under armed guard to various destinations to be scattered "diversas Regni partes."[167] The destruction of this city ended to all intents and purposes the long history of the Muslims of southern Italy, a population that had lived in Sicily and the peninsula since the ninth century, augmented and renewed by contact with North Africa.[168]

After the eradication of Muslim Lucera, Charles II initiated plans for the resettlement of the city. The initial proposal had been to settle refugees from the Aragonese raids in Calabria there, but by 1300 these families had mostly found refuge elsewhere.[169] The better Muslim houses were reserved for Pipino and his trusted Angevin retainers, while others were assigned to various religious orders and to clerics.[170]

Renamed Civitas Sanctae Marie, the re-Christianization of Lucera was to be accomplished not only by the importation of displaced persons, but also by the construction of new churches initiated under the supervision of Giovanni Pipino. The new city included foundations for the Franciscans, Dominicans, Augustinians, and Celestinians, as well as a new cathedral. Of these first churches, all erected in the first two decades of the fourteenth century, only San Francesco and the cathedral retain their medieval appearance.

Lucera had possessed an earlier cathedral purportedly located outside the city walls and perhaps erected under Byzantine rule.[171] On 24 August 1300, immediately after the removal of the Muslim population, plans were put forward to build a new cathedral inside the walls on the

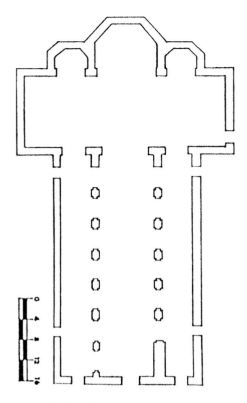

108   Lucera, cathedral, plan (from Brivio 1986)

site of the old mosque.[172] The dimensions of the new cathedral were larger than the original piece of land, however, and in January 1304 various citizens were reimbursed for properties requisitioned for the completion of the building.[173] Indeed, the famed architect and builder of fortifications, Pierre d'Angicourt, *praepositus*, reappeared at Lucera to provide estimates on the value of the property that was being requisitioned for the construction of the cathedral.[174] In May 1304 columns were transported from Frederick II's *palacium* to the site, and these can still be seen in the central west portal, the entrances of the apses and the crossing piers (pl. 109).[175] By 1304 timbers were being imported from Bagnoli and Schiavonia for the roof, and it can be supposed that in May 1311 the structure was largely complete.

The cathedral is in many respects a simplified version of the cathedral of Naples, reduced in both scale and complexity. The plan (pl. 108), with its strongly projecting transept and three absidial chapels, imitates the disposition of the Neapolitan church (without, however, the rectangular outer chapels added to the original cathedral by Archbishops Minutolo and d'Ormont). Although Lucera is lower and broader than the cathedral of Naples, the design of the piers is identical, but because the aisles are not vaulted the shafts

are reduced to two and coursed with the rectangular core. Ancient columns are inserted only in the crossing piers and the entrances to the chapels (pls. 109, 111, and 112). The structure is built out of brick and re-used Roman blocks (pl. 110). The capitals of the apse chapels support keeled ribs in the main apse and chamfered ones in the lateral apses, and the capitals are a mixture of debased palmettes, crockets (pls. 111 and 112), and heart-shaped perforated leaves. Several of these have exact counterparts in some of the nave chapels of San Lorenzo in Naples, and are also similar to those of the Cappella Tocco in the Neapolitan cathedral (pls. 113 and 95).

Perhaps the most striking and unique aspect of Lucera is its façade, which incorporates a single tower on the south (pl. 110). Apart from the tower, the three lower portals and the rose window (now blocked) would have been virtually the only decorative elements in an otherwise unarticulated field of brick.

The portals are in concentrated form striking testimony to the vigorous mixture of cultures of southern Italy. In the central portal the projecting gable is supported by antique columns that carry imitation acanthus capitals where the crisp and delicate foliage is distinct from the more ponderous decorative elements of the apse (pls. 77 and 114). The latter, like the design of the church itself, is instead related to Neapolitan workshops. In the side portals of the west façade the capitals are decorated with birds pecking grapes and long, delicately carved acanthus leaves, all closely related to the refined Apulian and Abruzzi workshops that must have come to Lucera to complete the west end of the cathedral. The contrast of the styles raises the intriguing possibility that some members of the first workshop (the apse capitals at the cathedral of Lucera) may have come from, and/or returned to, Naples. Could they have been Muslim slaves with special skills in stone carving? Bertaux published a document of 1301 in which Charles II requested that his agents in the area of Bari send him any further "Saracen" craftsmen available, including: "omnes sarracenos artistas quos vobis . . . ostenderit vel suxerit nominandos . . . magg. muratores . . . magg. carpentarios . . ."[176] There is other evidence of movement across the peninsula and workers present at both places, for in 1305 the Neapolitan builder Francesco di Vico was sent to Lucera to supervise the restoration of some of the towers of the castle.[177]

The cathedral was marked east and west with the arms of Charles II. Fleur-de-lys shields appear over the main portal (pl. 115) and in the keystones of the eastern apses, associating the king with the new cathedral and perhaps with the substitution of the Christian faith for that of

109 (*facing page*)   Lucera, cathedral, view of the nave from the west (Barbara Bini)

110   Lucera, cathedral, west façade (Barbara Bini)

the Muslims. In its deliberate evocation of the cathedral of Naples, and in particular in its use of ancient columns, Lucera is an explicit evocation of the capital, the best evidence we have of an attempt by Charles II to create uniformity in the religious monuments of the kingdom by systematizing certain essential characteristics in large-scale (cathedral) architecture. In this he would of course have been following the example of the architecture of the religious orders, not only that of the Cistercians in the thirteenth century but also, and much more importantly because it was urban, not rural, that of the Franciscans and Dominicans.

The church of San Francesco at Lucera, to the north of the cathedral, is a simple rectangular box with a polygonal apse in the east. It is also conspicuously marked by the Angevin royal arms (pls. 116 and 117). The birds and leaves that decorate the south portal, and the leaves and sculptural decoration of the west portal, closely reflect models in the Abruzzo, and are also related

to the west doors of the cathedral (pl. 118). The capitals of the *piscina* on the right side of the apse, however, are identical to the heart-shaped perforated leaves of the left apse in the cathedral. Here again one has the sense that the first workshop may have been replaced with the distinct and delicate style of carvers trained in both Apulian and Abruzzi work-shops who perhaps specialized in the execution of portals. As we shall see below, the same style appears in Charles II's chapel dedicated to the Magdalene at San Domenico in Manfredonia.

It is difficult to determine whether any fragments of secular Muslim buildings remain in Lucera, although the city plan would appear to reflect that of the Muslim city. As noted above, Muslim houses were assigned after 1300 to French administrators. Others were demolished to make place for the new cathedral, set at an angle in the center of an otherwise roughly orthogonal plan. It seems safe to assume that by and large the new Christian population of Lucera must have moved into and absorbed

111 (*above left*)   Lucera, cathedral, apses from the west (Chester Brummel)

112 (*above right*)   Lucera, cathedral, north transept arm from the crossing (Chester Brummel)

113 (*right*)   Naples, San Lorenzo Maggiore, capital from nave chapel (Jill Caskey)

115 (*above*)   Lucera, cathedral, gable over central portal (Barbara Bini)

116 (*right*)   Lucera, San Francesco, west façade (Barbara Bini)

114 (*facing page*)   Lucera, cathedral, detail of capital, central portal of west façade (Barbara Bini)

117 (*following page*)   Lucera, San Francesco, west portal (Barbara Bini)

118 (*page 115*)   Lucera, San Francesco, detail of capital, south portal (Barbara Bini)

the fabric of the Muslim city, whose plan probably underlies that of the present town. In February 1341 Robert sent instructions to refortify the new city, of which the most conspicuous surviving remains is the Porta di Troia.

There were other important Angevin foundations in Lucera, such as the church of San Domenico and the Celestinian monastery of San Bartolomeo, but no medieval remains are preserved. They were probably similar to San Francesco in style and character. The loss is especially regrettable in relation to San Bartolomeo, which was founded by Giovanni Pipino da Barletta, who was also the moving force behind the construction of the chevet at Santa Maria Maggiore in Barletta and the church of San Pietro a Maiella in Naples.

L'AQUILA AND ITS CHURCHES

High in the Abruzzi mountains, the city of L'Aquila retains a unique flavor that recalls the history of its creation. Founded with the support of the papacy in the second quarter of the thirteenth century, it was destroyed by Manfred in 1259 and rebuilt after 1266 by the French kings. When initially re-established some three decades before, L'Aquila had formed part of the larger political and territorial struggle against local feudal lords whose interests were closely allied with those of the empire. The later reconstruction of the city was part of a larger attempt to strengthen its role as a center of power on the northern borders of the kingdom.[178]

L'Aquila consists of a conglomeration of transplanted local towns united to form the new city.[179] In the 1250s it grew rapidly, and by 1257 it was the seat of a bishop. Although Charles of Anjou proposed to reconstruct it as early as 1266, it seems little was accomplished before the 1290s when Charles II took an active role in the rebuilding of the city.[180] L'Aquila thrived economically because it was on the Via degli Abruzzi, the major north–south artery that connected Florence to Naples; it was one of the main gateways to the kingdom, important for trade, the collection of customs duties, and defense.

Some aspects of the city plan must have been established before the 1290s, but the development of the town with active royal support led to the imposition of a grid (to the extent that this was permitted by the undulating terrain) that united the regional quarters, or *rioni*, each consisting of the population of one of the surrounding towns. These individual neighborhoods centered on church, fountain, and piazza dedicated to the saint transplanted from the local parish: San Pietro di Coppito, San Pietro di Sassa, Santa Maria di Paganica, Santa Maria di Roio. To these were added a number of churches for the new orders, including the Carmelites, Franciscans, Clares, Dominicans, and above all, outside the walls of the city, the mother house of the Celestinians, Santa Maria di Collemaggio, founded by Celestine V and erected from 1287.

The impression of an intact medieval fabric in the city of L'Aquila is belied by the almost complete destruction or redecoration of the church interiors – only the exterior shells of the churches are medieval. Repeatedly afflicted by earthquakes, beginning with those of 1315 and 1349, these monuments have been repaired or rebuilt on many occasions. Later, virtually without exception, they were covered with Baroque decoration,[181] which in turn was ravaged by the restorations of the 1950s and 1960s that stripped off the Baroque and much that was medieval as well.[182]

In spite of this devastation, certain characteristics emerge to suggest the existence of a well-formed and independent school of stonemasons who worked in a strongly developed local tradition. Particularly striking is the taste for crossing and absidial piers that consist of four heavy shafts on the main axes and four smaller rounded shafts on the diagonal axes (a form of the French *pilier cantonné*, a pier with four attached shafts), as can be seen at Santa Giusta, San Silvestro, and Santa Maria di Collemaggio, among others. Nave piers are almost always octagonal. Both of these features may today be seen best in the highly restored interior of Santa Maria di Collemaggio, begun in 1287 and consecrated, unfinished, in 1289.

Façades are generally square or rectangular and at times articulated by shallow pilasters (pl. 120). Insofar as can be judged from surviving evidence, decorative energy was reserved entirely for the portals and fresco decoration (only small fragments survive of the latter). The portals often include row upon row of archivolts, decorated with twisted columns, rosettes, floral spirals, biting animals, and other exuberant ornamental motifs (for example, pl. 119). They are the product of a number of local sculptors, some of whom, such as Raimondo di Poggio (Santa Maria di Paganica) and Tancredi di Pentima (the fountain of the Novantanove Cannelle), signed their work. There are often close ties to the sculptural workshops of Apulia.

Since Aquila had been recently refounded, the highly skilled workmen who executed the portals of the numerous churches there must initially have come from elsewhere. Since the style appears throughout the Abruzzo, however, it is likely that the workshops were local ones that traveled from town to town. The variety of sculpture at L'Aquila also suggests that there were a number of different shops, some more archaic in style

120   L'Aquila, façade of San Marciano (Barbara Bini)

(as at San Marciano, of about 1350, pl. 120) and some more current. The evidence suggests that the sculptors who worked on the portals at L'Aquila may have been present at Città Sant'Angelo, Lanciano, Atri, Sulmona, and numerous other sites in the region. The sculptors of the portals of San Francesco and the cathedral of Lucera may also have come from these Abruzzi workshops or been in contact with sculpture teams in the Capitanata in the decades between about 1280 and 1310.

In 1300 the royal palace and gardens were given to the Dominican order. According to Bernardino da Fossa, Charles II made a donation in 1309 for the construction of a new church to be dedicated to the Magdalen (pls. 122–28).[183] The Dominican church seems never to have been completed, perhaps because of the earthquakes of 1315 and 1349; campaigns seem to have consisted as much of repairs as new building. San Domenico was again catastrophically damaged in the earthquakes of

118

121　L'Aquila, detail of the west portal of Santa Maria di Paganica (Barbara Bini)

1456 and 1703 and was rebuilt again after years of semi-abandonment (pl. 122).[184] Since 1976 part of the interior has been turned into a concert hall. The monastic buildings (initially the royal palace) on the north flank of the basilica were transformed in the nineteenth century into a penitentiary. Only the partially destroyed chapel to the left of the apse, the cappella del Rosario, retains its vault departures and some fragments of fresco decoration (pl. 124).

The exterior walls and the remains of the three eastern apses (pl. 123) and the south transept of San Domenico are vivid testaments to the elegance and high quality of the initial phase of construction. Along with the ground plan (pl. 127, exterior walls only), these surviving elements indicate that the church was established to conform to the style seen at the cathedral of Lucera and the large-scale churches founded by Charles II in Naples. The polygonal apse chapels, finely constructed

of ashlar masonry, recall the plans of San Domenico and the cathedral of Naples, although the poor state of preservation of this church prohibits further analogies. On the other hand, the exterior wall of the south transept, constructed of horizontal bands of colored stone (pl. 125), seems uniquely related to the Abruzzo, as at Atri (San Domenico) as well as in a number of churches in the Principality of Taranto, such as Santa Croce in Brindisi. The most striking feature of the south transept, however, is the magnificent portal encased in a design of columns and archivolts separated by a pattern of coffered squares (pls. 125 and 126). This portal has been occasionally described as "Burgundian," but the design has to my knowledge no precedents in either Burgundy or any other French source. It is instead an elegant and imaginative reconfiguration of ancient vault coffering applied to the flanks of a portal by an anonymous and original master.

122 (*above left*)   L'Aquila, San Domenico, interior (Soprintendenza per i Beni Ambientali e Architettonici dell'Aquila)

123 (*above right*)   L'Aquila, San Domenico, exterior of the apses (Soprintendenza per i Beni Ambientali e Architettonici dell'Aquila)

124 (*right*)   L'Aquila, San Domenico, upper walls of the left apse, seen from below (Soprintendenza per i Beni Ambientali e Architettonici dell'Aquila)

125 (*facing page top left*)   L'Aquila, San Domenico, south transept façade (Soprintendenza per i Beni Ambientali e Architettonici dell'Aquila)

126 (*facing page top right*)   L'Aquila, San Domenico, detail of south transept portal (Barbara Bini)

127 (*facing page bottom*)   L'Aquila, San Domenico, plan (Soprintendenza per i Beni Ambientali e Architettonici dell'Aquila)

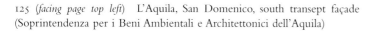

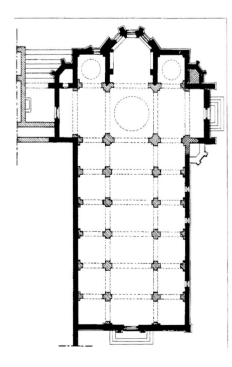

The plan of San Domenico is a reduced version of that of the Dominican church and the cathedral of Naples, with the projection of the main apse and the length of the nave reduced (pls. 96 and 127). The chapels that flanked the main apse seem to have been almost square, and these are flanked in turn by small polygonal chapels. As at the cathedral of Naples, the main entrance to the church from the city seems to have been the transept arm, which at Lucera faces the city center. Here, as in San Domenico in Naples, there are strong similarities to the plan of Santa Maria sopra Minerva in Rome and Santa Maria Novella in Florence.

In L'Aquila the building tradition is one of rich local artistic preferences and tastes, exceptional in the beauty of its sculptural decoration. An abundance of good limestone assisted in the development of well-established and highly skilled schools of masons who received ample employment in the reconstruction of the city in the late thirteenth and early fourteenth centuries. Both master masons and sculptors seem to have been for the most

128 L'Aquila, San Domenico, detail of capital of north transept portal (author)

part regional, although they were in contact with, and were perhaps called to work at, sites that spread down the east coast of Italy towards Larino, Lucera, and further south.

THE CHEVET OF THE CATHEDRAL OF ROSSANO AND SAN FRANCESCO IN GERACE

The geographical isolation of Calabria, the two decades of war and depopulation between 1282 and 1302, and innumerable earthquakes in the intervening centuries have meant that few monuments in this region survive from the Angevin period. Those that remain, however, are interesting testaments to distinct episodes of French rule, and in one instance reflect the importation of French tastes and architectural expertise from abroad. As shall be seen in the last chapter, the church of Altomonte confirms spurts of large-scale and ambitious building projects. At an earlier date, however, the reconstruction of the apses of Rossano cathedral is the earliest testimony of architectural importations.

The eastern apses of this cathedral are, as far as I know, unpublished, unstudied, and essentially undocumented (pl. 129). Insofar as they have received attention, they have been dated to about 1330 and attributed to the rule of Robert the Wise. There does not appear to be historical foundation for this attribution, however, which also seems unlikely in view of Robert's limited interest in church building apart from the projects of his queen, Sancia of Mallorca, in Naples and Provence.[185] Historical circumstances and the architectural evidence instead support a date in the early fourteenth century for the cathedral apses of Rossano. Calabria, which had been invaded by Spanish and Sicilian troops in the 1290s, was returned to the possession of Charles II with the Treaty of Caltabellotta in 1302. In the intervening decade the region had been devastated and depopulated, and it was at least in part to accommodate these refugee Calabrians that Lucera had been evacuated, as noted above.

In the period after the treaty of 1302, as part of the process of reasserting Angevin dominance, reconstructing destroyed and damaged churches, and setting a "Latin" stamp over a culture that had historically been

129 (facing page)   Rossano, cathedral, exterior of eastern apses (Chester Brummel)

130 Rossano, cathedral, detail of capitals on the portal to the episcopal complex behind apse (author)

firmly allied with Greek interests and culture, one may suppose that Rossano was reconstructed for the new Roman liturgy. It is possible that these apses formed part of a reclaiming of these territories undertaken under Charles II, possibly by Bishop Rogerius, who had been confirmed by Clement V in 1307.[186]

This dating in the decade after 1302 is suggested by the fragmentary structural remains. The eastern apses of Rossano are large-scale polygonal structures constructed of ashlar masonry, similar in many respects to the east ends of Lucera cathedral and San Domenico in L'Aquila. Although the dimensions of the volumes are adjusted to those of the pre-existing (?twelfth-century) nave and aisles, and are therefore small in scale, the adoption of polygonal and rib-vaulted volumes attests the reassertion of Angevin presence in this part of Calabria.[187]

Various details in the partially preserved episcopal buildings behind the apse suggest that the rebuilding of the chevet formed part of a larger project to reconstruct the entire episcopal complex, and that this, too, dates from the period around 1300. The execution of moldings and capitals, as well as of the small portal that leads into the episcopal palace behind the apse (pl. 130), suggests French expertise. Whereas Lucera and L'Aquila were in or near areas with abundant local workshops of masons, there are no indications of established schools of indigenous construction labor in this part of Calabria.

In any event, the population of Rossano had been devastated by the war of 1282–1302. Building campaigns of any significance almost certainly would have required the importation of an architect and stonemasons (we shall see that this seemed to have occurred at a later date at Filippo Sangineto's reconstruction of Santa Maria della Consolazione at Altomonte).

The profiles of the bases in the choir are similar in some respects in scale and type to those in the lateral chapels and chevet of San Lorenzo Maggiore and Santa Maria Donnaregina in Naples (App. 5, figs. 2, 4C and D, and 5), but the portal to the episcopal palace is attributable to a building tradition closer to French traditions and workmanship. Although there is no documentation of such a master working in Rossano, it is perhaps worth recalling that French architectural expertise continued to be present at the Angevin court in the fourteenth century: Eudes de Crespy is recorded at Castellamare in 1309 and in Naples in 1317, for example.[188]

The Franciscan church of Gerace presents more difficult problems (pls. 131–33). The house was founded in 1252,[189] but was damaged by the war, and in 1294 Charles II gave the Franciscans some houses for the reconstruction of their monastery.[190] The church is now presided over by the handsome tomb of Nicola Ruffo of 1372 in the style of Tino da Camaino.

The plan of the building, a simple rectangular hall with a rectangular, flat-ended chevet, is typical of Franciscan architecture everywhere. Only the portal on the south flank is distinctive: decorated with a pattern of pal-

131 Gerace, San Francesco, detail of south portal (author)

132 (facing page)   Gerace, San Francesco, interior view from the west (Chester Brummel)

133   Gerace, San Francesco, south portal (Chester Brummel)

mette, diamond, and interlace patterns, its decoration and capitals are closer to Sicilian models than other monuments in Calabria (pls. 131 and 133). But in this region, where so much has been lost to earthquakes as well as to war damage, it is hazardous to make assumptions on the origins of the sculptural style.

MANFREDONIA

Charles I supported the construction of a new tower and staircase to the grotto and shrine of the archangel at Monte Sant'Angelo, as we saw, but his son was a patron of the Franciscan and Dominican establishments in the port of Manfredonia at the foot of the mountain. Charles II was particularly devoted to the Dominicans here, whose church – also at first dedicated to Mary Magdalen – he helped to construct in 1294.[191] According to the chronicle of Sarnelli of 1680, the Dominican church of Manfredonia was one of the twelve houses of the order that he had sworn to construct while in prison in Barcelona.[192] Only the west portal, fragments of the outer shell, and an eastern chapel (now storeroom) dedicated to the Magdalen survive (pl. 134).

In spite of the fragmentary survival of the building, there is clear evidence of different phases of construction: the west façade portal, with its original and elegantly "fluted" colonettes and door jambs that play on the idea of vertically disposed cavets and fillets (pls. 135 and 136), seems substantially earlier in date, and different in style, from the fragments of ribs, vaults, and the altar niche in the Magdalen chapel to the east (pls. 137 and 138). This chapel may be an addition to the original church, perhaps executed in a last campaign early in the fourteenth century, because the shafts and moldings of the altar niche are related to the sculpture in the portals of the cathedral and San Francesco at Lucera.

In 1309 Charles II gave an ancient bronze statue from Barletta to the Dominicans in Manfredonia for the construction of a bell tower and a bell, "in subsidium campana et loci." The ancient statue has been associated with the monumental bronze of an emperor now located beside the church of San Sepolcro in Barletta, which would suggest that the bronze (if it was the same) was never transported north to Manfredonia.[193]

AVERSA

Charles II seems to have had special affection for what is now the ravaged, abused, and neglected city of Aversa. Here fragments of a number of important churches and monasteries affirm his patronage and to the lost splendors of this city. The most important of these foun-

134   Manfredonia, San Domenico, west façade (Barbara Bini)

dations was the Dominican house of San Luigi re di Francia, at present abandoned and inaccessible. The interior was entirely redecorated in the Baroque period and is now in a state of collapse; only the remains of a pointed arch can be seen from behind the apse (pl. 139).[194] The king made numerous donations to this house from 1304 until his death in 1309, and Robert made further gifts in 1309 and 1316.[195]

In 1305 and 1306 Charles II also subsidized the enlargement of the Clarissan church of San Francesco, and gave thirty gold once to the monastery of Sant'Agostino. Perhaps most importantly, he also established a commu-

127

135   Manfredonia, San Domenico, west portal (Barbara Bini)

136   Manfredonia, San Domenico, detail of west portal (Barbara Bini)

nity of Celestinian monks in the royal palace of Aversa, where an older church within the palace complex was provided for the use of the new community.[196] Nothing survives of this medieval complex and a Baroque church is now dedicated to Saints Philip and James.

CHARLES II'S FOUNDATIONS IN APULIA

After his return to Naples in 1294, Charles II attended not only to the foundation, reconstruction, restoration, and completion of numerous churches in Naples and Campania,[197] but to the foundation, repair, and reconstruction of churches in Apulia. In particular he supported the construction of the Dominican churches of Bari, Brindisi (also dedicated to the Magdalene), Trani, and, as we have seen, Manfredonia.

With the creation of the Principality of Taranto for his fourth son, Philip, Prince of Achaia, however, the architecture of Apulia developed along an independent course, as can be seen most strikingly in the Dominican church of Brindisi (now known as the Chiesa del

Cristo), Santa Maria del Casale outside Brindisi, and in numerous smaller churches (Ugento, Alezio). The distinct style of these monuments, closely related to monuments in Hungary and Achaia, means that they must be the object of a study that concerns Apulia and the East in ways in which this one cannot.

Conclusion

In the many sermons composed after his death, Charles II was eulogized for having rebuilt many churches and for his attention to the spiritual welfare of his people. Although we might be tempted to discount these as typical of the rhetoric of funerary orations, both the documents and the monuments confirm that Charles II was indeed an extraordinary patron and supporter of religious architecture, one of the most active medieval kings in this respect, surpassing perhaps even the great generosity of his uncle, Louis IX of France. "Many were the churches and monasteries, . . . many were the convents that he built and endowed."[198] In another sermon on the king, Giovanni da Napoli said "[Charles II] showed that he had love of God or charity in many and great works, but especially in two . . . for the worship of God flourished greatly where he stayed . . . and he greatly increased the worship of God in the lands of his domain by building churches and monasteries and religious places and endowing them."[199] There may in the history of the Middle Ages be few kings who were as energetic (or as obsessive?) as founders and builders of churches.

Although it is clear that Charles II had particular devotion to the Dominicans, after about 1295 there was also royal patronage for the Franciscan order. In Naples this is evident not only in Mary of Hungary's involvement in the reconstruction of Santa Maria Donnaregina, but also in the royal donations to San Lorenzo Maggiore of the 1290s, and the burial of several members of the royal family in this church. As noted above, the addition of Franciscan patronage to the list of favored orders can probably be associated with the return of the young princes from prison and especially the influence of Louis of Toulouse, who after years of education at the hands of Franciscan friars dedicated to the ideals of apostolic poverty, adopted this form of life himself.[200] This tale has been marvelously told by Toynbee, Manselli, Pásztor, and others, and need not be repeated here.[201] The return of the princes represents the first stage of what was to become a dominant fact of Angevin patronage in the following decades: devotion to the Franciscan order but in particular to the Spiritual Franciscans, as will be seen in the next chapter on Santa Chiara.

What is especially striking, of course, is that Charles II did so much with so little. The finances of the kingdom, always in a precarious state, worsened sharply with the war of 1282–1302 and the king's captivity. We can imagine that with the outbreak of the war projects underway were mostly interrupted, and in 1284 the incomes of all religious establishments were tithed for two years to support the war effort.[202] Bartolomeo da Capua was repeatedly involved in negotiations with the Holy See on the postponement or forgiveness of the royal debt towards the papacy, with mixed and unpredictable results. And yet in spite of the repeated outbreaks of hostilities against Sicily and Aragon, church building went on – and on, and on, after Charles II's return to the

137 (*above right*)   Manfredonia, San Domenico, altar niche of the Magdalen chapel (Chester Brummel)

138 (*right*)   Manfredonia, San Domenico, detail of capital in the altar niche of the Magdalen chapel (author)

139　Aversa, San Domenico, view from the east (Jürgen Krüger)

king's personal piety, but probably also the real need in the kingdom for new and increased liturgical spaces, especially for the new orders, the Dominicans, Franciscans, Augustinians, Celestinians, and Carmelites. Furthermore, in a late reflection of the shift in the nature of medieval religious movements that had already occurred elsewhere, these were urban rather than rural foundations. Charles II was concerned with the populations of the cities, and in bringing to those populations the comforts and joys of the faith.

It has often been noted that the architecture of Charles II represents the "italianization" of Angevin building practice.[203] To this we might add that almost all the projects were clearly designed by local architects using local labor and local building traditions. In the area of Naples, and especially at the cathedral, which replaced an Early Christian basilica, there was the explicit desire to record and remember the past through the conspicuous reuse of columns and the revival of certain types of ancient building techniques. Other features, however, such as the adoption of high transepts in various churches in Naples (Sant'Eligio, the cathedral of Naples, and San Domenico) and elsewhere (Lucera) suggest that there was also an urge to evoke an affiliation with Rome, a kind of *romanitas*.[204]

The architecture of Charles II should therefore be understood not only in a vague and general way as "Italian" (and specifically "Roman"), but also as distinctly Campanian. Even the emphasis on Roman prototypes recalls earlier Campanian traditions, such as Abbot Desiderius's rebuilding of Montecassino in the eleventh century. The "localization" of Angevin architecture also of course included elements of importation both mendicant and ultramontane, such as the Dominican plan and elevation type that seem to have been used in so many of the major monuments.

In the reconfiguration of Naples as a major European capital during the reign of Charles II, the cathedral was to play an important role in shaping a historical past that embraced both the traditions of the apostolic foundation and Constantinian patronage.

It is probable that individuals in the Angevin administration, such as Bartolomeo da Capua, *protonotario*, legal theorist, negotiator, and counselor to the king, were central figures in this process. Educated at San Domenico and a disciple of Thomas Aquinas, Bartolomeo (d. 1328) was the great Neapolitan personality of his age – and it was a long one. We may even suppose that the equilibrium of ancient and modern of the cathedral of Naples reflected in physical form aspects of the intellectual climate around Aquinas, which reconciled Christian doctrine to the ancients.

kingdom after 1294. If the Angevin soldiers had lamented the young prince's excessive piety in the early years of the War of the Vespers, how his accountants must have wailed at his religious profligacy after his return after 1294.

Yet although the surge of church building under Charles II seems striking, it should be remembered that little had occurred in terms of the construction and repair of churches since the early thirteenth century. The great Norman projects were for the most part eleventh and twelfth century in date; from the time of Frederick II's hostilities with the papacy onwards, there was little new religious architecture in the Kingdom of Sicily: in Campania, for example, the last major monuments before the arrival of the Angevins were the transepts of Caserta Vecchia and the porch of Sessa Aurunca. As has been seen, Charles I of Anjou was also not a particularly energetic patron of church architecture. So the numerous churches built by Charles II reflected not simply the

Archbishop Filippo Minutolo was also part of the local elite that assisted the king in his most complex negotiations. At Charles II's request Minutolo worked with Bartolomeo da Capua on the new constitution of the kingdom that recognized the previous customs and laws of the different populations of the *regno*, suggesting, as it were, an acceptance of the multicultural and multiethnic character of the kingdom. But there was also in all this a specific emphasis on things Italian, as we have seen in the buildings. And this too is reflected in Bartolomeo da Capua's thought, for after the death of Umberto d'Ormont, he pronounced two sermons on the late archbishop in which he exhorted the chapter and canons to elect a new archbishop of Italian origin.

It is with these men of action and culture that we might associate the essential elements of the architectural and cultural policies of the kingdom. The cathedral of Naples is dominated by this approach, and although French elements are also present, for example in the fine moldings of the rib vaults and the bar tracery of the windows, it is a generic "Frenchness," one that may enhance the idea of the sacred through its focus on decorative elements around the apse, but secondary to the overall concept of structure and space.

It may be worth considering whether in some ways the important shift in tone within the Angevin administration may not have been a distant and considered reflection of the rapidly crumbling Crusader kingdoms and the loss of the Holy Land in 1291. The funds collected in the six-year crusading tithe declared at the Council of Lyons in 1274 had largely disappeared into the papal-Angevin campaigns in the Sicilian War after 1282, and the devastating financial consequences of expansion must have been more than clear. Naples was not even able to reassert its dominance over the renegade island.[205] One solution would have remained: to "plant" the Angevin regime as fully as possible within the local intellectual and administrative hierarchy of southern Italy.

And so as we gaze at the architectural remains of Charles II's building campaigns, we may be gazing at the legacy of such figures as Bartolomeo da Capua and Filippo Minutolo, who stand in the shadows of the columns. And perhaps another shadowy presence, though more in terms of pious rather than practical inspiration, can be seen in the figure of the king's uncle, Louis IX of France, who was canonized in 1297. There were many parallels between the lives of the two kings: both deeply pious, both captured in battle and held captive for huge ransoms. Both were deeply involved in issues of justice and reform within their realms. Charles II's second son was named Louis in honor of his uncle, and this son also became deeply attracted to the Franciscan movement (and was in turn canonized). Yet if Charles II followed the example of King Louis, we might note that he did so emphatically within the architectural traditions and artistic preference of southern Italy.

As with Louis IX in France, the mendicant orders played an especially important role. In Naples, at least until the late 1290s, the dominant players were the Dominicans, heavily patronized by Charles II even before the outbreak of the war of 1282. His personal devotion to the Magdalen, whose relics he had discovered at Saint-Maximin, was combined with his attachment to the order, and many of the new churches he built for them, including those of L'Aquila, Naples, and Brindisi, were dedicated to her. The Magdalen, as a penitential saint, must in some ways have reflected Charles II's own struggles in the troubled years of his reign.

The siege of Lucera can perhaps be seen above all in the dual perspectives of financial exigency and religious prejudice, as an attempt to increase the king's sources of income through the sale of Muslim grain and Muslim persons, as well as the elimination of heterodoxy. Here again there are some vague parallels with Louis IX: in each case the king's intense piety led to religious intolerance. In the Kingdom of Naples religious bigotry may have been aggravated in no small measure by the reputed ferocity of the Aragonese Almogávar troops who raided and devastated the southernmost parts of the kingdom.[206]

Finally, like Louis IX, Charles II seems to have been a ruler genuinely devoted to the ideals of justice and reform. The edicts formulated at the plain of San Martino, where in 1823, as Prince of Salerno, he had summoned a parliament to codify a series of reforms, were reissued after the king's release from captivity in 1288. These testify to his concern for the well being of his subjects and the principle of justice in his kingdom. Yet not only did circumstances weigh heavily against his success, but also, if historiography can be a measure, these were not achievements valued by historians (in contrast, for example, to the military conquests of his father). Although in Charles II the Kingdom of Naples may have found one of its few genuinely well-intentioned rulers, his achievements have been largely forgotten and ignored.

Chapter 4

ROBERT THE WISE, SANCIA OF MALLORCA, AND THE CONVENT OF SANTA CHIARA IN NAPLES

> . . . When the construction of Sta. Chiara was almost complete, Robert brought his son Charles
> Duke of Calabria to take a look at it, and asked him how he liked the sacred temple. To this
> question Charles replied that the great nave made it seem like a stable and the side chapels
> were like so many horse-stalls. Robert, almost prescient of the future, replied, "May it please
> God, my son, that you not be the first to feed in this stable!"[1]

Charles II died in 1309 leaving a legacy of new churches that he had founded or supported throughout the kingdom, and his son Robert inherited the throne. Whereas Charles in 1288 came to rule a kingdom in which – apart from the rare and episodic foundations of his father – there had been almost no religious building since the early thirteenth century, Robert was crowned at a time when new churches recently completed or under construction could be seen on all sides. Naples in particular was densely packed with new monastic foundations, so that if Robert was to become the "re da sermone," Charles II had certainly been the "re delle chiese." Naples and the other chief cities of the realm were indeed covered with a "white robe of churches," the number and scale of which may well surpass the religious patronage of any other medieval monarch. And most of these, as we have seen, were devoted to the mendicant orders.

So when the newly crowned Robert and Sancia arrived in Naples in 1310, the city must have been dotted with recently consecrated churches and others still under scaffolding. Everywhere there were new and conspicuous monastic complexes: San Domenico Maggiore, San Lorenzo Maggiore, San Pietro Martire, Sant' Agostino alla Zecca, San Pietro a Maiella, San Pietro a Castello, Santa Maria Donnaregina as well as the continuing work on the cathedral. The religious foundations were particularly dense on the east and south edges of the city (see plan of Naples, page xiii).

During Robert's reign new religious foundations were therefore few. The king's interests in any event were largely embedded in the worlds of literature and theology, as well as in the art of the finest Tuscan painters and sculptors. Insofar as there were new buildings, the initiative can be attributed to the passionate religious convictions of Robert's second wife, Sancia of Mallorca, whose personality and piety will dominate this chapter.

The new religious foundations were to be few but magnificent. Above all others, the Franciscan double convent of Santa Chiara not only exceeded in scale any other church in the kingdom, but, as we shall see, may even have been part of a short-lived program to propose a Franciscan alternative to the authority of the papacy, by this time of course displaced to Avignon. The new project of Santa Chiara, initiated soon after the arrival of Robert and Sancia in Naples, reflected a new trend in the spiritual life of the kingdom – now strongly inclined towards the Franciscans and in particular towards the Spirituals.[2]

The primary stimulus for the foundation of Santa Chiara was to create in Naples a home for the one religious group that had specifically not benefited from Charles II's generosity: the "poverty-minded" faction of the Franciscans. Robert's brother, Louis of Toulouse, had renounced the throne in order to become a Franciscan friar with strong inclination in this direction, probably as a result of the years of contact with Spiritual Franciscans as tutors during his captivity in Aragon. Whereas the poverty-minded friars had been the object of Charles II's contempt and dismay (a view depicted with delicious pungency in Ambrogio Lorenzetti's fresco of the ordination of Louis of Toulouse in San Francesco in Siena), they were now to receive the rapt devotion of the new queen and considerable, if intermittent and perhaps ambivalent, support from Robert also. I shall propose here that the foundation of Santa Chiara, created as a double convent for the Poor Clares and Franciscans, was conceived from the start with views embedded in the religious and philosophical principles of the Spirituals to which both sides of the royal family – not only the three princes in captivity, but also Sancia and the royal family of Aragon and Mallorca – were closely allied. Yet in spite of its dedication to the Franciscan ideal of apostolic poverty, the insertion of a series of elaborate royal tombs and cycles of fresco painting by Giotto and others transformed the complex into one of the most lavish monasteries of medieval Italy. The tombs of nobles and members of the court, in the chapels down both flanks of the church, re-created the structures of the palace itself in the sacred space of the church. So it may have been for these reasons, or as a response to the renewed wave of Franciscan austerity brought to the court of Naples by individuals such as Sancia's brother Philip of Mallorca, or her lady-in-waiting, Delphine de Sabran, or through them of Angelo Clareno, that the queen much later in life founded the smaller and more modest convent of Santa Croce, to which she eventually retired after her husband's death in 1343. As we shall note below, she also founded two other religious houses in Naples, as well as a number of convents in Provence. Of this large group of monuments, only Santa Chiara in Naples survives.

A discussion of the architecture of the kingdom under Robert and Sancia inevitably focuses on the Franciscans because their foundations were the main objects of the queen's attention. But, as Boyer and Kelly have demonstrated, it would be a mistake to extrapolate from this the conclusion that these friars dominated intellectual and court culture.[3] To the contrary, Robert was deeply ingrained with political theory and philosophy largely Thomistic and Dominican in its origins; these currents flow deep in his sermons and in the intellectual culture of the court, and may even be seen to underlie certain themes in the conception of his tomb. In architecture we see little if any demonstration of this, however, because Charles II had already and so assiduously occupied himself with Dominican projects in the preceding twenty years of rule, and after, as we shall see, the queen was deeply involved in her own Franciscan projects.

* * *

Santa Chiara

Rarely is the anomalous neatly encapsulated by legend. Yet in Naples the perplexities presented by Santa Chiara required comment. So in a tale that dated at least to the sixteenth century, the church was compared to a stable, and the lateral chapels to "so many horse-stalls" (pls. 140 and 141).[4] Until its embellishment in the eighteenth century, this vast and austere convent was as inexplicable as it was inescapable, perhaps especially so to a Neapolitan public famous for excess in dress and embellishment.[5] How was one then, and how is one now, to explain the bare and steep mural surfaces of this building? What is one to make of the evaporation of the apse, which denies the heightening of light and intensifying of space characteristic of Christian monumental architecture and which, in its rejection of that single and central element of church design, has the unsettling effect of a body without a head? How is one to account for the absorption of the chapels into the nave, so that the upper walls rise from the back of broad galleries stretching down the length of the building, establishing a rigorous rectangularity of plan and external elevation (pls. 141 and 142)? Above all, what is one to make of a religious architecture that so emphatically and in every way refuses to ingratiate itself, and that rejects with puritanical rigor any sense of spiritual and aesthetic exaltation?

At the same time that it is strange, Santa Chiara is also huge. The convent loomed over medieval Naples and still presides over the modern city (pl. 143). It surpassed by far the scale of any other Clarissan convent; it was larger even than the church that serves as a shrine to Clare in Assisi.[6] Whereas other convents of the order were poor and small, often founded in abandoned churches or older monasteries (often Benedictine), converted for the use of the sisters and a small local lay population, Santa Chiara in Naples stood apart as a vast and monumental stage for royal presentation.[7] Larger than the cathedral, it came to serve in the fourteenth century as the setting for court ceremony: burials, coronations, and state functions took place in the convent church rather than in the cathedral.[8] Although the community of sisters was strictly enclosed, as in all Clarissan convents, the abbess of Santa Chiara nonetheless came to hold the remarkable title of "Queen of Pozzuoli," and carried the royal insignia at certain public feasts.[9] The convent was a veritable citadel of women, separated from the world by the force of papal legislation and by high walls, spiked grills, grates, screens, and turning wheels, yet it was also, and at the same time, intended by its royal founders as a monumental and public expression of certain religious ideals. Strict enclosure required the sisters to be invisible to the

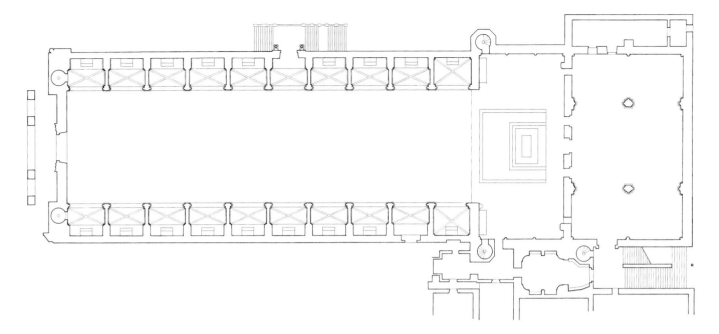

141   Naples, Santa Chiara, plan (from Venditti 1969)

exterior world, entombed in the convent and rendered mute by the regulations concerning speech within the cloister.[10] But within this world of silence and withdrawal there was presented a new world view: I will suggest that Santa Chiara was perhaps nothing less than the setting for a brave and doomed attempt to reform the Church.

Before 4 August 1943, the medieval interior of Santa Chiara was invisible, encased in a sumptuous Baroque decoration designed by Domenico Antonio Vaccaro and executed by Giovanni del Gaizo and others (pl. 145).[11] The original structure underneath was revealed to modern eyes only in August 1943 after Allied incendiary bombs caused a fire that burned continuously for thirty-six hours. In the process, the eighteenth-century stucco was entirely destroyed and the medieval walls behind severely calcinated (pl. 146). In keeping with the post-war preferences for streamlined design, and because of the cost and complexity of re-creating the splendors of the Baroque interior, the church was restored instead to an austere medieval shell (pl. 140), a loss still lamented by Neapolitans and lovers of the Baroque. The building in its present restored state has much of the harsh modernism of the architecture of the 1950s and 1960s that can be seen in other churches rebuilt after the Second World War (the cathedrals of Benevento and Teano, for example).

The destruction and restoration of the monument are important for an understanding of the previous scholar-

ship on Santa Chiara. From 1744 to 1943 the medieval walls were hidden from sight; those who wrote about the church before the war could see only the Baroque, and were limited to vague inferences about the appear-

142   Naples, Santa Chiara, section (from Venditti 1969)

143   Naples, Santa Chiara, view from the Castel Nuovo (author)

ance of the Gothic structure underneath. The eighteenth-century decoration also modified the relationship
of the main body of the church to the nuns' retrochoir:
it concealed the large lancet window behind the altar
and also blocked two of the three grilled openings between the nave and choir (pls. 144 and 145). Only the
central grill under the tomb of Robert the Wise remained visible. Because the community of nuns continued in the cloister and the rules of strict enclosure
prohibited entry into the retrochoir, studies of the
convent before the war were restricted to glimpses into
this space through the spiked openings under Robert's
tomb.[12] The church was therefore experienced as two
distinct structures, one of which was inaccessible, and it
was as a result usually described as consisting of two separate and individual parts (pl. 144). The literature thus
tended to focus on which part was built first.[13]

The restoration permits a different interpretation: in
spite of the abrupt severity of the wall between nave and
choir, some modifications or simplifications that took
place during construction, and the differences in the
types of spaces of the two parts, Santa Chiara was clearly
conceived and built as a unified whole (pl. 141). Although at least two architects are named, we are not presented here with two separate visions of plan and space:
on the contrary, as we shall see, the church is characterized by striking conceptual unity. The distinct character
of the choir responds to the requirements of enclosure
as well as to the particular piety of the patron (especially
her devotion to the consecrated host).

Although the destruction of the Baroque decoration
in the Second World War revealed the long-forgotten
medieval shell underneath, thus permitting some sense
of the original monument, it also imposes great constraints on any study (pl. 146). Moldings, base profiles, and
wall surfaces are for the most part modern, and therefore
no chronology can be established that depends upon this
type of detail for the sequence of construction.

The losses are not confined to buildings but also
include the archive and library of the convent, which
burned with the same fire that consumed the church.
Many documents had already been lost in previous
fires in the sixteenth century, however, and little of the
surviving material concerns the early history of the
foundation.[14] The Angevin Registers rarely mention
the construction of the convent.[15]

These misfortunes notwithstanding, Santa Chiara is a well-documented building in medieval terms, and the destruction of the documents is somewhat mitigated by a number of early studies that published texts now lost. The remarkable and indefatigable Franciscan historian, Lucas Wadding, included the papal bulls concerning Santa Chiara in the *Regesta pontificium* at the back of the *Annales minorum*, and other documents are included in the *Bullarium franciscanum*.[16] The fundamental dates are provided by the inscriptions on the adjacent bell tower. There are also several colorful anecdotes that add glimmers of information about the monument (and its reception), as do also the royal tombs and the documents that concern their construction. These have recently been the objects of splendid new studies by Enderlein and Michalsky, while a young Neapolitan scholar, Mario Gaglione, combing through archives and libraries, has found further important new information on the tombs and their inscriptions.[17]

★   ★   ★

FOUNDATION, ATTRIBUTION, AND SITE

The monastery was founded in 1310 as one of the first acts of the newly crowned Robert of Anjou and Sancia of Mallorca, a date recorded in the laconic fourteenth-century inscription on the bell tower that precedes the church:

ILLUSTRIS CLARUS ROBERTUS REX SICULORUM SANCIA REGINA PRELUCENS CARDINE MORUM/ CLARI CONSORTES VIRTUTUM MUNERE FORTES VIRGINIS HOC CLARE TEMPLUM STRUXERE BEATE/ POSTEA DOTARUNT DONIS MULTISQUE BEARUNT VIVANT CONTENTE DOMINE FR[ATR]ES Q[UE] MINORES SANTA CUM VITA/VIRTUTIBUS ET REDIMITA ANNO MILLENO CENTENO TER SOCIATO DENO FUNDARE TEMPLUM CEPERE MAG[IST]RI.[18]

The earliest texts refer to the convent of Santa Chiara by a variety of names that emphasize its eucharistic dedication: Corpus Domini, Sancti Corporis Christi, or Hostiae Sacre. Yet a few decades later, by the time of the inscription on the bell tower, the church is referred to simply as Santa Chiara.[19]

144   Naples, plan of Santa Chiara (from Dell'Aja, 1980)

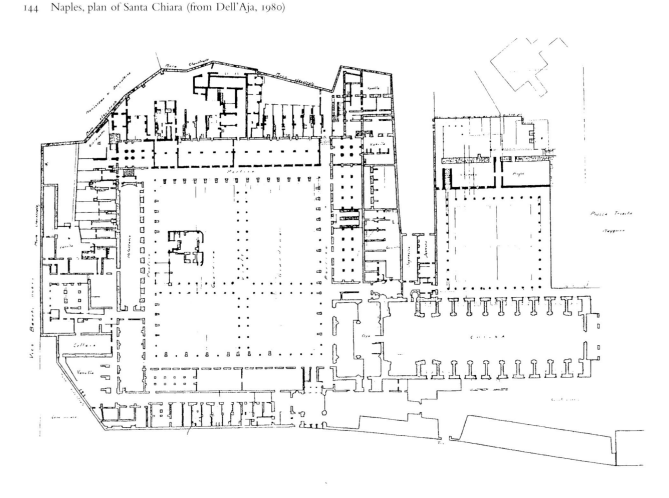

137

145   Naples, Santa Chiara before 1943 (Soprintendenza per i Beni Ambientali e Architettonci di Napoli e Provincia)

Most of the literature attributes the foundation of Santa Chiara to Robert, as also indicated by the inscription on the bell tower.[20] The papal bulls that concern the convent, however, refer for the most part to Sancia as the foundress: papal letters are usually addressed to her alone, and they specifically refer to the convent as her project: *opus manuum suarum*.[21] Sancia herself revised the rule by which the sisters were to live.[22] From the start in 1310 she dedicated her large dowry of 3,000 once for

the construction of the complex, and specified that she planned to retire to the convent at her husband's death. In 1317 she anticipated this plan by asking the pope's permission to leave her husband and enter religious life (the request was denied).[23] Petrarch, deeply familiar with the currents and tastes of Robert's court, also refers to Santa Chiara as the queen's undertaking.[24] And it was certainly Sancia who obsessively and repeatedly requested special permissions and indulgences from

146　Naples, Santa Chiara after 1943 (Soprintendenza per i Beni Ambientali e Architettonci di Napoli e Provincia)

Clement v and John xxii for her new foundation. The striking number of papal bulls issued on behalf of the convent suggests that the queen was a fanatical correspondent on matters important to her, and chief among these was this convent.[25] Her engagement in the foundation – as well as her need for papal sanction in this enterprise – far exceeded that for any of her other and later Clarissan foundations in Naples, Marseilles, Aix, or elsewhere.[26]

The site of the monastery is at the western extension of the *decumanus inferioris*, located to the southwest of the ancient center of Naples. The street, commonly known as Spaccanapoli (now Via San Biagio dei Librai), ended at what once was the Porta Puteolana (see map on p. xiii). Even today one experiences the release from the constraints of the ancient grid by the sudden spaciousness of the Piazza del Gesù. The area occupied by the convent is described in numerous documents as "in loco

147 Naples, Santa Chiara during the restoration showing new masonry (Soprintendenza per i Beni Ambientali e Architettonci di Napoli e Provincia)

qui dicitur extra hortos."[27] Archaeological excavations undertaken during the restoration of the monastic complex in 1951 revealed remains of the Roman water supply systems and some foundations; although located outside the walls, there is evidence that the site had been inhabited since ancient times.[28]

The negotiations for the acquisition of these various properties by royal agents, and the subsequent clearance of the land, must have been a lengthy process. It is likely that the first groups of friars and sisters were housed in these older structures at the site until the new monastic buildings were available. The use of pre-existing houses

as temporary quarters, and the creation of temporary enclosure for the Clares, would explain the different dates for the arrival of the male and female communities, as we shall see below.

The church is planted on a northwest–southeast orientation that roughly parallels that of San Domenico in the old city to the east: the altar is thus in the southeast.[29] As we have seen, deviation from standard orientation is not unknown in Naples since most medieval churches in the old city conformed to the exigencies of the Greek grid underneath. But Santa Chiara was founded outside the walls of the city where there had never been an ancient grid, and where the terrain, even if partially inhabited, was far more open than that of the ancient city. It is likely that the orientation of the church was established to permit the presentation of a majestic façade towards the most densely used commercial artery of Naples, so integrating it and the friars' community with the intense urban life of the medieval city.[30] The Franciscan-Clarissan convent thus formed a gateway to the entrance to old Naples as one moved towards the city from the southeast, and its high eastern gables faced the royal residence in the Castel Nuovo, from which it would have been a highly visible landmark, as it still is.

Apart from the inscribed date of the foundation of 1310 on the bell tower, the first document recorded is the papal bull of 1311, in which Clement V gave Sancia permission to found and build a Clarissan convent for 100 sisters "cum Ecclesia et Officinis etiam opportunis construere proponebas propriis sumptibus et expensis, ac possessiones accommodas, seu alios redditus ex quibus possent commode sustentari, de propriis bonis tuis acquisitis iam vel in posterum acquirendis eisdem monasterio, seu loco et sororibus concendere et etiam assignare."[31] At this early date the exact location and size of the site may not have been firmly established. By 20 June 1313, however, at least its general outline was settled and a request was made to Clement V to establish the Clarissan convent.[32] The first group of nuns arrived in late 1317 or early 1318, by which time some friars were already living in part of the new foundation, or at least at the location.[33] Clement V's approval of a community of 100 sisters (12 July 1311) was expanded to 120 by John XXII in July 1317, and soon increased again by this same pope to 150 (15 January 1318).[34]

The most detailed text concerning the site dates from 1321. It confirms the properties and incomes belonging to the abbey, and in particular lists the houses to the south of the monastic buildings which had become part of the convent's domain.[35] Land empty to the south and west of the monastery, land to the west where the orchard of Santa Maria Donnalbina was located, various houses that were on the south side of the convent, among them the house of the doctor Guido de'Viola to the west, and the house of the goldsmith Rostagno di Rainaldo to the east, now belonged to the monastery.[36] Another orchard towards the Pozzuoli gate, roughly at right angles to the public street, in a place called Sommario, which belonged to Matteo Ravignano, was also acquired.[37] It is impossible to be precise about the locations and extent of each of the properties mentioned, but the description of land to the east and west suggests that the original plot was rapidly expanded in those directions. The land first acquired may thus have been

located roughly at right angles to what is now the Via Benedetto Croce, the area presently occupied by the church, which perhaps corresponded to the size of the large plots acquired in 1311 or 1312. Later acquisitions made room for the expansion of the sisters' cloister.[38]

There has been considerable discussion as to whether the convent was founded for men or for women. The separate papal bulls for the founding of the friars' (1317) and the sisters' (1311) cloisters have fueled the debate, as have also the numerous suggestions that the church represents two separate and unrelated building campaigns.[39] Yet it seems likely that Sancia intended a double house from the outset. The document of 1321 in particular speaks of the foundation of a monastery for both nuns and friars: "Monasterium in civitatis Neapolis, in loco qui dicitur extra hortos, pia fecimus intentione fundari, quod Sancti Corporis Christi vocabulo providimus nuncupandum, ubi Sorores Ordinis Sanctae Clarae et Fratres Ordinis Minorum ordinavimus collocari."[40]

Further evidence that the complex was always intended for both men and women may be adduced from other aspects of the foundation. Sancia took care to specify that the pre-Urbanist rule of Clare herself be used at the Neapolitan convent. Clare's rule, established on her deathbed in 1253 and approved by Innocent IV, specified a close relationship to the friars.[41] Ten years later, however, Urban IV freed the friars from most spiritual and economic obligations to their female counterparts. Its successor, the so-called Urbanist rule, became obligatory for most convents and stipulated an independent chaplain to be appointed by the cardinal protector instead of an adjacent small friary.[42]

Sancia's insistence on the pre-Urbanist rule of 1253 is fundamental to the concept of the original program because it envisions a double foundation. Only after her death was the Urbanist rule of 1263 imposed.[43] Sancia's use of the original rule would have required the planning of an adjacent community of friars from the outset, and through her generous support she freed them from the more onerous aspects of this sort of arrangement: not least the financial burdens of the female community that caused much of the friction between the two orders elsewhere.

The concept of double monasticism may well have had roots in the early history of the Clares, although the phenomenon has rarely been discussed. C. and R. Brooke suggested that when Francis encouraged Clare to join him in 1212, he may have intended that she and her eventual female companions form a female counterpart to the friars in some sort of joint community.[44] Whether this was meant to be a joint mission serving the needs of the public, as is suggested by Jacques de Vitry's description of a Milanese community of Franciscans and Clares in 1216, or as the meditative and enclosed counterpart to the open and active life of the friars, remains unclear.[45] In any case, it is evident from her letters that Sancia was well informed on Franciscan history, and familiar with the early years of the order through written sources and perhaps oral tradition.[46]

By the time of the construction of the Neapolitan convent, enclosure was of course integral to the rule of the Clares. At Santa Chiara it was to lead to an episode concerning Robert, who on several occasions received permission to enter the enclosed choir with twelve retainers and four Franciscans (in April 1324 and again in 1336). In late 1338, on the anniversary of the translation of Saint Louis's relics, however, the king opened the entrance to the choir so that many more could enter, it is said because he prided himself on the sermon and was anxious for those clustered around the grills (*ante cratem*) to be able to hear it. This incurred the wrath of a pontiff whose patience was perhaps already strained by the royal couple's obdurate protection of Spiritual Franciscans in the monastic complex.[47]

As a double complex with separate cloisters for the Poor Clares and Franciscan friars, Sancia's Neapolitan convent can also be seen as the embodiment of two striking aspects of Saint Francis's life: his engagement in social action on one hand, and his need for prayer, solitude, silence, and meditation on the other. The convent with its two cloisters might be seen in effect as embodying both: the former were the province of the friars' cloister, whereas the latter prevailed in the domain of the sisters.[48] In her own life, Sancia may herself have swayed between these divergent aspects (or tensions) of the Franciscan model. In her first years in Naples, she created something of a convent within the palace by surrounding herself with a retinue of Clarissas who lived with her in the Castel Nuovo, a sort of court monasticism not uncommon at the time. In 1317, as we have seen, she had unsuccessfully petitioned the pope for a separation from her conjugal duties to enter Santa Chiara.[49] Yet in the 1330s, perhaps under the influence of the recently arrived Philip of Mallorca, she adopted what we might perhaps see as a more "activist" spirituality, founding two houses in Naples for reformed prostitutes, Santa Maria Maddalena and Santa Maria Egiziaca.[50] Her later decision to found a second double monastery (or closely placed but separate Franciscan houses for women and men) called Santa Croce and Santissima Trinità, where she retired after Robert's death in 1343, was perhaps inspired by the rigorous interpretation of religious poverty of Philip and others (such as Robert of Mileto and Delphine de Sabran).[51]

Santa Chiara would have been similar in some respects to several other royal double monasteries, such as the French foundations of Fontevrault and Saint-Louis-de-Poissy in France.[52] With their personal Franciscan and Clarissan retinues in attendance within the palace, it is even possible to imagine that to some extent the royal couple were perhaps living in a quasi-double-monastic arrangement themselves, although there is considerable debate as to Robert's own desires in these matters.[53]

Although construction of the complex extended well into the 1340s, and although the plan may have expanded as further property was acquired, the first priority was probably the construction of the church and the enclosed precinct for the nuns: both texts and architectural evidence suggest that church and convent were built rapidly. Since the bull of 1311 refers to the site of the convent in the future tense, the date of 1310 recorded on the bell tower refers to the foundation in a general sense, not yet the beginning of work on the buildings.[54] But by 1313 the rough perimeter of the site was established, and work may well have been underway.

Various details indicate that the complex was planned from the outset as an integrated whole, such as the windows on the right flank of the church towards the friars' cloister, which were designed in relation to the arcading of that cloister. As noted above, by late 1317 enough had been erected to permit the arrival of the first group of Clares, for by January 1318 they were at the convent.[55] The friars may have arrived earlier, since privileges and indulgences issued on 12 July 1317 mention them as already present,[56] and a small initial core of them perhaps conducted services in provisional arrangements somewhere within the complex as early as 1316.[57] In 1326 the painter Bartolomeo da Aquila received 20 gold once to paint "nella cappella della S. Eucaristia quelle istorie che gli sono state commissionate dalla Regina Sancia e dal Duca di Calabria," suggesting that some parts of the church – perhaps the nuns' choir? – were soon be put into use.[58] The first tomb dates from 1325.[59] As noted in the *Cronaca di Partenope*, the church was finished in 1338 and consecrated in 1340.[60] Work began in 1338 on the massive detached tower to the north: its four inscriptions record the dates of 1310 (the inception of construction of the church), 1330 (the concession of papal indulgences by John XXII), and the consecration in 1340 (although the tidiness of the round numbers of the dates may give us pause for thought).[61]

Rapid construction was facilitated by the simple design of the church and the immense sums provided by Sancia for construction. Building costs for the early fourteenth century are difficult to calculate, although, as we have seen, from about 1282–4 through the 1290s the sum of 40 gold once was adequate for the cost of labor in constructing a chapel. Assuming a reasonable rate of inflation for labor and materials over a few decades, the 3,000 gold once provided annually by Sancia, in addition to other later donations to the convent, could have supported a large crew at the site and permitted the rapid construction of the church and monastic complex.[62] Although the simplified structure, with flat and rectilinear wall surfaces, restriction of vaulting to ancillary spaces (chapels and aisles), and the absence of elaborate architectural detailing, meant that the church was relatively inexpensive to construct (at least in relation to a structure such as the choir of San Lorenzo), at the same time its scale meant that this was nonetheless a lavishly expensive undertaking.

Sancia's repeated petitions concerning increases in the number of sisters suggest that the precise dimensions of their quarters were not fixed until 1319. Did her ambitions grow as the project emerged from the ground? Had there been papal resistance to the scale of the initial plan that was gradually overcome? The nuns were probably first installed in temporary quarters, perhaps pre-existing houses at the site protected and enclosed by new perimeter walls. Sancia herself resided occasionally in the convent, for in January 1318 she received permission to enter and spend up to three nights at a time.[63]

In March 1318 an indulgence was issued for those who visited the church of *Hostiae Sanctae*, indicating that some portions were in use and accessible to the public.[64] On 4 August 1320 a letter was written concerning the acquisition of roof beams for the church.[65] In that same year John XXII issued another indulgence of 100 days on the feast of Corpus Christi.[66] Subsequent letters indicate that construction was still underway and that property was still being acquired. In 1319 Sancia promised an additional 1,000 once a year to the works until the structure was complete.[67] On 16 October 1320 Guglielmo Brancaccio conceded to the abbess an orchard that he possessed adjacent to the monastery in order to assist with the construction.[68] Yet another document, of 28 March 1321, issued by Charles of Calabria, gave permission for wood of the necessary size for the truss roof to be taken from any forest in the kingdom.[69] The same document gives precise instructions for where the materials could be stored until they were placed in the building.[70] Further documents were issued in 1325 and 1326 concerning roof beams to be delivered at the rate of five per year.[71] As the upper walls of the nave were completed, the structure was rapidly being roofed; the immense width of the nave must have made this a formidable enterprise. The inscription on the west side of the bell

tower records that in 1338 the church was covered with lead and in 1340 was consecrated.[72]

By 1338 several major tombs had been installed within the church and a few state ceremonies had taken place. Santa Chiara was well on its way towards becoming an integral part of the spiritual and courtly life of Naples.

THE BUILDING

The plan of Santa Chiara consists of a long nave flanked by nine lateral chapels on each side (pl. 141).[73] The nave terminates with the rectangular friars' choir at the far end of the church where the main altar is located, behind which there is an abrupt, flat wall penetrated only by a series of windows and three grated openings, now partially concealed by the supports for Robert's tomb. Beyond this wall is the nuns' choir, different in plan from the remainder of the building (pl. 148). Here two piers on either side divide the choir into three spaces not unlike the standard form of a chapter house. These piers support the rib vaults of the side aisles, and interrupted shafts against the exterior wall indicate that the main volume of the choir was also at one point intended to be rib-vaulted, a project abandoned in mid-course. The three grilled openings that face the altar from the nuns' choir are deeply flanged to enhance their view of the priest and the liturgy on the other side of the wall.

In the nave, the lateral chapels support a long tribune or gallery that extends the entire length of the church

148   Naples, Santa Chiara, view of the nuns' choir (Massimo Velo)

and sets the upper nave walls back in depth (pls. 140 and 142), creating a completely flat and contained exterior shell. The rectangularity of the plan is thus reinforced by the rectangularity of the enclosing walls: the building is in every way a box (pls. 141 and 142).

It has often been suggested that the design of the nave is inspired by southern and southwestern French single-nave churches, such as that of the Franciscans at Notre-Dame de Lamourquier in Narbonne or the cathedral of Albi. It is also common in Catalonia. This was the home territory of Sancia, whose early life was spent between Perpignan, Montpellier, and Catalonia, while Robert, who was raised in the Angevin domains of Provence, also of course spent time in the Spanish and Catalan domains.

By this time it was usual in Naples (and elsewhere) that naves would be flanked by lateral chapels; they appear in almost all the buildings erected in the previous generation, including the cathedral, San Domenico, and San Pietro a Maiella. But Santa Chiara reflects the more austere model of the Carmelite church (and perhaps Sant'Agostino) in disposing of aisles altogether. But the emphatically rectangular character of Sancia's church differs from its predecessors in the absorption of the chapels into the main body of the church and the raising of the clerestory wall from the back of the upper gallery (pl. 142). Although the galleries reflect the arrangements of Provençal churches, they may also have had some liturgical or ceremonial function. Lateral galleries are found in some Clarissan convents (Santa Chiara in Ravello, for example) and are certainly present in earlier architecture for monastic women, but at Santa Chiara the doors that provide access to the tribune connect with the public spaces of the church, not the enclosed spaces of the convent.[74] They must have served the friars and overflow crowds on state occasions.

Above the nave tribunes stretch the clerestory windows (pl. 140), entirely rebuilt since the Second World War. In the area that corresponds to the friars' choir, there are large relieving arches on either side and the gallery expands slightly at this point.

Two further observations: the final two chapels of the nave near the main altar are larger than the others and different in both plan and vaulting, and the second chapel from the friars' choir on the right (facing the altar) serves as an entrance from their cloister (pl. 141). This probably corresponded with the location of the rood screen, but no traces remain of this structure.[75] The doorway into the church on the left flank in the sixth chapel is new.

★ ★ ★

SANTA CHIARA IN THE CONTEXT OF CLARISSAN ARCHITECTURE

We are still in the infancy of studies on the architecture of the women's orders.[76] Where work has been done, it has rarely concerned itself with the liturgical use of space and the architectural implications of strict enclosure. The absence of a centralized administration in most women's orders meant that there was rarely any consistency between houses on architectural matters – in other words, the typical monastic model of repetition and consistency does not apply. And as noted above, convents were usually small and poor, often established in older or abandoned monastic foundations, as at San Damiano, restored by Francis in anticipation of the "ladies" who would some day live there.[77]

The reuse of older buildings, rather than the construction of new ones, was of course Francis's preference. Convent churches were often in fact inherited from male communities, and so there was wide variety in the types of buildings and in the solutions to establishing a suitable location for an enclosed choir. Filipiak demonstrated that each site found a different solution, the location of the choir and other ancillary buildings depending on pre-existing structures, the character of the topography, and the resources of the community. Ad hoc solutions characterize most Clarissan establishments (and perhaps much of the architecture of women's monasticism in general), and some fine examples survive at Alatri and Anagni, for example. At the former, the well-preserved abbey at San Sebastiano, the choir is an upper room adjacent to the church, which probably served as a dormitory as well. At San Pietro in Vineis in Anagni, the choir was set over the north aisle, and services could be heard through the slit windows of the older nave. In many instances, rooms were either added behind, beside, or even above a pre-existing church, and at times older adjacent rooms or cloister walks were converted into choirs. Indeed, the position of the retrochoir at San Damiano and of other early convents is modeled on anchoritic cells rather than the systematized organization of liturgical choirs in men's orders.[78] Seclusion and separation led to the adoption of hermetic rather than communal models.

A related issue is the relationship between the choir and the altar. At San Damiano there seems to have been a small grated window between the two, not aligned with the present disposition of the choir stalls in the "Coro delle Clarisse."[79] Nuns' choirs usually communicated with the churches by small grated windows and occasionally by doors. I have found no surviving Italian example of a Clarissan church before about 1310 where the choir is positioned for a view of the altar and the liturgy; on the contrary, this seems to have been discouraged by special planning as well as the regulations of the order. Grills and screens are positioned so that the female experience of the mass was auditory rather than visual, and of course this also meant that there was no possibility of the priest in turn seeing the religious women.[80] Although the mass is often described as sacred drama, and recent studies emphasize the importance of seeing the elevated host, architectural evidence suggests instead that vision was often difficult or impossible, not only for religious women but indeed also for large segments of the laity.[81]

The absence of direct visual access from the nuns' choir to the nave reflected the requirements of strict enclosure, requirements that were imposed with particular rigor upon the followers of Saint Clare. There are exceptions, however: in Milan in 1300 a Benedictine convent was remodeled to conform to the regulations of Boniface VIII's bull, *Periculoso*, by the erection of a wall between the nuns' choir and the church. This, however, contained a window so that the sisters could specifically witness the elevation.[82] In contrast, most of the early churches of the Clares suggest that from early on there were strong prohibitions against women's vision of the main altar, and the rules imposed on them enforced an auditory rather than visual experience of the mass.[83]

Santa Maria Donnaregina presents an interpretation of strict enclosure in striking contrast to that at Santa Chiara (pls. 102 and 103). Here the choir is placed in a deep upper gallery over the entrance to the church, an arrangement that permitted a view of the altar below only for those at the balustrade, thus effectively prohibiting a view of the mass and ensuring the complete invisibility of the female community to the laity and the clergy below.[84]

The contrast between Donnaregina and Santa Chiara is no doubt deliberate. On opposite sides of Naples, the two convents represented two opposed interpretations of the character of religious space for enclosed women, as well as of visual access to the mystery of the Eucharist. It would be tempting to situate the difference in the personalities of mother and daughter-in-law, each of whom seems to have had a direct hand in their respective Clarissan foundations, but for such an opposition of views there is no historical evidence. On the basis of a purely structural analysis, however, it can be observed that the choir at Donnaregina excluded the sisters from a vision of the public liturgy below, whereas at Santa Chiara this was facilitated (pl. 148). Through the three broadly flanged openings towards the nave of Santa Chiara, the female community could see the mass and

have a privileged view of the elevation of the host, especially since the celebrant would have performed with his back to the laity, facing the nuns on the other side of the wall. Presumably the enclosed community would also have been able to contemplate the reserved host on the altar, but perhaps this was also kept in the choir or an oratory within the convent, as at San Damiano.[85]

The emphasis on vision at Santa Chiara led also to a fundamental reordering of liturgical space. Church architecture consists traditionally of a longitudinal volume in which the lay population faces the altar in the east. But here the church is bifurcated; both laymen and nuns face the altar, which becomes a "hinge" in the center. There are two audiences who face – but must not see – each other. Each sector is focused on the consecrated host on the altar in the symbolic middle of the church.

There is perhaps here some sort of subtle reference to the issue of the Beatific Vision, the concept that the beatified can view the divine prior to the Day of Judgment. It cannot be my task to enter into this complex subject, but certainly the extent to which the church was designed to guarantee vision to its female monastic community relates to ideas about the attainment of certain kinds of sacred knowledge through the faculty of sight. Musto has observed that some of these concepts emerge in Robert's sermons: for example, in the *Introductio in librum de semine scripturarum* the seventh day of creation was associated with the exalted life of the Virgin and the contemplative, tied to the Transfiguration and the "claram visionem" of this state.[86] The king dedicated at least one of his sermons to the theme of the Beatific Vision, in which he connected it with the altar and the Resurrection of the Dead.[87] By the end of this chapter I shall have shown that these themes seem to connect with other sources of inspiration for the program of the building.

The Historical Context

The peculiarities of the architectural disposition reflect of course the original dedication of the convent to Corpus Domini or Hostie Sancte, a dedication quite new in the early fourteenth century.[88] Sancia's personal devotion to the consecrated host is well attested.[89] For example, in her letter to the Franciscan General Chapter of 1334, she stated:

> Since I am a sinner and insufficient and unlettered, and I speak literally, I know nothing except from the grace and intimacy of God, and I trust nothing of my

own, on Thursday the eighteenth day of April, I entered the small chapel next to my chamber in the Castel Nuovo in Naples, where well through three candles before daybreak, with the door closed, alone with the body of Christ, which was upon the altar, I commended myself to him and afterward began to write as the Lord directed me, without any counsel, human or earthly.[90]

In 1331 Sancia received permission to keep the consecrated host in her chapel at all times, a privilege previously accorded her mother, Esclaramonde de Foix, Queen of Mallorca.[91] This may have been one of the reasons that led Sancia and Robert in 1336 to purchase the Cenaculum in Jerusalem, where they installed a community of Franciscan friars;[92] through their intervention, the host thus came to be venerated anew in Jerusalem (now of course under Muslim control) on the same table where Christ had celebrated Easter and instituted the Eucharist.

Eucharistic veneration was one of the many ways in which Sancia's piety reflected the strongly formed religious preferences of the royal house of Mallorca. In the letter of 1334, cited above, she described in detail her family's long and ardent support of the Franciscans.[93] Her dedication to family tastes in these matters is also indicated by the names of her religious foundations, which echo those of her parents in Perpignan and Palma: Santa Croce, for example, echoes the dedication of the palace chapel in Perpignan.[94] In Perpignan and Palma the royal family patronized the convents dedicated to Clare and the Magdalen. Esclaramonde de Foix was a devoted patron on the Clares, and supported their houses in Perpignan and Montpellier as well as in Palma.[95] She, like her daughter, received permission (in 1308) to be accompanied by two Clares within the royal palace.[96] Sancia herself continued to maintain close ties with her Mallorcan family long after her move to Naples and continued to support the Clarissan convents in Palma and Perpignan.[97]

As is well known, both Sancia and Robert were descended from families with numerous saints distinguished for their devotion to poverty, chastity, and the Franciscan ideal.[98] The marriage of Robert and Sancia brought into conjunction two royal dynasties whose ranks were studded with saints and *beati*. Among the most conspicuous saintly members of the two sides were Elizabeth of Hungary and King Louis of France, but there was also a constellation of Hungarian saints on Robert's side through his mother, Mary of Hungary.[99] Holy lineage was an important political tool for the Angevins and provided the embattled dynasty with par-

ticular authority and prestige.[100] With these interests in mind, the Angevin throne had actively promoted the canonizations of Louis of France, Louis of Toulouse, and Margaret of Hungary.

But the Mallorcan royal house had strong ties to the Spiritual Franciscans and their dedication to the concept of apostolic poverty.[101] Narbonne, Perpignan, and Montpellier were among the most important centers for the Spirituals, and these cities were closely associated with its charismatic leaders, especially Peter John Olivi.[102] We have already had occasion to mention the correspondence between Olivi and the young Angevin princes while they were captives in Aragon. He declined the boys' invitation to visit them because he feared opposition from Charles II.[103]

Among his many other teachings, Olivi had success in promoting the concept of marital celibacy among his lay followers. Some of these ideas were further promulgated by Arnald of Villanova, a distinguished physician who treated several popes and whose writings were translated into Tuscan as well as Neapolitan.[104] His teaching appears to have had significant impact on the royal family of Mallorca and was probably familiar to Sancia even before her marriage – indeed, it may not be irrelevant that the family died out within two generations, one of the consequences of this doctrine. In the court of Naples itself, Delphine de Sabran was a strong proponent of marital celibacy and famously converted her husband Elzéar, to this view.[105] (The irony is that it was he who was canonized.)

Mallorcan involvement with the "poverty-minded" Franciscans and with the teachings of Olivi and Arnald of Villanova seems to have been established early in the reigns of James II and Esclaramonde and was expressed through ties to important Spiritual Franciscans and their supporters, in particular Raymond Lull and the ubiquitous Arnald of Villanova. The paths of Lull and Villanova crossed those of the Mallorcan, Aragonese, and Neapolitan royal families in Perpignan, Avignon, Palma, Naples, and elsewhere.[106] In asserting her family's long-term adherence to the Franciscans, Sancia in her letter of 1334 noted that both her elder brother James and her brother-in-law Louis had renounced their respective rights to their thrones to join the order.[107] Although she mentioned that both James and Louis (as well as another brother, Philip of Mallorca) were supporters of the Spirituals, the predilections of these princes were well known, as were Sancia's own, and it is in this context that we should understand the queen's exhortations to the Franciscans to return to the "original" teachings of Francis.[108] Through Prince Philip, who maintained close ties to Sancia after her marriage in 1304, and who moved to Naples in 1329 to take up a life of preaching and begging, the court was linked to one of the central leaders of the movement, Angelo Clareno, who corresponded with Philip and Delphine in Naples, and whose letters refer to Sancia.[109]

Royal support for the Spiritual Franciscans reached a critical point in 1329. In December of that year Philip preached a virulent sermon against John XXII in support of apostolic poverty.[110] Other events, such as John XXII's condemnation of belief in the Beatific Vision, gave powerful new impetus to the pope's enemies in Naples and Avignon. These controversies seem to have enhanced Philip's role as champion of an anti-papal movement. For a brief moment there may even have been a movement to declare Philip a new pope, a pope of apostolic poverty.[111]

The convent of Santa Chiara was a center for the Spiritual Franciscan movement in the Kingdom of Naples, probably from the start but at least in the years after the election of John XXII in 1316. It was increasingly the site for events that led to the papal–Angevin dispute on poverty.[112] Edicts against Robert and Sancia's protection of the Spirituals came fast and furious after Robert's sermon on this subject in the spring of 1323, a sermon that stated that Christ and the apostles had owned nothing; perhaps in partial response to such prestigious opposition, John issued the bull *Cum inter nonnullos* against the Spirituals in November of that year, a bull that rejected the premises of the Franciscan ideal of poverty and declared heretical the view that Christ and the apostles owned nothing.[113] Subsequent papal letters and recriminations flowed in a steady stream against Robert and Sancia's protection of heretical Franciscans in Naples in February and May 1325, with further letters in March 1327, and in January, July, and December 1331.[114] In 1335 Benedict XII ordered that the Franciscans in the short ragged habits associated with the group be expelled from Santa Chiara.[115]

Even before John XXII's letters against the Spirituals in Naples, however, his bull *Gloriosam ecclesiam* of 1318 describes the royal milieu within which the plan of Santa Chiara had been conceived:

There are many other things that these very presumptuous men are said to babble against the sacred sacrament of matrimony; many things which they foolishly believe concerning the course of time and the end of time; many things which they propagate with lamentable vanity concerning the coming of the Antichrist, which they declare even now to be close at hand. All these things, because we recognize them as partly heretical, partly senseless, partly fabulous, we

decree must be condemned together with their authors. . . . .[116]

Gloriosam ecclesiam brings out the extent to which the intellectual and spiritual milieu of the Spirituals and their supporters was deeply infused by the millenarian ideas of Joachim of Fiore.[117] Joachim's prophecy of a Third Age of the Holy Spirit predicted that the sinful and corrupt Church would be overthrown and a new Church would be created in a state of grace by barefooted monks, bringing about a new age of the Holy Spirit. The new age implied not only reform, but also, and more importantly (especially in radical Franciscan circles), the pursuit of the holiness (poverty, asceticism, celibacy) that would at last bring about the reform of the Church and end the era of the prelates.[118] By the early fourteenth century, Joachite thinking had evolved into a powerful vehicle for the critique of the papacy and parts of it became the ideological basis for opposition to John XXII.[119] It was nothing new, of course, to identify Joachite ideas with Francis – John of Parma himself, who had taught in Naples in the 1240s, was a proponent of Joachite ideas, but these views acquired special urgency with the persecution of the Spirituals that intensified in the early fourteenth century, as the Spirituals themselves seemed to be the "barefooted monks" who would bring about the Age of the Holy Spirit. The analogy was made clear by their ragged clothing and refusal to wear shoes or sandals, and this identification was promoted by many of the most articulate and effective supporters and advocates of the cause, including Olivi and Philip of Mallorca.[120] Arnald of Villanova, who has been mentioned as an influence in the courts of Aragon and Naples, was a powerful but controversial advocate of these ideas, as was Angelo Clareno, who wrote about them at length to Philip in the court of Naples.[121] Arnald and others in his circle certainly would have encountered Robert and Sancia while they were at Avignon before 1310, but probably the royal couple had already encountered these ideas long before. In any event, it would appear that Arnald was in Avignon in the critical period from May to August 1309, when Clement V was deciding the question of Robert's succession to the throne.[122]

And for those imbued with millenarian ideas, the events of the late thirteenth and the fourteenth century seemed to predict the arrival of the new Age of the Holy Spirit.[123] Several Joachite texts were interpreted as announcing the rule of Robert in Naples: the *Liber de flore* and the *Vaticinia de summis pontificibus* prophesied that the first of the four angelic popes would be aided by a French king who would be crowned emperor, end the schism, conquer Jerusalem (Robert purchased the holy sites in it instead), and end his days as a Franciscan.[124] Before the election of John XXII in 1316, the papacies of Celestine and Boniface had been thought to personify the sequence of angelic pope and the papal Antichrist, but after his election all previous contenders for the distinction of papal Antichrist faded into obscurity by comparison. In addition, this pope's persecution of the Spirituals seemed to fulfill the widely disseminated prophecy of a false pope who would attempt to destroy the evangelical way of life.

There is a tantalizing connection between the plan of Santa Chiara in Naples and one of the diagrams produced in Joachite circles to explain Joachim's historical system (pls. 141 and 149).[125] In the Joachite manuscript of Reggio Emilia, a rectilinear diagram illustrates his theory of the Three Ages and consists of a long boxlike shape with a series of lateral rectangular compartments

representing the main stages of the parallel ages of the Father and the Son.[126] Along the central longitudinal axis of the rectangle is a long trumpet-like shape identified as the *clarificatio spirito sancto*, culminating in the wider space at the end of the first and second ages. This last space corresponds to the Third Age, the Age of the Holy Spirit, and it is in a position that is analogous in the ground plan of the church to the friars' choir. Beyond this space there is a final compartment separated by a straight line, which represents the Resurrection of the Dead. In the plan of the church, this space corresponds to the location of the nuns' choir. In one of his writings on the Third Age, Angelo Clareno refers to the concordances between the Old and New Testament prophets and the angelic figures of the Apocalypse and Francis of Assisi; he noted that the fulfillment of the prophecies and concordances was to be attended by the choir of female anchorites and virgins prefigured by Elijah who await

149　Diagram from the *Liber figurarum* of Joachim of Fiore (Reggio Emilia, Biblioteca del Seminario Vescovile)

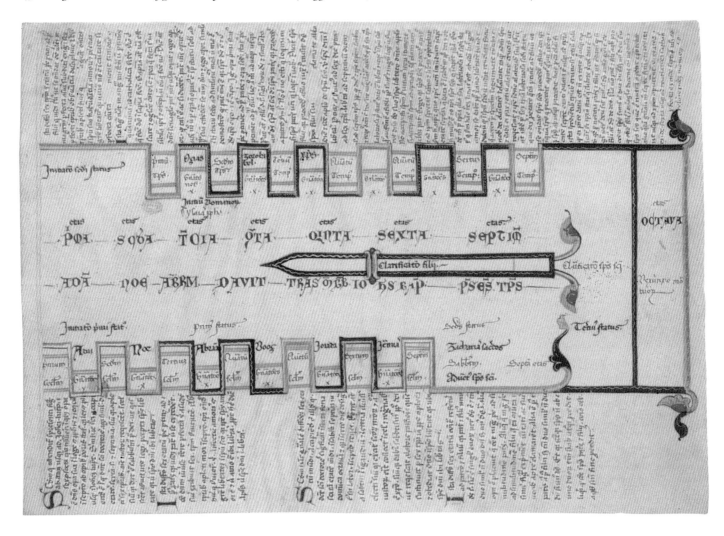

the resurrection of Francis and his restoration of the Church.[127] Musto has further observed that the theme of a choir of virgins associated with the Resurrection is also mentioned by both Olivi and Robert of Anjou.[128]

It is not clear that Sancia was in possession of any copies of the *figurae* of Joachim, but they must have circulated among the supporters of the Spiritual Franciscans at court. At her death a cache of "heretical" books was discovered in the nuns' choir of Santa Chiara; this included the writings of the former minister general of the order, Michael of Cesena (deposed because of his sympathy for the Spiritual cause),[129] and there were also Neapolitan copies of Joachim's treatises, some produced for court circles, as is demonstrated by Santi's list of Joachite manuscripts associated by Arnald of Villanova.[130]

It is also interesting to note in this connection that according to the *Anonimo Magliabechiano* of about 1536–46, Giotto's fresco cycle in the choir of Santa Chiara depicted an Apocalyptic program, one supposedly devised with the assistance of Dante.[131] This theme would of course have been in keeping with a Joachite interpretation of the plan in relation to the diagram of the Three Ages of Mankind, for the Apocalypse would have been found in that space occupied by the nuns and identified as the Resurrection of the Dead.

In his discussion of these matters, Musto also observed in 1997 that both Arnald of Villanova and Angelo Clareno placed particular emphasis on "enshrining into concrete form" the community that would make up the Third Age. In one of his letters, Clareno stated that spiritual preparation should result in some sort of *habitatio*,[132] and, similarly, Villanova made a precise analogy between verbal prophecy and architectural projection.[133] There was strong emphasis on the notion that, as Musto has put it, "mystical experience must immediately be transformed for human understanding by constructing some sort of 'tabernacle' to commemorate the intangible event in tangible, visible, form."[134]

The medieval universe was impregnated with symbolic order and everything had the capacity to signify something else: biblical texts were an inspiration for the conceptualization of liturgy and the spaces in which it occurred. As Crossley has noted, architecture played a fundamental part in "this polyphony of signs and references."[135] Abbot Suger and Durandus both use biblical symbolism as a generating force in the interpretation of churches, and there are a variety of buildings, especially in Romanesque southwest France and Spain (Tavernoles and Planès, for example), where tripartite plans clearly reflect the dedications to the Trinity, cruciform plans are dedicated to the Holy Cross, and circular plans are dedicated to the Virgin.

Given both the iconographic and literary evidence, it seems probable that the unusual plan of Santa Chiara may have been conceived as a secret (or not so secret) Joachite project, a plan hotly embedded in contemporary concerns that had special resonance in Naples. In some senses the project conceived in 1310 seems almost to have predicted, or anticipated, the subsequent confrontation with the papacy, which reached a dramatic climax for the Spirituals in general in 1318 and for the court of Naples with the disputes with John XXII in the 1320s.[136] The arrival of Philip of Mallorca in 1329 turned up the heat even further, presenting the papacy with an explicit challenge that was responded to with the inquisitorial investigations of the friars Andrea da Gagliano (Philip's friend and Sancia's chaplain) and Adhemar de Mosett in 1337 and 1338. From the testimony presented at the trials it is clear that Philip had pronounced at least one sermon in which he connected criticism of the papacy with strongly apocalyptic and possibly Joachite views.[137] Although the trial concerns events that occurred in the 1320s and 1330s, and arose out of the increasingly congested relations between the Neapolitan court and the papacy on issues such as the protection of the Spirituals, Apostolic Poverty, and the Beatific Vision, there seems to have been above all a ripening of the ideas and ideals (and conflict) with which the convent of Santa Chiara had been embedded from the start.

It will be recalled, too, that Santa Chiara represented an important departure from the previous architecture of the Clarissan order. The plan was specifically designed to provide women religious with a privileged view of the elevation of the host, modifying or even rejecting prior practice within the order, with the exception of Clare's own rule at San Damiano. The new design of a church with a retrochoir reflected the growing importance of Eucharistic veneration, and specifically recalled the initial dedication of the church to Corpus Domini.

But on an additional level the church of Santa Chiara responded to the powerful currents that dominated early fourteenth-century piety: it was envisioned as a center for the return to a Franciscan spirituality based on the original ideals of Francis and his first companions. The concept of a joint community, with coexisting male and female segments, may have been a deliberate attempt to return to some aspects of the first years of San Damiano. Furthermore, the possibility of a Joachite inspiration for the plan of the church suggests that the monastic complex might have been intended to form part of a larger attempt to reform the church along Joachite lines, and that the convent itself was perhaps to be the "stage" for the New Age of the Holy Spirit. The events of John

XXII's papacy, and the struggles between the Neapolitan Spirituals and the pontiff, put this programmatic vision into operation.

Finally, the Angevin cultivation of their own dynastic saints and the notion of a *beata stirps* largely dedicated to Franciscan ideals provided the perfect "sponsorship" for Joachim's Third Age. The church, its decoration and its tombs, would have existed as the center and symbol of the new revitalized Church (which at least for a moment might have been led by none other than Sancia's brother, the Spiritual Franciscan prince, Philip of Mallorca) in conjunction with a monarchy that defended and promoted the concept of apostolic poverty. The fusion of the Franciscan pedigree in the families of Robert and Sancia with the ideas of Joachim of Fiore seemed to sanctify the enterprise of the great double convent as well as that of Robert's rule.

But as Crossley also reminds us, some of the "polyphony of signs and references" may have been contradictory.[138] At Santa Chiara the many intersecting programmatic concerns revealed in the design and conception of the church suggest that the convent was established as an expression of the singular and personal concerns of its founder, as well as of the historic moment in which it was conceived. But at the same time the vast scale of the church, its decoration in the form of its tombs and frescoes, and its function as the setting for grand state ceremony, hardly seem in accordance with notions of apostolic poverty. In this way perhaps it parallels the phenomenon in late medieval book illumination known as "one-off" manuscripts, whose idiosyncratic and unique decorative programs within the constraints of standardized religious texts correspond to the personal whims of the individual patron.[139] Is it possible to think of such an enormous building as the exceptional and eccentric expression of an ideological program and personal whim? The unusual character of Santa Chiara would suggest that this was so.

And who was the author of this project? In the fourteenth century, there seemed to be little doubt that the project was Sancia's. Among the early sources, only the tower inscription links Robert to the origin of the complex, and this dates to the end of construction, not the beginning; it is possible that since the "program" for the church evolved by the 1330s to include state ceremonial, Robert may have wished to make a public declaration of his involvement. This convent was only the first of Sancia's many pious foundations in Naples, however, for she went on to found three other Clarissan houses in the city, and several more in Provence. That the queen acquired the reputation of having some expertise and competence in directing architectural pro-

jects is evident from later assignments that she was asked to undertake by Robert: after the death of Charles of Calabria in 1328, he asked her to take over supervision of the work on the abbey of San Martino; in 1333 she attended to the erection of the tombs of the King of Hungary and his wife in the cathedral of Naples; and finally she took charge of Robert's tomb after his death in 1343.[140]

Yet in all these varied projects, Santa Chiara held special place. Built at the beginning of one of the most radical and ambitious periods of Neapolitan history, the convent reflected the political and religious program of the early years of Sancia and Robert's reign in Naples. Its plan responded to the desire of religious women to participate in Eucharistic devotion, at the same time that it maintained their strict enclosure. These multiple and contradictory concerns, developed in an atmosphere steeped in millenarianism, led to the design of a church that is in some ways unique in the building traditions of Christian architecture.

Other Franciscan Foundations in Naples

None of the other Franciscan foundations established in Naples by Sancia survive. The most important of these was the church of Santa Croce, established with papal permission in March 1338 to the west of the Castel Nuovo (pl. 150).[141] This too was part of a double community, for a Franciscan house, dedicated to the Holy Trinity (Santissima Trinità), was established nearby, separated from the convent by an orchard.[142] A document of November 1343 guaranteed the isolation of the new foundations from other buildings, and a year later land was appropriated from the Arcamone family to add to the monastic complex.[143]

The convent was destroyed early in the fifteenth century. A sketch plan has survived, however, that reveals Santa Croce to have been a reduced and simplified version of Santa Chiara (pl. 150): the nuns' choir is a retrochoir behind the altar and there is a row of chapels along the right flank of the nave.

By the time of Robert's death in 1343, Sancia had changed her original plans to retire to Santa Chiara, and entered Santa Croce instead. We do not know why the queen shifted her allegiance, but we might wonder whether it was a result of the influence of Delphine de Sabran or Phillip of Mallorca, who may have introduced her to an even more simplified and austere view of Franciscan poverty. But by this time too Santa Chiara had become a "state monument:" the first burials there in the 1320s had initiated the role of the church as a royal

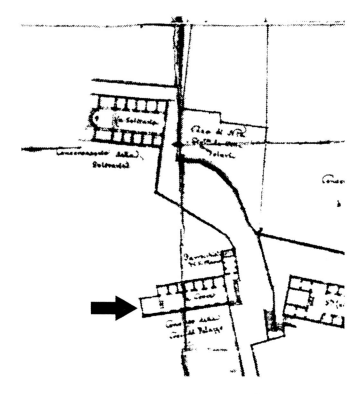

150   Naples, Santa Croce, plan of 1636 (from Colletta 1985)

necropolis, and the convent by the 1340s was invested with all the pomp of royal ceremony. At her death in 1345 Sancia was buried at Santa Croce behind the altar adjacent to the nuns' choir in a position analogous to that of Robert at Santa Chiara (pls. 151 and 152). Her body was found to be uncorrupted, it is said, when her remains were translated in June 1352 to the completed tomb in the presence of Queen Joanna and a group of bishops.[144]

The nuns and friars of Santa Croce and Santissima Trinità abandoned the monasteries when the Aragonese invaded in 1424. Joanna II transferred the nuns of Santa Croce and the mortal remains of Queen Sancia to Santa Chiara.[145] As Gaglione has noted, a well-preserved body, discovered accidentally in 1656 in the large cloister of Santa Chiara, was thought to be that of Sancia, but it seems more likely that she would have been interred within the church itself. Santa Croce was restored in the 1440s, and remained in place until its destruction in the late eighteenth century to make way for what is now Piazza Plebiscito and the associated buildings around it.[146]

Perhaps Santa Croce was intended by Sancia for her own, long-postponed, retirement from conjugal life and the court. Well before this, however, she had also established two other Franciscan foundations, Santa Maria

Egiziaca (1342) and Santa Maria Maddalena (1324) for indigent women. For the latter foundation, she exchanged the site of the church of the Annunziata, founded in 1304, with that of her new foundation inside the walls of the city. There are no medieval remains of either foundation.

The Carthusian Monastery of San Martino

The role of Charles of Calabria as collaborator in Sancia's projects and as an agent for royal enterprises of all types, from the cathedral to Santa Chiara, has emerged sporadically through the previous pages. The Carthusian monastery of San Martino, however, was his own creation built on the hill of Sant'Elmo and begun in 1325. It was left unfinished at the prince's untimely death in 1328, and Sancia in 1333, who had often worked closely with the prince on various projects, was asked to attend to its completion: "quod perfeci faciat monasterium."[147] Charles of Calabria purchased the land from two brothers in the Caracciolo family for 170 once. From the outset, Francesco di Vito and Tino da Camaino (Teni da Senis) were to act as supervisors along with the master, Matteo di Bolotto of Naples.

Robert assured the financial well-being of the house with the tithe on the church of Santa Maria in Termoli and the income from the customs of Castellamare for a total of 200 once a year, this to maintain thirteen Carthusian monks. Work on the complex was eventually completed by Joanna I and the church was con-secrated in 1369 in the presence of this queen, her consort Louis of Taranto, and many members of the royal family and court.

The choice of the Carthusian order seems to have been inspired by the Sanseverino foundation at Padula (see the next chapter). The counts of Sanseverino were closely allied with the royal family, and the splendid new complex at Padula perhaps stimulated Charles of Calabria's decision to erect a monastery for this eremitical order at the top of the hill above the city of Naples. The entire monastic complex was rebuilt and redecorated in the sixteenth century and later, however, and little more than the occasional vault or window survives of the medieval complex.

★   ★   ★

151   Tomb of Sancia of Mallorca (destroyed), from the album of Seroux D'Agincourt (Bibliotheca Apostolica Vaticana)

152   Tomb of Sancia of Mallorca (destroyed), from the album of Seroux D'Agincourt (Biblioteca Apostolica Vaticana)

Conclusion

It may be that the construction of a series of social and pious projects with a character that was aggressively associated with a certain brand of Franciscan spirituality was intended, or evolved into, an attempt to provide a new identity for the city of Naples. The *Cronaca di Partenope*, probably composed in the 1320s or 1330s, provides perhaps some illumination on these matters, since the narrative contains elements that cast a new and Franciscan light on some of the foundation legends of the city. The *Cronaca* in particular configures and interprets the Constantinian origins of the first cathedral as the "poison" of imperial wealth and pomp that was thus introduced into the Early Christian Church and led to its decline. As Monti pointed out in 1935, the *Cronaca di Partenope*, although based on the slightly older text that had emanated from the Cathedral Chapter (the *Cronaca di Santa Maria del Principio*), specifically associated imperial patronage of the church with its corruption.[148] The official history of Naples thus had a specifically Spiritual Franciscan cast which, if considered in the light of the foundation and construction of the vast convent of Santa Chiara, seems to have participated in the rather startling notion that the foundation was embedded with ideas associated with the rejection of the papacy in Rome (a legacy of the Constantinian transformation) and the reform of the Church. Carried one step further, the allusions to Constantinian decadence in the *Cronaca* could have formed part of a strategy to undermine the carefully cultivated pretensions of the canons at Santa Restituta, discussed in the preceding chapter. It will be recalled that the canons and bishops had recently cultivated the Constantinian antiquity of the building as part of a program to aggrandize the newly rebuilt cathedral and the restoration of Santa Restituta. The emphasis on distinguished "apostolic" and "Constantinian" origins had been used to add considerable luster to the cathedral complex and the historical foundations of the church in Naples.[149]

The historical chronicle of Naples thus seems interwoven with the fate of its two largest buildings. The shift of royal attention away from the cathedral (while it was still under construction) to Santa Chiara, and the use of the latter not only for state ceremonial but also for royal burial, may have been part of a larger movement to pull the center of attention in Naples towards the southwest, away from the old core of the city towards the new elite quarters around the Castel Nuovo and the arsenal. It also pulled the center of religious power and authority away from episcopal authority and its connections to the papacy in Rome towards a vision of a new Franciscan ideal. Some of this thinking was perhaps embedded in the plan of the Clarissan concept, if we can accept its inspiration based on a Joachite diagram.

In that light, the tower begun in 1338 at Santa Chiara may also take on special significance. Its massive forms marked the entrance to the old city from the southwest as well as to the monastic citadel of the convent. It marked the beginning of the southern *decumanus*, now Via Benedetto Croce, similar to the manner in which the northern *decumanus*, Via dei Tribunali, was marked by the foundations of the bell tower of the cathedral (when the latter was rebuilt after the earthquake of 1456, its greatly enlarged scale may have been an attempt to rival that of the Franciscan establishment across town). If there were power politics to be played out behind the programs of the cathedral and Santa Chiara in Naples, the two unfinished towers, each in its own way stunning in its scale and magnificence, might have been ambitious and doomed attempts to claim primacy and authority.

Chapter 5

THE PATRONAGE OF THE COURT
AND THE ARISTOCRACY IN
THE EARLY FOURTEENTH CENTURY

The traditional focus on the Angevin kings as patrons has diverted attention from the role of the court, aristocracy, merchant communities, confraternities, and the new religious orders in the foundation and construction of churches.[1] The interest in kings and court culture has tended to leave out of the equation other elements that were active forces in the configuration of the spiritual centers of the cities, and has overly simplified the mixture of interchange and collaboration that existed in the kingdom: it presupposes a top-down structure for cultural and artistic forces. This focus has also exaggerated the break between the first and second halves of the thirteenth century, that is to say, between the period before and after the arrival of the French, and perhaps too it has exaggerated the differences in terms of lay patronage between northern and southern Italy. For not only did certain workshops and artists move from working for one dynasty to the next, but also civic and ecclesiastical patrons continued the course set by their predecessors, maintaining traditions that had been established in the previous half century. Indeed, in some contexts, as we have seen, the Angevins seem to have inserted themselves into extant monuments and traditions of local importance, or to have patronized buildings designed with a strong sense of local tradition in the shaping of space or use of materials. For the most part there was, at least in architecture, hardly a French or Francocentric "revolution."

Most striking are the many Franciscan churches established in the towns of Campania; almost every center of habitation of any significance seems to have had at least a small settlement of the order.[2] There were also of course a few new monumental monastic complexes, sometimes founded in remote areas, the most spectacular of which is the Charterhouse of Padula. The Benedictine order, and especially its reform branches in the

form of the Virginians and the Celestinians, also continued to be an important focus of royal and noble piety.[3] Indeed, in her will Mary of Hungary listed the Virginian house of Montevergine before the mendicant orders, leaving them substantially more money than either the Dominicans or the Franciscans.[4] In Apulia, as in the cities of the Amalfi coast, strong traditions of merchant and civic patronage that date at least back to Norman times continued well into the fourteenth century, as we shall see at Barletta. A similar phenomenon can also be found in some of the towns along the Amalfi coast, notably Amalfi and Ravello, where there is also evidence of sumptuous private palaces and baths.[5] In all this pious work, however, evidence of bequests from civic patrons or members of the court to the Cistercian abbeys of Realvalle and Vittoria is strikingly absent.

This chapter will present some of these buildings and their patrons as a preliminary sketch of this rich aspect of the cultural and spiritual life of the kingdom. Because we are concerned here with a wide variety of sites and monuments, most of which are only partially intact or visible and some completely destroyed, the discussion will focus on the network of families who were patrons as much or more than the monuments themselves.[6] There can be no pretense here to completeness – some new and important studies are underway and in press for Naples, while more work needs to be done elsewhere. I hope here only to sketch a broad overview of civic and aristocratic patronage in the last decades of the thirteenth and first decades of the fourteenth centuries, mostly in Naples, with a view to suggesting that this reflects a much larger whole.

In the aggregate these foundations attest to the vital, and sometimes highly charged, spiritual life of the kingdom. And although the major royal monuments of Naples clearly had an influence on the types and dedi-

cations of foundations found outside the capital, some of which appear to be small-scale "copies" of Neapolitan models, it is also true in turn that the aristocracy had a role in shaping the spiritual tastes and views of the royal family (noteworthy examples might be Elzéar and Delphine de Sabran in relation to Queen Sancia, or Tommaso Sanseverino's influence on Charles of Calabria's foundation of San Martino). Bishops, as we saw with Filippo Minutolo at the cathedral of Naples, also played a fundamental part in shaping the character of pious patronage in conjunction with private patrons or confraternities, as did the Dominicans and Franciscans. Within Naples itself patronage was often tied to neighborhood or to the local *seggio* and was therefore "territorial;" the nobles of the region of Nido, for example, were for the most part buried at San Domenico and often used the conventual buildings to conduct affairs of common business.[7] The same is true of San Lorenzo Maggiore, closely allied with a *seggio* once located underneath what is now the chapter house.

Before proceeding with our story, it may be useful to reflect further on the character of the population of southern Italy from the advent of the French in 1266 to about 1350, for this type of information helps to place the patronage and execution of architectural projects in a broader context. Estimates of the population have varied from roughly 1.5 million (Galasso) to double that number (Filangieri, Percy).[8] It is reasonable to suppose that a good part of the population was concentrated in the larger cities (Naples, Salerno, Aversa, Capua, Bari, Brindisi, Trani, Barletta, for example) and the rest dispersed among the smaller towns, with scant habitation of the countryside. Among the poor, famine seems to have been endemic, so it is all the more reasonable to imagine that the voluntary participation in religious projects occurred only in the context of the upper classes and merchant communities, primarily where there were sources of external wealth in the form of trade (Apulia and the Amalfi coast) or significant feudal sources of income from fiefs.[9] Yet the feudal aristocracy of the kingdom was also small: Durrieu estimated 4,215 nobles in the kingdom as a whole between 1268 and 1282, a number revised by Galasso to 3,500.[10] Pollastri in her recent work has estimated that, among the French, 351 knights from 248 families received about 470 fiefs or parts of fiefs between 1268 and 1274.[11] But after this initial period, the war of 1282–1302 caused much disruption and displacement to those living south of Salerno, bringing a refugee population into the larger, safer cities such as Naples and causing a severe strain upon already limited resources. Durrieu and Pollastri have both noted the "fragility" of the ultramontane pop-

ulation in the kingdom, and, as we have seen, Charles of Anjou's attempts to attract settlers, and to legislate disincentives for the return to France, attest to this continuous difficulty.[12] Well into the fourteenth century, Robert continued to promulgate edicts intended to attract Provençal and French settlers to the kingdom.

Skilled construction labor probably continued to be in short supply even after the reign of Charles I, when masons were moved from one site to another, by force if necessary. There does, however, seem to have been a reduction in the number of large-scale projects, especially of course in the decade between 1282 and 1294, which must have meant that the crisis in construction labor evaporated for a time. But with the renewal of building after 1294 a shortage of skilled labor must certainly have been an issue again: we know, for example, that Charles II wished to reacquire some of the skilled Muslim workers sold into slavery after 1300.[13] It is also as evident as it is logical that there were clusters of skilled workers (and master builders) in locations where there were good supplies of stone, as at Andria, Naples, Aversa, and Cava de' Tirreni. As during the reign of Charles I, the vast bulk of the workforce in the fourteenth century probably still consisted of manual labor fairly unskilled in sophisticated construction techniques. Building practice was adjusted accordingly, with skilled labor producing those parts of structures where structural or technical considerations required their presence, and unskilled manual labor the surfaces in between. The use of *spolia* elements in foundations or in the quoins of walls, as at the cathedral of Lucera, might have solved some of these problems. Meanwhile, the records attest on occasion to the arrival of new architects from beyond the Alps: mention is made of Jean de Reims, supervisor and master mason, at Montecassino in 1349; Jean de Haya, architect, working in 1329 at the castle of Belfort; Pons de Toulouse, carpenter, working in 1328 at the castle of Salerno; and Eudes de Crespy, builder, in Naples in 1317.[14] This presence of ultramontane masters is occasionally attested in some monuments, as in the portal of Santa Maria della Consolazione at Altomonte (pl. 154). But beside the imported French expertise there were many Italian masters, both local (and in particular the Primario and de Vito or de Vico building families in Naples) and imported (a certain Angelo de Urbe, working in 1332 at the Castel Nuovo, Lando da Siena, Pietro di Gregorio di Siena, and, of course, Tino da Camaino).[15]

In Naples in the 1320s, for example, Tuscan sculptors were brought in to produce projects of special prestige: tombs and the portals of major monuments, such as those of San Domenico and San Lorenzo Maggiore.

154 *(facing page)* Altomonte, Santa Maria della Consolazione, detail of west portal (Chester Brummel)

These imported experts brought not only up-to-date artistic developments, but were perhaps also associated with special expertise in certain kinds of projects and materials: the Sienese masters in particular were especially skilled in marble carving, the materials themselves often brought from Rome.[16] These projects had a profound influence on other and somewhat later monuments in the Regno, such as the portals at the chapter houses at Sant'Agostino and San Lorenzo in Naples, San Biagio in Nola (pl. 155), and the church of Montevergine (pl. 157), the latter two of the middle or second half of the fourteenth century.

At the same time, I strongly believe that the religious orders, and in particular the Franciscans, brought their own architectural experts to supervise and quite probably design the churches of their order.[17] The similarities of the window moldings between the Franciscan churches of Campania (Teano, Eboli, Nocera Inferiore, Nola, Aversa, etc.) suggest that similar templates were used from place to place. As already seen, Franciscan friars supervised the works at Santa Maria Donnaregina and Santa Chiara in Naples – they were also almost certainly present in the various phases of San Lorenzo – and it is highly probable that similar individuals moved quietly and anonymously from site to site in Campania and elsewhere as the designers and building supervisors of other, smaller-scaled Franciscan establishments.

For the Franciscans there is often evidence, sometimes solid, sometimes circumstantial, to associate their houses with the patronage or support of local aristocratic families. These patrons either formed part of the surviving local nobles (the Filangieri at Nocera de' Pagani, for example), or the imported French nobility (the Estendart or Del Balzo families), or sometimes the Catalan or Aragonese aristocrats (such as the Della Ratta) who had settled in the kingdom. Although it is not surprising that the aristocratic patrons often mimicked various currents present in the royal family, the Angevins themselves provided a wide range of models and influences, from the predilection for the Dominicans evident in the patronage of Charles II and Bartolomeo da Capua, to the radical Franciscanism of Sancia at Santa Chiara. In between (and perhaps far more important as a broad phenomenon) there was also the more tempered Franciscan faction represented by the *studium* at San Lorenzo Maggiore and by Santa Maria la Nova.

Yet the inspiration worked both ways, as noted above. The foundation of the Charterhouse at Padula by the Sanseverino may well have inspired Charles of Calabria's monumental foundation of San Martino in Naples. As often as not, given the state of the evidence and the destruction of monuments and documents, one can infer some of these personal predilections through the choice of burial site.

Among the families who were conspicuous patrons of religious foundations or works of art were the Sanseverino (Eboli, Teggiano, and Padula), the Orsini at Nola, the Rufolo at Ravello, the Filangieri at Nocera Inferiore, and others, such as the del Balzo, della Ratta (de la Rath), and Estendard families.[18] Some of these families were French or Provençal (the del Balzo and Estendard) in origin, some Catalan (de la Rath or della Ratta), and others were local (Sanseverino, Filangieri, Rufolo), or Roman (Orsini).[19] In spite of their diverse origins, the families presented a small and in some ways a tightly knit group, alternately marrying with or feuding against each other, or both.[20] Because of the high mortality rate, a husband or wife might remarry two or three times, joining different constellations of families in rapidly shifting succession.[21] These are fascinating stories, centered on lives often filled with intrigue and drama, but only a small fraction of them can be discussed here.

Bartolomeo da Capua

Bartolomeo da Capua has been discussed already in connection with the reconstruction of San Lorenzo Maggiore, a church where his intervention seems to have been dramatic and fundamentally reconfigured the present nave and transept. Perhaps no individual was as important in the court and diplomatic affairs of Naples as he, and his long service in the court intersected with the rule of the three kings discussed in this study.[22] Born in 1248 in Capua into a family tightly connected with the administrative affairs of Frederick II and Charles I, he was educated at the University of Naples, where he became in 1287 a professor of law.[23] In those years he was integrated into the innermost circles of the court as counselor and familiar of the king, and as such was present at the siege of Messina in 1282. By June 1290 he was signing documents as *protonotaro* of the kingdom. He continued to serve as the right hand of Charles II, and in 1296 was appointed to the office of *Logoteta*. In these capacities he was vitally involved in the most pressing affairs of state during the reign of Charles II, above all the negotiations with the papacy over the debt to the Holy See and negotiations for the freedom of the three princes held hostage in Catalonia. After 1309 he continued to serve Robert. He was richly rewarded by all three monarchs, acquiring an immense estate, and when he died in 1328 he was buried on the left side of the choir of the cathedral.[24]

155 (*above left*)   Nola, San Biagio dei Librai, west portal (Barbara Bini)

156 (*above right*)   Nola, San Biagio dei Librai, west portal (author)

157 (*right*)   Santa Maria di Montevergine, west portal of medieval basilica (Barbara Bini)

Da Capua was devoted to Thomas Aquinas, to whom he dedicated a chapel in Capua, and he was closely tied to Dominican intellectual traditions.[25] He testified in 1319 in the canonization proceedings of Aquinas, and was one of the primary agents representing Angevin royal interests in this matter.[26] His sermons articulated a series of theories on kingship and various ideologies of legit-imization for Capetian royal authority in the Kingdom of Naples, especially during the reign of Charles II.[27] With Archbishop Filippo Minutolo, he was also part of the commission that wrote the new Constitutions for the Kingdom of Naples, promulgated in 1306.

The *protonotaro* was an active patron of religious estab-lishments in both his native city of Capua and in Naples. He founded the monasteries of Santa Maria di Montevergine in Capua and in Naples (Monteverginella), both in 1314, but there are no medieval remains of either monastery.[28] Both Virginian foundations had certain obligations regarding charity for the poor.[29] Until the end of the sixteenth century Monteverginella in Naples preserved a fresco on the portal that represented Da Capua kneeling beside the Virgin, holding in one hand a model of the church and in the other an inscription.[30] In Capua he also founded the chapel of San Nicola, sometimes known as San Nicola a Logoteta, as well as the chapel dedicated to Thomas Aquinas in the Dominican church of Capua.[31] In the Franciscan church of San Pietro in Capua he established a chapel for the burial of his father, as well as another chapel in the cathedral of this city dedicated to Saint Andrew. About 1300 he was given permission by Charles II to found a hospital and chapel dedicated to the Magdalen in Capua.[32] His chapel in the cathedral of Naples was dedicated to the Holy

Apostles. In Capua, Bartolomeo also founded a hospital dedicated to the Virgin, and a public bath in Pozzuoli.

Da Capua's fundamental role in the enormous project of the reconstruction of San Lorenzo in Naples was inspired by the need for a private family chapel in that church, as we saw in Chapter Two, and in that connection it is interesting that not only was he historically much more closely associated with San Domenico, but also that he chose to be buried in the cathedral. The patronage at San Lorenzo pertained perhaps more to broader family predilections than his own, which on the evidence of his writings and sermons was instead dominated by a Dominican intellectual tradition. The Da Capua palace, however, is in the *insula* of San Lorenzo, which was also the original site of the *seggio di Montagna*, which may have been decisive. The multitude of projects and range of orders that were the objects of his support suggest that Da Capua had a wide and practical view of

158   Naples, San Lorenzo Maggiore, west portal, detail of the left jamb (Giovanni Genova)

the role of the various churches and religious groups in the city, and that in some way he felt it his duty to support a number and variety of them, especially the orders associated with learning and reform.

Of this extraordinary patronage, the primary remains are the entrance portals of San Domenico (pls. 159–61) and San Lorenzo (pls. 72–73, 153 and 158). These are elegant testaments to the patron's taste and artistic predilections, in keeping with up-to-date trends in Tuscan and specifically Sienese artistic currents. Both portals once carried the shields of their common patron (although those in relief in the center are later additions); the original shields, like those still visible at San Domenico, were in mosaic or painted.[33]

The portals date respectively from 1324 (San Lorenzo) and 1325 (San Domenico). The former consists of three flat marble fascias of varied colors, separated by attenuated clusters of shafts, which continue into the pointed arch above as part of the archivolts. The pointed arch of the portal as a whole begins at the midpoint of its total height where the inner fascia becomes a three-part broken pediment. The lower third of the pointed arch above is stilted, thus creating a tall and spacious tympanum above the broken pediment. This area seems to have been specifically designed to contain sculptural ornament, possibly figures of the donor and the patron saint of the church, but no record of sculpture survives. The motif of the broken pediment, or tripartite lintel, is unique in Naples and may have derived from tomb designs in Tuscany.

This portal is strikingly original. Its beauty is particularly evident now that it has been cleaned, and the limpid and richly colored pink marbles can be seen. It is closely related in its design to the portal of Santa Chiara in Naples (pls. 162 and 164), which also uses antique colored marbles in the flat panels between the slender shafts. At Santa Chiara, however, the lintel is flat, which creates a somewhat more static design, and the marbles are used in alternating bands of color to create a more overtly coloristic effect. The capitals at Santa Chiara are somewhat heavier and more prominent, but in both the flat panels on the flanks of the door on either side terminate in delicate trefoil arches. It is almost certain that the portal of San Lorenzo is the earlier of the two, for work was still underway at Santa Chiara in the 1320s, and may not yet have extended to the entrance of the church, but it may not be unreasonable to attribute the two portals to the same master or workshop.

The portal of San Domenico has been partially mutilated by the addition of the Baroque porch in 1605 (pls. 159–61).[34] What remains is different in style and charac-

159 Naples, San Domenico, west portal, general view (author)

ter from the portals of the two Franciscan churches and the work of a different master and workshop. At San Domenico there is a deliberate play of black and white marbles placed in quatrefoil or diamond patterns in the fascia between the colonettes. The capitals of the door jambs are placed at the upper part of the lintel. The outermost jamb pilaster continues above the capital to form the point of departure for a gable with crockets, and the innermost arch is decorated with half-length figures of

163   Siena cathedral, detail of the baptistery portal (author)

the apostles in quatrefoils that rise to a central quatrefoil of Christ at the apex of the arch. The lintel is set over the flat surfaces of the innermost door jamb, so that the portal itself is conceived as a rectangular form, in some respects quite classicizing, set into a sharply pointed and gabled Gothic frame. In this it is close to the baptistery portals of Siena Cathedral, begun in 1317 or thereabouts, and the simplified design of the San Domenico portal seems to derive from this model (pl. 163). In the far more ornate decoration of Siena, there is a similar play of black and white marble inlay along the plinth of the baptistery façade, and a gable also surmounts the entire composition. But the portal of San Domenico also lacks the particular emphasis on classical motifs, such as the imitation of pedimental elements, that are ostentatiously present in Siena.[35]

We know, of course, that various Sienese masters were at work in Naples in the 1320s. Leaving aside Tino da Camaino, whose energies were concentrated on tomb sculpture, Filangieri also lists the Sienese master Lando di Pietro, who traveled widely and worked in Milan (1311) as well as Florence (1322–3), and who was called back to Siena in 1334.[36] Others have attributed the portal of San Domenico to Ramulo da Siena (or Ramo di Paganello).[37]

Although little remains of Da Capua's religious foundations apart from the reconstructed San Lorenzo, it can at least be said that the two portals in Naples attest to the sophisticated and eclectic taste of this patron and give an inkling of the many wonders that have been lost in the destruction of his other projects and commissions. The protonotary had traveled widely in Italy and France in the service of his king, and may, one feels, have taken a personal interest in selecting the artists to be involved in each project and bringing them to Naples. And so the fact that the workmanship and style is consistently Italian is noteworthy. Compared to the extravagant decoration of the portals in Siena, with their twisted columns, light pink marbles, and more elaborated sculptural decoration, the portals of San Domenico and San Lorenzo are decidedly muted and restrained, and we might find in their sober monumentality some reflection of the spirit of the buildings of Charles II. Was this an echo of the tastes of the mendicant communities for which they were commissioned, the style of the sober faction of the court, or a personal preference expressed by Da Capua himself? We have no way of knowing, of course, but the sense of historical reference in the design of the cathedral, the broad volumes of San Lorenzo, and the refined and delicate taste for equilibrated design and colored marbles in the portals of both mendicant churches would suggest that the patron may have had a decisive role in the character of the projects that he commissioned or supported.

Giovanni Pipino da Barletta

Giovanni Pipino da Barletta is remembered with infamy for his role as Charles II's agent in the extermination of the Saracen community of Lucera in August 1300.[38] But Pipino was also an active church builder. He probably founded the church of San Pietro a Maiella in Naples,[39] where he was buried, and established the monastery (now Baroque and transformed into a boarding school) of San Bartolomeo in Lucera, both of the Celestinian order. He was an important force behind the reconstruction of the choir at Santa Maria Maggiore in Barletta (pls. 165–67), having obtained a papal indulgence from Clement V in 1307 for the completion of the church.[40] For Charles II he also supervised the early stages of work on the cathedral of Lucera,[41] closely related stylistically to the cathedral and San Pietro a Maiella in Naples.[42] As we shall see, his patronage followed closely the taste and aesthetic established in royal projects, but was also marked by conspicuous favor for the Celestinians.

According to Matteo Villani, Giovanni Pipino came from humble origins, the son of a notary in Barletta, and

164   Naples, Santa Chiara, main portal, general view (Giovanni Genova)

began his own career as a notary.[43] His acquaintance with the royal family, first with Charles I and then in particular with Charles II, seems to date from the years around the outbreak of the War of the Vespers in the early 1280s.[44] Among the earliest documents to cite Pipino are the records of the dramatic trial of the families of Della Marra and Rufolo in 1283, accusations in which Pipino was implicated but of which he was to be acquitted.[45] His risky association with the Della Marras notwithstanding, he came to be much favored by Robert of Artois, regent between 1285 and 1289, who knighted him in 1290 and probably appointed him *magister racionalis* the same year.[46] In 1291 Pipino accompanied Robert of Artois to Provence, but by 1292 was back in Naples and well integrated into court circles. Royal favor was such that Pipino received permission to change the course of a road in the city of Barletta in order to enlarge his house.[47] He went on to become one of Charles II's most trusted agents and advisors, and was a witness to and one of the three executors of the king's will in 1309.[48]

In early 1300 Pipino was entrusted with the plan to destroy Muslim Lucera.[49] His triumph, obtained, it is said, with "sagacità ed inganno," led to many titles and rewards.[50] But the meteoric rise of Pipino was matched by the equally dramatic fall of his grandsons, who died in prison on account of their violent feud with their Della Marra cousins (once also close business associates of the family) and general brigandage in Apulia. As a result of these later events, work on Santa Maria Maggiore in Barletta, a project pursued with energy and determination by their grandfather, may well have been interrupted.[51]

The first project undertaken by Giovanni Pipino was the reconstruction of the chevet of the church in Barletta. Santa Maria is best known for its Romanesque nave and sculptural decoration, but in the early fourteenth century the original apse was replaced by a new, expanded chevet that terminated in a crown of five radiating chapels (pls. 165–67).[52] The expansion of the east end was initiated only twenty-five years after the consecration of Santa Maria Maggiore in 1267, for sometime between 1288 and 1292 a group of thirty-six wealthy citizens of Barletta made a collective donation for the "enlargement and beautification" of the church.[53] It is possible that Pipino formed part of this civic initiative from the outset, because in November 1292 he gave a house by the cemetery to the canons "ad opus dicte ecclesie."[54]

Yet in 1307 Pipino was still promoting the project for the extension and construction of the new chevet, as attested by the papal bull that gave him permission to

165   Barletta, Santa Maria Maggiore, interior from the west (Chester Brummel)

"ampliare e dilatari" the "opere sumptuose" with an indulgence of 100 days for all those who visited Santa Maria.[55] The indulgence granted by Clement V suggests that although projected two decades before, actual construction of the new choir may have been delayed until the first decade of the fourteenth century. That some progress was made at that point is suggested by a bequest of a woman of Barletta in 1313 requesting burial in the "cammerella" with the image of the Virgin, a location identified by Santeramo as one of the radiating chapels.[56] The first phase, the ambulatory and chapels, may at that

166   Barletta, Santa Maria Maggiore, exterior from the east (Chester Brummel)

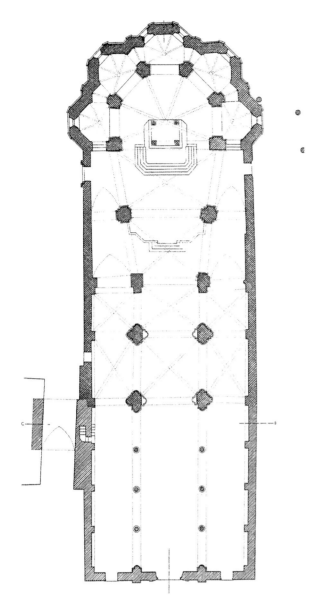

167 Barletta, Santa Maria Maggiore, plan (Soprintendenza di Beni Ambientali e Architettonci di Bari e Provincia)

width was maintained, however, until the (slight) projection of the first pair of radiating chapels (pl. 165).[59] Yet since the new extension had only two stories and no gallery, it was much lower than the twelfth-century nave (pl. 165). The effect of a change in scale is exaggerated both inside and out by the open wooden truss ceiling over the nave, as opposed to the vaults tightly capped with masonry cone roofs *a chiancarelle* of the chevet. There is no ambulatory strictly speaking, but rather a passageway inserted within the spurs of wall of the chapels that contain the hemicycle, so that the chapels seem to emerge from the polygonal volume of the apse in the manner of some churches in southwestern France (Cahors, Souillac).

In spite of the changes in design and in scale, the general effect of the interior at Santa Maria Maggiore is one of harmony and equilibrium. This is in large measure the result of the use throughout of white local limestone. The conjunction of an older nave with a new Gothic choir might even have recalled the disposition of the Franciscan church of San Lorenzo in Naples, but the evidence at Barletta suggests that the chapels at Santa Maria Maggiore served above all as burial chapels.

The Gothic extension to Santa Maria Maggiore and the career of Pipino both reflect the mercantile culture and rapid growth of the city of Barletta in the twelfth century as it grew to prominence and wealth. Barletta was an important harbor for access to the Holy Land and later the central haven for the Christian communities displaced by the Muslim reconquest of Palestine.[60] Like many other refugees from the Holy Land, the Emperor of Constantinople, Baldwin II, made Barletta his home after his escape, and at his death in 1274 Charles of Anjou commissioned his tomb.[61] The city was also to become the seat for the displaced Bishop of Canne, who followed the relics of Saint Ruggiero of Canne that were removed, or translated, to Santa Maria Maggiore in 1276.[62] The Bishop of Nazareth also took refuge in Barletta after the loss of his seat in the East.[63] The city was thus the permanent home of two displaced bishoprics and their attendant clergy, a rather cluttered state of affairs where issues of protocol must have been complex indeed.[64] One can imagine that in these crowded circumstances the canons of Santa Maria Maggiore were anxious to demonstrate their own importance with regard to these various and prestigious squatters.

In the late thirteenth and early fourteenth centuries, Barletta also enjoyed the special favor of Charles II of Anjou, who enlarged the port, repaired and enlarged the walls, and paved the streets.[65] All this was a reward for the city's fidelity at the outbreak of the War of the

point have been complete, but it is possible that the Romanesque chevet remained in place, and that the chapels remained as some sort of retrochoir behind the older apse for some time, for at his death in 1316 Pipino endowed the church with the handsome sum of 100 once for the continuation of the work.[57] His son and heir, Niccolò Pipino, Count of Minervino, had difficulty, however, in fulfilling the terms of the legacy, and perhaps for this reason the connection of the new choir to the nave remained incomplete until centuries later.[58]

The chevet of Santa Maria Maggiore almost doubled the total length of the recently consecrated church. Its

Vespers, but it no doubt was also stimulated by the need to present a *bella figura* to the expatriate communities from the Holy Land. The rapid growth of the population and the growing significance of the city were reflected not only in these public works, but also in a thriving community of money changers, tradesmen, and merchants whose financial resources in large part derived from trade with the East.[66]

So along with some of the merchant communities of the Amalfi coast, Barletta stands out in the kingdom as an exceptional example of vibrant civic and commercial life and of mercantile patronage. In this it continued a tradition of civic patronage that was also conspicuously present in other Apulian cities, such as Bari. And indeed there were many ties between the merchants of the Amalfi coast and those of Barletta, for we have already noted the links between Pipino and the Rufolo and Della Marra families.[67]

In connection with the civic character of Barletta, we may wish to recall that the five radiating chapels at Santa Maria Maggiore were apparently intended from the start to serve as private family memorial chapels.[68] This is indicated by the blank shields carved over the entrance arches to the chapels (once painted with family arms), as well as by the many transactions ceding to, or exchanging property with, the canons of the cathedral chapter, transactions that also stipulated burial in the cathedral.[69] Some of these transactions seem to have concerned property to the east of the apse, between the cathedral and the castle, which was once densely packed with narrow streets and houses. This part of the urban fabric (which included many churches and religious foundations) was destroyed in the sixteenth-century enlargement of the castle, however, so that the locations of the sites exchanged can no longer be determined.[70]

In spite of its unusual plan of an ambulatory with radiating chapels, the chevet of Barletta does not have many connections with the monuments in Provence and Paris that Pipino would have known well from his travels north in the company of Robert of Artois and Charles II (in 1291 and again in 1305–07, at the very least). The absence of any arcade moldings, the shallow three-sided chapels with few and small windows, the restricted number of colonettes attached to each hemicycle support (three), and, above all, the massive hemicycle piers and exterior walls that correspond in their dimensions to the pre-existing parts of the Romanesque church to the west (pl. 167), all suggest a continuity with local, rather than with imported, building traditions. There is little here that recalls French architecture either Northern or Provençal, which in the decades between 1290 and 1310 was characterized by strongly projecting

spur buttresses on the exterior and elaborate and complex surfaces made of complex groupings of slender shafts, gables, pinnacles, and tracery both inside and out.[71] Nor in the flat mural surfaces of Barletta do we find a relationship to the fluid and transparent spaces of the French systems of ambulatories and radiating chapels of late thirteenth and early fourteenth centuries. At most, we might look to the choirs of Cahors and Souillac in southwestern France, where radiating chapels open directly on to the hemicycle without an ambulatory in between, but even here the connection is remote.

However, in a general sense the austerity of the elevation of the new chevet at Santa Maria Maggiore is related to the other monuments associated with Pipino. Although nothing medieval remains of his foundation of San Bartolomeo, the cathedral of Lucera and San Pietro a Maiella in Naples may attest to Pipino's taste (pls. 109, 168 and 169), one that clearly reflects the models of Naples. In these buildings the rectangular piers flanked by semicircular shafts support an arcade, clerestory, and wooden truss ceiling: there are two such shafts attached to each pier at Lucera, and three at San Pietro a Maiella. The inner volumes of the naves are flat, because no vaults were intended to cover the central vessels. Although only the eastern apses are vaulted at Lucera, at San Pietro the aisles and lateral chapels are vaulted as well. The structural and aesthetic system, as we saw in Chapter Three, was derived from the cathedral and perhaps ultimately evolved from Dominican sources.

San Pietro a Maiella was founded at the west end of the Via dei Tribunali, the ancient *decumanus maior*. This part of the city had recently been enclosed in the new city walls erected by Charles II, and it is quite possible that the church and its tower were meant to mark the new boundaries of the city (pl. 171).[72] The site was fitted between the *decumanus* and buildings to the south and as a result the dimensions of the church were constrained: it was originally practically square in shape. The east end consists of a series of narrow rectangular chapels flanking the main altar. The outermost chapels formed part of a second campaign that expanded the transept one bay in depth and permitted the addition of the lateral chapels along both flanks of the nave, a project that dates from the 1330s. The broad outlines of the plan and elevation can be related to the general type of mendicant planning that has been found at San Domenico and the cathedral in Naples; the flat-ended chevet should be seen not so much as Cistercian as a reflection of the constraints of the site and of local practice in a monastic setting.

The documents of the monastery were lost in 1799, and there is no evidence for the date of foundation.[73]

168 Naples, San Pietro a Maiella, portal on east wall of nave (Giovanni Genova)

169 Naples, San Pietro a Maiella, interior towards altar (Giovanni Genova)

This is not a matter that can be resolved here, but we can safely assume that the project was in some way associated with Pipino, who died in 1316, and that its style is consistent with that of other monuments erected by Charles II and his circle. It is interesting to note that the outermost chapels of the transept, as well as the lateral chapels of the nave, were added in the mixed brick and tuff technique that appears in sections of the walls of the cathedral in the work of the first decade of the thirteenth century. Similarly, the portal on the south flank, facing the cathedral, is identical to the south nave portal at the cathedral of Naples (pls. 91 and 168). The extension of the transept and nave by the additions of chapels, on the other hand, would seem to date from the 1320s or

later, because the capitals are not unlike other examples that can be found between about 1315 and 1325 (pls. 172–74).

Two of the three churches known to have been patronized by Pipino were established for the Celestinians, and his apparent predilection for this order might invite some reflection on the character of his patronage. Although interest in the order has lately tended to focus on Celestine's absorption of the schismatic branch of the Franciscans (the Spirituals, or Fraticelli) into the order,[74] it seems improbable that this was the motivating factor for Pipino, an ambitious and self-promoting royal retainer who was rapidly acquiring great riches. The Fraticelli by 1300 were struggling to survive various and multiple

170

waves of persecution, and we know that Charles II (as well as his father before him) took a dim view of these ragged Franciscans.[75] The Celestinians were a reform and revival of Benedictine monasticism with a special emphasis on poverty and hermeticism. The order was organized along the lines of traditional monastic culture rather than the model of the itinerant, poverty-minded associations of friars that the Spirituals represented, and it may indeed have been above all this traditionalism and conservatism that Pipino favored.[76] In this connection, it might be noted that Pipino's tomb in San Pietro a Maiella is exceedingly austere, consisting of a plain sarcophagus decorated with the family shield.[77]

Pipino may also have supported the Celestinians because they were a local order, the most important founded in the second half of the thirteenth century, and "twice" (Benedict and Peter of Morrone) associated with southern Italy.[78] Given his intimate ties to the court

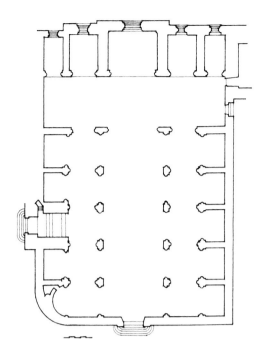

171 (*below*) Naples, San Pietro a Maiella, view of east flank and entrance portal from Via dei Tribunali (Massimo Velo)

170 Naples, San Pietro a Maiella, plan (after Filangieri 1884)

171

and to political circles, however, it is also possible that Pipino's patronage reflected that of Charles II and perhaps even formed part of the local opposition movement, or antipathy, to Boniface VIII.[79] The canonization of Peter of Morrone, promoted by the Angevin–French alliance and initiated in Naples, surely came out of the climate of the capital, which continued to venerate him, and which had found in his complacent residence in Naples a tidy arrangement with the papacy.[80] We might also wonder whether the ambitious former notary from Barletta was in the company of Charles II when he greeted the reluctant Peter of Morrone after his election to the papacy by the College of Cardinals in 1294.[81] In any event, Pipino would certainly have come to know Celestine during the latter's sojourn in Naples during his brief papacy.

If these suppositions are correct, it may be possible to see in Pipino's patronage concerns for local building traditions, local materials (both at Santa Maria Maggiore in Barletta and San Pietro a Maiella in Naples), and even local saints, as well as a general and deep-set commitment to austerity. These were tastes already associated here with Charles II, even if these choices might be a reflection of the astute suggestions of advisors as a response to the specific situation of the kingdom in the 1290s and later. The foundations of Pipino echo those of Charles II (the cathedral and San Domenico of Naples, the cathedral of Lucera) in the same way that Pipino's apparent devotion to Celestine may have echoed the king's personal intervention in bringing the new pope to Naples in 1294 and the later promotion of his canonization. In searching for an understanding of these matters, we may wish to ask ourselves whether the shaping of such a well-defined aesthetic in architecture was not the result of a collaborative shaping of taste between local individuals with roots deeply planted in the Italian south, such as Giovanni Pipino da Barletta, Filippo Minutolo, and Bartolomeo da Capua, and the austere tastes of their ruler, Charles II. What is interesting, of course, is that this strongly defined taste exists in spite of the broad exposure of all these individuals to the delights and luxuries, the exquisite refinement and delicacy, of Gothic north of the Alps.

Nocera de' Pagani and the Filangieri Family

There is a medieval church underneath the dense Baroque ornament in the Franciscan church of Sant' Antonio in Nocera Inferiore (pls. 175 and 176). But only the rib vaults in the chancel and the west portal attest to this older structure, whose presence can be imagined

172   Naples, San Pietro a Maiella, right chapel of the right transept arm (Massimo Velo)

as a single-nave church under the present layers of stucco and ornament.[82]

The portal of Sant' Antonio is, however, a fascinating example of the impact of French models on the Kingdom of Naples, and specifically of the "translation" of French Rayonnant forms, possibly even Rayonnant templates, into a local architectural language (pls. 177 and 178). For in the dense clustering of slender shafts at Nocera there is a direct relation to the clusters of shafts on the portals of the monuments most closely connected with France, Sant' Eligio and the displaced portals of Santa Maria della Vittoria. At Nocera, unfortunately, the lintel and tympanum have been destroyed, but the bases and keeled and undulating shafts create a series of deep concavities and projections that suggest that the template for the portal was designed by a Frenchman. The capi-

173   Naples, San Pietro a Maiella, vaults of the far right chapel of the right transept arm (Massimo Velo)

tals, on the other hand, could be the work only of local expertise, for the abstracted, elongated, and schematic leaves bear only a cursory resemblance to their French counterparts (pl. 178).

The models for the portal at Nocera date from the second half of the thirteenth century in France, and were brought to Italy in the retinue of Charles I after 1266. By the third decade of the fourteenth century, this type of elaborate portal was long out of date in southern Italy, since it had been replaced by the more classicizing taste for flat panels of marble interspersed with shafts, as seen at San Lorenzo and San Domenico in Naples. So the portal at Nocera bears witness to the moment of impact of French sculptural and architectural expertise in southern Italy and its influence upon secondary monuments outside the capital.

That this should have been the case is not surprising. The Castle of Nocera, the hereditary stronghold of the Filangieri, passed to the royal family with its confiscation from the Filangieri, who had sided with Manfred in 1266.[83] Elena, the widow of Manfred, was imprisoned there after her husband's defeat and died there in 1270. Until 1284 the castle was one of the preferred residences of the Angevin royal family, when at the intercession of Martin IV it was returned to Pietro Filangieri, who lived there until his death in 1290 or 1291.

The Franciscans at Sant'Antonio had been for some time the recipients of Filangieri generosity. Of Norman descent, they had been loyal retainers of Roger II and continued as vital members of the feudal aristocracy under Frederick II. Guidone Filangieri was buried in Sant'Antonio at his death in 1256, and an inscription in the cloister referred to him and his brother Pietro as founders.[84] This was confirmed by Wadding, who referred to both Guidone and Petrus as founders of the church.[85]

175   Nocera Inferiore, Sant'Antonio, façade from west (Barbara Bini)

174 (*facing page*)   Naples, San Pietro a Maiella, detail of capital, far right chapel of the right transept arm (Massimo Velo)

176 Nocera Inferiore, Sant'Antonio, interior from west (Barbara Bini)

Is it possible to see in the almost ostentatiously Rayonnant forms of the portal of Sant'Antonio a gesture of fidelity to the new regime? Its style is certainly consistent with other monuments erected in the first two decades of Angevin control in southern Italy, and its specific and deliberate evocation of Rayonnant models cannot be accidental. One might imagine that the portal of Sant'Antonio represents a form of homage in stone, a submission to the tastes of the French rulers, but specifically to the tastes of the first generation under Charles I, and datable between the return of Pietro Filangieri in 1284 and his death in 1290 or 1291.[86] And yet at the same time the clear reproduction of French types of moldings and sculptural decoration also characterized many Franciscan projects, as can be seen in the upper basilica of San Francesco in Assisi itself.

★ ★ ★

The Sanseverino and their Relations at Eboli, Padula, Teggiano, and Cuccaro Vetere

The church of San Francesco at Eboli, badly damaged in the Second World War and almost completely reconstructed, exemplifies in some ways the transition from French types of detailing, as can be seen in the rib vaults and axial window at the end of the church, to the profoundly Italian portal at the west (pls. 179–82).[87] The east window, with its heavy series of moldings, keeled shafts and arches, and tall, tubular capitals, recalls in many respects the portal of Sant'Antonio in Nocera Inferiore (pls. 177 and 181). In the chancel the rib vaults and the capitals are part of the same project. But between the chancel and the west portal there stretches a nave still partially covered with Baroque decoration and whitewash on the interior and plaster on the exterior, so that it is impossible to determine whether the church was extended to the west in a subsequent campaign, whether

177 Nocera Inferiore, Sant'Antonio, west portal (Barbara Bini)

178 Nocera Inferiore, Sant'Antonio, capitals of the portal, left jamb (Barbara Bini)

completion was delayed, or whether the portal was simply replaced at a later date.

The chevet probably coincides with the date of a papal indulgence in 1292, and would therefore be roughly contemporary with the portal of Sant'Antonio at Nocera. The eastern end of the Franciscan church of Eboli thus also seems to attest to the first wave of French influence in the kingdom, and so also do the battered capitals of the responds, similar to the equally battered capitals in the west end of Sant' Eligio al Mercato in Naples.

The portal, on the other hand, can be compared with the "plain style" fourteenth-century portals ubiquitous in Naples, and can be seen, for example, in the minor portals of the cathedral and at San Pietro a Maiella, both of about 1300–10 (pls. 176 and 182). The portal at Eboli, in the center of the lintel, bears the arms of the Sanseverino family, one of the great noble families of southern Italy and one that was especially devoted to the Franciscans. The arms of another family, as yet unidentified, are on the upper door jambs. The doorframe is enclosed in a handsome acanthus

179   Eboli, San Francesco, view of interior (Barbara Bini)

ornament that also once passed across the length of the lintel.[88]

The Sanseverino, along with their cousins the Filangieri, were among the older established local nobility of southern Italy. Unlike the Filangieri, however, the Sanseverino cast their lot with the French and from the outset were closely allied with Angevin affairs of state. Ruggero Sanseverino fought at the right hand of Charles of Anjou at the battle of Tagliacozzo in 1268, and he and his progeny were richly rewarded for their service with fiefs and properties throughout Campania, Lucania, and Calabria.

The area south of Salerno was devastated after 1282 by Aragonese troops, and the foundations connected with the Sanseverino can probably all be securely dated to the following decades (but especially after the treaty of 1302) as part of a process of reconstruction and restoration. The Charterhouse of Padula was founded in 1306 by Tommaso Sanseverino, Count of Marsico, on

property that had belonged in part to the abbey of Montevergine. In negotiations finalized in October 1305 the land was ceded to Tommaso Sanseverino in return for other holdings, an agreement confirmed in April 1306 by Charles II.[89] De Cunzo and De Martini have observed that there may have been pragmatic reasons for the choice of the Carthusians, because Padula is located on swampy ground that required the concentrated effort at systematic drainage that this order could provide. The area had been depopulated in the unsettled years of the war, which may have meant that the previously existing canals needed to be restored or re-established.[90]

The Charterhouse of Padula was splendidly rebuilt beginning in the 1560s, and only fragments of the original structures remain (pl. 183). The vaults of the church (covered with stucco) are fourteenth century, as are the various fragments of cloisters and dispersed capitals. An inscription over the door of the church (1374) attests to

180   Eboli, San Francesco, exterior from west (Barbara Bini)

the fact that work continued well into the second half of the fourteenth century.

Enrico Sanseverino, eldest son of Tommaso, Constable of the kingdom and Count of Marsico, married Ilaria de Loria (the daughter of the famous admiral Ruggiero Loria), who in 1319 founded the Franciscan church at Cuccaro, a small village now deep in the Cilento. She was buried in the church, now reduced to rubble with no trace of the tomb (pl. 184).[91] Antonino's description of the church in 1745 notes an inscription with the name of the countess, as well as a fresco in the cloister that represented her as benefactress of the monastery. He also relates that the church was filled with the tombs and private chapels of the local nobility, and mentions the date of 1333 on a pilaster.[92] All this is gone, and the rough

181 (*right*)   Eboli, San Francesco, detail of axial window in presbytery (Barbara Bini)

179

182   Eboli, San Francesco, detail of west portal (Barbara Bini)

rubble walls are collapsing under the weight of vegetation.

Enrico Sanseverino was buried at his death in 1336 in the church of Santa Maria Maggiore in Teggiano in a tomb designed by the school of Tino da Camaino (pl. 187). But the churches of Teggiano seem on the whole to have benefited from local patronage as much or more than that of the Sanseverino family, and the church of San Francesco at Teggiano, the portal of which bears the date of 1307, for example, has no indications of Sanseverino patronage (pl. 185). But a later generation of the Sanseverino family renewed the family tradition of generous patronage, especially to the Franciscans, at Padula, where, for example, Giovanni Tommaso Sanseverino in 1380 founded a Franciscan monastery near the Charterhouse. The family was also involved in the construction of the Franciscan house in Mercato Sanseverino to the north.[93] We can imagine close connections between these communities, not only through the friars themselves, but also the patrons and artisans. The sculpture in the apse of Santissima Pietà at Teggiano (pls. 186 and 188) bears striking resemblance to that of the nearby church of San Francesco at Padula (pl. 189) founded in 1380, and both can almost certainly be attributed to the same sculptor working in the late fourteenth century. These two apses are among the most vivid evocations of the development of the Gothic style in the latter part of the century, and attest to the continued wealth and abundant patronage of the Val di Diano.

★ ★ ★

183 *(facing page)*   Padula, Charterhouse, fragment of the cloister (author)

184 Cuccaro Vetere, the remains of the Franciscan church (author)

185 Teggiano, San Francesco, detail of portal (Chester Brummel)

Nola and the Orsini

The Del Balzo Orsini of Nola also played a dual role in reflecting but also perhaps inspiring royal patronage in Naples. Of the two Franciscan establishments in Nola, the earlier is Santa Maria Iacobi (also known as Santa Chiara), a Clarissan convent reconstructed by Count Roberto Orsini, whose arms decorate the keystone of the rib vault of the chancel and the frontal of the portal towards the courtyard (pls. 190–94).[94] The family arms represent the fusion of two important families of southern Italy: the Des Baux of Provence (italianized as Del Balzo) and the Counts of Orsini, lords of Nola from 1290, with the marriage of Roberto Orsini to Sveva del Balzo in 1333. The Orsini brought to Nola a powerful economic and cultural revival tinged with Franciscan overtones. This is attested not only in the architectural remains of Santa Maria Iacobi and San Biagio (formerly San Francesco), but also in the fragments of painted and sculptural decoration that adorned these churches and related to contemporary developments in Naples.[95]

As with many Clarissan churches, Santa Maria Iacobi was an older structure adopted and adapted by a settlement of the Clares who arrived probably in the second half of the thirteenth century. It has recently been suggested that the site had previously been occupied by a Basilian community, and that the dislocation of the nave in relation to the axis of the square chancel is the result of the earlier existence of the altar area. But as seen now, both parts of the building were reconstructed in the fourteenth century.[96]

The reconstruction of the convent was undertaken by Roberto Orsini between his marriage to Sveva del Balzo in 1333 and his death in 1350. His son Nicola proceeded with the work after 1350, constructing – or reconstructing – a dormitory for the monastic community, as recorded by a fragmentary inscription at the site. In 1394 Nicola Orsini was again involved with Santa Maria Iacobi, petitioning Boniface IX to authorize urgent repairs to the church. It was also Nicola who commissioned many of the frescoes that still decorate the walls of the church and the choir.[97] Evidence of these repairs can be seen in the shallow arch supporting the opening of the nuns' choir and its flanking capitals on either side (pl. 193).

The disposition of this small church, with a double-storied nave and tall chevet, reflects that of the recently completed church of Santa Maria Donnaregina in Naples. The nuns' choir at Nola, however, covers the entire length of the small nave, a situation that reflected the extremely reduced dimensions of the central vessel (11.10 by 6.90 m.), a scale no doubt determined by the

186   Teggiano, Santissima Pietà, chancel arch (Barbara Bini)

187   Teggiano, Santa Maria Maggiore, tomb of Enrico Sanseverino (Chester Brummel)

exigencies of the site and the popularity of the convent (pls. 193 and 194).

For all its rustic simplicity, Santa Maria Iacobi at Nola entered into traditions of Neapolitan construction in the early fourteenth century. The original capitals supporting the rib vaults of the chancel, with their long leaves rising from the base to the abacus (pl. 190), reflect similar types of capitals in the nuns' choir of Santa Chiara and at Santa Maria Donnaregina. The ribs are keeled like many of those in Naples. The framing of the exterior portals, with a broad single or double fascia that rises from flat door jambs, is typical of Angevin building throughout the kingdom, and can also be found in a number of secular structures.

The intense devotion of the Del Balzo Orsini family to the Franciscans is attested by some of their later

188 (*right*) Teggiano, Santissima Pietà, detail of capital, chancel arch (Barbara Bini)

189 (*below*) Padula, San Francesco, detail of capital, chancel arch (Barbara Bini)

projects. In Nola itself the court chapel of the counts of Nola, Santa Margherita, was given in 1372 to the Franciscans and transformed into the church of San Francesco, now San Biagio (pls. 195–98). The chapel was probably the work of Roberto Orsini, perhaps around the 1340s, but I know of no analogies for the richly patterned ribs of the chancel vault that are so striking in this gracious and elegant space.

The chevet is distinctly different from the nave portal, and this confirms that it was once part of the original comital chapel. It is covered by an ornately decorated rib vault supported by conical corbels and tall lancet windows, the bar tracery of which has been destroyed (pls. 195 and 196).

The west portal coincides with the donation of the chapel to the Franciscans. All that survives today

190 (*right*)   Nola, Santa Maria Iacobi, detail of capital, chancel (Barbara Bini)

191 (*below*)   Nola, Santa Maria Iacobi, entrance to complex (Barbara Bini)

192   Nola, Santa Maria Iacobi, lower church towards altar (Chester Brummel)

are the door jambs, the lintel, and eccentric capitals; tympanum and archivolts have been replaced. The door type derives in some respects from the Neapolitan type of San Lorenzo and Santa Chiara: lavish marble side panels set off by a series of slender shafts (pls. 155, 156, and 197). But the capitals, with their elaborate crisp leaves that project from tall conical tubes behind, suggest that this sculpture is late fourteenth century, probably of the 1370s.[98] The forms of the capitals have become highly stylized, even baroque. The fragments of frescoes that still survive in the church and its ancillary spaces, in particular a seated image of an Enthroned Christ, attest to the fact that the Del Balzo Orsini at San Biagio participated in up-to-date artistic currents emanating from Naples.[99]

The importance of Franciscan projects in Nola may have been particularly encouraged by its bishop, Fra Pietro Angerio, counselor and confessor to Queen Sancia. But the Orsini counts had for decades also been intimately allied with the Franciscan order, as indicated

193 (*right*)   Nola, Santa Maria Iacobi, view towards west (Chester Brummel)

194 (*below*)   Nola, Santa Maria Iacobi, the nuns' choir (author)

195   Nola, San Biagio dei Librai, chancel vault (Barbara Bini)

by their patronage of two chapels in the transept of the
lower church of Assisi. Their patronage in southern Italy,
and the model of Assisi, was to find a much later expression in the remarkable church of Santa Caterina in
Galatina, but that is part of another narrative.

The influence and patronage of the Del Balzo Orsini
was not restricted to the order, however, for Nicola
Orsini also supported the construction of a new cathedral of Nola with the decision in 1370 to return the epis-

copal seat from Cimitile back to Nola. This is confirmed
by an inscription recorded by Remondini dating from
1385.[100] Nothing survives of this project, but one
wonders if there were not some similarities with the
contemporary church of San Biagio.

Nicola Orsini deserves a footnote in this chapter for
two other reasons. He played a vital role as host and
guide to Saint Bridget of Sweden during her two years
in Naples and its vicinity, for she passed through Nola

in 1365 on her way to the capital.[101] Nicola Orsini later promoted her new order at the papal court in Avignon, and in 1391 he testified on behalf of her canonization. He was part of the intellectual elite of the second half of the fourteenth century; a famous orator and student of Cicero, he was also in correspondence with Boccaccio and Coluccio Salutati, and closely tied to Niccolò Acciaiuoli, with whom he collaborated in a request to Petrarch to publish his *Africa*.

★ ★ ★

196 (*left*) Nola, San Biagio dei Librai, corbel of chancel (Barbara Bini)

197 (*below*) Nola, San Biagio dei Librai, west portal, detail (Barbara Bini)

189

198   Nola, San Biagio dei Librai, exterior of apse (Chester Brummel)

break of pious foundations dedicated to the Annunciate Virgin in the first quarter of the fourteenth century, and often these were hospitals or hospices. One of the earliest examples was the hospice and hospital of the Annunziata founded in Naples in 1318.[102] Two years later the majestic hospital of the Annunziata was founded in Sulmona. Other hospitals dedicated to the Annunziata were soon after founded in Aversa and Capua, and indeed throughout the kingdom.

It is tempting to associate the chapel of the Annunziata with the Count of Caserta, Francesco della Ratta, who died in 1359 and whose tomb is in the north transept arm of the adjacent cathedral (pl. 201). His father, Diego della Ratta (or de la Rath) was a Catalan immigrant who arrived in Naples in the service of Iolanda of Aragon, first wife of Robert the Wise. Diego was present at the siege of Pistoia in 1306 and was involved in the defense of the realm against the emperor, Henry VII, in 1311. He served as Robert's vicar in the Romagna, and he was rewarded for his service by the royal family with the gift of the county of Caserta.[103] Noted as a famous *coureur de femmes*, whose reputation was mentioned by Boccaccio, Diego della Ratta was a fine figure inordinately fond of women.[104] Unlike his

199   Caserta Vecchia, L'Annunziata, view of the interior (Chester Brummel)

Caserta Vecchia and the Della Ratta

Tucked behind the magnificent cathedral of Caserta Vecchia is a small chapel dedicated to the Annunziata, a building that is unpublished except for brief mention in histories and guidebooks to Caserta (pls. 199 and 200). The chapel consists of a square chancel preceded by a rectangular nave. Only the altar area is rib-vaulted, and the triumphal arch is supported by capitals that seem above all to have been inspired by the floral designs in wall paintings.

The fragmentary remains of the entrance portal and the details of the architectural structure suggest a date in the middle of the fourteenth century. And in this connection it is interesting to note that there was an out-

son, Francesco, born sometime between 1317 and 1319, Diego spent very little time in Caserta itself. Francesco inherited the title at his father's death in 1325.[105] The young count was first married to Beatrice del Balzo, the sister of Sveva del Balzo, wife of Roberto Orsini (both Del Balzo sisters were buried at Santa Chiara in Naples at their deaths). Francesco then married Catherine d'Aulnay, the widow of Beltrando del Balzo, who died in 1360.

It also may be possible to consider the chapel of the Annunziata as a quotation or small-scale copy of the royal palatine chapel of Santa Barbara in the Castel Nuovo in Naples. The simple rectangular structure, the flat wall surfaces decorated with fresco (traces survive in the chancel arch of Caserta Vecchia), and the character of the rib vaults of the chancel all suggest a deliberate attempt to evoke the royal chapel in Naples. Most striking is what would appear to be the influence of wall painting on the character of the capitals, which with their winding vines are more pictorial than tectonic, to my knowledge unique in the Kingdom of Naples.

200 (*left*) Caserta Vecchia, L'Annunziata, detail of a capital (Chester Brummel)

201 (*below*) Caserta Vecchia, cathedral, tomb of Francesco della Ratta (Chester Brummel)

Montevergine

Of the many sacred sites in the Kingdom of Naples, few were more important than the shrine of Montevergine. But nothing more than two portals and fragments of sculpture are visible after the Baroque remodeling of Giovanni Ciacomo Conforto in the seventeenth century (pls. 157 and 202). A new basilica erected between 1952 and 1961 extends to the west and transformed part of the older church into a retrochoir behind the bleak modern structure. The Baroque and modern reconstructions surely represent one of the most terrible losses of a medieval site for the Kingdom of Naples; its lost

202 Santa Maria di Montevergine, portal, detail of capital (Barbara Bini)

marvels are only partially revealed by the beauty of the few surviving tomb effigies, now in the museum, and the monumental panel of the Virgin in the church.

Founded as an order dedicated to the Virgin in 1119 by William of Vercelli (1085–1142), Montevergine became a focus for local pilgrimage, the mother house of a series of monasteries founded by William and his followers in southern Italy and Sicily.

Although the initial phase of Angevin control presented a series of difficulties for Montevergine, the patronage of Charles II transformed the fortunes of the community. In a series of privileges Charles II declared his special devotion to the Virgin and monastery.[106] As Prince of Salerno he had already assigned an annual income of 25 once to the abbey from the customs duties at Salerno.[107]

A first church, consecrated by William of Vercelli in 1124, was enriched with the large icon of the Virgin attributed to Montano d'Arezzo.[108] The king exchanged lands with the abbey for the construction of baths at a hospital in Pozzuoli.[109] His devotion to the Virgin of Montevergine was continued by Robert, who as prince confirmed a donation from the customs tolls at Salerno, but the most conspicuous patrons of the shrine were Philip of Taranto and Achaia and his wife Catherine II of Courtenay. Philip in 1296 began a series of donations and bequests to the abbey, including in 1309 his lands in the fief of Tartareto near Sarno.[110] He also commissioned paintings from Montano d'Arezzo for his palace chapel, which was dedicated to the Virgin of Montevergine.[111] The fourteenth-century reconstruction of the church has also been attributed to the patronage of Philip of Taranto, and indeed the medieval portals that remain may date from his lifetime (1276–1331) or from the years just after his death. In the portals is seen the attenuated style of the central third of the fourteenth century, as in the portal to the chapter house of San Lorenzo in Naples. An additional royal brother, John of Durazzo, was also a patron of the abbey, and, as we have seen, Mary of Hungary notably remembered Montevergine in her will at her death in 1323.[112] Royal patronage was followed by that of the court: both Giovanni Pipino of Barletta and Bartolomeo da Capua were patrons of the monastery and the latter, already noted, founded several new houses of the order, among them Monteverginella in Naples.

The warm support of Charles II, Robert, and Philip of Taranto, however, could not match that of Louis of Taranto, second husband of Queen Joanna I, who ranks as one of the greatest patrons of Montevergine.[113] In 1346 he buried his mother, Catherine II of Courtenay, in a sumptuous tomb in the church and left generous bequests to the abbey.[114] Two years later he buried his sister Maria at the abbey, and placed her in a tomb next to that of her mother. At his death in 1362 he too was buried there.[115] Recently, Vitolo has suggested that the patronage of the house of Taranto at Montevergine was intended as a counterweight to the royal mausoleum created at Santa Chiara, and this observation suggests an attempt to destabilize the Franciscan hegemony of the court under Sancia and perhaps but to a lesser extent Joanna I.[116]

The museum next to the church at Montevergine contains fragments of several tombs, among them three members of the Lagonesse family. The Lagonesse (in Italian known also as Leonessa or Lagonissa) had come to Italy with Charles I in 1266; Jean de la Gonesse was buried in Montevergine in 1288. His two children, Charles and Catherine, were buried there in 1304.[117] In 1335 Berterado di Lautrec, another nobleman of French extratcion, was buried in the church with the remains of his son Giovanni.

★　★　★

Altomonte

The church of Santa Maria della Consolazione, in one of the most evocative and beautiful parts of Calabria, affirms that powerful ties to France survived and were renewed at regular intervals. The church was constructed at the site of an older foundation by Filippo Sangineto, Count of Altomonte, who as founder was buried in a magnificent tomb under the axial window of the chancel (pls. 154 and 203–07). Filippo became Count of Sangineto at the death of his brother in 1338; the brothers were the sons of Ruggiero, Count of Belvedere and Sangineto, and Cobella Sanseverino, a niece of Thomas Aquinas.[118] Noted as a warrior on behalf of King Robert, Filippo had accompanied Charles of Calabria to Tuscany in 1326, first as *capitano generale* and then as Vicar.[119] He was appointed Justiciar of the Kingdom and Seneschal of Provence and Forcalquier from 1330 to 1343 and again in 1346–7, and Robert on his deathbed appointed Filippo to the Regency Council for the duration of Joanna's minority.

It was during his years in Provence that Filippo Sangineto took on the project of enlarging the church of Santa Maria de' Franchis at Altomonte. He prepared

203   Altomonte, view of the city from the west (author)

204   Altomonte, tomb of Filippo Sangineto (Chester Brummel)

a will in Nice in 1336 in which he stated that the church should be repaired and enlarged.[120] He designated 200 once of gold for the work, adding that if this was not sufficient his heirs should attend to its completion. That plans were already underway in 1336, however, is suggested by the inscription on the bronze bell now preserved in the right transept of the church, which records the patron, the date, and the name of the founder, Cosma de Laurino (the bell was perhaps intended for an older tower attached to the previous church at the site).[121] In 1342 Clement VI issued five bulls in favor of the reconstruction.[122] Work probably proceeded rapidly, for the church is a simple aisleless structure with low projecting transepts, built out of rubble masonry. Some scholars, such as Caruso, have supposed that Sangineto's contribution consisted only in the addition of the chancel, transept, and west end to a small original structure.[123]

It is above all at the west end of the church of Altomonte that one finds evidence of renewed French influence and specifically of French workmanship. The west portal is among the most striking of the surviving examples of imported northern forms in the eighty years of Angevin domination since 1266, along with that of Sant'Eligio and the monument of Cosenza. The elegant and undulating moldings of the portal, in which austere and undecorated capitals alternate with crisp and crinkly leaf forms, and the rich floral medallions of the inner archivolt, are very similar to mid-fourteenth-century works in central and southern France. The leaf capitals appear only in the supports of the two statue niches on either side of the portal. Although battered and damaged, the work is of remarkable quality, in keeping with the delicate tastes of fourteenth-century France. The pattern of the rose window and eastern lancet windows (although also entirely restored) are also among the most original tracery designs that can be found in Italy, evidence again of the presence of French workmanship.

Altomonte is an impressive surviving testament to continued contact with French models during the eighty years of Angevin domination, and indeed in this it is far

194

205 Altomonte, interior from the west (Chester Brummel)

more "French" in its detailing than the cathedrals of Naples, Lucera, or any of the other royal buildings of Naples after about 1280 (pls. 203–07). This can be attributed directly to Filippo Sangineto, who seems to have imported master masons and sculptors from France to work on the church (pls. 206 and 207). But if the count was more "uninhibited" in his Frenchness than the royal family, he was like them in his eclecticism, for the tombs

206   Altomonte, west façade (Chester Brummel)

207   Altomonte, detail of west portal (Chester Brummel)

and paintings attest to his refined tastes with regard to Italian workmanship (pl. 203). Sangineto's own tomb is one of the masterpieces of the workshops of Tino da Camaino, and while in Tuscany he must have encountered Simone Martini, from whom he commissioned the small panel of Saint Ladislao, now in the museum of Altomonte. And the surviving *gisant* of another striking tomb in the church, perhaps that of Sangineto's brother Giovanni or his nephew, Ruggiero, indicates his patronage of other sculptors whose work is close to that of tombs in Santa Chiara.[124]

Sangineto's taste for things French might be compared to the strong element of courtly taste for French language and literature. As Sabatini has observed, there were a number of translations of Latin texts into (clumsy) French for the local nobility, one for the so-called "Conte de Militrée" and another for Bartolomeo Siginulfo, Count of Caserta until 1309.[125] The prologue to the former says that the translation has been produced "pour ce qu'il set lire et entendre la lengue fransoize et s'en delitte, a fait translater par ordre, secont la lettre, en françois la devant ditte cronique, et especialment pour sa delectation et pour la delectation de ses amis."[126] The emphasis on delectation suggests a world of courtly pleasures powerfully dominated by the French style in language and literature.

Some Conclusions

This brief overview demonstrates the vitality of the secondary noble courts of the Kingdom of Naples, as well as their important role in contributing to the shape of royal taste. Far from being provincial, the cities of Nola, Caserta Vecchia, Eboli, and others not only participated actively in the propagation of the styles of the court of Naples, but also helped to shape those tastes. There are suggestions that these patrons also had considerable independence and at times wide-ranging and eclectic interests as well, as we have seen with Filippo Sangineto at Altomonte. This was mixed with what we might consider the more emphatic and "traditionalist" view of individuals such as Bartolomeo da Capua, whose patronage also favored local traditions and local building methods.

In this connection, we might do well to close this chapter with a brief reflection on the particular difficulties of architectural "imitations" in matters of style. The elements of clear importation tend to be portals, capitals, and tracery, all elements that can be produced by a small, moveable workshop. We saw this in the Sienese elements of the portal of San Domenico, and see it as well in the portal at Altomonte. Behind and around these doors, the architectural language remains one that can be efficiently produced with the labor force and materials at hand. Unlike the other arts, architecture, therefore, participated only with some difficulty in some of the more fashionable tastes of the court, as it was almost always planted in the more practical and material exigencies of the place.

Conclusion

> What the court is, God knows, I know not. I do know however that the court is not time; but temporal it is, changeable and various, space-bound and wandering, never continuing in one state. When I leave it I know it perfectly; when I come back to it I find nothing or but little of what I left there . . . the court is the same, its members are changed . . . the court is constant only in its inconstancy.[1]

For some decades now it has been fashionable to frame the cultures pertaining to kings and royal patronage in terms of court styles. Implicit in this has been the concept of the stability and continuity of court cultures and their approach to the visual arts, as well as a certain equation between the concepts of courts and a "high style" of elegance. Royal and court production in the arts was identified with one overriding taste, usually that of the monarch, which was then echoed by his entourage.[2] These views tended to assume also that the taste of the king was unchanging, that the ruler himself was the principle generating force of the court style,[3] and that artistic taste filtered top down. But even in the long reign of Louis IX of France, which would seem to provide the ideal model of such consistency and continuity, there is clear evidence that there was a variety of different styles simultaneously in existence in Paris and the Ile-de-France, and that this variety existed in spite of well-established traditions and stable political conditions. Indeed, the highly international character of medieval court (and clerical) life in mid-thirteenth-century France and England meant that a monarch, his advisors (both secular and religious), and the court had many options open to them, options that could be deliberately and consciously cultivated to achieve certain ends. We are in the presence of a sophisticated and urbane clientele, deliberate in its selection of styles and the messages that those styles were to convey.[4]

Although the setting of king and court in Naples was similar in some ways of that of other European courts, there were also profound differences. For long stretches Angevin rule in southern Italy was relatively unstable, and this especially in the decades between the conquest of Charles of Anjou in 1266 and the definitive return to Naples of Charles II in 1294. French rule in Naples was also essentially colonial in nature and often at the mercy of the large-scale forces working throughout the Mediterranean that were beyond and outside its control. Most notable among these forces was the irrevocable loss of the Holy Land in 1291 to Islam, with great loss of life and misery but there was the more immediate issue of Aragonese ambitions for control of Sicily and southern Italy. Charles of Anjou's plans for eastern conquest were repeatedly trapped in networks of opposed schemes that moved against his domains, both from the East (Islam) and from the West (Aragon). His political maneuvers and those of his successors were in large measure tied up with those of the papacy, chameleon-like and unpredictable in its own way, as well as the pressure felt throughout Europe to recapture the Holy Land.

Thus, if northern courts can be described as complex and rapidly changing structures, the court of Naples was perhaps much more acutely so. Not only were the rulers equally itinerant and peripatetic, but they also spent many years entirely outside their Italian domains, attending the papal court in Rome or Avignon, making political alliances and borrowing funds in Florence, or as prisoners (Charles II and then his sons in Aragon), attempting either to negotiate treaties (in Rome, Paris, and elsewhere), and finally, raising funds for continued war (Charles I and Charles II again, in Paris and Florence and in between). When the ruler was absent from the realm large segments of the court went with him, so if courts are to be defined as where the ruler is, for the Kingdom of Naples this was often, and for long stretches, a court out of Italy, or at least out of the kingdom.

208   Magliano de' Marsi, right portal (Barbara Bini)

209   Magliano de' Marsi, detail of the right jamb on the right portal (Barbara Bini)

The more conspicuous aspects of the material culture that we might be able to associate with the court were, furthermore, ephemeral: clothing, tapestries, heraldry, spectacle, etc. None of this survives, and there are only shadowy suggestions of its importance from the notations in the Angevin Registers. Vestiges of the wealth and color of what would have constituted court culture in Naples remain only in manuscripts, in the fragments of wall frescoes, especially those, for example, in the church of the Incoronata in Naples, or in the dry use of sculpted shields on tomb monuments and church portals. The palatial residences that would have housed and contained king and court have been almost entirely obliterated or reconfigured; the gardens and courtyards, with elaborate fountains and waterworks, no longer even a memory.

The subject of religious architecture is far from representing a significant echo of this court culture: indeed to the contrary – as the result of recent research, monuments such as San Lorenzo Maggiore and Sant'Eligio al Mercato in Naples now seem more the product of the mercantile and aristocratic communities, both Italian and foreign, than the result of concerted and long-term royal

patronage. Occasional monuments attest the influence of royal projects and northern taste, for example the portal of Magliano de' Marsi (pls. 208 and 209), not far from the ruins of Charles of Anjou's foundations for Santa Maria della Vittoria (pl. 29). But in the long run, these could not compete with the vigorous local tradition of stone carving, exemplified in the Abruzzo by the richly decorated portals in L'Aquila.

The peripatetic and international character of the court of Naples, and its position in the heart of the Mediterranean, may also have meant, however, that the royal household served even more effectively than the other European courts as a venue for the exchange of ideas and information. This was a two-way enterprise: not only, and famously, did Tuscan and French artists work for the king and court in a series of splendid projects, but Southern masters also went North, in one instance as far as Flanders to produce the fountains and waterworks in the gardens of Hesdin for Robert of Artois.[5]

The research of Warnke and Vale reminds us that not only did the status of artists within the royal household vary widely in relation to their particular art form, but also that painters were far more likely to be absorbed into the household than sculptors and architects, whose work took them to shops or the site, and these quite possibly remote from the ruler and the court.[6] At the Angevin court, however, it is also true that certain individuals, such as Pierre de Chaules, described as familiar and "beloved clerk" of the king, represented the king's interests, and supervised particularly important projects. Clearly there was great fluidity and flexibility in these relationships and one individual might occupy a number of roles.

There was also fluidity in the extent of royal interest in large-scale projects. Charles I probably had little consistent or sustained interest in the arts – or, if it existed, such interest was difficult to maintain in the face of other more pressing concerns; his architectural projects were mainly oriented towards a network of control and defense, as well as palaces worthy of his rule. Charles II, once settled in Naples after 1294, is the only one of the three kings actively to have pursued a policy of systematic church building, and this was conceived and executed within the frame of a kind of mendicant austerity and spirituality. We cannot really think of Charles II as a patron of the arts, but rather as a patron of the devotional and didactic interests of the faith. Of the three generations, perhaps only Robert can truly be described as a "patron of the arts" in the sense in which we normally think of the term, perhaps in some ways among the first of the medieval kings to exhibit the kind of ostentatious splendor and cult of great artists that we associate with the courts of the Renaissance. But, ironically, it is also under Robert's rule, and certainly its most costly project by far, that the monumental and slightly fanatical enterprise of the monastic complex of Santa Chiara was constructed.

In all these projects, however, the Angevins were plagued by acute and persistent shortages of funds, even though Charles II and Robert shifted their priorities to focus more on national concerns and were less ambitious in schemes of conquest than Charles I. The powerful forces unleashed by the thirteenth-century religious movements, and especially those associated with reform and the mendicant orders, were to dominate the religious life of the court and the architectural projects of the kingdom: we need only remind ourselves how Prince Louis's decision to become a Franciscan friar and renounce the throne affected the course of its history. Thus, combined with a culture of ostentatious display and splendor, there was also the "mendicantization" of the court and its structures: this complicated and not entirely compatible coexistence of austerity and

display is today perhaps most visible in the royal and aristocratic tombs in the mendicant churches, where the court in the afterlife clusters around the tomb of the ruler as it must once have placed itself before him in life. In that sense, king and court appropriated sacred space and reshaped it to create a form of "replica" of the structures of the court.

The issue of burial brings with it, of course, the issue of French influence, because the Angevins brought to Italy, or at least actively participated in, the French custom of dividing the body of the deceased and burying different parts at a variety of sites.[7] This began with the tragic aftermath of the Crusade to Tunis in 1270–71 with its plethora of royal bodies (Louis IX, Jean Tristan, Isabelle of Aragon, among others) subdivided and transported up the length of Italy on the long route home. It is interesting that this particularly French custom, although continued by Charles II, seems to have been abandoned in Naples by the time of the deaths of Robert and Sancia in 1343 and 1345 respectively. By then, Italian tradition as well as papal proscriptions on the division of the body had reasserted themselves.[8]

In this respect we might cast one last look at the issue of "Frenchness" in Naples. Although this concept is fundamental to the literature on the subject, I hope that I have conveyed the idea that it was of fleeting interest and difficult execution. What is more, "Frenchness" was a concept broadly under attack in Italy by about 1280, not only for the political reasons outlined in the early sections of this book, but also for literary and cultural ones.[9] Although Italian architecture has been effectively described as eclectic and tolerant of complexity, it appears to have been, after about 1280 at least, distinctly *not* accepting of an ostentatiously French architectural idiom.[10]

Yet at the same time French continued to dominate the language and much of court culture in Naples. In literature, in other art forms such as metalwork (and no doubt in clothing and tapestries, etc.), as well as in court protocol, the Frenchness of the court must have been an overwhelming fact for much of our period. So it may be reasonable to distinguish between public monuments and private (insofar as the term makes sense in the social structures of the court) environments.

In architecture, in any event, even the fleeting taste for a French aesthetic would often have been constrained by the local exigencies of labor and materials, as has been considered in some detail. Furthermore, the importation of forms seems to have led rapidly as much or more to their ossification as their long-term influence, for certain structural and decorative elements associated with French Gothic entered the artistic vocabulary and remained essentially unchanged for decades. This is evident in tracery patterns and capitals, especially those at the cathedral and San Lorenzo in Naples. At times the imported forms gave birth to marvelous new variants, such as the flattened, disk-like crockets of the portal of San Domenico in Naples, but more often they came to coexist with a local way of thinking about space and construction. In this regard it is also interesting to note that the court was at times more overtly "Frenchifying" in its tastes than the monarch: the portal of Altomonte constructed in the 1340s by Filippo Sangineto is an example of this.

An important part of this book has concerned the observation that the rulers did not always play a generating force in the pious projects that have been attributed to them. Indeed, many of the most successful aspects of the Angevin legacy were those generated by mercantile and civic powers, as well as by the ecclesiastical hierarchy and the court administration. The role of the urban elites of the Kingdom of Naples has generally been left out of historical narratives, but Sant'Eligio and San Lorenzo Maggiore in Naples and Santa Maria Maggiore in Barletta, for example, are vigorous attestations to the roles of the local civic aristocracy and upper merchant class. These communities, separately and together, and of course in relation to the religious authorities of the various institutions, had a vital and conspicuous role in shaping the aesthetic agenda, at times clearly moving the king and his public presentation in the direction of locally understandable and acceptable idioms. How else are we to understand the cathedrals of Naples and Lucera? During the reign of Charles II, individuals such as Archbishop Filippo Minutolo of Naples, and the protonotary Bartolomeo da Capua in particular, seem to have been the advisors who conceptualized the new public and religious image of the regime, not only through the rhetoric of speeches and sermons, as has been well noted, but also through the rhetoric of architecture. The cathedral of Naples, with its references to a splendid Early Christian past in the reuse of ancient materials, in its evocation of traditions that tied Naples to the Apostle Peter and to the first Christian emperor, Constantine, through the language of construction (columns and building techniques) and painting, is the most striking example.[11] We might go further, and consider whether these men did not in some way *themselves* create Naples as a capital by providing the city with buildings worthy of this new role. The cathedral is one notable example of this, but so is also the extraordinary reconfiguration of San Lorenzo Maggiore assisted by Bartolomeo da Capua in the 1320s.

These developments in Naples were echoed by the projects of Giovanni Pipino at Barletta and Lucera, and the creation of the distinct identity of towns such as Cittaducale and L'Aquila in the north, although it is probably important to note that the tradition of lay contribution had a long history in southern Italy. We might then wonder if the creation of an identifiable Angevin character in the architecture of early fourteenth-century Naples is not as much, or more, the work of the cities and the court than the king, at least in terms creating an architectural language, a *rhetoric of building*, suitable to the circumstances of the country, its people, its ambitions, and its rulers.

I have proposed that a pro-Angevin historical tradition born in the anti-Aragonese movement of the sixteenth century emphasized the role of the French kings in shaping the material culture of the Kingdom of Naples.[12] The most conspicuous example of this redirection of the narrative is the example of San Lorenzo in Naples, where the building has been variously considered as a royal burial church, a conspicuous example of royal patronage, and an architectural testament to the profound importance of the French in Italy. My view is quite different, one that combines with the intermittent patronage of the royal family the important role of the Franciscan order and of the patrician families of Naples. San Lorenzo, for all that it is an exceptional monument in every way, is one also deeply embedded in the goals of the Franciscan order as well as those of the neighborhood and *seggio* in which it was planted. Here, as it were, it is the Angevins who come knocking on the door of the local institution, and who achieve through their collaboration an integration into a well-established local context, rather than the reverse.

The *Decameron* in its delicious and scabrous stories brings alive the world of fourteenth-century humor and delights, and some of these stories touch on Naples. But in a discipline that concerns itself with the material remains of buildings, and with stones and walls, the human element remains much more elusive, and the personalities emerge only with far greater difficulty. It is difficult and no doubt foolish to write about ghosts, but nonetheless this book is filled with them: the men and women who, moved by faith and ambition, created places for prayer and burial, as well as the prelates, friars, and nuns whose spiritual example inspired these patrons in the present life and whose prayers would guarantee salvation in the next. Above all there are here the ghosts of buildings, some gone forever, some waiting quietly to be revealed within their Baroque dress, others known only from foundations.

Appendix 1

CONSTRUCTION AND LABOR

A full discussion of labor, wages, and building practices in southern Italy would require an entire volume and the training of an economic historian. This is not possible here, but a reconsideration of some aspects of the labor force in relation to the churches illuminates the appearance of some of the buildings. Experience derived from the workshops of Charles I no doubt informed the projects undertaken by his successors.[1]

The Angevin Registers were one of the major sources on the medieval building trade.[2] The texts published before the Second World War provide insights into how the king's agents established building projects, organized the labor force, and administered ongoing projects. Although our interest here is in the construction of religious foundations, there are many parallels between religious architecture and the construction of palaces and fortifications. In the context of the relations between Italy and Europe north of the Alps, the texts that concern construction in the Angevin Registers provide an important example of the intersection of separate populations working together, often unhappily, on royal projects.

The wealth of the documentation on the labor force from the archives of Naples is unusual for the thirteenth century. Almost no documents survive of the great wave of Gothic building in the twelfth and thirteenth centuries. Most surviving texts on medieval construction date from the later Middle Ages, and, though instructive, reflect different historical situations and different social and economic conditions from those that prevailed in southern Italy. The English Pipe Rolls are the best-known exception, and have stimulated a wealth of scholarship on the practice of medieval building in England.[3]

The Angevin Registers are not construction accounts, however, and in this respect they differ from their English counterparts.[4] They are instead the chancery's instructions to royal agents at the building sites, and thus represent the king's responses to situations and problems that presented themselves on site. The nature of the documentation may therefore in part account for the impression one has of enterprises riddled with difficulties, delays, shortages of money, corruption, incompetence, and frustration.

The registers are also remarkable because we often seem to hear the clear voice of the patron. The king was impatient at delays and irritated by the day-to-day vicissitudes of the work sites. He had particular ideas about which materials should be used and where; he sent letters of great specificity about details of the projects, including wall widths, room dimensions, and the quality of stonework that should be employed. He harassed his building supervisors and threatened them with fines or imprisonment when things did not go smoothly.

The texts are dominated above all by the difficulties of finding a skilled and stable workforce, and workers were rarely willing to remain for long. At Realvalle and Vittoria there are suggestions that, as construction progressed, Charles began to compromise on the level of quality he had insisted upon at the beginning; this may be visible in the upper aisle walls at Realvalle, where the rubble masonry, which is organized into horizontal bands divided by smaller stones below becomes a disordered mass with no evidence of the systematic placement of stones above (pl. 30). The decline in the precision of the rubble wall seems to coincide with Charles's repeated letters urging greater speed to the works.

While some work was accomplished as regular wage labor, much of the workforce was conscripted. Specialized aspects of construction, such as capitals or roof tiles, for example, were commissioned as piecework (*in appalto*, *ad extalium*), and in those instances we often have the names of the masters in question.[5] The nature of specially contracted work varied widely in scale and was commissioned for different purposes, from the walls of the castle of Manfredonia built by Maraldo di Monte Sant'Angelo,[6] to the specifically carved elements (shafts, capitals, and ribs) at the abbey of Realvalle.[7] Wages, however, were standardized throughout the kingdom, so that workers were paid at the same rate from Campania to Calabria and through Apulia, irrespective of local differences in the availability of workers or the cost of living.[8] But almost everywhere workers were scarce, and some were brought to work at one site at the apparent expense of the completion of another.[9]

LAYOUT AND SETTLEMENT

As seen in Chapter One, the abbeys of Realvalle and Vittoria were established by the combined forces of Cistercian monks and royal agents, some of whom seem to have been friars in other orders. Although the agreement on the foundations dated from almost a year before, at neither site was action taken until the two pairs of French monks from Royaumont and Loroux arrived in Naples. Then planning teams were sent out to each of the sites, with the pairs of monks accompanied by an abbot from one of the local Cistercian houses and three or four royal representatives.[10]

The first monks arrived in January 1274 to establish the abbey of Vittoria in the Abruzzo, near the battle site on which Conradin was defeated. These were the Frenchmen Peter and John from the abbey of Oratorio (Loroux) in Angers; the royal representatives were Fra Giacomo, Pierre de Chaules,[11] Simon de Angart, and Pietro de Carrellis.[12] Also included in the initial party was the abbot of Casanova, a Cistercian abbey in the Abruzzo. The group left Naples for the Abruzzo early in January to establish the exact location of the abbey and to estimate the number of workmen and materials necessary for construction.[13] This was done with exemplary efficiency, for on 6 February 1274 Charles was able to establish the administrative structure for the project.[14]

The team who set out the project at Tagliacozzo thus consisted of four representatives of the king, one of whom was a friar, and three representatives of the Cistercian order. When the permanent administration was established at Vittoria, a balance between royal and monastic interests was maintained, for the Cistercian monk Peter of Oratorio and the judge Angelo da Foggia were named as accountants (*expensores operis*). By this time, the second monk, John, disappears from the records, and we can probably assume that he died or returned home, since the instructions in the founding documents had specified that two Cistercian monks were to represent the prerogatives of the order in the disposition of the buildings. The two *expensores* at Vittoria worked under the direction of the general supervisor, Pierre de Chaules, who subsequently took over that function at the abbey of Realvalle as well.

At Vittoria the layout of the site and the estimates of cost were accomplished quickly, and by 6 February Charles was in a position to appoint the administrators of the project. The *praepositus*, or general supervisor, was Pierre de Chaules, "beloved cleric" of the king and familiar of the court. His name appears in the Angevin Registers over the next decade in connection with the supervision and possibly the design of a large number of royal building projects including the Castel Nuovo in Naples, but he is never designated as *prothomagister*, or architect.[15] Under Pierre de Chaules one of the two accountants, Angelo da Foggia, was replaced in March 1274 by Giovanni de Variano, who in turn was removed from office in disgrace in 1278.[16] Giovanni de Variano and Peter of Oratorio had to approve of all expenditures together, and their accounts had in turn to be supervised by Pierre de Chaules.[17]

The plan of Vittoria (pl. 28) must have been established by the monks from Oratorio, who probably brought it with them from France. In spite of the homogeneity of the architecture of the order, Cistercian regulations for the layout of new abbeys were few and usually consisted of broad prescriptions consisting primarily of proportional relationships

and building "after our manner."[18] The plan of Vittoria is the first (and only) example in Italy of the expanded rectangular east end.[19] Unfortunately, Loroux, the mother house of Vittoria and a daughter of Cîteaux, is completely destroyed, so it is unknown whether its plan conformed to the expanded rectangular chevet of Vittoria.

This may mean that Peter of Oratorio was the architectural designer, a hypothesis perhaps supported by the apparent absence of an architect (*prothomagister*) at Vittoria until 1277. At Realvalle, on the other hand, neither of the monks seems to have had particular architectural expertise, and *prothomagister* Gauthier d'Asson was named from the outset and was present at the site until 1278.[20]

We might observe that although the Cistercians acquired great fame in Europe as builders, and were especially important in this respect in Italy, the numbers of monks or *conversi* (lay brothers) who had expertise in construction seem to have been in decline by the middle of the thirteenth century, in spite of occasional evidence for a continued monastic role in the building trade.[21] The situation at Vittoria, of course, may also reflect the general circumstances of Angevin building projects in general, where the shortage of trained masons and supervisors often required a certain flexibility and fluidity of responsibility. Pierre de Chaules, for example, who appears as general supervisor at Realvalle and Vittoria, perhaps assumed the role of architect for the Castel Nuovo in Naples by 1279, though he is not given the title of architect in the documents.[22]

Elsewhere we noted the lacuna in the documents from 1274 until 1277. However, it seems that the sums of 100 once were sent to each site every month, albeit often late.[23] Charles wrote in early July 1277 to the abbots of Loroux and Royaumont requesting twenty monks and ten *conversi* to come to each of the new foundations, asking that they arrive at the sites by the feast of Saint Martin (11 November).[24] At the same time, in a flurry of other letters, the king wrote to the abbots of the Cistercian order informing them that of the two abbeys Realvalle had precedence because it was founded in honor of his first victory at Benevento. He also wrote to his bailiffs in the Anjou instructing them to cover the travel expenses of the monks from Oratorio and Royaumont as far as Marseilles.[25] Exactly a month later, on 3 August 1277, he wrote again to his bailiffs in Angers ordering eight missals, eight graduals, eight antiphonaries, and four lectionaries, two for regular days and two for feast days.[26] At the end of December 1277 a brother Nicholas was appointed abbot by Charles, Prince of Salerno.[27] A document of 4 September 1278 mentions that at Realvalle there were now thirty-seven monks and *conversi*.[28] With the arrival of the Cistercian monks from Oratorio to the abbey of Vittoria, their abbot, Bartholomew, replaced the monk Peter as *expensoris operis* and the latter disappears from the documents.[29]

By April 1278 great progress appears to have been made at Realvalle, for a request was sent to the king to send eight additional carpenters for the lifting devices for the large stones and for the construction of all other elements in wood required by the masons and stone layers.[30] At Vittoria in May 1278, however, the workforce was small, and construction seems to have proceeded slowly. A request went out on 12 May 1278 for twenty-four wall builders, ten carpenters, twenty-five stone carvers, eight rough cutters, eighty manual laborers, twelve *incisores nemorum*, one locksmith, and six smiths, as well as men for the quarries and wagons.[31] But no workers appeared on the scene. The king's agent, Gualtiero, expecting his return in June, sent his *prothomagister*, Henry d'Asson, to Rome to explain the urgent need for workers at the abbey. On 6 June Charles renewed his orders for the workmen for the site, and went into some detail on the quality of construction to be achieved: "the construction of the church should be accomplished in formwork, but with cut stone used in the corners, the windows, the arches, ribs, and pillars . . ."[32] Much later, in 1282, however, when the structure was close to completion, Charles seems to have modified his standards for the quality of construction, stating that the vaults could be constructed in any sort of stone ("de omnibus lapidibus"), but that the pilasters, the arches, the windows, and the doors should be built "of cut stone of the best and strongest quality suitable to the ornamentation of the work."[33] Did he also mean the flat wall surfaces? At Vittoria the walls have been razed almost to the foundations, but old photographs suggest that they were of rubble masonry (pl. 29). The aisle walls at Realvalle, which were built of a mixture of large and roughly shaped stones combined with finely cut responds (pl. 30).

On 31 March 1279 a document was issued by the royal chancery concerning the assignment to the work at Realvalle of 8 once and 24 tari for each month of work from 1 April for eight stonecutters (*tagliapietri*), eight wagon drivers, and six helpers.[34] But clearly this was not a large enough workforce to permit construction to continue with sufficient speed. On 21 May 1279 the king issued a long document for the rapid completion of Realvalle "si que en icelle soit ovré plus diligemment et plus hastivement et mieuz que l'en i a accoustumé."[35] For the construction of the wall ("en l'euvre des meurs"), on which by that time there were working fifteen masons, should be added eight, for a total of twenty-three. These were to be assisted by ninety-two maniples, that is: four assistants per mason, and twelve laborers to carry the stones to the wall ("pour aporter les grosses pierres entalliées au mur"). For the cutting of stone ("pour entailler pierre"), there would be added to the eighteen at the site twenty-two others, thus providing a total of forty stonecutters. To extract and rough shape the stone, "pur eschapler pierre," there should continue to be twelve quarriers/rough shapers (*eschapleurs*) at the quarry of Sarno, but at the quarry of Moulins where there had been no quarriers, ten should be appointed, and at the quarry of Munchières les Crétiens (Nocera dei Cristiani) four additional scapplers (rough shapers) should be added to the twelve at the site, for a total of thirty-eight scapplers/quarriers at the three quarries. The sixteen quarriers at Nocera would each receive an assistant.

In the same document, the king specified that there should be at Realvalle one smith with three assistants, and four new carpenters "pour faire argaz et rapareillier et fere les buarz et autres lengnemenz necessaires pour icele euvre." These were to be in addition to the two carpenters already at the site, one more whose responsibility lay specifically with the repair of the wagons. The document then goes on to specify the types and varieties of barges that are to be constructed to bring stone from the quarries to the site.

Thus, in May 1279 the workforce at Realvalle consisted of the following

23 wall builders
40 stonecutters
38 scapplers/quarriers
92 assistants for the wall builders
16 assistants for the scapplers/quarriers at Nocera
12 manual laborers for the carrying of stones to the walls under construction
7 carpenters
1 smith
3 assistants to the smith
35 wagon drivers

There was a total of 267 workers, all under the supervision of two *expensores operis*, two superintendents, one *prothomagister*, and one notary. These workers were all paid a *per diem* fee.

But clearly the workforce was still not sufficient, and in particular it does not seem to have had an adequate number of skilled stonecarvers. Therefore, on 30 June 1279, the king specified that four masons, Iohannes de Zalono, Guillielmo de Blesi, Iohannes de Maloctis, and Robertus de Reus, should carve stones *ad extalium* (by the piece) in accordance with the instructions of the master mason.[36] The document goes on to give the price of the different elements in question:

For a full capital in the nave, 15 tari
For an engaged capital against the walls, 10 tari
For double capitals, 20 tari
For all the "charges" (vault departures and ribs), 1 once each

Furthermore, the carving of plinths, bases, and shafts was contracted out to two Neapolitan masons, Berutus de Vico de Principatu and Michael de Neapoli, at the rate of 25 onces each, at the rate of 2 auri and 15 tari per support, for ten columns.

The workforce of 267 laborers was thus increased by six "specialist" carvers assigned to the sculpting of columns, capitals, and vault departures. We can still see their work at Realvalle in the shafts that rise to the vault departures, carved from grey tuff, as well as in the capitals and the few surviving beds of the vault departures (pls. 35 and 36).

Another document, of 15 February 1282, modified the disposition of the workforce at Realvalle and increased it to the following:[37]

40 stonecutters in the lodge (*incisores lapidum*)
18 quarriers in the quarry of Nocera de Cristiani (*scappatores lapidum*)
10 manual laborers to assist the quarriers at Nocera

15 quarriers at the quarry of Sarno
10 manual laborers to assist the quarriers of Sarno
24 stone cutters (*magistris fabricatoribus*)
4 stone layers for the walls (*magistris assettatoribus lapidum in fabrica murorum*)[38]
96 manual laborers
16 manual laborers to make the lifting devices and hurdles
3 smiths
6 assistants to the smiths
4 master carpenters
41 drivers of the wagons and carts
3 boatmen assigned to leading and steering one boat and two barges
1 other boatman for another barge
10 drivers of the barges/skiff
8 manual workers to dig foundations
4 French supervisors
1 master mason
1 steward
2 accountants
2 master mortar makers

and for the beams to be brought from Calabria:

33 carpenters ("personis deputatis ad laborandum et assettandum lignamen quod delatum est a Calabria")
1 bargeman ("alio gubernatore et ductore unios alterius scafe facte de novo et assignate per Iustitiarium Principatus")
4 boatmen

Thus, a total of 352 workers at different levels was employed in the construction of the monastery of Realvalle. The manual laborers were increased slightly on 17 April 1282 at the quarry of Nocera to eighteen.[39] A document of 1279 regards the employment, "ad extalium," of a certain Thomas *tegularius* who was to provide the roof tiles "ad modum francie" for the covering of the church, refectory, dormitory, and all other buildings of the monastery.[40] The production of the roof tiles does not mean that the buildings were complete, but rather that the wooden beams for the roofs were soon to be in place and that work on vaulting would then begin. Presumably the production of the tiles would have taken place at the site, and it would have taken some time to build a kiln and produce the numbers of tiles required. One can assume that roofing was projected for 1280 and 1281, with the vaults of the church to follow afterwards.

In May 1284 the two accountants at Realvalle were asked to submit their final accounts.[41]

There were variations between winter and summer at the work site, and these were especially notable at Vittoria, which is about 700 meters above sea level and where winters would have been far more severe than at the site of Realvalle. In January 1280 there were only five wall builders and three stonecutters at Vittoria.[42] But from April onwards, the king ordered that there should be present:

38 quarriers
30 wall builders

7 rough shapers (*spuntatori*)
38 stonecutters
3 stone layers (*asseeurs de pierres*)
3 carpenters
3 smiths
162 manual laborers
14 cart drivers
38 bull drivers
4 supervisors

For a total of 336 workmen,[43] directed by four supervisors and a master builder.

As work neared completion at Vittoria there was an acceleration of the pace and an increase in the numbers of workmen. In 1280 at Vittoria the workforce shifted in the wintertime to the quarry, where it was adjusted in the following fashion:

50 quarriers
27 rough shapers
40 fine shapers (*scalpellini*) working in the lodge
10 more carpenters

But there were no wall builders, and manual labor was reduced from 162 to 60.[44] In March 1281 the numbers at Vittoria swelled to more than 450 workers:

45 quarriers
27 rough cutters
40 fine cutters
40 wall builders
3 preparers
8 carpenters
4 smiths
8 waggon drivers
30 bull drivers
2 custodians for the bulls
253 manual laborers
4 supervisors
1 master mason
1 steward
1 guard on horseback
1 accountant

As work came close to completion at Vittoria, the pace picked up. A text of 6 March 1282 details the following division of the labor force:

at the quarry of Carcii:
   30 quarriers
   12 rough shapers
   60 manual laborers
at the quarry of Montis Sicci:
   20 quarriers
   10 rough shapers
   20 manual laborers
and at the site of the abbey:
   50 fine shapers "in loggia"
   1 stone layer
   16 carpenters

30 *muratori*

4 smiths

120 manual workers assigned to the 30 *muratoribus*

10 *bayarderiis*

1 "manuale pro mundanda loggia"

4 supervisors

and there were also twenty-two cart drivers with their horses, twenty-five wagon drivers with their bulls, two guards for the bulls, and four straw carriers, not to mention the superintendent, the accountants, and the *credencerius*.[45]

There were thus large numbers of workmen at the sites, ranging from almost 300 at Realvalle to more than 500 at Vittoria. As noted in Chapter One, the king's projects were, however, plagued by absenteeism and fleeing workers.

The king was not reticent in expressing his frustration and impatience with the progress of work at the building sites, and viewed the workers as lazy and incompetent.[46] He imposed an armed guard who would force the masons and manual laborers to work a full day and place in chains any workmen who attempted to flee or who was uncooperative or slow:

> Unum de stipendiariis nostris tecum morantibus magis discretum et providum . . . qui . . . compellat magistros et alios in eodem opere laborantes ad laborandum die quolibet diligenter, et si qui eorum aufugerent ab opere ipso, vel difficiles se ostenderent ad veniendum et laborandum, seu negligerent et minus bene in eo procederent, eos ponat in bonis compedibus, et sic compediti in penam fraudis et nequitie ipsorum in opere ipso continuo faciat laborare . . . Et si aliquis ipsorum operariorum tempestive in hora competenti ad opus ipsum non venerit, vel ante horam debitam . . .[47]

As noted in Chapter One, in the late 1270s Charles of Anjou had as many as ten or fifteen major construction projects underway simultaneously, at times with a total of 300–500 workers apiece. If this figure is roughly correct, then as many as 5,000–7,000 men could have been employed in construction, a number that comprised a significant proportion of the population.

Two observations might be made. Workmen obtained by conscription would rarely have had skills in the building trade, and were reluctant to go far from family and farms or vineyards. Famine and poverty were often acute even in the best of circumstances.[48] The presence of men from various regions at the sites would have meant that a variety of dialects would have been in use, and there were probably problems of comprehension and rivalries between these different groups, as well as tension with the French administrators. It is easy to imagine problems of morale and a high potential for strife and misunderstanding under these circumstances.

Yet it is difficult not also to feel some sympathy for the supervisors. They were under constant pressure to find workers. The supervisors were responsible for the costs of the travel of workers to and from the site, and they were to be transported by force if necessary:[49] "quas si non receperis, ipsos [magistros] ad predictum opus per omnem cohercitionis modum quem videris expedientum, districte compellas . . ."[50]

The king also stipulated that three masons with their four assistants should build "cannam unam quadratam," equal to 2.646 meters, per day.[51] Henri d'Asson, master mason of Vittoria, was able to persuade the king that four masons would be needed for this building unit.[52] This adjustment did not seem to have lasted long, for a later document reversed the decision and brought the rate of pay per square unit of wall back into accordance with all other building projects.[53]

However, the amount of a wall that can be built by the day depends not only on the types of materials being used but also on the weather conditions. The rough rubble walls flanking the aisle windows at Realvalle could presumably have been erected with greater rapidity than the more careful construction in horizontal beds of the mixed rubble below. In the event of poor weather, shortages of materials or workmen at the quarry or in other parts of the chain of production, neither laborers nor masons would receive their pay.

SALARIES

Wages for construction projects were standardized throughout the kingdom.[54] The general supervisor (*praepositus*) and the senior supervisors were paid 4 tari per day. Accountants and master mason (*prothomagister*) received 1 tari a day. Supervisors received 10 grani a day, and all masons, carpenters, and quarriers received 15 grani in the summer and 12 grani in the winter. Manual laborers received 7 grani in the summer and 6 in the winter.

Small has observed that the wages of 7 grani in the summer is not much above subsistence level, roughly equivalent to what a castellan received each day for the upkeep of a prisoner.[55]

THE ORIGINS OF THE LABOR FORCE

As noted, much labor for the king's projects was conscripted, preferably from the surrounding region, but, if not, from neighboring provinces. Workers unwilling to work at royal building sites were often delivered in chains; workers who walked off the job were to be captured and returned with force to the projects. Labor, both skilled and manual, was in short supply.

It is tempting to suppose that this was more of a problem in isolated areas, such as the site of Vittoria, than in large cities like Naples. But in fact the records for the construction of the Castel Nuovo in Naples are also full of references to masons and manual workers who abandoned the project in midstream.[56] Even though the level of construction of the Neapolitan buildings attests to a higher quality of materials and workmanship (Sant'Eligio al Mercato, the Castel Nuovo, San Lorenzo Maggiore), skilled masons seem never to have been in abundance.

Was this situation new to the Kingdom of Naples? Under Frederick II there had been recourse to Cistercian masons, but it is uncertain how significant this monastic labor force might have been. There are suggestions that in some parts of thirteenth-century Europe, such as Poland and elsewhere, the presence of Cistercian architects and masons was still a signif-

icant element, but there is little evidence that this was also the case in the Kingdom of Sicily;[57] the only example within our study is Peter of Oratorio at Vittoria, who may well have had some architectural expertise.

Charles of Anjou also employed Muslim masons and workers, sometimes in large numbers. At Melfi, for example, he requested, in September 1278, one hundred laborers and fifty drivers from the Saracen community at Lucera.[58] For the curtain walls of Lucera itself, he employed 300 Muslim *manipoli*.[59] The architecture of Campania attests to the vigorous presence of Muslim building labor in that region, no doubt especially valued because they were able to come up with glamorous architectural effects with rubble, as can be seen still at Ravello, Amalfi, and any number of other sites (pl. 210).

But in general it is difficult to establish evidence of nationality among the manual laborers. This is possible only for the higher levels of expertise in the building force, often hired to provide work by the piece, such as the French at Realvalle employed to carve the capitals and ribs (pl. 36) and the Neapolitan masons hired to carve the plinths, bases, and shafts (pl. 35). It seems safe to assume that this type of specialized labor was employed to produce as piecework the elements that were not possible to achieve with normal wage labor.

Small has observed that the shortages of labor might be the natural result of the large number of royal projects simultaneously under construction.[60] It is also true that it would have been difficult to sustain a stable and well-trained workforce in times of economic instability and social disorder, such as those that prevailed for long stretches of Frederick II's reign or that of his successors, Manfred and Charles. Although the building trade is among the most mobile of professions, workers would tend to congregate where the wages were acceptable,[61] and they may emphatically not have been in the Angevin kingdom of Naples.

CONCLUSIONS

If the tone of the Angevin Registers can be interpreted to reflect the voice of the king, then the impression is one of an immense capacity for details, great impatience (especially with human frailty), and general suspiciousness.[62] The abbot, the *credenziere*, and the accountant were each required to maintain a notebook with all expenses recorded, and each account book had to be checked against the other two with a signature and a seal.[63] The Registers suggest episodes of micro-management of the workforce (how many workers, where they should be working; how much work they should accomplish in a day irrespective of the weather) that must have been a cause of great stress to the supervisors.[64] If work done by the piece was judged to have been contracted out at too high a price, the administrator was held responsible and had to pay the difference.[65] Workmanship or materials judged to be defective were to be replaced at the supervisor's own expense: "de pecunia

tua pro servittis upsius operis assegnata" (the king to Rinaldo Villani at Vittoria on 30 March 1282).[66]

In many parts of southern Italy the nature of the stone militated against an imitation of French Gothic structural concepts, either because it could not be adapted to sharply cut details with elegant cavets and fillets or because it did not have the properties of the absorption of compression and weight of French limestone. Tuff is too soft and porous, piperno often too friable, to permit the execution of sharp profiles and elegant cavetto and roll moldings. Daily experience of the French building experts as they worked at the sites in Italy must have led to a certain number of modifications to designs as work was underway, as noted in the rejection of vaulting over the nave of Sant'Eligio al Mercato in Naples, where the initial design for rib vaults and flying buttresses was abandoned.[67] On the other hand, in areas where there was a good supply of stone, as in Apulia, there were also local stone-cutting workshops, as we have seen at San Francesco in Bitonto.

There was also, of course, an economic element in the construction of vaults. The cost of cutting each of the "charges" (vault departures) at Realvalle was double the cost of carving each capital, and many more "charges", of course, were needed. If money was tight, as it always was in the Kingdom of Naples, then rib vaults were also an expense and a luxury. Apart from the issue of the quality of the stone available, it is no wonder that they were suppressed at Sant'Eligio and that rib vaults appear only in the chancels of later churches.

The Angevin Registers also reveal a great deal about the vicissitudes of the work sites. In the late 1270s Charles of Anjou issued repeated instructions that workers who had run away were to be brought back by force, in chains, and fed bread and water. If they could not be found, their houses and vineyards were to be burned and their families thrown in prison. Armed guards were positioned at the sites, not only to protect the materials, but also to keep the workers from escaping. Sometimes the supervisors were required to keep the armed guards at the site at their own expense.

The difficulties of the labor situation may explain to some extent why the architectural legacy of the first generation of the Angevin conquest was so ephemeral. Skilled masons were hard to find and a large proportion of the workforce was conscripted and worked for minimal wages, often far from home. Under these circumstances the quality of work produced might well have been poor. This would have been particularly problematic if supervision were not adequate during the mixing of mortar. Rubble masonry as at Realvalle is particularly vulnerable if mortar is poor (one colleague has described the situation like that of a cardboard box filled with wet pebbles), but even in buildings erected in ashlar masonry, exposure to water can rapidly damage the adhesion of the wall surfaces. In the case of the two Cistercian abbeys, maintenance of the monastic complex in the perennially underpopulated abbeys always presented difficulties.

Appendix 2

THE RUFOLO FINE
AND THE COSTS OF CONSTRUCTION
AT SAN LORENZO MAGGIORE

It has recently been established that the Rufolo donation of 1284 consisted of 400 once. What might this sum have meant in relation to the costs of construction? As it happens, the documents from Realvalle and Vittoria provide some possible conclusions on the expenses of building in Naples in the 1270s: a document from Realvalle of 1279 in particular lists the cost of piecework and can be used as a rough index for construction costs relative to a monument such as San Lorenzo.[1] The rate is 30 tari to each once.[2]

Engaged capitals at Realvalle cost 10 tari each. If multiplied by the number of engaged capitals (thirty-two) in the choir chapels at San Lorenzo, these elements would have cost roughly a total of 320 tari or slightly over 10 once. At Realvalle double capitals cost 20 tari, while freestanding capitals cost 15; the heavy clusters of capitals between the chapels at San Lorenzo might therefore have cost a maximum of about 30 tari each, which, when multiplied by the number of such capitals at the Franciscan choir (eighteen), would come to about 540 tari, or 18 once. At Realvalle the construction of responds, including plinths and bases, to the level of the capital cost 2 once and 15 tari apiece; at San Lorenzo the partial costs of the more complex forms of the engaged and freestanding supports might therefore be estimated at about 125 once. Crossing capitals at Realvalle cost 40 tari each; at San Lorenzo we may consider that there were at least two of these in the first phase of the work, thus costing about 80 tari, or slightly over 5 once.

Exclusive of the cost of materials, the construction of foundation walls or the erection of flat wall surfaces, the carving of bar tracery, and of course exclusive of other costs such as scaffolding, materials and labor for glass, and supplies of lumber and lead for the roof, and the expenses of the vaults, the cost of labor just for the construction of the carved vertical elements at San Lorenzo, that is to say shafts and capitals, would probably have required at least 160 once. If we were to add in the elements excluded above, this would at least triple to somewhere between 450 and 500 once, and perhaps significantly more.

Other kinds of comparable data come from the abbey of Vittoria, where in 1280 work on the church and the monastic complex cost over 160 once each month. Burial or memorial chapels and their decoration regularly seem to have cost in the neighborhood of 40 once: in 1293–94 the Bishop of Capaccio made a donation of 50 once for the construction of a burial chapel at San Lorenzo, for example,[3] and this seems to be a fairly standard sum. Thus Matteo Rufolo's donation of 400 once would have covered a large part of the costs of the new east end of San Lorenzo, but certainly not by any means all of it.

The new chevet, in relation to the sixth-century basilica and the street plan of Naples, reveals that it was constructed to the east of the old Vico Gigante, which ran north–south and must have abutted the ancient *seggio* to which it would have provided access. The extension of the church was on the other side of this narrow street, the rights to which must have been acquired by the convent for the extension of the church. The street in an earlier form can, of course, still be seen below in the excavations, or *scavi*, of the Roman market underneath the church and cloister. It must have been repaired and renewed at a much higher level behind the apse of the sixth-century church constructed over the market.

Although we cannot be certain at what point in the construction of the chevet the funds from Matteo Rufolo came into play, it is likely that they were intended to be sufficient for the entire project. Were they intended to complete the choir after the work was interrupted by the war of 1282, a project that, however, was to remain incomplete until Charles II's donations in the late 1290s? The significance of the sum may also suggest a discreet attempt to commemorate or remember the lost Rufolo son, Lorenzo, hanged as punishment as a result of the notorious trial of 1284.

THE DOCUMENTS ON THE RUFOLO FINE

The texts that refer to the construction of the choir of San Lorenzo in 1284 have been published in various sources, but I include them here:

1. 15 January 1284, Foggia

Scriptum est Mattheo Rufolo de Ravello etc. . . . Cum intuitu Divinae Pietatis Custodi, et Fratribus Minoribus morentibus Neap. in loco, qui dicitur S. Laurentius pro complenda Ecclesia ibi constructa uncias auri quadragentas ponderis generalis providerimus exhibendas; devotioni tuae pracipimus quatenus de summa unciarum auri duorum millium quadragentarum promissarum per te pro compositione facta inter Curiam nostram, et te per quientantiam officiorum, quae dudum tempore Domini Patris nostri, tu, et Laurentius filius tuus gessisti; uncias auri quadrigentas eisdem ponderis praedicti Custodi, et Fratibus solvere, et exhibere procures. Eecepturus de iis, quae eis dederis ad tui cautelam idoneam exhibere procures. Eecepturus de iis, quae eis dederis ad tui cautelam idoneam apodixam. Datum Foggiae anno, et die 25 Ianuarij 12 Indit.[1]

2. 6 May 1284, Naples

Carolus etc. Tenore presentium, notum facimus universis presentes licteras inspecturis quod pridem, divine pietatis intuitu, ad nostrorum et predecessorum remissionem peccaminum, religiosis viris, Fratribus Minoribus, Neapoli commorantibus, in subsidium reparationis Ecclesie, uncias auri quatrigintas de nostre munificentie liberalitate, donavimus percipiendas per procuratorem earum a Mattheo Rufolo de Ravello, qui . . . Datum Neapoli, die VI. maii, XII indictionis.[2]

Appendix 4

CHECKLIST OF SITES

This is a list of churches and religious foundations in the Kingdom of Naples that date roughly from the mid-thirteenth to the mid-fourteenth centuries. Some are mentioned in the documents, some are simply fragments (doors, windows), and a few are intact buildings. In some cases the monuments listed are destroyed without trace, in others the names of the dedications have been changed; in a few instances the actual location of the site is uncertain. Since issues of dating are often complex and controversial, no discussion of dating is included here.

Acerenza (Basilicata)
The cathedral, dedicated to the Assunta and San Canio, is late eleventh century. In 1281 Charles I proposed to reconstruct the church on a new site, but there is no evidence that any work was undertaken on the project.

Agnone (Molise)
Sant'Antonio Abate, Gothic portal
San Francesco, Gothic portal and rose window

Alézio (Apulia)
Santa Maria della Lizza. The episcopal seat of Gallipoli was moved to this site after the siege and destruction of Gallipoli in 1268–69.

Altamura (Apulia)
Cathedral of the Assunta. Begun *circa* 1228–32, this was extended and embellished on several occasions. There is an inscription of 1316 on the north flank attributing repairs to Robert.

Altomonte (Calabria)
Santa Maria della Consolazione, on site of earlier church, Santa Maria de' Franchis. In 1336 Filippo Sangineto acquired the *jus patronatus* and initiated the partial reconstruction of an earlier church, which includes the west portal and transept arms and the elongation of the chevet. The church includes several important medieval tombs, including that of Filippo Sangineto.

Amalfi (Campania)
The tower of 1276 adjacent to the cloister
The cloister (Chiostro del Paradiso) and its various chapels, decorated with frescoes, dated 1266–1268

Sant'Antonio, formerly San Francesco, now Albergo Luna
Cappuccini (formerly Cistercian), now Albergo Cappuccini

Andretta (Campania)
Annunziata, Gothic portal

Andria (Apulia)
Sant'Agostino, belonged to the Templars, then passed to the Augustinians from 1230 to 1358
San Francesco, inscriptions with dates of 1230 and 1346
Annunziata, Gothic portal and rib vaults on interior
Cathedral of the Assunta, various fragments of Gothic arches in interior and parts of the tower

Ascoli Satriano (Apulia)
Augustinians
Franciscans. Later became the cathedral; fragments of Gothic remains

Atri (Abruzzo)
San Domenico; remains of west façade
San Sabino (Poor Clares)
Cathedral of the Assunta: complex chronology (see Aceto, 1998)
  tower, dated 1268
  portals on south flank: dated and signed; eastern: 1302, Raimondo di Poggio; central: 1288, Raimondo di Poggio; western: 1305, Rainaldo d'Atri.
Sant'Andrea

Aversa (Campania)
Sant'Agostino
Sant'Antonio (Franciscans)
Sant' Eligio (destroyed)
San Francesco delle Monache (Clares), founded 1310
San Domenico (formerly San Luigi re di Francia)
La Maddalena
San Pietro Morrone, Celestinian
Il Carmine, founded 1315

Bari (Apulia)
San Domenico
Cathedral of San Sabino, repairs to tower after collapse of 1267 and further modifications 1310–37
Santa Chiara
San Nicola, repairs and donation of reliquaries by Angevins

Barletta (Apulia)
Sant'Agostino
San Domenico
Santa Maria del Carmine
Santa Maria Maggiore (collegiate church, later elevated to Cathedral), east end extended late thirteenth–early four-teenth centuries (see Chapter five)
San Giacomo
Sant'Eligio (Celestinians)
Palace chapel

Benevento (Campania)
San Domenico (also known as San Vincenzo)
Cathedral, inscription on tower 1278; baldachin of 1311
Annunziata
Clares
San Marco. Charles proposed to found such a church at the battle site of Benevento; project never executed

Bisceglie (Apulia)
Santa Margherita

Bisignano (Calabria)
Cathedral

Bitetto (Apulia)
Franciscans
Cathedral of San Michele rebuilt 1328–36 with support from Robert of Anjou

Bitonto (Apulia)
San Francesco d'Assisi, formerly Santa Maria Maddalena (see Chapter One)

Brindisi (Apulia)
Santa Croce
San Domenico (now Chiesa del Cristo)
Santa Maria Maddalena (Dominicans)
San Paolo (Franciscans)
Santa Maria del Casale

Capri (Campania)
Clares

Capua (Campania)
Santa Maria di Montevergine
Santa Maria Maddalena (Augustinians); see Chapter Five on Bartolomeo da Capua
San Nicola a Logoteca
San Domenico (now San Tommaso d'Aquino)
San Pietro ad Monterone (Franciscans)

Casaluce (Campania)
Santa Maria (Celestinian)

Caserta Vecchia (Campania)
Annunziata, see Chapter Five
Cathedral of San Michele, shafts and vaults of the transept, *circa* 1230–40?

Castellamare di Stabia (Campania)
Franciscans, medieval portal survives

Castellaneta (Apulia)
Cathedral of the Assunta, fragments of tower

Castelvecchio Subequo (Abruzzo)
Franciscans. Consecrated 1288

Castrovillari (Calabria)
Franciscans
Santa Maria del Castello

Catania (Sicily)
San Francesco

Chieti (Abruzzo)
San Domenico
Franciscans, San Francesco della Scarpa
San Benedetto (Celestinians)
Sant'Agostino, founded 1316

Cimitile (Campania)
Church of Saint Felix, new portal of the *basilica nova*

Cittaducale (Lazio)
Franciscans
San Ludovico

Citta Sant'Angelo (Abruzzo)
San Francesco
Collegiata (San Michele)

Civitella del Tronto (Abruzzo)
San Francesco

Conversano (Apulia)
Cathedral, parts of façade

Cosenza (Calabria)
Clares
Cathedral, tomb of Isabelle of Aragon

Crotone (Calabria)
Franciscans (destroyed by the construction of the castle)

Cuccaro (Campania)
Franciscans, see Chapter Five, founded by Ilaria di Loria, 1333

Eboli (Campania)
San Francesco, see Chapter Five
Sant'Antonio

Foggia (Apulia)
Dominicans
Franciscans

Francavilla Fontana (Apulia)
Church, order unknown; here Philip of Taranto discovered a miraculous image of the Virgin in 1310; indulgences to the church were granted by John XXII in 1332.

Gaeta (Lazio)
San Domenico
San Francesco
Cathedral, paschal candlestick of *circa* 1340
Annunziata

Gagliano Aterno (Abruzzo)
Santa Chiara
San Martino

Gerace (Calabria)
San Francesco, see Chapter Three
Cathedral of the Assunta, portal into crypt

Gioa del Colle (Apulia)
Franciscans

Giovinazzo (Apulia)
Sant'Agostino
Santa Chiara

Goriano Sicoli (Abruzzo)
Clares

Guardiagrele (Abruzzo)
Celestinians
Santa Maria (Clares)
San Francesco

Guglieto (Campania)
Santa Maria

Isernia (Molise)
San Francesco
Clares

Lanciano (Abruzzo)
Annunziata, one surviving portal installed in the Seminanio
San Francesco
Sant'Agostino
Santa Maria Maggiore, portal of 1317

L'Aquila (Abruzzo)
Cathedral of San Massimo destroyed
Sant'Agostino
San Domenico (formerly Sta. Maria Maddalena), begun 1309
San Flaviano
San Francesco
Santa Maria di Collemaggio
Santa Giusta
San Marciano
San Marco
Santa Maria di Paganica
Santa Maria di Roio
San Pietro in Sassia
San Pietro di Coppito
San Silvestro
Sant'Antonio
Corpus Domini (also known as Beata Antonia)

Larino (Molise)
Cathedral of the Assunta and San Pardo, portal dated to 1319
San Francesco

Laurito (Campania)
San Filippo d'Agira

Limosano (Molise)
San Francesco
Santo Stefano

Limatola (Campania)
Annunziata

Lucera (Apulia)
Cathedral, Santa Maria Assunta, begun 1300
San Bartolomeo (Celestinians)
San Domenico
San Francesco
San Leonardo (Augustinians)

Maddaloni (Campania)
San Francesco d'Assisi
Annunziata

Manfredonia (Apulia)
San Domenico (see Chapter There)
Franciscans

Magliano de' Marsi (Abruzzo)
Santa Lucia

Mercato Sanseverino (Campania)
Dominicans
Sant'Antonio (also known as San Francesco and first dedicated
    to Santissima Annunziata founded 1358)

Messina (Sicily)
San Francesco
Clares

Miglionico (Basilicata)
Santa Maria Maggiore, portal by Nicola da Melissano

Mileto (Calabria)
Museo Diocesano, tombs of the Sanseverino family

Monopoli (Apulia)
San Domenico
San Francesco

Monte Piano (Abruzzo)
Clares

Monte Sant'Angelo (Apulia)
San Michele (see Chapter One)
San Benedetto, originally San Giovanni Evangelista
San Francesco
Celestinians

Montevergine (Campania)
Santa Maria di Montevergine: church, portals, tombs, painting
    by Montano d'Arezzo

Naples (see text)
Santa Chiara (also Corpus Domini)
Santa Croce di Palazzo
Santissima Trinità
San Martino
Santa Maria Donnaregina

Santa Maria Maddalena
San Lorenzo Maggiore
San Domenico Maggiore
Cathedral
San Pietro a Maiella
San Pietro Martire
San Pietro a Castello
Sant'Antonio Abate
Santa Maria di Montevergine (Monteverginella)
Santa Maria Egiziaca
Santa Maria Incoronata
Annunziata
San Giovanni a Mare
San Giovanni a Carbonara
Sant'Agrippino a Forcella
Sant'Eligio al Mercato
Santa Maria del Carmine
Chapel of Santa Barbara, Castel Nuovo
Chapel of San Martino, Castel Nuovo
Sant'Agostino alla Zecca
Santa Maria Donnaromita; became Cistercian in 1278
Santa Maria la Nova

Nardò (Apulia)
Cathedral of Santa Maria
Sant'Antonio
Santa Chiara

Nocera Inferiore (Campania)
Sant'Antonio (formerly San Francesco: see Chapter Five)

Noci (Apulia)
Chiesa Madre

Nola (Campania: see Chapter Five)
Cathedral of San Felice
Clares, now Santa Maria Iacobi
Franciscans, now San Biagio

Ortona (Abruzzo)
San Tommaso
San Domenico

Ostuni (Apulia)
San Francesco

Padula (Campania)
Charterhouse of San Lorenzo
San Francesco

Palermo (Sicily)
Augustinians (San Agostino)
San Francesco
Clares

Penne (Abruzzo)
San Domenico
Clares

Picerno (Basilicata)
Annunziata

Piano di Monte Verna (Campania)
Santa Maria a Marciano

Potenza (Basilicata)
San Francesco
Santa Eucaristia

Ravello (Campania)
Santa Chiara
San Francesco
Cathedral of San Pantaleone, liturgical furniture

Rossano (Calabria)
Cathedral
Annunziata
Patirion, central portal

Sant'Agata dei Goti (Campania)
San Francesco

San Flaviano (Abruzzo)
Franciscans

San Giovanni Rotondo (Apulia)
Sant'Onofrio

Santa Maria di Realvalle (Campania)
Cistercians (see Chapter One)

Santa Maria della Vittoria (Abruzzo)
Cistercians (see Chapter One)

Santa Severina (Calabria)
Cathedral of Sant' Anastasia

Salerno (Campania)
Dominicans
Franciscans
Santo Spirito (Clares)
San Pietro a Maiella
San Giacomo dei Padri Celestini

Scala (Campania)
Cathedral, tomb, mitre

Scurcola Marsicana (Abruzzo)
Sant'Antonio
Santa Maria

Senise (Basilicata)
San Francesco

Sessa Aurunca (Campania)
Dominicans
Augustinians

Somma Vesuviana (Campania)
Dominicans
Cappella San Ludovico

Squillace (Calabria)
Santa Maria della Pietà

Stilo (Calabria)
La Matrice, central portal

Sulmona (Abruzzo)
Sant'Agostino, portal reused on façade of San Filippo
Santa Chiara
San Domenico
San Francesco della Scarpa
Santo Spirito del Morrone
Cathedral, tomb in crypt
Santa Maria della Tomba

Tagliacozzo (Abruzzo)
Franciscans

Taranto (Apulia)
San Domenico
San Francesco
Santa Maria della Giustizia

Teano (Campania)
San Francesco

Teggiano (Campania)
Sant'Antonio
Cathedral of Santa Maria Maggiore
San Francesco
San Domenico
Santissima Pietà

Teramo (Abruzzo)
Franciscans, first San Francesco, then Sant'Antonio

Terlizzi (Apulia)
Santissimo
Rosano, portal by Anseramo da Trani
Termoli (Abruzzo)
Franciscans
Chiesa del Purgatorio

Termoli (Molise)
Franciscans

Trani (Apulia)
Dominicans
Franciscans
Cathedral, burial of Philip of Thessalonika, 1277

Tricarico (Basilicata)
Santa Chiara
San Francesco

Tripergole (Campania)
Santa Maria Maddalena
Santa Marta

Tropea (Calabria)
Clares
San Francesco

Ugento (Apulia)
Santa Maria del Casale

Vasto (Molise)
San Giuseppe
San Pietro

Venosa (Basilicata)
Dominicans
Trinità

Viano (Abruzzo)
Santa Maria (Clares)

Vibo Valentia (Calabria)
Franciscans: Capella del Rosario

Zagarise (Basilicata)

Appendix 5

BASE PROFILES

Right and left are determined facing main altar.

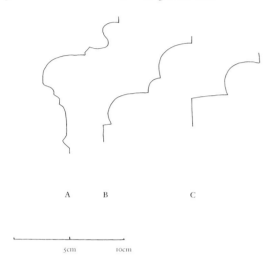

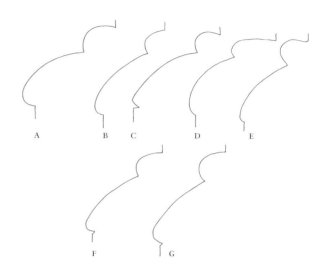

1 Naples, Sant'Eligio al Mercato
    A. Portal, south flank of church, left jamb.
    B. Interior, southwest pier of nave (damaged).
    C. Interior, northwest pier of nave (damaged).

2 Naples, San Lorenzo
    A. Nave, first (double) chapel, right side of nave
    (Krüger, R1–R2) – formerly Da Capua Chapel.
    B. Nave, fifth chapel on right (Krüger, R5).
    C. Nave sixth chapel on right (Krüger, R6).
    D. Nave fifth chapel on left (Krüger, L5).
    E. Nave seventh chapel on left (Krüger, L7).
    F. Chevet, second chapel on left (Krüger, CH 4L).
    G. Chevet, fourth chapel on left (Krüger, CH 2R).

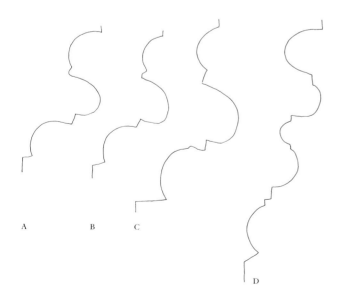

3 (*left*) Naples, cathedral.
    A. Cappella Tocco.
    B. Cappella Tocco.
    c. Cappella Tocco.
    D. Nave, westernmost bay, north side (ancient base reused).

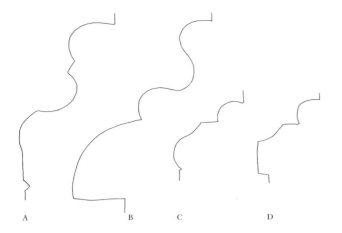

4 Various monuments
  A. Barletta, Sta. Maria Maggiore (cathedral), chevet.
  B. Lucera, cathedral of Sta. Maria Maggiore, left chapel, left side.
  C. Rossano, cathedral, east end, right chapel (damaged).
  D. Rossano, cathedral, east end, right chapel (damaged).

5 Naples, Sta. Maria Donnaregina (possibly restored by Chierici)
  A. Apse.
  B. Left pier at entrance to apse.
  C. Nave, octagonal column supporting gallery.
  D. Nave, octagonal column supporting gallery.
  E. Nave, octagonal column supporting gallery.

6 (below) Naples, Sta. Chiara (possibly restored after 1943)
  A. Nuns' choir, west wall.
  B. Nuns' choir, east wall.
  C. Nuns' choir, south wall.
  D. Nave, interior chapels, left side.

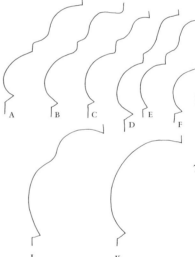

7 San Pietro a Maiella
  A. First chapel to right of central apse.
  B. First chapel to left of central apse.
  C. Second chapel to left of central apse.
  D. Nave, crossing pier, left side of nave.
  E. Nave, respond of left aisle adjacent to transept.
  F. Nave, respond of left aisle adjacent to portal.
  G. Nave, third pier from transept, right side of nave.
  H. Nave, pier adjacent to facade, right side.
  I. Nave, pier adjacent to facade, left side of nave.
  J. Nave, thord pier from facade, left side of nave.
  K. Nave, second pier from facade, left side of nave.

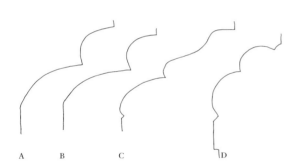

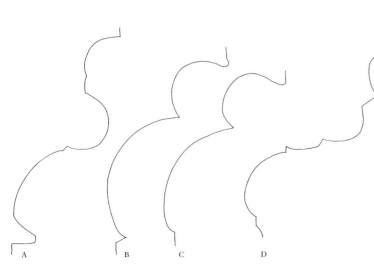

8 Larino cathedral
  A. Nave, westernmost bay, south side.
  B. Nave, second pier from west, south side.
  C. Nave, pier at juncture of chevet, south side.
  D. West portal.

Notes

INTRODUCTION

1 Bologna 1969 is a majestic study, and exceptional in its incorporation of historical material with works of art. See also Leone de Castris 1986. On the architecture, Venditti 1969 is excellent and represents the most important analysis to date.

2 De Frede 1969, pp. 16–17; Del Giudice 1863–1908, II, p. 44; Summonte 1601–43, I, p. 202.

3 Herde 1992; Barbero 1983, pp. 71 ff.; Merckel 1888.

4 See Reeves 1976, p. 66; Zeller 1934, p. 286, who observed that Joachim of Fiore had predicted that a new emperor Charles would come from the Carolingian race, reign over all Europe, and reform the Church and Empire. It is interesting to note in this connection the recent emphasis on the Carolingian ancestry of the Capetian line in the royal tombs of Saint-Denis installed about 1264. Charles himself cultivated this mythology (Herde 1992, p. 181).

5 Clement IV reflected on the conquest as "a great exaltation of the whole French nation." Cited by Housley 1982, p. 152. Urban IV also compared Charles to Charlemagne.

6 Camera 1840–60, I, p. 275: "Malcontento generale da per tutto il regno – Continuava tuttavia il re Carlo ad aggravare il suo popolo d'imposte, di balzelli e di vessazioni d'ogni genere, tanto che papa Clemente prendendo in considerazione le funeste consequenze che ne avrebbero potuto derivare, si vide nell'obbligo d'indirizzargli de' severi rimproveri per la strana condotta di governare."

7 See Léonard 1954, p. 58, and Vitolo 1986, p. 14, on Clement's reproaches after the atrocities of the Battle of Benevento in 1266.

8 Barbero 1983, passim, and see above, note 2, and for example Gardner 1972, p. 136, for observations on Cardinal Annibaldi's shift of allegiance from fierce loyalty to Charles to a promoter of the imperial rival Frederick of Thuringia. Also Herde 1992, pp. 181–84.

9 Salimbene 1986, pp. 657–58, at the end of his narrative concludes by describing the French as "an extremely proud and foolish people, terrible and accursed, a people who hold all other nations of the world in contempt . . ."

10 Riccetti 1996, pp. 214 ff.

11 Waley 1961, pp. 207–08. In Apulia and especially the Salento resistance to Charles of Anjou's conquest continued through March 1269 when Charles finally defeated the last hold-outs at Gallipoli. See Massa 1907, pp. 139 ff., and, in general, Vitolo 1986, pp. 15–20 and 42. Opposition was also strong in clerical circles at the highest level: Herde 1992, p. 184. On the issue of the "self-identity" of the Sicilians as either the island or as the entire population of the *regno*, in their appeal for help to Aragon in 1282, see Reynolds 1997, p. 300.

12 Dunbabin 1998. The description of Charles as a "driven, chilly thug" is from the book's jacket.

13 Barbero 1983, *passim*; Herde 1992, also Herde 1977. For a recent and more positive assessment, see Dunbabin 1998.

14 Benevento was of course a papal city, which accounts for Clement's extreme irritation. See Barbero 1983, pp. 94–99, for a full discussion of Clement IV's relations with Charles, and also Housley 1982, pp. 222–30. Clement's dismay is easy to understand when we also consider that the loans he negotiated for Charles were on the security of the churches of Rome and the liturgical vessels of the papal chapel: Percy 1964, p. 36.

15 On the response to the decapitation of Conradin, see De Frede 1969, p. 28.

16 Housley 1982, pp. 67–68, observes that southern Italy and the east were locked together in crusading policy, and that it was assumed that the conquest of the Kingdom of Sicily was a prelude to a crusade to reinforce the Christian domains in Syria and reconquer Constantinople.

17 Insofar as the project would have entailed some level of financial planning, of course. On the assessments of the economy, see Abulafia 1997, pp. 6–8. It seems probable that Charles was counting on this vague reputation for immense wealth in order to finance the Italian campaign and subsequent eastern projects. Herde 1992, p. 184, noted that Saba Malaspina saw the economic difficulties and the imposition of heavy taxation as the direct result of the plans for conquest in the east. The dissertation of 1964 by William Percy is perhaps the most useful source on the economy and taxation of the Kingdom of Sicily.

18 Léonard 1954, *passim*; De Frede 1969, pp. 1–224; Galasso 1992, pp. 38-43.

19 On the essential insecurity of Charles's position, as well as the heterogeneity of his troops, see Herde 1980, pp. 43–44.

20 Kiesewetter 1995, pp. 39–41.

21 Ibid.

22 On Angevin ambitions in the Mediterranean, see Manselli 1974.

23 The revolts included the entire peninsula of Apulia, particularly devoted to the Swabian dynasty (Kiesewetter 1995, p. 37; Palumbo 1989, pp. 323 ff.). Rebellion broke out again after the defeat of the Angevin navy and the capture of Charles II (then still Prince of Salerno) on 5 June 1284.

24 French settlers were exempt from taxation, for example, which must have added to the tensions and resentments between the local populations and the newcomers. On the problem of retaining settlers in Italy, see Housley 1982, pp. 154–55, and Bruzelius 1991, pp. 407–08; for the analogous situation in the Holy Land, Prawer 1951, pp. 88 ff.

25 For example, Durrieu 1886, pp. 189–228, esp. pp. 213 ff., who described the "impitoyable répression" of the kingdom. See also Pontieri 1950, pp. 149–52.

26 See Egidi 1911 (part 1), pp. 649–50.

27 Minieri-Riccio 1882, p. 243.

28 Vitolo 1986, pp. 20–21.

29 In his wonderful article on the construction of galleys for Charles of Anjou, Pryor 1993, p. 88, notes the rise of costs of labor and materials after 1282.

30 On the heterogeneity of the troops and difficulties between the different groups, see Herde 1980, pp. 43–44. I return to anti-French attitudes and their consequence for this topic in the Conclusion.

31 See the next chapter on the discussion of the theft of stones by the king's relative.

32 Runciman 1958, pp. 125 ff.

33 For example, in Robert's renewal of the work of draining the swamps around Naples in 1309 it is stated that the project had been abandoned with the death of Charles I and the imprisonment of Charles II. See Minieri-Riccio 1882, pp. 216–17.

34 The disappearance of the engineer Jean de Toul from the records in the sieges of Hungary is a good example.

35 Lognon 1957, pp. 173–86, in his review of Léonard, notes that Charles I was "hanté par le souvenir de Frederick II" (p. 175).

36 The French contribution has been emphasized in the literature since the work of Bertaux and Enlart, both of which remain fundamental sources for the study of Angevin architecture in the Kingdom of Naples.

37 Clement IV wrote to Charles: "This is how your country is constituted: on this side the Saracens, on the other the Greeks; elsewhere famed port cities; still in other spots, the Germans; all people who can love neither you nor your country" (Jordan 1909, p. 369).

38 On the important subject of tombs and burials, see the new studies of Enderlein 1997 and Michalsky 1998.

39 Del Giudice 1863–1908, I, p. 230, and II, pp. 192–93, section iv.

40 Del Giudice 1863–1908, I, pp. 230–31.

41 Camera 1840–60, I, p. 324 and p. 332. By 1302 Charles II owed the papacy 93,340 once (Camera 1840–60, II, p. 138), which increased by 1307 to 366,000 once. See Vitolo 1986, pp. 12–13 and 62.

42 Percy 1964, pp. 28–40.

43 On this see the immensely interesting article of 1969 by Buczek on medieval taxation, especially pp. 58–63 on the Cistercians and the crusading tithes declared for Charles of Anjou.

44 Herde 1992, p. 184.

45 Percy 1964, p. 247.

46 Jordan 1909, pp. 536 ff.

47 Percy 1964, p. 246.

48 My discussion of labor in this volume is only a very partial consideration of the subject. For detailed considerations, see Small 1989, and Pitz 1986.

49 Small 1989, p. 328.

50 Bruzelius 1991. For a more positive assessment, see Dunbabin 1998, pp. 211–13.

51 Most recently on Realvalle, see De Sanctis 1953, pp. 153–96 with a complete bibliography. The fundamental work on Santa Maria della Vittoria are the articles by Egidi published between 1909 and 1911. See also Bruzelius 1991. On Vittoria, see also Pesce 1994.

52 For Naples the best study is the excellent and thorough analysis by Venditti 1969. My views on French influence are in contrast not only to other studies of the subject (for example Enlart 1894), but also to the terminology currently in use, which identifies Gothic work in southern Italy as "angioino".

53 For the secular architecture, see Small 1989, *passim*. A wealth of documents on this is published in the volumes of Sthamer; also Egidi 1909 and Egidi 1910; Francabandera 1932; and most recently Aceto 1996.

54 A document of 1269 in the archive of Salerno also mentions a Master Peter of Salerno who was commissioned to provide "tabulis vitreis" for the chapel at the palace of San Lorenzo. See Carucci 1931, I, p. 345.

55 On the cult of the Magdalen, see now Jansen 2000.

56 See on this the interesting and important analysis of Trachtenberg 1991, esp. pp. 27–28.

CHAPTER 1

1 Excerpts from a sermon by Federico Franconi on the text "The Lord our King shall sit Forever" (Psalm 28:10), quoted and translated by D'Avray 1994, pp. 90–91.

2 See for example Charles's letter to Pierre d'Angicourt, Filangieri 1950–, XI, p. 184, and his instructions for the castle at Brindisi. See also Pitz 1986, p. 42.

3 A letter of 8 March 1277 specified at great length wall widths and all other details. See Sthamer 1912–26, II, pp. 92–94 and Bertaux 1905, XXXIV, pp. 94–95.

4 Among his predecessors who were active in defending the rights of the cathedral was Peter of Sorrento, who

brought the Franciscans and Dominicans to Naples. See below, Chapter Three, in the discussion of the cathedral of Naples. Ayglerius's intelligence and sensitivity to local tradition may be reflected in the fact that he took the interesting step of moving the festival of San Gennaro from 19 September to 8 May so that it would not interfere with the harvest; see mention of this in M. del Treppo, "Aiglerio," *Dizionario biografico degli italiani*, 1960, I, p. 520.

5 Buczek 1969, p. 62.

6 Here I have in mind the king's apparent taste for austerity that emerges in his instructions for the royal palace chapel at Bari: Dunbabin, 211, where he specified that the chapel should be like that at the castle of San Lorenzo near Foggia, with clear glass and decorated with neither pictures nor statues. Unfortunately, none of the royal chapels survives.

7 Minieri-Riccio 1874, p. 63; Schulz and von Quast 1860, I, p. 332; IV, p. 19, no. XLVIII; Del Giudice 1863–1908, I, pp. 112–13 and 185–90.

8 This apparently aborted foundation has been connected with the later foundations of Realvalle and Vittoria in 1274, which were explicitly intended to commemorate Charles's two victories. But the later foundations were also clearly prompted by the settlement of the contested crusading debt of the Cistercians.

9 Minieri-Riccio 1872, *Itinerario*, p. 4.

10 On the uprisings that accompanied Conradin's descent into Italy, see Léonard 1954, pp. 105–06.

11 Minieri-Riccio 1875, p. 5; Bertaux 1903–04, p. 326.

12 Enderlein 1997, pp. 24–39.

13 Carucci 1931, p. 481.

14 This is of course in contrast to ongoing projects along the Amalfi coast, many of which are strikingly Islamic, such as the Villa Rufolo in Ravello and the cloister and tower of Amalfi cathedral.

15 Villari 1967, pp. 34–36 and 104–09. Also guidebooks to the city of Naples, mostly written in and after this period of Neapolitan history, reflected this political and intellectual climate and thus also tended to promote the idea of the Angevin contribution to local monuments.

16 Bertaux 1905, XXXIV, p. 313, goes so far as to describe Charles d'Anjou as presenting himself as the "roi des moines."

17 Del Giudice 1863–1908, I, pp. 230–31; Filangieri 1950–, I, pp. 52–53; Minieri-Riccio 1874, p. 18.

18 Venditti 1969, p. 712; see also Rossi 1997, pp. 165–74, who notes the "marcata vocazione sacra del territorio." On the area of the market as the object of royal patronage, see the discussion of the Carmine below.

19 Camera 1840–60, I, p. 302. See also De Seta 1981, p. 42.

20 Galante 1985, p. 296, describes an inscription, now lost: IOANNES DOTTUM GULIERMUS / S. BURGUNDIO ET IOANNES / LIONS TEMPLUM HOC CUM HOSPICIO A / FUNDAMENTIS EREXERUNT ANNO DOMINI MCCLXX. The document is published in Minieri-Riccio 1878–83, I, p. 34; also Schulz and von Quast 1860, III, pp. 35–37, and Summonte 1601–43, II, pp. 264–66. The description of subsequent repairs and restorations at Sant'Eligio in Venditti

1969, pp. 710–21, is excellent and the reader is referred to this text. The remarks on Sant'Eligio here will concern themselves with the character of the original plan and elevation, with some hypotheses on the chronology.

21 See the essay by Giovanni Vitolo, "La piazza del mercato e l'ospedale Di Sant'Eligio," in Vitolo and Di Meglio, forthcoming.

22 It is no coincidence, in this connection, that two of the three French saints are associated with battle and victory, and all three were bishops: Denis was evoked in the famous French battle cry, "Montjoie Saint Denis," apparently used by Charles himself in Italy, and Martin had been a Roman soldier in Gaul. D'Engenio Caracciolo 1624, p. 439, states that the regulations for the confraternity date from 1268, which suggests that the organization was founded just after the Battle of Tagliacozzo.

23 Filangieri 1950–, XXI, pp. 39–40: "Scriptum est . . . Inter cetera caritatis opera que devote pro Christi nomine dispensantur in terris, illud Deo gratissimum credimus residere quod locis ecclesiasticis in quibus laudatur incessanter Altissimus pia miseratione largimur, considerantes . . . Hospitali venerabilis ecclesie Sancti Eligii de Neapoli, ad quam pure mentis devotionem gerimus et habemus pro salute nostra et animarum omnium parentum et filiorum nostrorum bone memorie in helemosinam concessimus, donavimus et tradidimus . . . de solo vacuo in campo Moricini dicte civitatis Neapolis contiguo ipsi ecclesie pro ampliando hedificio domus infirmorum et cimiterii defunctorum et corpore ipsius ecclesie dicte hospitalis in larg. can. III et in long. can XLI, incipientes a cruce lapidea fixa prope ipsum hospitale in loco ubi fit forum et finientes quantum superius protenduntur ex recta linea mensure descendentes versus septentrionem et iuxta menia civitatis predicti ita quod in constructione amplificationis murorum ipsius edificii nulle alie fenestre seu porte fiant set addantur de novo pro logiis seu apothecas aliquibus faciendis ex quibus platea ipsius fori occupari et devastari possit quamquam ille tamquam sunt ad presens in longitudine muri hospitalis eiusdem."

24 This is in keeping with other aspects of the reign of Charles, for the French rarely settled in the kingdom with their families, and in any event there was a high level of mortality among the immigrants. Maintaining a permanent presence of loyal French retainers was always a problem. See Dunbabin 1998, p. 61. See also D'Engenio Caracciolo 1624, p. 439, and De Falco 1549, p. 53.

25 See Minieri-Riccio 1876, *Studi storici estratti*; also, Minieri-Riccio 1876, *Studi storici fatti*, p. 115, for the donation of Charles II in the Campo Moricino in 1302, followed that same year by the construction of a house by the king "pro comoditate mutilatorum in servitiis nostris." The important and continued patronage of the French nobility is attested in the will of Giles de Montreuil of 1306: see Bridges 1955, esp. p. 192. The nobles described by Bridges maintained strong ties to various aspects of French tradition and associations, and these,

as we shall see below, sometimes included architectural matters. As regards later patronage, for example, Don Pietro of Toledo rebuilt and enlarged the hospital that then included for the first time female patients. See Di Giacomo 1892, "Le chiese di Napoli: S. Eligio al Mercato," p. 153.

26 D'Engenio Caracciolo 1624, p. 439. On San Giovanni a Mare, see Radogna 1873; see also Venditti 1968, pp. 522–29.

27 Chioccarello 1643, p. 178, states that the bishop's arms were visible on the exterior of the apse. Episcopal documents indicated continued support until Ayglerius's death in 1282, including a conspicuous donation in 1276.

28 Mentioned above, n. 25.

29 Venditti 1969, pp. 712–13, dates this reconstruction to *circa* 1360, thus in the reign of Joanna I.

30 Lavagnino 1947, pp. 66–67. The nineteenth-century decoration was added by Orazio Angelini between 1836 and 1843; see Venditti 1969, p. 714 n. 71.

31 A canna is 2.646 meters. The lot was therefore 7.938 by 108.486 meters, a long and narrow strip that can perhaps be identified in the Duca di Noia plan of 1775 (pl. 10). The new triple apses of the chevet extend about 6.60 meters beyond the transept, which would have occupied the location of the first apse, and thus roughly correspond to the donation of 1279.

32 As noted above, an apse was found in the restoration after the Second World War, but I have found no documentation of this discovery.

33 The total width of the nave and aisles is 17.97 meters in the second bay west of the transept, and the nave alone is 8.78 meters wide. The truss ceiling is at present placed at approximately 21 meters from ground level. It should be noted, however, that because the church is asymmetrical, most measurements are irregular.

34 Venditti 1969, p. 714: Chierici 1934, "Il restauro della chiesa di S. Maria di Donnaregina," pp. 30–31, has noted the low resistance of tuff to the pressures and thrusts of vaults.

35 Hartmann-Virnisch 1996, pp. 345–50; Esquieu 1988. Beatrice was originally buried in the cathedral of Naples in the old basilica of the Stefania. Her will, however, stipulated that her remains be moved to the church of the Hospitalers in Aix, and after the completion of the Provençal church in 1277 her body was moved from Naples, although leaving intact there a tomb (no longer extant), which, the king instructed, was still to contain her "dust." On the burial of Beatrice, see Enderlein 1997, pp. 211–12, and Michalsky 2000, pp. 243–47. We shall return to her tomb and burial again in the discussion of the cathedral of Naples. The possibility that Saint-Jean-de-Malte was a model for Sant'Eligio finds an interesting parallel in the use of a Provençal galley as the prototype for the production of boats in the Kingdom of Sicily, Pryor 1993, p. 37.

36 Minieri-Riccio 1857, p. 11.

37 The best study of Larchant is that of Henriet 1978.

38 Michael Davis is presently working on this material; see Branner 1965, *passim*.

39 *Congrès archéologique de France: Pays d'Aix* (1988), *passim*, for a number of these buildings, as well as Carraz 1966, p. 22, who attributes this taste to Charles of Anjou as Count of Provence.

40 The chapel was to be simple, illuminated by windows of clear glass in a cupola. The documents on the reconstruction of the castle of Bari are among the most vivid testimonies to the king's "micromanagement" of building operations; see for example the letters of 1276 in Sthamer 1997, II, pp. 3 ff.

41 Bruzelius 1985, pp. 161–71.

42 Bruzelius 1987, pp. 635–40. For a stylistic dating, see Davis 1984.

43 There are no affinities with the Cistercian workshops suggested by Venditti 1969, p. 721, and Wagner-Rieger 1961, "San Lorenzo Maggiore in Neapel," p. 136.

44 Venditti 1969, p. 720.

45 Di Giacomo 1892, "S. Maria del Carmine," p. 18.

46 Minieri-Riccio 1857, p. 124: ". . . ut in dicto loco dicti fratres construere possint Ecclesiam, horatorium et domos pro habitatione ipsorum volentes, quod inter predictum locum et viam publicam nullus construere possit domos, et hoc pro remissione peccatorum nostrorum inclitae memoriae quondam parentum nostrorum Domini Ludovici Illustris Regis et dominae Blancae Reginae Franciae."

47 Branner 1965, p. 89.

48 Di Giacomo 1892, "Santa Maria del Carmine," pp. 19–20. A statue of a crowned female figure attributed to Tino da Camaino which stood adjacent to a house in the Piazza until 1662 was said to represent Elizabeth of Bavaria, mother of Conradin and benefactress of the church. Valentiner 1952, demonstrated that the figure represents Saint Catherine of Alexandria, and that it was probably taken from the tomb of Philip of Taranto in San Domenico executed by Tino after the prince's death in 1327. On the traditions of the patronage of the two queens, see Summonte 1601–43, II, pp. 262–63.

49 Minieri-Riccio 1876, *Studi storici fatti*, pp. 83–84 and p. 94. The importance of the monastery is attested in the late sixteenth century by its wealth (an annual income of 5,000 ducats a year) and the number of friars (120): see Strazzullo 1968, p. 100.

50 Emery 1953, p. 260, Cannon 1987, and De Falco 1549, p. 54.

51 Monaco 1975. The image is one of a group of Carmelite pseudo-Byzantine images that tended to emphasize the Eastern origins of the order.

52 Venditti 1969, pp. 721–22; Blunt 1975, p. 126. On the damage in 1456, see Quagliarella, pp. 245–50.

53 Venditti 1969, p. 724.

54 Venditti 1969, pp. 724–28; Schulz and von Quast 1860, III, p. 51; D'Engenio Caracciolo 1624, p. 383, states on p. 384 that there were ninety friars at Sant'Agostino; during the reconstruction of the church in the late sixteenth century the number had been reduced to sixty. See Strazzullo 1968, p. 98.

55 Filangieri 1950–, XXI, p. 38; D'Engenio Caracciolo 1624, p. 383.

56 Minieri-Riccio *Studi storici fatti*, 1876, p. 42. See also Amodio 1941, p. 150, and Camera 1840–60, II, p. 69.

57 See below on the discussion of the chapter house. Against this longer period of construction, see Venditti 1969, p. 724; Minieri-Riccio 1857, p. 79.

58 Bertaux 1896, p. 24; De Lellis 1654, pp. 67–92.

59 Bertaux 1896, pp. 24 ff.; Venditti 1969, p. 724.

60 Strazzullo 1968 published a census of 1585 of the monastic establishments of Naples. At that date, among Angevin foundations, the income of Sant'Agostino was exceeded only by that of the Carthusians at San Martino (18,000 ducati), the Dominicans at San Domenico and San Pietro Martire (8,000 ducati each), and the nuns of Santa Chiara (7,000 ducati), all royal and Angevin foundations.

61 On the later phases of construction, see Venditti 1969, p. 724.

62 Alisio 1980, p. 403.

63 Bertaux 1896, pp. 24–26. Venditti 1969, p. 726, also describes these as Swabian capitals of "exceptional interest." The chapter house measures 12.26 meters in depth by 16.24 in width.

64 A good summary of the medieval history of Santa Maria la Nova can be found in Capone 1978, pp. 11–21. On the rebuilding of the Castel Nuovo, see Aceto 1996, and Palmieri 1999.

65 On this see Palmieri 1999, *passim*, and Aceto 1996.

66 The old site had been badly damaged by the siege of Naples of 1251–53. See Palmieri 1999, p. 505.

67 The monument was rebuilt between 1596 and 1599 by Giovanni Cola di Franco; see Blunt 1975, p. 53, and Da Napoli 1927.

68 Sbaraglia, 1759-1804, IV, p. 194. In January 1280 Charles ordered that none of the masons at work on the church of Santa Maria or on the conventual buildings of the friars minor should be disturbed in their work. Minieri-Riccio 1879, "Il regno," IV (1879), p. 8.

69 Strazzullo 1968, p. 99.

70 Venditti 1969, pp. 728–30.

71 The exiguous physical remains notwithstanding, both abbeys have been the object of several important studies. For Realvalle, see De Sanctis 1993, Amarotta 1974, De Boüard 1937; and Francabandera 1932. For Vittoria, see most recently Pesce 1994, pp. 47–80, and above all the magisterial work of Egidi 1909 and Egidi 1910; Bruzelius 1991; and most recently Cuozzo 1994, esp. pp. 256–69, and, more generally, the entire volume *I Cistercensi nel mezzogiorno medievale*, ed., H. Houben and B. Vetere, 1994.

72 Cuozzo 1994, p. 256, emphasized the need to use the new abbeys as unequivocal symbols of the new regime. Although Summonte 1601–43, II, p. 319, described Realvalle as "suntuosissimo," a text of the seventeenth century mentioned the church as "non però finita" (Cuozzo 1994, p. 260). Already *circa* 1600 he described the abbey as "ridotto di serpenti e rane, essendo tutto ingombrato d'acque, di rostine, e di sterpi . . ."

73 Here see Sthamer 1926, II, pp. 3–39. For the general tone of urgency in Charles's instructions, see also Egidi 1909–10, *passim*.

74 Jordan 1909, pp. 386, 488, 493–94, 537–41; Léonard 1954, pp. 51–56; Housley 1982, p. 39; Marc-Bonnet 1948; and Purcell 1975.

75 And, indeed, one must imagine that this tithe, following close upon the heels of the tithes declared for Louis IX's crusades in the Holy Land, was not eagerly received by any religious foundation. The Cistercians and Templars were exceptionally fortunate in having established the precedent of immunity, but, as Buczek 1969 points out, this was part of a long struggle that pitted the Cistercians against the other ecclesiastical institutions in France as well as the papacy. See Buczek 1969, pp. 56–63, on Charles of Anjou and the Cistercians.

76 Hence Charles may have been especially put out by what would appear to be Cistercian ingratitude. On the Cistercians and the Capetian family, see Branner 1965, pp. 32–33. The abbey of Royaumont, thus founded in 1228 in fulfillment of Louis VIII's will, became one of the most important royal abbeys established within the order and was also the burial place of Louis IX's children. See here also Bruzelius 1979, pp. 90–110.

77 Del Giudice 1863–1908, III, p. 93: "Grave nobis est plurimum et molestum quod vobis, pro quibus est ecclesia Romana obligata non est de mutuatis nobis penitus satisfactum licet nobis vel nostris officialibus ascribi non possit ad culpam set potius cisterciensibus Regni Francie qui nobis ad solvendum decimam suorum proventuum per sedem apostolicam sententialiter condamnati solvere ipsam decimam vobis iuxta tenorem sententie in locis et terminis debitis non curarunt." See also the documents of 4 August 1268 and 11 February 1269 that are cited by Minieri-Riccio 1874, pp. 28, 39; and De Boüard 1926, pp. 10, 14, 31–32, 36, 163, 209. On Charles's financial situation and his debts, see Monti 1932, and for a summary of the controversy between Charles and the Cistercians, Housley 1982, pp. 216–19.

78 The same four abbots and the abbot of Citeaux had been involved in negotiations on this issue with papal authorities for some years, at least since 1265: see Buczek 1969, pp. 59–62. The statutes of the Cistercian order concern this matter in some detail. See Canivez 1933–41, III, for the deliberations of the order in 1264 (p. 18) and 1267 (p. 49), and p. 116 on their capitulation in 1273: "Item, cum super solutione illius pecuniae tangentis decimam regis Siciliae, de qua venerabiles patres quatuor primi abbates cum illustri rege Siciliae composuerunt, et super hoc seipsos et domos suas pro se et illis omnibus, quos tangit negotium dictae decimae, obligaverunt; quia ipsorum curialitati et caritati dignum est modo debito responderi, statuit et ordinat Capitulum generale, ut summam cuilibet a patre abbate impositam usque ad feriam quintam infra octavam Paschae praesentibus abbatibus solvere non omittant."

79 Amarotta 1974, and De Boüard 1937 have suggested that there were also political considerations behind the foundation of the two abbeys. Amarotta observed that the foundation of the Cistercian abbeys in 1274 coincided with a particularly difficult period of Angevin relations with Gregory X, who was eager to resume peaceful

coexistence with Michael VIII Paleologus, Emperor of Constantinople. This would have put a sudden halt to Charles's well-developed plans for invasion and conquest in the East. Amarotta also noted that the monks arrived in 1274, the year of the Council of Lyons, and that it was only in 1277, shortly after the election of the anti-Angevin pope, Nicholas III, that Charles wrote to the mother houses requesting the arrival of the full compliment of monks for each of the abbeys. The timing of each phase of these activities, Amarotta suggested, was in keeping with Angevin negotiations and political maneuvers relating to the papacy. In addition, it is probably important to recall that underlying the events of these years was the rapid decline of Crusader control of the Holy Land. Although few may have foreseen in the conquest of Krak des Chevaliers in 1271 the subsequent loss of the last stronghold (Acre) in 1291, there was much evidence for the need for a rapid reordering of priorities and the consolidation of alliances. See also, for example, Venditti 1969, p. 699.

80 Guillaume de Saint-Pathus, 1899, p. 71.
81 And indeed it is interesting to note that Charles places Blanche's death in the Cistercian convent of Maubuisson, rather than in Paris where she actually died. Riant 1884, pp. 169 and 175.
82 Egidi 1910, p. 127; De Boüard 1937, p. 150; Francabandera 1932, p. 46.
83 De Santis 1652, p. 153.
84 The entire text is in Del Giudice 1863–1908, III, pp. 335–41. Herde 1980, pp. 44–45, notes that the French army itself was not sufficiently homogeneous to permit a clear sense of nationality, and even the Provençal soldiers were considered by royal French chroniclers, such as Primat, to be barbarians. The victory of Tagliacozzo was won by the elite French corps that Charles concealed until a final and decisive attack that transformed the battle into a French victory.
85 Although even within this group, as Herde 1980, p. 44, notes, there were distinctions based along national lines, with the French from the Ile-de-France apparently considered those most clearly fulfilling the role of a conquest predicted in the *Song of Roland* and other sources of Capetian ideology. See here Barbero 1983, pp. 107 ff.
86 Schulz and von Quast 1860, IV, p. 50. One wonders if Charles's experience in this matter did not derive from the mixtures of populations in his army, which Saba Malaspina described as filled with discord. See Herde 1980, p. 65, n. 230.
87 Egidi 1910, p. 126.
88 Herde 1980, p. 45: "Deus, sub cuius nomine gens Gallica semper pugnat, non patiaris nunc Gallicos tuos animo deleri, sed exhibe nobis ex his improbis hostibus hanc tantam miraculose victoriam, ut igiter, sicut solemus, in tuis possimus laudibus delectari." The text is taken from Saba Malaspina. One imagines that this did not go over well with the soldiers and knights of other nationalities who participated in the battle.
89 Enderlein 1997, pp. 32–34 and 204–25.
90 Egidi 1909–10, and see most recently Pesce 1994.

91 A first excavation was published by Fiocca 1903. A new survey of the site, which has led to the recent publication of Pesce, was undertaken under the direction of the late Professor A. M. Romanini and Professor M. Righetti Tosti-Croce of the University of Rome "La Sapienza."
92 But not accessible; the owners of the land, conscious of being in contravention of the law, also prevented photographs or a close examination of the excavation.
93 See for example Branner 1965, p. 135.
94 Del Giudice 1863–1908, III, p. 337; Schulz and von Quast 1860, IV, pp. 50–53.
95 Egidi 1909, p. 262; Schulz and von Quast 1860, IV, pp. 41–42.
96 Egidi 1909, p. 263, n.2: "Ecce quod ad providendum de loco et situ loci in quo mon. ipsum melius construi valeat et edificari de novo, una cum ven. Ab. Casenove . . . vos ad partes ipsas duximus transmittendos . . . quatenus . . . provideatis de loco . . . extimetis per quantam pecunie quantitatem construi poterit et que res necessarie sint ad construendum de novo mon. ipsum et pro quanta pecunie quantitate." A preliminary survey was standard procedure for all building projects. In the same year, at the meeting of the General Chapter of the Cistercian order in September, instructions were given for two monks from the abbey of Loroux, and two monks from the abbey of Royaumont, to travel to Naples to establish the two new monasteries in accordance with the strictures of the order.
97 Unfortunately nothing survives of Loroux in the Anjou.
98 Egidi 1909, p. 264, n. 2, notes that in the original documents the name of Angelo da Foggia is substituted over an erasure, and he presumes that the original partner to Peter of Oratorio would have been the other monk, John, who by 6 February 1274 has disappeared from the records.
99 Egidi 1909, p. 265, document of 8 March 1274.
100 This issue is discussed at length and with great intelligence by Egidi 1909, pp. 266–69, but the inclination to consider Pierre de Chaules an architect has been such that even recent authors revert to this designation. Elias 1983, p. 1, notes overlap and the lack of specialization in the duties and functions of the royal household.
101 Egidi 1909, p. 273; Schulz and von Quast 1860 IV, pp. 43–44.
102 Egidi 1909, p. 273; Schulz and von Quast 1860, IV, p. 44.
103 Egidi 1909, pp. 273–74. The document dates from 1 May 1274.
104 Filangieri 1950–, XI, p. 229, doc. 165. The document is dated 27 May 1274. The first master at Realvalle was Gauthier d'Asson, who was present at the site until April 1278, when instead Thibaud de Saumur is named as *prothomagister*. See Francabandera 1932, pp. 19–20.
105 On the account books, see also Egidi 1909, pp. 739–40.
106 Filangieri 1950–, XI, p. 248, docs. 222 and 223.
107 Filangieri 1950–, XVIII, p. 109, doc. 212.
108 Egidi 1909, p. 275.
109 Egidi 1909, p. 278.
110 Egidi 1909, p. 281.
111 Egidi 1909, p. 282, n. 1.

112 Egidi 1909, pp. 284 ff.

113 Egidi 1909, p. 287, n. 4.

114 Egidi 1909, pp. 288–89.

115 Egidi 1909, pp. 290–91. Although of course covering a roof usually precedes the erection of vaults. There is no way of knowing if at either abbey the vaults over the main spans were ever erected.

116 De Boüard and Durrieu 1933–35, II, pp. 224–45.

117 Bonaini 1887, p. 240: "minabantur . . . monasterium S. Marie de Victoria . . . demoliri, circa quem locum . . . Corradinus hostis ecclesis fuit devictus . . ."

118 Amarotta 1974, pp. 171–72.

119 Known as Cîteaux III. See Aubert 1947, I, pp. 190 ff. for this type of ground plan.

120 Exact dimensions of the church are difficult to obtain because the site is so overgrown and the walls ruined to foundation level.

121 Proportional relationships were fundamental to the Cistercian aesthetic. See Bruzelius 1979, pp. 87–89.

122 As in De Sanctis 1993, p. 153.

123 Wagner-Rieger 1961, "S. Lorenzo Maggiore in Neapel." There is no evidence that the plan of Realvalle was in any way different from that of Santa Maria della Vittoria, and Krüger 2001 rightly has instead placed the San Lorenzo plan in a Franciscan context, as we shall see in the next chapter.

124 This issue is especially significant in view of the importance accorded to Cistercian masons and sculptors in the building campaigns of Frederick II and as importers of French Gothic to Italy. The emphasis on Cistercian influence is a current in almost all Italian scholarship on medieval architecture in central and southern Italy. Yet it seems unlikely that there was more than a handful of trained lay brothers in the order after the middle of the thirteenth century. Far more viable in my view is the concept of a "utilitarian Gothic" that was adopted throughout Europe and the Holy Land for structures that were above all utilitarian in nature (the crusading castles of Syria and Palestine, not Cistercian but surely deeply similar to what was being constructed in Italy in the same decades).

125 In considering the evidence from the Registers, it should of course be remembered that we have only one side of the correspondence; letters to the king about conditions at the site, which might well have presented full details of the local situation, no longer survive. The Registers provide only the king's responses and his instructions, and these are sometimes startling in their preoccupation with detail (micromanagement at its most egregious).

126 De Boüard 1926, p. 332. This sudden profusion of texts and the intensity of the king's concern lead one to wonder whether there had not been an arrangement with the Cistercian abbots sent to Italy to resolve the matter of the tithes that the monks would arrive within four years of the accord, thus by the end of 1277. For a discussion of the tithe in relation to the foundation of the abbeys, see Bruzelius 1991, pp. 410–11.

127 Francabandera 1932, p. 29.

128 Egidi 1909, p. 287.

129 Egidi theorized that the problem of absenteeism derived from the substitution of silver for gold in coins after 1278. However, Francabandera 1932 notes that the ordinances on absenteeism continue after gold is reintroduced, and therefore suggests that the reason why the workers fled was because of the harsh conditions of labor and the penalties imposed upon them when they were ill or the weather prohibited a full working day.

130 Egidi 1909, p. 284. As Egidi notes, when in September 1278, the king discovered that the abbot and accountants of Vittoria, having been deserted by the local workmen, hired foreign laborers at a higher rate (18 grani rather than 15), these were to be sent away unless they would accept the receipt of 12 grani a day until the difference in rates of pay had been compensated for. See Egidi 1909, p. 759, n. 1.

131 Egidi 1909, p. 283, n. 7.

132 For impressed construction labor in England, see Colvin 1983, pp. 134–35.

133 Egidi 1909, p. 745.

134 This figure is cited by Galasso 1988, p. 34; Percy's study on taxation suggests a figure of 3–4 million (Percy 1964, p. 247).

135 All the following is based on Egidi 1910, pp. 125–28.

136 The reader familiar with later Cistercian history will already know that in the middle and late thirteenth century there were many more incidents of internal strife in general throughout the order and an ever-growing shortage of lay brothers.

137 Minieri-Riccio 1863, p. 70. Unfortunately, the cure was of short duration.

138 Pina Belli D'Elia is currently engaged in a major study of this site. In the meantime, see Melillo 1989, pp. 71–75; Otranto and Carletti 1990; Piemontese 1997; Belli D'Elia 1975, p. 42; Corsi 1994.

139 Cavaglieri 1987, p. 26.

140 Filangieri 1950–, VII, p. 104.

141 Bernich 1898; Sthamer 1912–26, I, pp. 133 ff.; Angelillis 1949, pp. 248–50; Calò Mariani 1984, pp. 167–76.

142 A solution that can be proposed for the discrepancy of the dates is that of my students, L. Arcuri and M. G. Russo, that the tower was begun but left incomplete, and was in urgent need of repairs by 1278.

143 Sthamer 1912–26, I, pp. 133 ff.

144 Calò Mariani 1991, pp. 26 ff.

145 The church was originally dedicated to the Magdalen. Filangieri 1950–, XXVI, p. 14. "Religiosis fratribus Minoribus exequtoria concessionis cuiusdam loci in Botonto pro construendo oratorio et domo pro fratribus ipsis." See Krüger 1986, p. 186, for the full documentation.

146 The one exception is the brief discussion of Castellano 1982, pp. 263–82, esp. pp. 276 ff. Castellano attributes the construction of the chevet of San Francesco in Bitonto to a Magister Jocobus Tounches, or Iacobo de Tongo, who was the brother-in-law of Sergio Bove.

147 Sbaraglia 1759-1804, IV, p. 308, 22 November 1291.

148 Castellano 1989, p. 276.

149 Calò Mariani 1980, p. 300.

150 For the dangers and the defects, including the noxious fumes from the linen works nearby, see Palmieri 1999, pp. 508–9.

151 Palmieri 1999, p. 510; the connection with the spaces described by Boccaccio was first noted by Filangieri 1936-40, I, p. 49.

152 Filangieri 1950–, XCIII, p. 245.

153 On this see Freigang 1992, *passim*. And as will be seen in the next chapter, it is also difficult to support Branner's statement (1965, p. 135), that "San Lorenzo was a direct, formal extension of the Court Style to southern Italy, a conscious expression of Capetian hegemony by Charles, indicating that in the 1270s Royaumont more than ever retained its royal associations." By Branner's account the transference of the court style to southern Italy took place via the two Cistercian abbeys, a view that as we have seen was also adopted by Wagner-Rieger and many other writers.

CHAPTER 2

1 The major studies are Krüger 1986 (also review by Pace 1988); Berger-Dittscheid 1990; Wagner-Rieger 1958; Wagner-Rieger 1961, "San Lorenzo Maggiore in Neapel"; Wagner-Rieger 1961, "San Lorenzo Maggiore: Il Coro"; De la Ville sur-Yllon 1895, "L'abside della chiesa; Chierici 1929–30, "Il restauro della chiesa di San Lorenzo"; Bruzelius 1994.

2 De la Ville sur-Yllon 1895, "La chiesa ed il convento".

3 Ricciardi 1999 on a recently discovered plan for the conventual complex is extremely interesting in this respect, esp. pp. 195–98. After Masaniello's revolt of 1647 the Spanish viceroy removed the armory to Castel Nuovo and Castel Sant'Elmo and attempted to move the city offices away from San Lorenzo to new and more spacious surroundings. The city officials declined to move.

4 Divenuto 1975, p. 130.

5 Villari 1967, p. 110. See Summonte 1601–43, and D'Engenio Caracciolo 1624, p. 123.

6 Chierici 1929–30, "Il restauro della chiesa di San Lorenzo," p. 28. The choir stalls are now in the upper choir of Santa Maria Donnaregina.

7 De Lellis 1654, p. 68.

8 Ricciardi 1999, pp. 195–96.

9 Chierici 1929–30, "Il restauro della chiesa di San Lorenzo," pp. 27–29.

10 Chierici 1929–30, "Il restauro de la chiesa di San Lorenzo," pp. 24–39. No documents on the restoration apart from the article seem to survive. On the condition of the choir in the late nineteenth century, see De la Ville sur-Yllon 1895, "L'abside della chiesa," p. 40: "L'abside di S. Lorenzo sta nel più completo abbandono: è deposito di pietre, di vecchie tavole tarlate, di ogni sorte di brutture ed immondizie. Ragneteli secolari ne tapezzano le mura, i pavimenti sono rotti, le pareti scalcinate, gli altari e le tombe infrante e profanate: non fa certamente onore al nostro municipio, al quale la chiesa appartiene."

11 Berger-Dittscheid 1990. On the Early Christian basilica, see especially Rusconi 1965, and Rotili 1978, p. 55.

12 For a summary of the various phases of excavation, see De Simone 1986, pp. 235–36.

13 Summonte 1601–43, I, p. 54.

14 I thank Antonio De Simone for providing me with his excavation plans and a copy of a series of photographs taken in the 1950s before his own work at the site.

15 De Simone 1986, p. 251.

16 "Hirpinus" 1961; Johannowsky 1961; Rusconi 1965, pp. 709–31; and De Simone 1986.

17 Krautheimer 1986, pp. 195–96.

18 Recupido 1984. It is tempting to associate this gift with the energetic archbishop, Peter of Sorrento, who also brought the Dominicans to the city center.

19 Palmieri 1999, pp. 504–05.

20 See on this Nimmo 1987, p. 55.

21 Moorman 1968, pp. 90–91.

22 Moorman 1968, pp. 90–91.

23 Already in 1223 the *Regula Bullata* limited preaching to clerics. See Clarck 1969, p. 298.

24 Clarck 1969, pp. 301–04. The clericalization of the Franciscans accorded with a revised papal policy that called for their assistance in the fight against heresy. For this purpose the order was adapted to the juridical structures of the Church, and the General Chapter of Narbonne in 1260 was entirely clerical in nature.

25 Knowles 1948, p. 174. On this process, see also Pásztor 1988, p. 21.

26 Nimmo 1987, p. 54.

27 Apart from these Neapolitan examples, the reader might wish to consider in this category Jacopo Torriti in Rome.

28 On Franciscan architectural legislation, see for example Villetti 1982 and in the same volume the introduction by Bonelli, esp. pp. 7–10.

29 To date the best study of this phenomenon is Schenkluhn 1985, esp. pp. 76 ff.

30 Rusconi 1965, p. 712.

31 Recupido 1984, p. 18.

32 A student of John of Parma's when he was lector in Naples before he became Minister General. Salimbene 1986, p. 559.

33 Peter of Sorrento is discussed at some length in relation to the construction of a tower at the cathedral of Naples in Chapter Three.

34 On the role of the mendicant orders in relation to city environments, see Guidoni 1977; Romanini 1974 and Romanini 1978.

35 Salimbene 1986, p. 297, considers Giovanni of Parma an early exponent of Joachite ideas in Naples. Di Fonzo 1995, p. 182, states that John of Parma was in Naples roughly between 1240 and 1245. Other noted teachers of the studium of San Lorenzo are listed by Sabatini 1975, pp. 62–63.

36 Sabatini 1975, p. 16 and n. 4. Early descriptions or lists of the Franciscans in Naples always place San Lorenzo under the category of Conventuals, and Santa Maria la Nova in the category of the Observants.

37 A new cloister to the south of the main cloister was recently freed from later accretions.

38 An even more striking classicism of about the same years is noted in the discussion of the cathedral tower of Archbishop Peter of Sorrento of 1234 in Chapter Three. On these conventual spaces, see also Middione 1994 and Verrengia 1995, p. 175.

39 On the *seggi* of Naples, see the classic study Croce 1942.

40 D'Andrea 1994, p. 459.

41 One thinks here of Sant Maria d'Aracoeli in Rome, for example.

42 See on the palace most recently Radke 1996, esp. pp. 40–47.

43 De Rinaldis 1927, p. 72, states that the windows of the chapter house at San Lorenzo are modeled on those by Giovanni Pisano in the Campo Santo of Pisa. This seems remote.

44 Krüger 1986, p. 72, attributes the painting in the lunette to a master working in the style of Giotto. See also Bologna 1969, p. 280.

45 These might also, however, be later in date, since a description of 1631 before the reconstruction of the chapter house speaks of this structure as "tutto vecchio e guasto e invalido." Ruocco 1936, p. 433. I suspect the vaults, which are constructed in terracotta, are seventeenth century.

46 Vitolo 2000, "La Noblesse," p. 559.

47 Krüger 1986 records the documentation for a series of land transactions and the construction of various conventual buildings in the last decade of the thirteenth century and into the fourteenth. On later property acquisitions, see Capone 1993.

48 The estimate of seventy to ninety friars comes from Di Fonzo 1995, although the author does not state his source. The later figure is attested by a contemporary source and published by Strazzullo 1968, p. 99.

49 On Frederick and the mendicants, see Barone 1978, pp. 612 ff.

50 Barone 1978, pp. 616–18.

51 Kamp 1973–82, I, p. 319.

52 Rashdall 1958, p. 24.

53 Del Giudice 1863–1908, III, p. 252.

54 For example, "Il coro di S. Lorenzo è anche la testimonianza meglio conservata di quell'attività costruttiva con cui Carlo I d'Angiò durante il suo regno si studiò di sottolineare i nuovi diritti francesi sul territorio acquistato . . ." Wagner-Rieger 1961, "San Lorenzo Maggiore: il coro." Similar views were also expressed by Venditti 1969, pp. 704–10. Chierici 1929–30, "Il restauro della chiesa di San Lorenzo," p. 24, states that the choir was "ideata e condotta da architetti dell' mezzogiorno della Francia scesi in Italia al sequito di Carlo I . . ." See also J. Gardner's remarks on San Lorenzo in Gardner 1988, esp. pp. 31–32; Pace 1988, p. 1 (review of Krüger 1986). Against this, Bruzelius 1991.

55 The most recent and vigorous affirmation of this tradition is that of Pace 1988, p. 105, in his review of Krüger 1986; an association with Charles of Anjou was also suggested by Bertaux 1905, p. 323, based on Chioccarello's manuscript, *Notitia ecclesiarum et beneficiorum regiorum*, in the Archivio di Stato of Naples. Others of the same view include De Falco 1549, no page numbers; Celano 1692. III, p. 158; Wadding 1931–64, III, p. 113; D'Engenio Caracciolo 1624, p. 103; Wagner-Rieger 1961, "San Lorenzo Maggiore: il coro," p. 1; Berger-Dittscheid 1990, pp. 54–55; a sixteenth-century manuscript on the churches of Naples published by D'Aloe 1883, p. 502; De Stefano 1560, p. 131; Sarnelli 1685, pp. 128–29; and many others. Krüger 1986, pp. 110–17, however, was very specific and articulate on the limited royal contribution of the kings, also Gardner 1988, p. 56, and Filangieri 1884, II pp. 5–6: "non fecero altro che contribuire con larghe sovvenzione all'ingrandimento ed alla perfezione di detta chiesa."

56 The attribution of San Lorenzo to Charles I dates from De Stefano 1560. For example, in G. A. Galante's guide to Naples of 1872 (new ed., N. Spinosa, Naples, 1985, p. 114), the author states: "Tolta Napoli agli Svevi, Carlo I d'Anjou deliberò di mutarla in un tempio sacro a San Lorenzo . . . Il Maglione, discepolo di Niccolà Pisano, fu chiamato da Carlo I per architettare la nuova basilica di S. Lorenzo nel 1266 . . ." An inscription attributing the church to Charles of Anjou is published by Schulz and von Quast 1860, III, p. 39: "Templi huius, quod Christi martyri Laurentio Carolus I utriusque Siciliae rex anno MCCLXV vovit parique pietate Carolus II absolvit, frontem terrae motu anno MDCCXXXII labefactatam fratres huius coenobii minores conventuales reficiendam ingenio v[iri] c[larissimi] Ferdinandi Sanfelicii patricii Neapolitani exornandamque curavere anno MDCCXLIII." "Hirpinus" 1961, p. 17, recognizes the vow as spurious.

57 Schenkluhn 1985, p. 178, and Cadei 1985, *passim*.

58 The first member of the royal family to be buried in the church, Raymond Berengar, may have had special devotion to the Franciscans, because he was one of the three sons tutored by members of the order during their captivity in Catalonia. Separate burials for children would also be in the manner of the French practice, since for example the Cistercian abbey of Royaumont, founded by Louis IX, was used for the burial of royal children. For the interpretation of San Lorenzo as royal necropolis, see most recently Berger-Dittscheid 1990, pp. 54 ff.

59 See Appendix 2 for some observations on the costs of construction in relation to this donation. Also Berger-Dittscheid 1990, p. 44. I thank Rosalba Di Meglio for her resolution of this matter. See also Kiesewetter. De la Ville sur-Yllon 1895, "L'abside della chiesa," p. 37, erroneously states that Charles I conceded "500 once d'oro."

60 The subject has been thoroughly studied by Sthamer 1937, pp. 1–68. See also Camera 1875, II, pp. 374–85, Della Marra 1641, pp. 347–50; and now Kiesewetter 1999, pp. 117–19. For the structure of the Angevin administration, see for example Cadier 1891, pp. 97 ff.

61 Sthamer 1937, p. 3; Galasso 1992, p. 51, writes of the fate of the Rufolo and della Marra families with stringent pungency; see also Bresc 1982–84.

62 Sthamer 1937, p. 8. On the loans, see also Camera 1875, II, pp. 374–80.

63 Kiesewetter 1999, p. 119.

64 Percy 1964, pp. 77 and 84.

65 Sthamer 1937, pp. 11 ff. on the accusations, pp. 29–30 for the documents.

66 Sthamer 1937, p. 14.

67 Lorenzo Rufolo is referred to as deceased (*quondam*) in documents after 22 December 1283. The execution seems to have taken place early that month, between 6 and 22 December, at about the same time that Galgano della Marra was hung; Sthamer 1937, p. 20. Angelo della Marra had been put to death on 3 October 1283 (Sthamer 1937, p. 16). Camera 1875, II, pp. 382–83, suggests that Lorenzo was not executed, but this appears to be an error.

68 Although not, it seems, to the extent that Sthamer suggests purely on the basis of state documents. There was for example a funerary chapel founded by the family in the cathedral of Ravello in 1287: see Widemann 1991, esp. the documents on pp. 69–73.

69 Sthamer 1937, p. 24.

70 Camera 1875, I, p. 342, refers to Fra Abamodo as "Conventuali." The castle where Matteo was imprisoned was southeast of Tropea. Sthamer 1937, p. 34, doc. 13.

71 Schulz and von Quast 1860, II, p. 277. A Giovanni Rufolo is listed as archdeacon of the cathedral at Ravello by Camera 1875, II, p. 315.

72 Sthamer 1937, p. 17.

73 Sthamer 1937, pp. 36–37, and docs. 20 and 22.

74 Sthamer 1937, p. 62, doc. 105.

75 It might also be noted that Matteo Rufolo had a son named Francesco, whose name appears on the ciborium inscription in the cathedral of Ravello in 1271. Schulz and von Quast 1860, II, p. 270.

76 Sthamer 1937, p. 46, doc. 51. According to Camera 1875, II, pp. 382–83, Matteo died, again in disgrace but for other reasons, in 1291.

77 Sthamer 1937, p. 58, doc. 94; p. 59, doc. 96; p. 60, doc. 101; pp. 64–65, doc. 110.

78 Widemann 2000, p. 166.

79 Sthamer 1937, pp. 7–8. For the completion of San Lorenzo in 1324, see Krüger 1986, pp. 84 and 88.

80 Herde 1977, pp. 199–226. Charles returned shortly after the Prince of Salerno had been taken captive.

81 Kiesewetter 1999, p. 119.

82 Berger-Dittscheid 1990, pp. 50 ff.

83 "Hirpinus" 1961, p. 17.

84. Minieri-Riccio 1871, pp. 31–32; Camera 1875, I, p. 274.

85 As Stephen Runciman (1986, p. 129) noted, "no other medieval ruler, not even his brother King Louis, was so minutely concerned with all the activities of his government."

86 See for example the documents cited by Krüger 1986, pp. 176–77.

87 Berger-Dittscheid 1990, pp. 54 ff.

88 Erlande-Brandenburg 1975, pp. 30, 94; and Hallam 1982, p. 364.

89 Louis celebrated his first mass as a Franciscan at San Lorenzo in 1296: Krüger 1986, p. 131.

90 Charles II's will left 80 once to the Dominicans, 40 to the Franciscans.

91 Charles II was buried at Notre-Dame de Nazareth at Aix-en-Provence, and left his heart to San Domenico in Naples: Del Giudice 1863–1908, pp. 154–69.

92 On Louis, see Pásztor 1955, "Per la storia," pp. iv–88. It should be noted, however, that Charles II supported San Francesco alla Scarpa in Sulmona *circa* 1290; see Moretti 1983, pp. 580–83.

93 On Louis of Toulouse and the Franciscans, see first and foremost Bologna 1969, pp. 158–70, esp. pp. 161–67.

94 Bologna 1969, pp. 158–67.

95 Although both Krüger 1986 and Berger-Dittscheid 1990 suggest that some of the chapels may antedate the chevet, neither examines this issue in detail.

96 I question the association of San Lorenzo with the Cistercian abbey of Realvalle. The tendency in the literature has also been to interpret the plan with ambulatory and radiating chapels as cathedral type (see for example Cadei 1985) and with royalty (Berger-Dittscheid 1990, pp. 53–54), but one might note that this plan had also become standard in monastic churches where the multiple chapels served the liturgical needs of increasingly clerical communities.

97 Cadei 1985, pp. 475–78; Wagner-Rieger 1958, pp. 139–44; Wagner-Rieger 1961, "S. Lorenzo Maggiore in Neapel"; and Wagner-Rieger 1961, "San Lorenzo Maggiore," pp. 1–7. This is difficult to reconcile with her suggestion of a date of *circa* 1270 for San Lorenzo, for Realvalle was begun (and surely the conventual buildings first!) only in 1274. From this she proceeds to the suggestion of an entire group of similar buildings associated with Charles of Anjou's patronage, and thus of a homogeneous "court style." Also along these lines Raspi-Serra and Bignardi 1984, pp. 223–28. Realvalle has never been excavated and we know nothing of the choir plan.

98 As tenaciously reaffirmed by Pace 1988, p. 105. This supposition would situate San Lorenzo firmly within the context of royal building projects and bring it into relation with Realvalle and Vittoria.

99 Berger-Dittscheid 1990, p. 45; Wagner-Rieger 1961 "San Lorenzo Maggiore: il coro," p. 5. The "modernity" of the plan is relative, for a similar disposition existed at Longpont and at Royaumont in the early decades of the thirteenth century.

100. The oft-cited similarity to Saint-Louis in Poissy is not useful, for that church was begun only in 1297, nor are comparisons with the Cistercian abbey of Valmagne convincing.

101 As noted in the previous chapters, the documents attest that the capitals at Realvalle are largely the work of French sculptors. It is difficult to accept Pace's remark (1988, p. 105) that the chevet is "audace e moderna."

102 In Naples, flyers are unique to San Lorenzo, although they were initially projected at Sant'Eligio. The ambulatory roofs are terraces; these had been current in France since the 1230s (Saint-Denis; Beauvais Cathedral). Schenkluhn 1985, pp. 124–70, notes the similarities between the elevation of San Francesco in Bologna and that of the Cistercian abbey church of Pontigny.

103 Schenkluhn 1985, pp. 114–63. Also Cadei 1985 on this

same subject appeared at about the same time, although this author does not emphasize the role of San Lorenzo as a *studium*.

104 Although Fra Donato (d. 1308), whose tombstone can be found in the second chapel on the right of the hemicycle, has been associated with the construction of the church, he has none of the attributes of an architect; see Mormone 1973, pp. 33–4.

105 Krüger 1986, plates 35 and 36.

106 There is no mention of this tower in any of the sources, but it antedates the extension of the Gothic church of San Lorenzo to the west in the 1320s, and may date from the middle of the thirteenth century or before. The structure is covered with plaster, so it is impossible to analyze its construction, although the incorporation of an ancient column may suggest that it is of twelfth- or early thirteenth-century date.

107 Berger-Dittscheid 1990, pp. 50–52.

108 Chierici 1929–30, "Il restauro della chiesa di San Lorenzo," p. 28. When the choir was moved, the altars and tombs attached to it were destroyed.

109 Di Meglio, forthcoming in *San Lorenzo e San Domenico di Napoli*, eds S. Romano and N. Bock.

110 On the chapels, see now Freigang 2002, p. 539, who notes that in Toulouse the multiplication of chapels in the mendicant churches began in the 1260s, and that laity were being buried in these by the 1270s. Also, in the same volume, Gardner's remark, 2002, p. 554, that in many respects the patterns of chapel construction and burial in Naples seem to imitate Paris and London rather than Rome and Florence.

111 Schenkluhn 1985, pp. 136 and 146–63. In disagreement, therefore, with Pace's remark (1988, p. 105). "sono le allusioni 'francesi' . . . a contare nel messagio ideologico di questa architettura."

112 Little 1964. See also Schenkluhn 1985, pp. 76 ff.

113 Cade 1985, and Schenkluhn 1985, pp. 76 ff.

114 Thus that the church came to acquire this function, rather than having been designed with it as a point of departure, thereby contradicting Venditti 1969, p. 708, Wagner-Rieger, "San Lorenzo Maggiore: il coro," pp. 2–3, and Berger-Dittscheid 1990, pp. 54 ff.

115 A document of the early 1290s that mentions the transportation of thirty cartloads of wood may refer to the ongoing construction at San Lorenzo, but it could also concern another Franciscan site or the conventual buildings at San Lorenzo itself.

116 Bologna 1988.

117 Krüger 1986, p. 147.

118 Summonte 1601–43, II pp. 361 and 374–75 and D'Engenio Caracciolo, 1624, pp. 111–12. Camera 1840–60. II, p. 163, states that Montano d'Arezzo had painted two chapels in the Castel Nuovo of Naples in 1305 and two other chapels in 1306. He was also employed by Philip of Taranto.

119 Neither Michalsky nor Enderlein considers the frescoes part of lost tomb projects.

120 See Bologna 1969, pp. 99–107, and Leone de Castris 1986, pp. 196–99.

121 Aceto 1985, pp. 10–27, and Aceto 1988–89; Filangieri 1883–91, II, p. 57, Mormone 1973, p. 45; also Gardner 1988, *passim*, on the tomb.

122 Fragments of Giovanni's tomb are discussed by Aceto 1988–89, p. 134 ff.

123 Divenuto 1975, p. 130 and fig. 2, and also Maresca di Serracapriola 1992, pp. 17–20 and especially n. 28.

124 Krüger 1986, p. 130.

125 There are a number of chapels dedicated to the Virgin at San Lorenzo, and it is difficult to know which one this refers to.

126 Krüger 1986, p. 191.

127 D'Engenio Caracciolo 1624, p. 105.

128 Schulz and von Quast 1860, III, p. 39.

CHAPTER 3

1 Taken from a sermon by Federico Franconi quoted and translated by D'Avray 1994, p. 105.

2 On the travel and itinerary of Charles II, see Kiesewetter 1997, pp. 152 ff. On the life and reign of Charles II up to 1294, see above all now Kiesewetter 1999.

3 Kiesewetter 1997, pp. 153–55. Minieri-Riccio 1882, p. 18. He left Charles Martel as vicar, assisted by Robert of Artois.

4 Perhaps Charles II, captured and imprisoned, simply had not known about the bloody events that took place later that day, or his affection for Naples was part of the gratitude and pleasure he felt in returning "home." For example, the king's words in relation to his works in the city: "quanto speciali instinctus amore nos prohevit ad ampliationem et incremandum civitatis eisdem Neapolis," Cantèra 1894, p. 4.

5 In the return from the crusade of 1270, Charles was able to obtain Louis's entrails for burial at Monreale.

6 The cultivation of a specifically Early Christian antiquity and a Constantinian tradition was of special interest to the archbishops during the reign of Charles II, as will be discussed below.

7 See Chapter Five on civic patronage in general and that of Giovanni Pipino in particular.

8 For Charles II's sojourns in France, see Kiesewetter 1997, *passim*: Charles was in Paris from February to August 1279; late June 1280; late June 1282; and January, then from July to September 1290.

9 On Parisian architecture of the late thirteenth century, see most recently Davis 1998, *passim*.

10 On these artistic trends, see *L'Art au temps des rois maudits: Philippe le Bel et ses fils, 1285–1328*, exh. cat., Le Grand Palais, Paris, 1998, and the papers of the colloquium, *1300. . . . l'art au temps de Philippe le Bel*, Rencontres de L'Ecole du Louvre, XVI, Paris, 2001, *passim*.

11 The fragments of frescoes in Santa Restituta are fourteenth century and later and are mentioned only by Sorrentino 1909, p. 228.

12 See for example D'Avray 1994, *passim*, and Pryds 1993.

13 Historical tradition has attributed the cathedral to Charles I of Anjou, an attribution perhaps stimulated by

the inscription on the west wall of the cathedral under the tomb erected in 1580–81 by Domenico Fontana. The documents issued by Charles II, however, are unequivocal in their declarations of the latter's foundation of this monument, as has been noted by various authors, including Cantèra 1890, pp. 5–6, and Chioccarello 1643, p. 186, and at this point should now be beyond dispute. Nevertheless, the tradition has been an obstinate one and has recently been revived by Bologna 1969 in relation to the frescoes in the Cappella Minutolo. Venditti 1969, p. 740, seems uncertain on this issue, attributing the cathedral to Charles II but stating that Charles I may have been involved in some preliminary way. Summonte 1601–43, II, p. 345, states that when Charles I first arrived in Naples in 1266 he came through the Porta Capuana and celebrated a mass of thanksgiving at the cathedral with 400 of his French knights. In 1273 Charles I gave stones from the city walls for the construction of a chapel in the episcopal palace (Chioccarello 1643, p. 175); no evidence of this chapel survives. The now-lost seated statue of Charles II that was once in the interior of the Saint Louis chapel (the present sacristy) was perhaps confused with Charles I and this may have added weight to the tradition that the first Angevin king had been the founder of the new cathedral. The history of the cathedral complex has been the object of many studies, mostly historical, few archaeological or architectural. A useful summary is in Sorrentino 1909, but see also the many studies by Strazzullo and above all the several highly useful essays by Cantèra. The scholarship of Chioccarello and Mazzocchi forms much of the foundation for these later works and is an essential point of departure, though dominated by their views on the local disputes over the precedence of the two clergies. Fundamental new material on the cathedral, which includes many of these observations, has recently been published in eds, Romano and Bock 2002.

14 See Venditti 1969, pp. 738–40, and De Stefano 1560, pp. 26–49, on the restorations and reconstructions; also Strazzullo 1957. For a succinct and somewhat anguished summary of the state of the monument, see Strazzullo 1963–64. No doubt the many redecorations and reconstructions have discouraged detailed studies of the cathedral as a medieval monument. Also Romano and Bock 2002, *passim*, and in this same volume Bruzelius 2002, pp. 119–31; also Romano 2001.

15 Bruzelius 1999, "Columpnas."

16 A document issued by Robert in February 1310 states it thus, referring to his father, "Ad supplicationem domini Philippi tunc Neapolitani Archiepiscopi exponentis maiorem Neapolitanam Ecclesiam in perceptione annualium decimarum eidem Ecclesie debitarum . . ." Other documents, such as Charles II's letter of 1305 on the tithes for the cathedral (Cantèra 1892, pp. 25–26), refer to the donations "ad supplicationem bone memorie P. tunc Neapolitane Archiepiscopis . . ." Enderlein 1997, pp. 10 ff, in his recent study reminds us that in the lifetime of Charles I, Palermo and the royal Norman tombs nearby at Monreale were still considered the chief sites for royal identity. See also now Romano 2001.

17 On the king's devotion to the cathedral, see Cantèra 1894, p. 5, n. 3; the document of June 1294 is a request for an estimate for a piece of land and a cellar contiguous to the cathedral (Cantèra 1890, p. 7: "solum et cellarium ipsi ecclesie maiori contigua eidem constructioni et edificationi necessaria plurimum nec ea velit vendere de hoc ipsum Archiepiscoporum . . .").

18 Cantèra 1890, pp. 7–8. It is difficult to know, of course, how significant a proportion of the building costs 100 once would have represented, but the fact that donations of 40 once crop up for chapels (construction and decoration) may indicate that this was a handsome but not excessively large sum, by no means adequate for the total construction costs for a year. On this topic, see now Bock 2002, *passim*.

19 Michalsky 2000, pp. 241–47, 253–60. There was in the old cathedral of Naples not only the tomb of Charles I but also the empty sarcophagus of his first wife, Beatrice, both of whom had presumably been buried in the Stefania. Although Beatrice's body was moved to Saint-Jean-de-Malte in Aix-en-Provence, Charles specifically requested that the monument in Naples that contained her "dust" be kept intact. See also Enderlein 1997, pp. 26–28. In August 1295 the heir to the throne of Hungary, Carlo Martello and his wife Clemenza, both died and they eventually received burial in the cathedral. On the documentation for these monuments, see Enderlein 1997, pp. 36, 208. As Enderlein 1997, pp. 32–35, points out, Charles I insisted on French clergy for the memorial masses in honor of the deceased members of his family. This was the case not only in Naples, but also at the tomb of his son Philip in Trani, who died in 1276. The conjunction of kings and bishops might be seen as similar to the French royal necropolis at Saint-Denis, where the remains of the first bishop of Paris were placed adjacent to, but separate from, those of the French kings in the thirteenth-century rebuilding of the church. However, the shift within the royal family to patronage of the mendicant orders meant that preference for burial soon passed to the Dominicans and Franciscans, a process that culminated in the tomb of Robert at Santa Chiara. On all this, see Enderlein 1997 and Michalsky 2000, *passim*. See now also Bock 2002.

20 Romano 2001 has recently reexamined the issue of the cult of the bishops with extremely interesting results. The Stefania was erected in the late fifth or early sixth century: see Strazzullo 1973, pp. 226 ff. On the episcopal tombs placed in the Stefania under Bishop John II "Lo Scriba", see Strazzullo 1973, p. 229. One *arcosolium* is still visible under the pavement of the *curia vescovile* adjacent to the small apse within a structure erected by Bishop Vincent, and fragments of others can be seen elsewhere. Farioli 1978, p. 287, states that "in una basilica non si fanno arcosoli," but there is evidence for these in Naples and elsewhere. The archaeological remains suggest that the large pavement under the *curia vescovile* is that of the Stefania, as Farioli recognized in her contributions to Bertaux, in A. Prandi, ed, *Aggiornamento*, IV, pp. 153–59, which provides a useful summary of the literature and the debate on the location and ori-

entation of the Stefania. In the pavement under the *curia vescovile* there seem also to be indications of a chancel enclosure. See also Ambrasi 1967, pp. 726 ff.

21 On many of these aspects of the cathedral of Naples, see now Romano and Bock 2002, especially the introduction by Romano and the essays by Bock, Bruzelius, and Aceto.

22 On Minutolo, see Walter and Piccialuli 1964, pp. 647–704; Chioccarello 1643, pp. 180–90. Enderlein 1997, p. 10, observes that in 1270 and perhaps for much of the lifetime of Charles I, Palermo and the royal Norman tombs at Monreale were still considered the chief sites of royal identity, yet Beatrice's monument was placed in the old cathedral of Naples (the Stefania) from the outset.

23 Chioccarello 1643, pp. 180–81, quotes the documents from the Angevin Registers as describing Minutolo as "clericum familiarem e consiliarum a Rege Carolo primo."

24 Parascandolo 1874, p. 90.

25 Parascandolo 1874, p. 92.

26 On the earthquake of 1293, see Minieri-Riccio 1878, p. 14. Donnaregina is discussed below.

27 There are some slight suggestions in De Stefano's excavation that a first church may have been aligned with the apse of Santa Maria del Principio and thus placed transversely to the axis of Santa Restituta, with the altar therefore in the west.

28 Capasso 1984, p. 66 n. 1, refers to the Constantinian foundation as a "favolosa tradizione." Venditti 1969, p. 792, noted its North African characteristics, in particular the raised apse framed by columns, an arrangement that he associates with Sabratha. At the *basilica nova* at Cimitile, of the late fourth century, the niches placed at the beginning of the curve of the apse may have been derived from Santa Restituta. A useful study is also Ambrasi 1967. The Constantinian tradition was to play an important role in Naples, for not only did the Donation of Constantine justify the papacy's right to establish Angevin rule, but it also provided an imperial precedent for Angevin patronage. See for example the *Cronica di Notar Giacomo*, ed., P. Garzilli, 1845, p. 5.

29 "Apostolicity" is of course a topos of cathedral foundation myths. See for example Miller 2000, pp. 181–82 and 233–36.

30 See now Bock 2002, *passim*. Also Chioccarello 1643, pp. 181–82, 184–85; Zigarelli 1861, p. 64. The debt to Minutolo was part of a larger loan of 400 once, the rest from Tuscan bankers. Bartolomeo da Capua, who was buried in the cathedral at his death in 1328, was directly involved with many of the negotiations for the king's loans and debts, attempting at one point to borrow the staggering sum of 100,000 once from Clement V, and at the very least to have excused the ever-mounting Angevin debt to the Holy See. On this, see Walter and Piccialuti 1964, pp. 697–704, esp. 699.

31 Minieri-Riccio 1878–83, III, p. 105.

32 There were 20 grani in one tari, and 30 tari in each uncia. As Coulter 1944, pp. 144–46, notes, a head scribe

would be paid one tari (or 20 grani) a day for the production of royal books. Cantèra 1894, p. 5, and Cantèra 1890, p. 10. See the latter publication for further documents issued by Giacomo da Viterbo in 1303, 1305, and 1306 for the collection of the tithe. Members of the court also made contributions: for example, in 1302 a valet of Raymond Berengar left one uncia for the construction of the cathedral (Cantèra 1890, p. 10).

33 Some of the difficulties had to do with the extraction of the tithe from the citizens of Naples. In 1304 the archbishop (by now Giacomo da Viterbo) received 175 once and 8 tari "ratione decimarum maiori Neapolitanae ecclesiae per regiam curiam debitarum . . ." See Cantèra 1892, pp. 19, 23, and 26.

34 Chioccarello 1643, p. 199.

35 Cantèra 1890, pp. 16–17.

36 Kamp 1973–82, I, p. 311, gives the annual income of the cathedral in 1308–10 as 1,000 once. In the Kingdom of Naples, this was exceeded only by Salerno (1,300 once, p. 425), and equalled only by Capua (p. 109).

37 Loreto 1839, 100; Del Treppo 1960, p. 520.

38 Summonte 1601–43, II, p. 119. This tithe, added to the properties already in the cathedral's possession, may well have generated a considerable income.

39 On Giacomo da Viterbo (1302–07), see Glorieux 1933, II, pp. 308 ff.; and Cantèra 1892, esp. pp. 13–16. Giacomo da Viterbo had taught theology in Paris as the successor to Thomas Aquinas.

40 The reversion of episcopal tithes to the crown in times of vacancy was common in France and often assisted the monarchy in times of financial distress: the prolonged vacancy between the death of Ayglerius and the appointment of Filippo Minutolo, from 1282 to 1288, may thus have helped to sustain the crown at a time of extreme penury while funds were being raised for the ransom of Charles II and the prosecution of the war against Sicily. Furthermore, the presence of the papal legate in Naples as regent may well have diminished the urgency of the need for a new archbishop. The tithe received for 1303–04 was for 308 once, which may represent part of the sum owed to the cathedral also during the vacancy of the episcopal see. See also Parascandolo 1874, III, p. 102.

41 On the Minutolo family, see Della Marra 1641, p. 284, and Bock 2002, p. 135. The bishop's brother Giovanni participated in the extermination of the Saracen community of Lucera in 1300 and was rewarded by Giovanni Pipino with the use of houses in Lucera.

42 For example, on the Filomarino chapel, see De Lellis 1654, p. 13. Naples may have been one of the first cathedrals systematically to plan private family chapels along the flanks of the nave. On private chapels in general there is now a substantial bibliography, but see especially Hueck 1976, Hueck 1986, and Gardner 2002.

43 For the most recent detailed discussion of Stefania, see Farioli 1978, in Prandi, ed., 1978, IV, pp. 158–60.

44 It is possible to suppose that some part of the Stefania might have been kept in place for some years after the initiation of construction of the main apses and transept

of the new cathedral to the south. If so, then the tombs of Charles I of Anjou and his first wife, Beatrice, probably located near the altar, could therefore have been preserved *in situ* for some years, along with the relics of the most important of the bishop-saints, while work went forward on the southern end of the old basilica.

45 Charles II commissioned the reliquary of San Gennaro in 1304 from three French goldsmiths. There is a debate as to whether the new reliquary was intended to celebrate the millennium of the saint or the safe return from imprisonment of Philip of Taranto (Leone de Castris 1986, p. 163). The new reliquary has also been associated with the reconstruction of the cathedral by Romano 2001, pp. 213–14. On the vicissitudes of the cult of San Gennaro, see now Vitolo 2001, *Tra Napoli e Salerno*, pp. 38–43.

46 Cantèra 1890, pp. 11–12.

47 D'Engenio Caracciolo 1624, p. 37. De Lellis 1654, p. 13. This chapel was destroyed with the construction of the San Gennaro chapel in the seventeenth century, which led to the creation of the Filomarino altar at Santissimi Apostoli by Borromini.

48 Although it is also possible that the fragmented state of these columns represents repairs made after the various earthquakes that damaged or destroyed the façade from 1349 onwards.

49 Cantèra 1890, pp. 17–18.

50 As will be seen below, the architectural details of the Gothic remodeling of Santa Restituta, which can be seen in the spiral stair that gives access to the organ loft, are slightly later in date than the rest of the new cathedral. The use of abaci à *bec* may indicate the work of one of the French masters active in Naples.

51 Vitolo 2000, "Esperienze religiose."

52 The chapel was adjacent to the altar of Santa Maria del Principio. All that remains at the site at the present time is an inscription commemorating the location of the burial. Vitolo 2000, "Esperienze religiose"; Mazzocchi 1751, p. 72; and Cantèra 1894, p. 34.

53 Zigarelli 1861, pp. 67–69.

54 Cantèra 1892, p. 55: "sunt quasi consumpta . . ."

55 The palace of Quisisana no longer survives. But the width of the chapel at the Castel Nuovo at 10.22 meters does not correspond to that of the nave of the cathedral, over 14 meters wide. For the documents, see Cantèra 1892, pp. 4–5.

56 On the orders on the roof beams and other documents concerning their transportation, see Cantèra 1894, p. 6, Cantèra 1890, pp. 12–15; and Cantèra 1892, pp. 5–7.

57 Mazzocchi 1751, pp. 146–52; Galante 1874, p. 11. On d'Ormont, see Romano 2001, *passim*.

58 For a summary on the discussions of the columns, see Farioli 1978, in Prandi, ed., 1978, IV, p. 158 and n. 30.

59 Only an atrium could have provided the requisite number of columns on site for the new cathedral. For a discussion of the atria in front of either or both of the early basilicas, see Mazzocchi 1751, pp. vi–vii, and Venditti 1973, p. 185. The location of the tower of Peter of Sorrento, however, as well as the disposition of the other

buildings, suggests that atria did exist, and that these (like the atria at Capua and Salerno) might have been large and imposing. The best discussion of the ancient columns is in Mazzocchi 1751, p. vii, who describes the columns of the cathedral and discusses them as part of a dissertation on the fact that the Stefania was the church now known as Santa Restituta and vice versa. He suggests, pp. 40–41, that the ancient columns encrusted in the piers have been sliced vertically, but a close examination reveals that this is not the case.

60 Bertaux 1903–04, I, p. 30, n. 5, states that the longer columns came from the Stefania and the shorter from the atria of the two cathedrals. It is generally supposed in the literature that the Stefania had only twelve columns based on the evidence of the thirteen hangings provided for the church (Strazzullo 1973, pp. 226–27). See also Capasso 1984, pp. 71–73, who speaks also of a crypt "in capite catacombe," quoting from John the Deacon. Santa Restituta still preserves *in situ* twenty-nine columns.

61 Venditti 1969, p. 748; Chierici 1934, *Il restauro della chiesa*, p. 33.

62 On the ambos of Salerno, see Glass 1991, pp. 65–75.

63 Minieri-Riccio 1874, p. 6. Various texts mention ambos in the old cathedral, for example Chioccarello 1643, p. 73. The transportation of marbles is noted by Palumbo 1959, p. 98. See also De Boüard 1911, pp. 239–45.

64 Sersale 1745, pp. 5–6, 21, associates the location of this tower with an earlier one erected by the Duke-Bishop of Naples Stephen II, who erected two tall towers after 764, one of which had a chapel dedicated to Saint Peter and was probably in the location of what is now the Cappella Minutolo.

65 De Stefano 1975, p. 161.

66 On the cathedral of Caserta Vecchia, see D'Onofrio 1974, pp. 193–94, who states that the design of the bell tower here must have been based on a "lost" Campanian model. It seems likely that the prototype was the tower of Naples.

67 It is likely that many of these ecclesiastics would have been opposed to the policies of the emperor. D'Aloe 1861, p. 468, cites the rumor that Peter of Sorrento died imprisoned by Frederick II. Some sense of Peter of Sorrento's historical interests may be suggested by his commission for a life of Sant'Aspreno, first bishop of Naples. Zigarelli 1861, pp. 54–60.

68 Against this view, see D'Onofrio 1974, p. 193.

69 See Cantèra 1894, p. 12, n. 2, and Celano, 1692, I, pp. 111–12. Cantèra refers to a document where a marble column, pieces of *cipollazzo*, and an architrave were found in the foundations of the tower. This material, damaged in the earthquake of 1349 or 1456, seems to have been used as fill.

70 See Strazzullo 2000, p. 46.

71 Ughello 1973–87, VI, pp. 143–44. On the earthquake of 1456 and repairs, see Summonte 1601–43, III, p. 212, and Parascandolo 1874, IV, p. 43. The arms of Piscicello and other Neapolitans who contributed to the reconstruction are visible in the upper parts of the pier of the south

aisle towards the transept and the exterior of the south transept arm (pl. 91). In 1631 an obelisk designed by Fanzago was erected in the piazza. Structural difficulties seem to have plagued this side of the cathedral, and may have been caused by the rapid descent of the terrain at this point of more than 7 meters, as well as possibly inadequate or unstable foundations within and around the previous structures.

72 The bronze horse of the piazza, presumably of imperial Roman date, was melted to make a bell for the adjacent cathedral tower. The many reconstructions of this part of the cathedral can lead to uncertainty in the chronology, but it should be remembered that what can now be seen of the south transept seems to consist for the most part of repairs made after the earthquakes of 1349 and 1456. It may be that the transverse arch at the crossing was rebuilt after 1349; see Venditti 1969, p. 748.

73 Venditti 1969, pp. 744–45; De Stefano 1560, p. 150. The space underneath the Cappella Minutolo is heavily whitewashed but there is no evidence visible to suggest that it is older than the date of the chapel above. See also De Stefano 1560, pp. 149–50. Its pavement, unstudied and unpublished, may well be older, however, perhaps early thirteenth century or before.

74 Strazzullo 1973, p. 227. He further states that Bishop Paul III (800–21) decorated the tower before the church of Saint Peter with paintings. According to Strazzullo, the altar presently in the Minutolo chapel may be of the early ninth century, for he states that the chapel had not been completed at the death of Bishop Stephen II.

75 See Romano 2001, *passim*, on this chapel and its decoration. For another view, see Bologna 1969, pp. 88–90, and Leone de Castris 1986, p. 199, who attributes the cathedral project to Charles I, suggesting (p. 208, n. 36) that "una maestranza transalpina" initiated the apses during the lifetime of Charles I and then abandoned the project. He hypothesizes that the incomplete state of the monument permitted Charles II to later describe himself as the founder. See also Sorrentino 1909, p. 228.

76 Romano 2001, *passim*, and Romano 2002, pp. 7–20.

77 Summonte 1601–43, II, p. 380.

78 Galante 1874, p. 2. The capitals in the Cappella San Paolo are similar to those of the Cappella San Martino at San Pietro a Maiella, discussed in the following chapter.

79 Bologna 1969, p. 116; Leone de Castris 1986, pp. 266–67; Romano 2001, *passim*. On the tomb of Ayglerius, see Delfino 1991.

80 Sparano 1768, pp. 210–11; D'Aloe 1861, p. 484, state that the cathedral was consecrated in 1314. Venditti 1969, p. 749 and p. 865 n. 57, however, also notes that a donation was made for the cathedral in Mary of Hungary's will executed in 1325 and that other gifts were made "ad opus" later in the fourteenth century. On the new liturgy, see Mazzocchi 1751, p. 149.

81 Aceto 1995, *passim*.

82 Enderlein 1997, p. 37. Umberto d'Ormont, future Bishop of Naples, was deacon of San Giorgio at that time. The marble episcopal throne to the right of the main altar in San Giorgio may have been erected for this

occasion, if it was not added later by Archbishop d'Ormont in connection with the translation of the relics of San Severo.

83 Chioccarello 1643, p. 199, states that the chapel was initiated in 1306 at the request of Mary of Hungary. Apart from questions of personal preference, the burial of Raymond Berengar in the church of San Lorenzo Maggiore in 1306 may have occurred because the Saint Louis chapel was not yet complete. Cantèra 1890, p. 9, n. 1, includes a document that states: "pro ipsa decima persolvetur in opificio constructionis ipsius maioris ecclesie que fit nuper usque ad perfectionem eius debitam convertatur et post ipsius opificii complementum ad faciendas fieri certas cappellas in ipsa ecclesia in quibus pro animabus dictorum parentis et aliorum nostrorum divina celebrantur officia desolvatur dignum. . . ."

84 Chioccarello 1643, p. 199.

85 Only one battered head of a king survives of the tomb sculpture. See on the documents Cantèra 1894, p. 89, n. 1.

86 De Stefano 1974, pl. 152. The main entrance to the Saint Louis chapel was from the west, into the portal still extant in the chapel (pl. 92). Later reinforcements to the transept buttresses partially obscure the south side of this portal. The style of the doorway is like that of the portals in the Cappella degli Illustrissimi and the Cappella Minutolo, as well as those at the west end of the church.

87 The text is cited by Galante 1874, p. 4. The tombs were moved to the main apse after 1456, and perhaps as late as 1580. See Strazzullo 1957, *passim*.

88 Cantèra 1894, p. 35.

89 Farioli, in Prandi, ed., 1978, IV, pp. 153–58.

90 Galante 1875–77, p. 60; Vitolo 2000, "Esperienze religiose," p. 16.

91 Sparano 1768, pp. 211–12.

92 The several sets of cathedral clergy must have been of great importance for the organization and funding of the new work. For some of the documents, see Parascandolo 1874, III, pp. 196–205. Fonseca 1990 has discussed the chapter and other clergy.

93 See Monti 1931, "La Cronaca."

94 Vitolo 2000, "Esperienze religiose," pp. 16–17, and Romano 2002, p. 16.

95 Romano 2002, pp. 15–16.

96 Vitolo 2000, "Esperienze religiose," p. 17.

97 These various attributions are discussed by Venditti 1969, p. 739. Vasari 1991, pp. 118 and 130. Vasari also associated the nave of San Lorenzo with that of the cathedral, no doubt because of the integration of ancient elements. See also De Dominici 1840, I, pp. 60–61. De la Ville sur-Yllon describes the style as "gotico provenzale," (1894 p. 177), but there is little connection to surviving monuments in the Angevin domains of Provence.

98 Carabellese 1899.

99 Venditti 1969, p. 738, has emphasized the analogies with San Domenico in Naples. One important characteristic of all these monuments is the high transept, an element also seen at San Lorenzo and Sant'Eligio. The pier type is also, of course, a common one and can be

found not only in Cistercian foundations, but also in the great Norman cathedrals of Sicily and Apulia (Bari, Barletta). It is also worth noting that the pier type is not only one of importation, but in fact has its origins in Roman supports, such as those reused in the front porch of the cathedral of Sessa Aurunca.

100 The cathedral of Orvieto was also planned in 1288–89 with small lateral chapels down the length of the nave, and Charles II might have seen the early stages of the monument when he passed through Orvieto in 1288. See, on the general subject of chapels, Gardner 2002, and Romano 2001.

101 On Sessa Autunca and Caserta Vecchia, see D'Onofrio and Pace 1981, pp. 76–87 and 180–84, although they do not mention this feature in either building. Venditti 1969, p. 860, n. 110, notes that Bertaux and Wagner Rieger both dated the transept of Caserta Vecchia to the time of Charles I; see also Venditti 1968, pp. 55 ff.

102 On Early Christian Naples, see Ambrasi 1967, pp. 625–57. Some of the legends discussed here had recently been revived in Peter of Sorrento's life of Saint Aspren written *circa* 1230.

103 On the importance of this theme in the late thirteenth- and fourteenth-century program of the cathedral, see especially Romano 2001, *passim*.

104 Romano 2001, n. 59.

105 Summonte 1601–43, II, p. 345.

106 Corrado 1998, pp. 390–91.

107 On the De Vico family as builders, see Filangieri 1883–91, V, pp. 224–26, and on Francesco's father Berutus, VI, p. 522. Filangieri, II, p. 216, also mentions a "Nicola da Napoli, architetto," active in 1270. But there were also some French architects and masons working in Naples early in the fourteenth century, notably Eudes de Crespy working at Castellamare in 1309 and in Naples in 1317 (II, p. 223) and Giovanni de Haya in 1329 (II, 2). Could the particularly French features of the remodeling of Santa Restituta with an impost *à bec* be attributable to one or the other of these?

108 On Galiardo Primario, see Filangieri 1883–91, V, p. 270; for Attanasio or Anastasio, II, pp. 315–16; on Riccardo Primario, II, p. 316.

109 To my knowledge, only a few scholars have given adequate emphasis to the presence of Italian expertise in the construction of the Neapolitan buildings discussed here, among them Chierici 1934, *Il restauro*, pp. 27, 33, and 35, Carabellese 1898, and Nitto de Rossi 1898, pp. 129 ff. It is interesting to speculate on why the literature has tended to attribute much of south Italian construction to foreign architects: is this a form of modesty, a reaction to the nationalism of fascism, or did these attributions, especially to Frenchmen, in some way ennoble or enhance the "value" of the medieval monuments of Naples?

110 These references have to do with law and taxation; see for example Percy 1964, p. 84.

111 Zigarelli 1861, p. 64.

112 The Dominican site was established in 1231 in Naples with the support of Archbishop Peter of Sorrento and

Gregory IX at the site of a much older hospital Benedictine community at Sant'Angelo a Morfisa. Venditti 1969, pp. 731–38. Cosenza 1899, p. 155, states that construction was initiated in 1289, but there are various reasons why this is unlikely.

113 It would also seem likely that a certain amount of property acquisition had to take place to create this large complex. Perrotta 1830, pp. 1–2; Valle and Minichini 1854, pp. 143 and 183.

114 Savarese 1981, p. 131.

115 Cosenza 1899, pp. 135–38.

116 The documents concerned are in Naples, Archivio di Stato, Monasteri soppressi, vols. 709, 719, and 743.

117 Naples, Archivio di Stato, Monasteri soppressi, vols. 709, 719, and 743, and Cosenza 1899, p. 156.

118 These purchases and exchanges are summarized by Cosenza 1899, p. 156.

119 For the consecration of 1303, see Anderson 1995, p. 285 and n. 14.

120 Cosenza 1899, p. 157.

121 Cosenza 1899, pp. 187–90.

122 Cosenza 1900, pp. 23–25.

123 Naples, Archivio di Stato, Monasteri soppressi, vol. 754, fol. 14, published in Feniello, plate 3.

124 Krüger 1986, p. 177. The monastery was a Byzantine foundation and Basilian before it became Benedictine.

125 On Isabella, see Anderson 1995, p. 281 and n. 7; Minieri-Riccio 1857, pp. 35–36 and 119.

126 See Galante 1985, pp. 73–74.

127 Bertaux 1899, pp. 3–5. A full bibliography is given in Leone de Castris 1986, p. 291, n. 1.

128 Wolohojian, pp. 46–55 and 202–03.

129 Bertaux 1899, pp. 12 and 161. Wadding 1931–64, VI, p. 517.

130 The tomb had been moved to the new seventeenth-century church and was reinstated in the old church in the restorations of Chierici, who believed that it was always intended to be located on the left nave wall. See Chierici 1934, "Il Restauro," pp. 136–37. See also Aceto 1995, pp. 12–14. On the original location of the tomb, see Enderlein 1997, pp. 89–98, and Michalsky 2000, pp. 289–97.

131 See most recently Elliott 2000, part II.

132 There is a wide range of opinion on the attribution of the frescoes to Cavallini or his school, and it is not possible to review this question here. See most recently Leone de Castris 1986, pp. 240, 266–69, 286, and Aceto 1992, pp. 57–58.

133 Wadding 1931–64, VI, p. 517. Elliott 2000 also associates the expansion of the choir with the increase in the number of friars, MS. p. 91.

134 Leone de Castris 1986, p. 287.

135 Bertaux 1899, Appendix IV, p. 169; D'Engenio Caracciolo 1624, p. 170.

136 Bruzelius 1992, p. 87.

137 Bruzelius 1992, p. 86-87. See Makowski 1997.

138 The chapel, whose paintings are considered of inferior quality, has not received much attention. See, however, Leone de Castris 1986, pp. 290 and 292, n. 23.

139 Lorenzetti 1936.

140 Filipiak 1957; Bruzelius 1992.

141 For Longchamp, see the brief mention in Branner 1965, pp. 89–91.

142 See Kurmann-Schwarz 2002 on Königsfelden.

143 Such as the sermon by Federico Franconi cited in the opening to this chapter.

144 The most recent study of the Castel Nuovo and its palatine chapel is that of Palmieri 1999; the classic studies are those of Filangieri 1927, pp. 1–11; and 1936–40, 1964.

145 Palmieri 1999, p. 513.

146 Palmieri 1999, *passim.*

147 Palmieri 1999, p. 508. The delay was probably due to Charles ii's death in 1309.

148 Friedman 1988, p. 112; Guidoni 1992, p. 3.

149 Di Nicola 1981, pp. 94 ff.

150 Clementi and Piroddi 1986, pp. 25–37.

151 The history of Lucera is told in one of the most thorough and brilliant studies on southern Italy, that of Egidi 1911–14.

152 As we shall see below, the well filled granaries of Lucera were later much coveted by Charles ii, and the destruction of the Muslim community in 1300 may well have had to do with their abundant holdings of wheat.

153 Part of this structure still survives at the site. Its elegance is attested by the fact that in 1242 Frederick had ancient statues transported to his *palacium* from Naples and Grottaferrata.

154 Egidi 1911, pp. 642–44; Haseloff 1992, pp. 124–25.

155 For a succinct description in English, see Abulafia 1988, pp. 146–48; Tomaiuoli 1995, pp. 238–43; Calò Mariani 1984, pp. 113–16; Calò Mariani 1998, pp. 40–41. For Charles i's fortification, see Haseloff 1992, pp. 104–29.

156 Santoro 1982, pp. 59–60.

157 Charles was particularly interested in men who were "fabri, carpentatores, magistri lapidum, ingeniatores . . ." (Egidi 1911, pp. 649–50).

158 Egidi 1911, p. 623, and 1912, pp. 79–87. Egidi 1913, p. 703, states, however, that the population of Lucera could not have exceeded 20,000.

159 Egidi 1911, pp. 36, 616 and 634.

160 Egidi 1911, p. 636.

161 Egidi 1911, pp. 697–98.

162 Egidi 1914, p. 134.

163 See Egidi 1912, pp. 664–96; Egidi 1913, pp. 681–707, *passim.*

164 Egidi 1913, pp. 130–31.

165 Egidi 1913, pp. 681 ff.

166 Egidi 1913, p. 687.

167 Egidi 1913, p. 687.

168 Although under Robert there are a few references (1335) to Muslims requesting protection from abuse and persecution. See Minieri-Riccio 1883, "Genealogia di Carlo ii," p. 29.

169 Egidi 1914, pp. 734–38.

170 Egidi 1914, pp. 132–35.

171 The biographer of Gregory ix states that Frederick ii built his palace on top of the foundations of the old cathedral. But this was clearly anti-imperial propaganda, for in his will Frederick urged his sons to reconstruct the old cathedral, which was in ruins. See Egidi 1911, pp. 627–28.

172 Egidi 1914, p. 754. The document is quoted by Egidi in n. 1: "Set specialiter inter cetera tibi hoc unum imponimus, quod locum illum notatum arabice Musquitum, in quo saraceni predicti orant et ad orandum soliti convenire erant ad orandum statuas et facias servari et haberi pro maiori ecclesia in ibi construenda . . . et quod similiter domus que sunt circiter locum ipsum de quibus et prout expedire videris, pro futuris eiusdem ecclesie canonicis et clericis conserventur . . ."

173 Egidi 1914, p. 758. Egidi supposes that the land transactions meant a change of site, but since the location of the cathedral is in the center of the old city, it seems more likely that the documents of 1304 simply attest to the acquisition of further land. The author notes that fragments of Arabic inscriptions were found under the foundations of the cathedral.

174 Egidi 1914, pp. 759–60. For this reason he has been associated with the design of the cathedral.

175 Bruzelius 1999, "Columpnas marmoreas," *passim.*

176 Bertaux 1895, pp. 420 ff.; also Camera 1840–60, ii, p. 79.

177 Egidi 1914, p. 765.

178 See Fobelli 1991, pp. 196–202, esp. 196.

179 Clementi and Piroddi 1986, pp. 23 ff.

180 Clementi and Piroddi 1986, pp. 25–28.

181 For the earthquake of 1915; Gavini 1915, pp. 235–40.

182 See Pace 1971, pp. 71–82.

183 Recorded by Gavini 1927–28, p. 47; Krüger 1986, pp. 194–96.

184 Damage from the earthquakes of 1315 and 1349 may have occurred during construction.

185 Martelli 1955, esp. pp. 163 ff.

186 See Russo 1961, pp. 193 ff; and Carlucci 1932, pp. 1–17.

187 The nave has rectangular piers that support slightly pointed arches and can be associated with monuments produced in Byzantine southern Italy such as Santa Maria d'Anglona, for example. The surfaces of the nave are entirely covered with early twentieth-century stucco decoration.

188 See above in the discussion of the cathedral of Naples, n. 107.

189 Schulz and von Quast 1860, ii, 354; and now Spanò 2002.

190 Ruocco 1937, p. 139; Krüger 1986, p. 193; Russo 1961, p. 200.

191 The king's participation is attested by the Anjou arms over the west door, as well as by Sarnelli 1685, pp. 229–30. See also Krüger 1986, p. 199.

192 Sarnelli 1685, pp. 229–30.

193 Krüger 1986, p. 199.

194 Krüger 1986, pp. 181–83. Parente 1857, ii, p. 198, stated that the church was founded by Charles i inspired by Mary Magdalen, but this can be discounted.

195 Parente 1857, ii, p. 198.

196 Parente 1857, ii, pp. 183–84: "In Hospitio Regio in civitate Aversae sita erat ecclesia Sancti Petri, et in ea ecclesia Rex Carolus secundus Rectorem constituit, ex quo Ecclesia praedicta ad Regem jure patronatus pertinebat."

197 Charles ii also subsidized the construction of the church

of San Domenico in Sessa Aurunca, now known as San Pietro a Castello. Krüger 1986, pp. 208–09.

198 The sermon was by Federico Franconi and is quoted and translated by D'Avray 1994, pp. 147–48.

199 D'Avray 1994, pp. 148–49.

200 Anderson 1995, pp. 283–84.

201 On Louis of Toulouse see especially Toynbee 1929.

202 Chioccarello 1643, p. 198, mentions this.

203 See, for example, White 1966, p. 197, and Venditti 1969, *passim*.

204 On the transept of Old Saint Peter's, see, for example, Bozzoni 1997, pp. 63–72.

205 Housley 1992, p. 262.

206 On the invasions and the Almogávar troops, see Russo 1961, pp. 199 ff., and Carlucci 1932, pp. 3 ff.

CHAPTER 4

1 Camera 1840–60, II, p. 340, n. 1: "trovandosi allora quasi terminata la costruzione della chiesa di S. Chiara, re Roberto vi si condusse col duca Carlo suo figliolo a curiosarla, ed a questi dimandato avesse se gli piaceva quel sacro tempio. Al che senza adulazione Carlo rispose, che sembrava di essere una scuderia che avea una sola navata, onde le cappelle laterali rimanevano come tante mangiatoie. Roberto quasi presago dell'avvenire gli soggiunse: piaccia a Dio, o mio figliuolo, che non siete il primo a mangiare in questa scuderia." The spelling is his.

2 Ferdinando Bologna was the first to associate the Spiritual Franciscans with the complex of Santa Chiara, especially in the volume of 1969. There are many studies of the Spirituals in Naples, but see especially Musto 1997, pp. 419–86, and Paciocco 1998. Important new work is being done on Sancia of Mallorca by Matthew Clear, but this has not yet been published. For an alternate view on the importance of the Spiritual Franciscans within the court itself, see Boyer 2000, pp. 568 and 577, and Kelly 1999, *passim*.

3 Boyer and Kelly, as in the previous note.

4 The heir to the throne, Charles of Calabria, predeceased his father in 1328, so he was indeed among the first to "eat in the stable." On the tombs of Santa Chiara, see Fraschetti 1898; Morisani 1972, pp. 159–73; Gardner 1981; Bertaux 1895, "Magistri Johannes et Pacius," pp. 147–52; Michalsky 2000, pp. 125–52; and Enderlein 1997, pp. 99–105, 119–21, 124–26, 130–33, 168–70, and 193–99.

5 Bertaux 1898; De Rinaldis 1920; Spila da Subiaco 1901; Fastidio 1900, p. 144; and Gallino 1963. See also Di Montemayor 1895, pp. 65–67, 84–87, and Dell'Aja 1992. Speculations on the character of the church have included the suggestion of Bernisch, published by Spila da Subiaco 1901, that the nave was vaulted.

6 Meier 1990. The mother house of the order is about 55–60 meters long. The one convent that may have rivaled Santa Chiara in Naples in the number of sisters, if not the size of the church, was that in Kraków, which also had 250 nuns. More commonly, communities of Poor Clares numbered between ten and twenty sisters, although some were larger, as at Carcassonne, where there were eighty nuns in 1372, and Toulouse, with fifty-three sisters in 1330. On the sizes of Clarissan houses, see Moorman 1968, p. 210.

7 Clare's own convent, San Damiano at Assisi, is a good example of a small older church restored for the Clares. Since many convents were inserted into older foundations, the original dedications were often kept, as at San Sebastiano at Alatri. On this extremely interesting site, see Prehn 1971, pp. 5–11, and Scaccia Scarafoni 1916–18, pp. 5–52, 223–62, and Fentress 2004. The only extensive study of early Clarissan architecture is that of Filipiak 1957.

8 Including the nun's retrochoir, Santa Chiara is 110.50 meters long inside the walls; exclusive of the choir, it is 82 meters long. The cathedral of San Gennaro is 100 meters long. Both church and choir at Santa Chiara are 33.00 meters wide, the nave walls are 45.70 meters tall. On the traditions of Santa Chiara, see Spila da Subiaco 1901, p. 180. The coronation of Sancia and Robert's heiress, Joanna I, took place in the convent church on 29 August 1344.

9 D'Andrea 1980, pp. 39–78, esp. 75.

10 For strict enclosure, see Huyghe 1944.

11 The Baroque decoration was charmingly described by Di Montemayor 1895, II, p. 84, "Come un velo di neve sovr'ogni cosa," and by Bertaux 1868, p. 169: "une sorte de salle de fêtes." The designs were by Vaccaro in 1744, but because he died nine months later, the work was carried out by others, with considerable modifications to the original plans. See Mormone 1959, III, pp. 85–103; and Blunt 1975, p. 118, n. 21.

12 Only Bertaux was able to enter the choir, an achievement facilitated by the French Academy in Rome.

13 Most recently Dell'Aja 1992, p. 26. In my view the double monastery was integral to Sancia's project from the outset, as suggested also by Spila da Subiaco 1901, p. 317, and church and choir were constructed as part of one long campaign. The frequently made suggestion (for example, Bertaux 1868, p. 167) that the Franciscan cloister was an afterthought seems highly unlikely.

14 On the sixteenth-century fires, see Gaglione 1996, pp. 53–56, esp. n. 1. For surveys of the documents, see D'Andrea's three articles in the 1976, 1977, and 1987 volumes of the *Archivum Franciscanum Historicum*.

15 Dell'Aja 1980, pp. 48–56.

16 Wadding 1931–64, VI and VII and Eubel 1898-1904, VI and VII.

17 Enderlein 1997, Michalsky 2000, Gaglione 1995, and Gaglione 1996.

18 Gaglione 1998, p. 10.

19 In a document of 1316 Robert stated that "quod monasterium Sancte Clare de Neapoli, interdum *Sancti Corporis Christi*, interdum *Sancte Clare* et quandoque *Hostie Sacre* denominatur, et hac appositione sinonima essentia nominis non immutatur." Quoted by Camera 1840-60, II, p. 193.

20 Most recently Gardner 1988, p. 56. These views are sum-

marized by Celano 1692, III, p. 393, who states, however, that Robert was "fortemente incitato dalla piissima Regina Sancia . . ." Numerous authors have suggested that the foundation was a gesture of expiation not only for Robert's usurpation of his nephew's rights to the throne, but also for his purported poisoning of his eldest brother Charles Martel, who died in 1295 (see for example De Lellis, *Aggiunta alla Napoli sacra dell'Engenio*, 254 [MS. Biblioteca Nazionale, Naples]). But as Spila da Subiaco 1901, p. 28, and others have pointed out, this is highly unlikely, because at the time of Charles Martel's death the next brother in line to the throne was Louis, who had neither declared his Franciscan vocation nor renounced his rights to his inheritance. Sancia's primary role has been affirmed by Bertaux 1898, pp. 166 ff., by Spila da Subiaco 1901, *passim*, and most recently by Dell'Aja 1992, p. 15.

21 For example, Wadding 1931–64, VI, pp. 531–32, 543–47, 569–70, 622–23, and 630–46.

22 The letter dates from 1321. She states that the sisters will live "secundum regulam datam Sororibus Ordinis sancti Damiani a Domino Innocentio Papa IV . . ." Wadding 1931–64, VI, pp. 631–46; Spila da Subiaco 1901, p. 70. Because she specified the rule of San Damiano, which had its own rule, as distinct from the rule of Innocent IV of 1247, Sancia is referring to the rule that Clare wrote on her deathbed in 1253 *approved* by Innocent IV on 9 August 1253. This version of the rule reflected Clare's ideas on the matter of poverty, which had been mitigated (against Clare's wishes) in previous rules drawn up on behalf of the sisters by their advisors. See Armstrong 1988, pp. 109–21. Moorman 1968, pp. 32–39, 205–15, 406–13, especially 211–12, provides a useful summary of the various versions of the rule and the development of the order. It should be noted that Sancia did not adopt the more lenient Clarissan rule previously developed for another prestigious royal convent, Longchamp, founded by Isabelle of France in 1261.

23 Robert's letter of 10 July 1315, agreeing to Sancia's financial contributions to the convent as well as her eventual retirement, is now destroyed, but is quoted by Bertaux 1898, p. 166, n. 3. "Posse contingere ipsam Reginam, contentis mundanis affectibus velle finaliter tempore apto suo habitum alicujus Sancte Religionis assumere ac in regulari observancia reddere Domino dies suos." As Bertaux noted, the document had an inscription in the margin that stated: "Pro Regina et novo monasterio Sancte Clare quod fieri facit in Neapoli." See also Spila da Subiaco 1901, p. 53, n. 1. The pope refused Sancia's request to leave her husband and enjoined her to heed her spouse.

24 Petrarch stated that "At Clarae virginis praeclarum domicilium, quamvis a litore parumper abscesserit, videto, reginae senioris amplissimum opus," quoted by Bertaux 1898, p.169, n. 1.

25 Musto 1985.

26 These other convents have all been destroyed. A certain number of documents pertaining to the Clarissan foundations in Provence survive in the departmental archives of the Bouche-du-Rhône in Marseilles. See also the documents in Wadding 1931–64, VII, pp. 567, 572–73, and Eubel 1898-1904, VII, pp. 48, 56, 96–98. Sancia eventually retired to Santa Croce, founded on 19 March 1338, after the death of Robert (Eubel 1898-1904, VII, 97–8). The convent in Aix was established on 14 May 1337.

27 Wadding 1931–64, VI, pp. 632, 645, 646.

28 Gallino 1963, p. 21. His attribution of the reused marbles on the portals to ancient remains at the site cannot be supported, however, because these marbles were imported from Rome.

29 Because of this anomaly, I shall refer to parts of the church by right and left as one faces the altar, rather than by the points of the compass.

30 Dell'Aja 1992, p. 4.

31 Wadding 1931–64, VI, pp. 531–32. On the same date he gave Sancia permission to have two Poor Clares among her attendants; and Eubel 1898-1904, VI, p. 87.

32 Spila da Subiaco 1901, p. 261.

33 The delay in the arrival of the sisters no doubt depended on a guarantee of enclosure. The enclosure of the sisters at Santa Chiara was reaffirmed by John XXII in the year preceding their arrival. We shall return to some of these questions below. In contrast with the permission for the foundation of a Clarissan house, papal sanction for the friars' cloister was given by John XXII on 11 January 1317. Wadding 1931–64, VI, pp. 544–45.

34 Wadding 1931–64, VI, pp. 531, 546–47; 568.

35 Wadding 1931–64, VII, pp. 631–46.

36 Wadding 1931–64, VI, pp. 631–46.

37 As we shall see below, the document goes on to specify where construction materials for the monastery could be placed. See Gallino 1963, pp. 22–23.

38 This would account for the successive increases in the number of sisters in the convent in 1317 and 1319.

39 For example, Bertaux 1898, pp. 167–68.

40 Wadding 1931–64, VI, p. 562

41 This in effect stipulated a continuation of the arrangement at San Damiano.

42 Moorman 1968, p. 213. On the rule of 1263, see also Fontette 1967, pp. 137–39. The rule of Urban IV also clarified the nomenclature of the Clarissas, with the pope designating the group as the Order of Saint Clare, rather than Poor Ladies, or Poor Recluses, of San Damiano.

43 D'Andrea 1987, pp. 60–63; Wadding 1931–64, VI, pp. 631–46.

44 Brooke and Brooke 1978, pp. 275–88. It has also been suggested that strict enclosure was part of Clare's intention from the outset: see Lainati 1973, pp. 223–50.

45 Brooke and Brooke 1978, p. 281.

46 Musto 1985 points out (p. 194) that her letters to the Franciscan order of 1334 make reference to the Franciscan rules, to the *Vita I* and *Vita II* of Thomas of Celano, to Bonaventure's *Legenda maior*, and there are probably also references to the *Legenda trium sociorum*.

47 Eubel 1898-1904, VII, pp. 18–19, and 55. Bertaux 1898 also provides a narrative account of the event and the document, pp. 170–71.

48 Although the phenomenon of double convents was in decline by the thirteenth century (Bynum 1987, p. 22), the Clares depended on various arrangements of associated Franciscans to administer the sacraments.

49 Wadding 1931–64, VI, p. 531; for Sancia's retinue of sisters acquired in June 1312, see Eubel 1898-1904, VI, p. 87. As late as 1337 Sancia seems still to have been planning to enter Santa Chiara, although six or seven years later she actually retired to Santa Croce. For her request to do so, see Di Montemayor 1895, p. 65.

50 Spila da Subiaco 1901, pp. 58–59. D'Andrea 1987, p. 62, has some observations to make on Sancia's evolving spirituality, which he describes, however, to confusion. Queen Esclaramonde of Mallorca, Sancia's mother, also founded convents with the same dedications and functions in Perpignan.

51 So it may be sensible to see Sancia's spiritual inclinations as shifting over the three decades of her rule in Naples. See also Musto 1997, *passim*, and most recently Paciocco 1998, *passim*.

52 On Fontevrault, see Crozet 1964, pp. 426–77; for the destroyed convent of Poissy, see Erlande-Brandenburg 1971, pp. 85–112.

53 By 1332 Robert was paying for the expenses of fifteen Franciscans living in the Castel Nuovo. Spila da Subiaco 1901, p. 41, n. 5. The Franciscan and Clarissan retinues bring up the issue of celibate marriage, which was widely practiced in pious circles at the time. See Vauchez 1987, pp. 83–92, and Musto 1997, pp. 435–36.

54 In any event, it should be noted that the tower postdates the construction of most of the church.

55 The gap in dates between 1313 and 1317 is attributable to the long vacancy between the death of Clement V in 1314 and the election of John XXII on 4 August 1316. The strict regulations on enclosure were reiterated in John XXII's bull of 11 January 1317. See Wadding 1931–64, VI, p. 547.

56 Spila da Subiaco 1901, pp. 80–81; Wadding 1931–64, VI, pp. 543–44.

57 The group of friars initially consisted of only twenty members. On 14 June 1316 the order was issued for a cloth "ad aurum tartarici coloris albi" offered by Robert during the mass celebrated in the convent church. Di Montemayor 1895, p. 67. In 1317 the number of friars increased to fifty.

58 Caggese 1922–30, II, p. 399.

59 Gaglione 1996, pp. 99–100.

60 The date of completion is based on the *Cronaca di Partenope*, and the dedication was recorded in the north inscription on the campanile. Gaglione 1998.

61 On the tower, see now Gaglione 1998, with the correct recording of the inscriptions, pp. 10–11.

62 Spila da Subiaco 1901, pp. 261–62.

63 Eubel 1898-1904, VI, p. 137.

64 Eubel 1898-1904, VI, p. 144.

65 Dell'Aja 1980, p. 59.

66 Eubel 1898-1904, VI, p. 190.

67 Gallino 1963, p. 27.

68 The orchard was "ipsi ecclesie seu monasterii immedi-ate conterminum, constructioni et hedificationi presertim corporis ipsius ecclesie necessarium et admodum oportunum." Fastidio 1990, p. 144. As he remarks, the text of the document undermines Bertaux's suggestion of two separate churches.

69 It states that the construction of the church was specifically undertaken by Sancia. It also refers to a contract of August 1320, in which Gabriele de Santo Petro of Bologna promised to provide Stefano Murillo of Naples, *praepositus*, for the construction of Santa Chiara, "trabes de abiete quatratas quinquaginta, quamlibet longitudinis cannarum quatuordecim latitudinis a duabus lateribus palmorum duorum et altitudinis in quolibet capite palmorum duorum et medii et in medio palmorum trium nec non cavallos de abiete similiter quatratos centum quemlibet longitudinis cannarum novem latitudinis palmorum duorum a duabus faciebus et a reliquis duabus altitudinis palmorum trium," to be taken from the forest of Mercurio in Calabria, which in 1310 had provided the timber for the reconstruction of the Lateran in Rome. The cost was 900 once to be taken from the sums provided by the queen for the construction of the church. Because of the danger of bandits in Calabria, Gabriele de Santo Petro and his associates were permitted to carry arms otherwise prohibited in the kingdom. See Fastidio 1990, p. 144, and Spila da Subiaco 1901, p. 71.

70 Wadding 1931–64, VI, pp. 631–46.

71 De Lellis *Parte seconda*, 1654, p. 176.

72 It is by now widely recognized that consecration dates can either precede or postdate by many years the completion of construction.

73 For what is known of the dedications and original family sponsors of the chapels, see Gaglione 1996, pp. 53–85.

74 However, in the Baroque remodeling under Vaccaro, the galleries were covered and separated from the nave by grills, so one can assume that by the eighteenth century the sisters did have access to the tribunes.

75 A guide to the subject of choir screens is Hall 1979. See also Hall 1974, pp. 325–41; Doberer 1956; Jung 2000.

76 The notable exception is the doctoral dissertation, Filipiak 1957.

77 Wadding 1931–64, II, p. 47.

78 It should be recalled that for a time before she could move to San Damiano, Clare lived with the anchorites at San Panzo outside Assisi.

79 The present choir may have extended to enclose the entire circumference of the apse, in which case the small window now partly concealed behind the later choir stalls would have opened on to the choir of the Clarisses.

80 Bruzelius 1992.

81 On the elevation, see Jungmann 1986, II, pp. 207–11; Emminghaus 1978, pp. 81–83. It should be noted that choir and rood screens may often have prohibited vision by the lay population as well.

82 Occhipinti 1978, pp. 197–212, esp. 211: "Fenestra vero maior . . . ut per eam videri possit hostia salutaris quia ibi ante illam fenestram in corpore ecclesie altare novum Domino construetur."

83 The rule of 1253 states: "Let a curtain be hung inside the grille which may not be removed except when the Word of God is preached or when a sister is speaking with someone. Let the grille have a wooden door which is well provided with two distinct iron locks, bolts, and bars, so that it can be locked, especially at night, by two keys, one of which the Abbess should keep and the other the sacristan. Let it always be locked except when the Divine Office is being celebrated." Armstrong 1988, p. 68. This author points out (n. 33) that Clare went beyond the strictures provided in the Rule of Ugolino and Innocent.

84 The character of the religious space for the nuns at Donnaregina, who worshiped in an upper tribune richly decorated with frescoes, parallels the general phenomenon in the late Middle Ages of an internalized process of silent perception and individual introspection. See Lewis 1990, p. 257, and Duby 1999, II, pp. 523–25.

85 At San Damiano there is a niche for the reserved host in the nuns' oratory, which is on the upper level, adjacent to the dormitory.

86 Musto 1997, p. 467.

87 Musto 1997, pp. 467–8.

88 One of the earliest such dedications is found in Verona by 1272, but they are rare. See Barbiero 1946, p. 203.

89 In this matter she was in concert with other women of her generation. See Bynum 1984, pp. 179–214.

90 Musto 1985, pp. 213–14.

91 On Esclaramonde, see Vidal 1910.

92 See Camera 1840-60, *Annali*, II, pp. 492–93, and Rigaux 1989, p. 145. On the subject of eucharistic piety and women, see Bynum 1984, *passim*. Sancia and Robert also obtained for the Franciscans the custody of the Holy Sepulcher and other sanctuaries in Jerusalem.

93 Musto 1985, pp. 207–14, esp. 208.

94 Vidal 1897, p. 76. The chapels were finished in 1292.

95 Archives départementales de Languedoc-Roussillon, Perpignan, docs. in B257 and B175, for example. Neither convent survives.

96 Eubel 1898-1904, VI, p. 50.

97 Archives départementales de Languedoc-Roussillon, Perpignan, B219. See also Rosellò Lliteras, 1989–90, III, p. 17.

98 Bologna (1969) was the first to understand the implications of these connections for the art of Naples.

99 The family saints are depicted at the foot of the Last Judgement scene in Santa Maria Donnaregina.

100 See now on this Michalsky 1998.

101 Pou y Martí 1930 and Musto 1985, pp. 191–202. On the Spirituals in general, see Douie 1932.

102 See for example Biget 1984, pp. 75–94.

103 This of course happened in any event in the case of the eldest son, Louis. Olivi stated: "Nam et michi a fide digno aliquo dictum fuit, quod eciam dominus pater vester timuerat vos imbeguiniri, seu ut proprius loquar in divinis infatuari per eloquia oris mei." Ehrle 1888, III, p. 539. Robert's views on the poverty issue are well-known from his sermons. See Baddeley 1897, pp. 151–53.

104 Musto 1997, pp. 434–35, especially n. 58.

105 See Vauchez 1987, pp. 83–92, and Strelke 1987, pp. 203–24.

106 A number of versions of Arnald's manuscripts survive in Neapolitan dialect and have been associated with the court of Robert of Anjou. See Santi 1985, pp. 977–1014, esp. 995–97. We know that Arnald was in Avignon in 1309 when Robert and Sancia were also there, and letters of his to some members of the Angevin royal family survive – for example, a letter to Blanche of Anjou of the summer of 1309. Santi 1985, p. 1002.

107 Musto 1985, p. 208.

108 On Philip of Mallorca, see Vidal 1910.

109 Vidal 1910, pp. 362 ff. See also Vauchez 1987, pp. 83–92. On the relations between Delphine de Sabran, Sancia, Philip of Mallorca and Angelo Clareno, see now Musto 1997, pp. 424–46.

110 Douie 1932, pp. 184–85; 211.

111 A useful if somewhat compressed account of these events can be found in Léonard 1954, pp. 267–69.

112 On Naples as a center for the Spiritual Franciscans, see in particular Ehrle 1888.

113 Douie 1932, pp. 163–64.

114 Ehrle 1888, pp. 65–69; also Eubel 1898-1904, VI, pp. 282 ff.; VII pp. 18–19.

115 The habits were described by John XXII as "curtos, strictos, inusitatos, et squalidos." Eubel 1898-1904, V, p. 128. For a discussion of the significance of Franciscan dress, see Lambert 1961, pp. 214–15; and Strehlke 1987.

116 Peters 1980, pp. 246–47.

117 For Joachimism at the court of Naples, see now Musto 1997. Also McGinn 1979, pp. 126–30. An excellent summary of Joachimism is provided by Bloomfield 1957. For the relation of Joachite ideas to the court circles in Naples, see Vauchez 1987, p. 219.

118 Oberman 1978, p. 91.

119 Oberman 1978, pp. 146–47.

120 On all this, see now Musto 1997, esp. pp. 442–46. Olivi clearly felt that he was living on the eve of the coming of the Third Age when the hierarchy of the Church would be replaced by the elect. See Oberman 1978, p. 90.

121 Manselli 1951, *passim*.

122 Charles II died on 4 May 1309. The decision in favor of Robert was made on 26 August of the same year, and the coronation of Robert and Sancia took place on 8 September. On the Spiritual Franciscans in general, see also Gratien 1928, p. 436.

123 Leff 1967, p. 170.

124 McGinn 1978, pp. 155–73.

125 See Tondelli, Reeves, and Hirsch-Reich 1954; and Reeves and Hirsch-Reich 1972.

126 On the wide dissemination of the *figurae* at an early date, see Reeves and Bloomfield 1954, pp. 772–93, esp. 780 ff.

127 Musto 1997, pp. 437–38.

128 Musto 1997, p. 439.

129 Pou y Martí 1930, p. 47. The books were sent to Clement VI in Avignon, and all trace of them has been lost.

130 Musto 1985 and Santi 1985. Another interesting example

of millenarian interests in the Angevin court can be found in the remarkable *Apocalypse* panel published by Schmitt 1970.

131 I thank F. Bologna for bringing this to my attention. See also Gaglione 1996, pp. 9–37, esp. p. 23 n. 2.

132 Musto 1997, pp. 423–24, 446–47.

133 "Cum vero geometria succedit, emancipatum instruit filium ut construende sibi domus accipiat certitudinem mensurarum in fundamentis et spaciis et lateribus parietum et terminius angulorum. Constructoque habitaculo prudentis induere habitum ad bene regendum insinuat astrorum peritia, ut ardua considerare non negligat et futura metiri." Musto 1997, p. 431, n. 45.

134 Musto 1997, p. 431, n. 45.

135 But see Crossley 1988, pp. 116–21.

136 In this regard, the remarks of Foucault 1970, p. 59, on the nature of knowledge are interesting: " knowledge resided entirely in the opening up of a discovered, affirmed, or secretly transmitted, sign. Its task was to uncover a language which God had previously distributed across the face of the earth; it is in this sense that it was the divination of an essential implication, and that the object of its divination was divine."

137 Vidal 1910; Pou y Martì 1930, *passim*; Auw 1979, pp. 173–80; and Musto 1985, pp. 195–8; as well as Musto 1997, p. 446. On the trial, Eubel, VI (1902), pp. 597–638, and Pásztor 1955, "Il processo."

138 Crossley 1988, p. 121.

139 See Brownrigg 1989, p. 237, and Lewis 1990, p. 224.

140 Camera 1840–60, II, p. 384.

141 Wadding 1931–64, VII, p. 572; Spila da Subiaco 1901, p. 58, n. 1. D'Engenio Caracciolo 1624, p. 556, associated the foundation with the death of Charles of Calabria's son Charles in 1327 and his burial in Santa Croce in Florence.

142 Wadding 1931–64, VII, pp. 260–62.

143 Camera 1840–60, II, p. 592; Minieri-Riccio 1883, p. 592; and Gaglione 2003, *passim*.

144 See most recently Aceto 2000, pp. 27–35, and Gaglione 1995, pp. 81–100, on the tomb of Sancia. Also D'Engenio Caracciolo 1624, p. 557, Minieri-Riccio 1883, p. 592.

145 Gaglione 2003, p.101; Gaglione 1995, p. 81.

146 Gaglione 2003.

147 All the documents are from Camera 1840–60, II, pp. 316–18 and 384.

148 Monti 1935, pp. 21–22.

149 See above, Chapter Three.

CHAPTER 5

1 For reasons of space, the notes are kept as succinct as possible in this chapter. See Vitolo 2000, "La Noblesse." The entire volume, *La Noblesse dans les territoires angevins à la fin du Moyen Age,* ed. N. Coulet and J.-M. Matz, is of great relevance to this chapter.

2 One of the few studies of this material is Raspi Serra 1981, pp. 605–47.

3 See Vitolo 2000, "La Noblesse," pp. 554–57.

4 For Mary's will, see Camera 1840–60, II, p. 290.

5 For the Amalfi coast and its merchant patrons, see Caskey, 2004.

6 See on the aristocracy and their administrative and social roles, Vitale 1998.

7 The *seggi* were centers of local government in the different districts of Naples. On the *seggio* of Nido, see Vitolo 2000, "La Noblesse," p. 564.

8 See Chapter One, n. 134.

9 Licinio 1989.

10 Durrieu 1933–35, II, pp. 217–400; Galasso 1992, p. 54. See most recently on this Pollastri 2000.

11 Pollastri 2000, p. 91.

12 Pollastri 2000, p. 93, notes that of the initial list of 351 nobles, 43 knights either died or returned to France after the conquest, with 42 more deaths between 1270 and 1272.

13 Venditti 1969, III, p. 764.

14 Filangieri 1883–91, II, pp. 2, 225, 308; V, p. 325.

15 Filangieri 1883–91, II, pp. 46, 282; VI, pp. 485–86, 496.

16 De Boüard 1911, pp. 239–45.

17 The topic of Franciscan and Dominican architectural expertise in the Kingdom of Naples has never been addressed.

18 For these families, see above all Della Marra 1641. For the Sanseverino, see pp. 65–88: on the Catalan family of Della Ratta, pp. 307–11; on the Estendard, pp. 400–06. See also Vitale 1996.

19 Among this group should also be included Bartolomeo da Capua, who was discussed in Chapter Two and whose patronage is notable not only in major religious monuments but also in secular architecture. The only article on a building related to Bartolomeo da Capua is that of Di Resta 1970, pp. 53–60.

20 For the anarchy that emerged by 1310 and the profound disruption of civic order in the Kingdom of Naples, Caggese 1922–30, I, pp. 233–354, is particularly effective.

21 The intermarriage of families, and often the French with the local nobility, formed part of a larger strategy that had to do not only with the "Italianization" of the settlers, but also with the acquisition of property and power. See on this Vitale 1996, pp. 192–94.

22 See the entry by Walter and Piccialuti 1964, VI, pp. 697–704, and Minieri-Riccio 1872, *Cenni Storici*, pp. 135–48.

23 Minieri-Riccio 1874, p. 136; Vitale 1996, pp. 190–91.

24 Minieri-Riccio, 1874, p. 143, who provides also his epitaph. By the sixteenth century the tomb had been destroyed.

25 Vitolo 2000, "La Noblesse," pp. 554–55.

26 Walter and Piccialuti 1964, p. 699.

27 See the many articles by Boyer, especially Boyer 1999, "Une théologie," and Boyer 1995.

28 Sabatini 1975, p. 18, notes the importance of the library at Montevergine in Naples. Tropeano 1978, pp. 55 and 60; Vitolo 2000, "La Noblesse," pp. 554–55; Pessolano 1975, pp. 17–29.

29 At Monteverginella, the monks were required to house,

feed, and lodge twelve paupers; at Capua the monks were required to distribute 100 tunics to the poor on the anniversary of the founder's death. See Vitolo 1998, p. 213.

30 Recorded by Summonte 1601–43, II, p. 381.

31 Walter and Piccialuti 1964, p. 700.

32 Di Resta 1985, p. 36; Di Resta 1970, pp. 1–2.

33 Maresca di Serracapriola 1992, pp. 17–20 and especially n. 28 (p. 24).

34 Maresca di Serracapriola 1992, pp. 12–14.

35 See I. Moretti, "Siena: Architettura," Romanini and Righetti, eds, *Enciclopedia dell'arte medievale*, X, 1999, p. 636.

36 Filangieri 1883–91, II, p. 46; Venditti 1969, p. 826. One might imagine that Lando could have been in Naples between 1324 and 1334. There are no documents, however, that connect him with the portal of San Domenico.

37 Savarese 1981, pp. 131–45.

38 The best study of the Muslim community of Lucera is still that of Egidi 1911–14. See on Giovanni Pipino and his heirs, Caggese 1926, pp. 141–56; Tirelli 1958, pp. 108–55.

39 For a discussion of the monument and its bibliography, see Venditti 1969, pp. 778–86, and Filangieri 1884, *Chiesa e convento di S. Pietro a Maiella, passim*.

40 Bruzelius 1999, "Giovanni Pipino," *passim*.

41 On Lucera cathedral, see Calò Mariani 1984, pp. 170–71; and Bruzelius 1999, "Giovanni Pipino," *passim*.

42 For a discussion of Pipino's patronage at San Pietro a Maiella, see Filangieri 1884, *San Pietro a Maiella*, pp. 2–3.

43 Matteo Villani noted: "Giovanni Pipino da picciolo Notaio, per haver'egli con sagacità, e con inganno tratto dal Regno i Saraceni di Lucera, & acquistato à Re Carlo vecchio quella Città, fu fatto da quel Rè uno de' maggiori Signori del Regno," cited in Della Marra 1641, p. 283.

44 This may have been the result of several protracted stays on the part of the royal family in Barletta, Pipino's home town. See Kiesewetter 1997, pp. 85–283. From 31 January to 8 February 1284, for example, Charles II was in Barletta (Kiesewetter 1997, p. 146) and it may be at that time that he encountered Giovanni Pipino, who was later to perform so many services for this king. Caggese 1926, p. 142, describes Pipino as a faithful servant of Charles I, citing the registers of 1292.

45 See above, Chapter Two. In 1283–84, the crown prince, then serving as viceroy in the absence of Charles I and enmeshed in attempts at revision and reform, sought to settle some of the issues that had led to the revolt (a process that also produced the Reforms of the Plain of San Martino). See Egidi 1913, p. 135. Jozzelino della Marra, with whom Giovanni Pipino was closely associated, was hung, however. In 1295 Pipino's daughter Angiola married Nicola della Marra (Caggese 1926, p. 143). On the trial and the fate of several members of the Rufolo and the Della Marra families, see Sthamer 1937, *passim*, esp. pp. 4ff. Camera judged the reforms of San Martino as the source for the later egregious behavior of the nobility in the Angevin kingdom of Naples, since it gave them rights and a level of independence that quickly led to abuse: 1840–60. I, p. 349.

46 Egidi 1913, p. 136; Della Marra 1641, p. 284.

47 Loffredo 1893, II, p. 310.

48 It is interesting to note that by *circa* 1300 most of the king's close counselors were Italian. See, on Pipino's role in the reign of Charles II, Camera 1840–60, II, p. 181; the other witnesses were Bartolomeo da Capua and Queen Mary of Hungary. See also Egidi 1913, pp. 137ff. Pipino was involved in the treaties with James II of Aragon and on several occasions represented or assisted the king in his negotiations with the papacy over the Angevin debt to the Holy See, as especially in 1306–07.

49 The siege of Lucera was discussed at length in Chapter Three.

50 Egidi 1913, p. 144.

51 For the effect of the Pipino brothers on Barletta, see Caggese 1922–30, I, pp. 473–75.

52 The consecration of 1267 probably marked the installation of the altar ciborium and pulpit, as well as the completion of the upper stories of the Romanesque nave. For the dating of the altar ciborium and pulpit, see Schäfer-Schuchardt 1987, I, pp. 114–15.

53 The dating of this document is that of Kappel 1996, p. 187. The reconstruction was perhaps inspired by the illicit acquisition of the relics of San Ruggiero of Canne, stolen from the cathedral of Canne, which seems to have been in ruinous condition: the Bishop of Canne rented some land in 1260 in order to obtain income to repair his church, "que in ruyna morabatur pro eo quod dicta ecclesia de suis proventibus non poterat reparari." Nitti de Vito 1914, pp. 361–62, doc. 281. On Giovanni's donation, see Santeramo 1924, I, pp. 197–200. For other donations and exchanges by Pipino, some concerning the same property, see pp. 140–42 (1287); pp. 194–96 (1292); pp. 287–88 (1302).

54 Santeramo 1924, I, pp. 320–21.

55 Santeramo 1917, p. 138.

56 Santeramo 1924, II, pp. 101–02, 103–06. The documents include discussion of the attempts of Giovanni's son, Nicholas, Count of Minervino, to raise funds.

57 Loffredo 1893, II, p. 90. For the documents on the donations in the late fourteenth century, see Santeramo 1924, III, pp. 102–03, 146–47, 179–80, 210–12, 212–13, 253–54.

58 Civita 1993, p. 71, attributes the new choir to Pierre d'Angicourt, as do various other authors, including Enlart 1894, p. 208.

59 The most cogent analysis remains that of Enlart 1894, pp. 207–09.

60 Loffredo 1893, II, pp. 318ff.; Ambrosi 1976, pp. 14–17; Filangieri di Candida 1927, pp. iii–iv. Ambrosi is particularly effective in his descriptions of Barletta as a center for travelers and refugees, and, as he observes, the church of Santo Sepolcro in Barletta is an excellent example of a monument that reflects both Northern (French) sources and architectural developments that emerged in the Holy Land. Also Belli D'Elia 1992. On Barletta and

the knightly orders, see *Barletta crocevia degli Ordini religioso-cavallereschi medioevali. Seminario di Studio: Barletta, 16 giugno 1996*, Taranto, 1997, especially Houben 1997, and Iorio 1997. On the medieval city of Barletta, see Iorio 1988. For the bishoprics of Canne and Nazareth, see also Nitti de Vito 1914, p. ii.

61 Kappel 1996, p. 187; Santeramo 1917, p. 131.

62 Santeramo 1917, p. 133; Kappel 1996, p. 187. The theft or "transfer" included an altar, the episcopal throne, and a clock. The letter requesting restitution of the relics and marbles to Canne is in Ughello 1644–62, VII, p. 795.

63 The seat of the Bishop of Nazareth was transferred to Barletta in 1310. See Filangieri di Candida 1927, p. vi, and Ughello 1644–62, VII, pp. 771–73. The see of Nazareth was eventually combined with that of Canne, and dissolved only in 1815.

64 Loffredo 1893, I, pp. 318 ff.

65 Were these urban works promoted by Pipino, so often at the king's side? See Batti and Barone 1904, pp. 21–22; Loffredo 1893, I, pp. 305–09, II, pp. 327–36, 321–22; Filangieri di Candida 1927, pp. 261, 286, 291.

66 Loffredo 1893, II, pp. 338–42; Filangieri di Candida 1927, pp. iii ff.

67 This is a situation typical of merchant cultures found more often in Tuscany and northern Italy than in the Kingdom of Naples, with the notable exception of the mercantile cities along the Amalfi coast: Del Treppo 1977, *passim*.

68 Kappel 1996, pp. 185–89; Schäfer-Schuchardt 1987, I, pp. 101–15.

69 Santeramo 1924, I, pp. 138–39, 144–45, 172–74, 183–84, 188–89, 211–12, 282–83, 284–85, 287, 288, and others. These documents date between 1287 and 1307.

70 Grisotti 1995, esp. p. 47.

71 Davis 1998; Freigang 1992.

72 De Seta 1988, pp. 44–45.

73 De la Ville sur-Yllon 1902; Filangieri 1884, *Chiesa e convento di San Pietro a Maiella, passim*; Venditti 1969, p. 780.

74 There is no good full study of the order as a whole, but extremely useful are: Herde 1979; Cattana 1975. On the Celestinians and the Fraticelli, see Frugoni 1991, pp. 127–55.

75 For the Spirituals in the context of the Celestinians in particular, see Frugoni 1991, pp. 130 ff. Charles II himself was not sympathetic to this movement, in spite of the fact that Franciscans of this persuasion were the tutors for his three sons in captivity. A review of the Angevin Registers reveals numerous episodes in which Charles I was attempting to eradicate the radical Franciscans from the kingdom, even though these occur long before the absolute polarization of the order.

76 Herde 1979, p. 403, notes that from the outset Peter of Morrone had no intention of forming a new order, but incorporated his followers under the Benedictine Rule. When in October 1294 Celestine attempted to absorb Montecassino into his congregation and impose the austere customs and gray habit of the Celestinians, he met with determined resistance and a number of the Benedictine monks went into exile. It should be remembered that there was also a strong Joachite trend in the Celestinian order and a number of the monasteries were dedicated to Santo Spirito (such as that at Sulmona). The monks were often known as the "Fratelli dello Santo Spirito." See Frugoni 1991, p. 130, and Cattana 1975, p. 731.

77 The tomb is illustrated in Filangieri 1884, *Chiesa e convento di San Pietro a Maiella*, plate XIV.

78 By 1294 there were 35 monasteries in the Abruzzo, Apulia, and Lazio, with about 600 monks, Cattana 1975, p. 731. The order was especially strong in Apulia and the Abruzzo.

79 See for example Vian 1988, p. 167; Herde 1979, p. 412. Charles II had made donations and conceded privileges to Peter of Morrone early in 1294, before his election to the papacy. Herde 1979, p. 406. See also on the hostility between Boniface and Charles II during the papal elections of 1294.

80 The canonization procedure began in Naples in May 1306.

81 Or Pipino might have encountered Peter of Morrone if he had been in the company of Charles Martel in 1293 at Sulmona. A number of Charles II's officials took over offices in the papacy upon the election of Celestine: Herde 1979, pp. 407–08. The most significant of these was Bartolomeo of Capua, who entered the pontifical court as apostolic notary.

82 See on this site Raspi Serra 1981, pp. 609, 632–35.

83 Orlando 1886, II, p. 48.

84 Orlando 1886, II, pp. 11–12.

85 Wadding 1931–64, V, p. 186.

86 Raspi Serra 1981, pp. 634–35 specifically associates this portal with Realvalle, but the sculpture is quite different from what remains at the latter site; neither the spindly tall leaves nor the wandering vine and leaf motif at Nocera have an exact model at Realvalle and are of decidedly inferior quality. It is unlikely that the portal of Nocera would have been the work of the French masters hired to carve capitals by the piece at Realvalle, work on which was probably near completion in 1282.

87 On this church, see Raspi Serra 1981, pp. 625–29.

88 Raspi Serra 1981, p. 645, states that the church was enlarged *circa* 1370, but the portal seems to date from the first half of the fourteenth century.

89 De Cunzo and De Martini 1985, p. 9.

90 De Cunzo and De Martini 1985, p. 14.

91 Wadding 1931–64, VI, p. 605.

92 Antonini 1745, pp. 339–40. The church was dedicated to John the Baptist and described as "opere sumptuoso" by Wadding 1931–64, VII, p. 122.

93 Raspi-Serra 1981, pp. 629–31, 635.

94 It is not known when Santa Chiara in Nola was established. On this church, see in particular Zampino 1957.

95 See most recently Toscano 1989, pp. 117–42. See also Leone 1934, and Guadagni, n.d., n.p.

96 Fusco 1997, p. 1.

97 Toscano 1989, pp. 119–21.

98 Toscano 1989, pp. 128–29.

99 Bologna 1969, p. 146; Leone De Castris 1986, pp. 290, 293.

100 Remondini 1747, I, p. 162.

101 Cecchetti 1963, pp. 484–95.

102 D'Addosio 1883, p. 14; see also Caggese 1922–30, II, pp. 42 and 395.

103 Caggese 1922–30, I, pp. 44, 221–22.

104 Tescione 1965, p. 103.

105 Tescione 1965, pp. 111–12.

106 Tropeano 1973, p. 27.

107 Tropeano 1973, pp. 28–29.

108 For an overview of the medieval history of Montevergine, see Tropeano 1973, p. 28.

109 Tropeano 1973, pp. 38–39; Bologna 1969, pp. 102–07; Mongelli 1957, passim; Mongelli 1976 and Mongelli 1965.

110 Tropeano 1973, pp. 39–40.

111 Bologna 1969, p. 102.

112 Vitolo 1998, p. 213.

113 See on this subject most recently Vitolo 2000, "La Noblesse," pp. 555–56.

114 Vitolo 1998, p. 215.

115 Vitolo 1998, p. 215.

116 Vitolo 2000, "La Noblesse," p. 555.

117 Aceto 1988, pp. 94–98; and Leone De Castris 1986, p. 62.

118 Caruso 1842, p. 98; Di Dario Guida 1984, p. 7.

119 Di Dario Guida 1984, p. 10.

120 Di Dario Guida 1984, p. 14.

121 Di Dario Guida 1984, p. 14.

122 For the architecture of the church, see Martelli 1955, pp. 157–75.

123 Caruso 1942, pp. 95–107.

124 Negri Arnoldi 1983, pp. 13–14.

125 See on this the wonderful essay of Sabatini 1974, pp. 38–40.

126 Sabatini 1974, p. 39.

CONCLUSION

1 Quoted from Walter Map's *De Nugis Curialum* by Binski 1995, p. 45; see this author's important remarks throughout the book regarding courts and court cultures.

2 See for example the remarks in Leone de Castris 1994, p. 239, concerning the "unico gusto . . . una sola lingua."

3 Years ago while working on Saint-Denis I came to the conclusion that royal patronage at the court of Louis IX, as at other European courts, seems to have been varied, changeable, eclectic, and in some respects opportunistic.

4 On court eclecticism, see Binski 1995, passim.

5 This in 1299 under Rinaldo Cognetto. See Vale 2001, pp. 279–80.

6 Warnke 1993, pp. 114 ff.

7 See Brown 1981.

8 Brown 1981.

9 See for example Brownlee 1996, pp. 259–69. Also, Herde 1992, p. 184, on clerical disdain for the French and descriptions of their rapaciousness.

10 See Trachtenberg 1991, p. 31.

11 See on the cathedral of Naples the recent volume of essays, Romano and Bock 2002.

12 As noted in Chapter Two, I owe the development of these reflections to conversations with Francesco Aceto and Rosario Villari.

APPENDIX 1

1 My observations here are based on the publications of two scholars in particular, Pietro Egidi on Santa Maria della Vittoria, Egidi 1909–10, passim, and Small 1989. See also on the Castel Nuovo, Aceto 1996.

2 The archive, taken outside Naples for safekeeping during the Second World War, was burned in 1943: see Jamison 1949, pp. 87–91. In an effort of remarkable patience and dedication, the archive was reconstituted under the guidance of R. Filangieri and is being published in an ongoing series, from 1950. See Mazzoleni 1987. Many documents were taken from Sthamer 1912–26 and Schulz and von Quast 1860, the many publications of Minieri-Riccio, and Haseloff 1920. Recently new documents have been discovered in the collections left by Sthamer, see Palmieri 1997, and Esch and Kiesewetter 1994.

3 See for example Knoop and Jones 1933; Salzman 1952; Pitz 1986.

4 Small 1989, p. 325.

5 Aceto 1996, p. 252. The high quality of the work at the Castel Nuovo may indeed be related to the number of masons (35 *scappatores*) paid by the piece (*ad extalium*). On the general proportion of skilled to unskilled, see Small 1989, p. 332.

6 On Giordano di Monte Sant'Angelo, see Sthamer 1912–26, I, pp. 133–68, and Calò-Mariani 1984, p. 170.

7 Bruzelius 1991, p. 414.

8 Small 1989, pp. 328–32.

9 This is especially striking in the construction of the Castel Nuovo in Naples: Aceto 1996, p. 252.

10 The history is summarized in Bruzelius 1991, pp. 402–16.

11 Pierre de Chaules went on to have an important career under Charles; this was his third project for the king. See Egidi 1909, pp. 265–74 and notes.

12 For Pietro de Carellis and Simon de Angart, see Durrieu 1933–35, II, pp. 273 and 300, and Egidi 1909, p. 263, n. 1.

13 The document is in Schulz and von Quast 1860, IV, p. 41; Egidi 1909, pp. 262 ff.

14 Egidi 1909, p. 264.

15 Filangieri 1964, pp. 3–10, and Aceto 1996.

16 Egidi 1909, pp. 280–82.

17 This organization parallels the situation at some building sites slightly earlier in thirteenth-century England. Taylor 1963, pp. 133 ff.

18 Fergusson 1984, p. 169.

19 Fraccaro de' Longhi 1958. On the subject of the expanded rectangular chevet, see more recently Kuthan 1994.

20 Amarotta 1974, pp. 163–82, esp. 164.

21 Fergusson 1984, pp. 165–72; Aubert 1947, I, pp. 98–99.

22 Egidi 1909, pp. 268–70 and 735–37.

23 Egidi 1909, pp. 274–75.

24 Filangieri 1950–, XI, pp. 301 and 305, docs. 106, 192, and 193. Charles also expanded on the personal qualities necessary for the community: "honestate conspicue, discretione mature, prudentia predite et providentia circumspecte . . ." At Vittoria, as will be seen in the conclusion of this essay, those personal qualities may have been absent from part of the monastic community.

25 Filangieri 1950–, XI, pp. 301 and 305, docs. 106, 192, and 193. See also De Boüard 1926, p. 332.

26 For the number and choice of the liturgical books, one supposes that Charles must have been instructed by the monks themselves. De Boüard 1926, p. 338: "Ballivo Andegavie et magistro Johanni de Villameroy, ut ad usum eorumdem monasteriorum, una cum subdecano Aurelianensi, magistro Henrico, canonico Cathalanensi et magistro Johanne de Marolio . . . , octo missalia, octo gradualia, octo antifonaria et quatuor lectionaria, duo videlicet de temporalibus et duo de festis . . ."

27 Filangieri 1950–, XIX, p. 116.

28 De Boüard and Durrieu 1933–35, pp. 110–11.

29 This also coincides more or less with the arrival of the architect at the site.

30 Schulz and von Quast 1860, IV, p. 63, doc. CLXI.

31 Egidi 1909, p. 281, n. 1; we know that in January 1278 there were to be twelve *scappatores*, fifteen *incisores*, sixteen *muratores*, and eighty *manipulos* at the site. Schulz and von Quast 1860, IV, p. 54, doc. CXXXV.

32 Filangieri 1950–, XIX, p. 218, doc. 364.

33 Filangieri 1950–, XIX, p. 289; XXV, p. 137, doc. 87.

34 Filangieri 1950–, XXI, p. 214. The document is also in De Boüard and Durrieu 1933–35, I, pp. 163–68.

35 Filangieri 1950–, XXI, pp. 221–23.

36 Filangieri 1950–, XXI, pp. 88–89. Also in Schulz and von Quast 1860, IV, pp. 85–86, doc. CCXXIII.

37 Barone 1885, pp. 430–31.

38 These individuals seem to be the template makers for the more complex structural parts and the vaults, because they come on to the scene at both sites towards the end of the construction process. Egidi 1909, p. 744, is also of this opinion. It may be supposed that they were masons with a higher degree of technical skill.

39 Schulz and von Quast 1860, IV, pp. 101–02; doc. CCLXVII. The French version of the document was published by De Boüard and Durrieu 1933–35, II, pp. 221–23, doc. 219.

40 Minieri-Riccio 1875–81, "Il Regno," II (1878), p. 358. Filangieri 1950–, XXI, p. 271.

41 Francabandera 1932, p. 34.

42 Egidi 1909, p. 286.

43 Egidi 1909, p. 286.

44 Egidi 1909, p. 287.

45 This document, one of the most complete, is in De Boüard and Durrieu 1933–35, II, pp. 224–27, and Egidi 1910, pp. 169–71. See also the discussion of the abbeys of Realvalle and Vittoria for further observations on the labor force.

46 Egidi 1909, p. 283, n. 7.

47 Egidi 1909, p. 753, n. 1.

48 Licinio 1989.

49 Schulz and von Quast 1860, IV, p. 73.

50 Document of 20 January 1279 for twelve *scappatores*, fifteen *incisores*, twelve *maconerii*, eighty *manipuli*. Schulz and von Quast 1860, II, p. 88.

51 Egidi 1909, pp. 748 ff.

52 Filangieri 1950–, XX, p. 245.

53 De Boüard and Durrieu 1933–35, II, pp. 146–50, esp. 150. The document dates from 24 January 1280.

54 The monetary units in the Kingdom of Sicily are the following: 1 uncia = 30 tari; 1 tarus = 20 grani

55 Small 1989, p. 328.

56 See Aceto 1996, pp. 252 ff.

57 Bialoskorska 1994.

58 Small 1989, p. 329.

59 Egidi 1911, p. 616.

60 Small 1989, p. 333.

61 Small 1989, p. 333, and Salzman 1952, p. 34.

62 This interpretation is based on a general reading of Filangieri 1950–; see also Egidi 1909, pp. 738–39.

63 Egidi 1909, pp. 740–41.

64 Egidi 1909, pp. 740–41.

65 Egidi 1909, p. 741.

66 Egidi 1909, p. 741, n. 3.

67 As noted in Chapter One, there is also the possibility that the work was initially interrupted by the War of the Vespers, and that when construction was taken up again, vaults and flyers over main vessels were no longer in fashion.

APPENDIX 2

1 Filangieri 1950–, XXI, pp. 88–89.

2 Coulter 1944, pp. 144–45; Egidi 1909, p. 755.

3 Presumably located in the nave: Ruocco 1938, pp. 224–25; and Krüger 1986, pp. 143–44.

APPENDIX 3

1 Krüger 1986, p. 129. See also Filangieri 1950–, XXVII, pp. 288, 292, 298.

2 Krüger 1986, p. 129, Filangieri 1950–, XXVII, p. 347.

Bibliography

Abulafia, D., *Frederick II: A Medieval Emperor*, London, 1988.

——, *The Western Mediterranean Kingdoms, 1200–1500: The Struggle for Dominion*, London and New York, 1997.

——, "Charles of Anjou Reassessed," *Journal of Medieval History*, XXVI (2000), pp. 93–114.

Aceto, F., "La scultura dell'età romanica al primo rinascimento," *Insediamenti Verginiani in Irpinia: Il Goleto–Montevergine–Loreto*, Cava de' Tirreni, 1988, pp. 85–116.

——, "Per l'attività di Tino di Camaino a Napoli: le tombe di Giovanni di Capua e di Orso Minutolo," *Prospettiva*, LIII–LVI (1988–89), pp. 134–42.

——, "Magistri e cantieri nel 'Regnum Siciliae': L'Abruzzo e la cerchia federiciana," *Bollettino d'arte*, LIX (1990), pp. 15–96.

——, "Pittori e documenti della Napoli angioina, aggiunte ed espunzioni," *Prospettiva*, LXVII (1992), pp. 53–65.

——, "Tino da Camaino a Napoli: una proposta per il sepolcro di Caterina d'Austria e altri fatti angioini," *Dialoghi di storia dell'arte*, I (1995), pp. 10–27.

——, "Le *castrum novum* angevin de Naples," *Chantiers médiévaux*, ed. R. Cassanelli, Paris, 1996, pp. 251–68.

——, "Novità sull'incontro dei tre vivi e dei tre morti nella Cattedrale di Atri," *Prospettiva*, XCI–XCII (1998), pp. 10–20.

——, "Un opera 'ritrovata' di Pacio Bertini: il sepolcro di Sancia di Maiorca in Santa Croce a Napoli e la questione dell' *usus pauper*," *Prospettiva*, 100 (2000), pp. 27–35.

——, "La Sculpture, de Charles Ier d'Anjou à la mort de Jeanne Ire (1266–1383)," *L'Europe des Anjou: aventure des princes angevins du XIIIe au XVe siècle*, Paris, 2001, pp. 75–87.

——, "Una proposta per Tino di Camaino a Cava dei Tirreni," *Medien der Macht: Kunst zur Zeit der Anjous in Italien*, ed. T. Michalsky, Berlin, 2001, pp. 275–94.

——, "Tino da Camaino nel Duomo di Napoli," *Il Duomo di Napoli, dal paleocristiano all'eta' angioina*, ed. S. Romano and N. Bock, Naples, 2002, pp. 148–55.

Alisio, G., *Napoli e il risanamento: recupero di una struttura urbana*, Naples, 1980.

Alomar, G., "Iconografia y heraldicas de Sancha de Mallorca, reina de Napoles (1309–1345)," *Actas del XXIII Congreso internacional de Historia del Arte, Granada, 1973*, I, Granada, 1976, pp. 265–74.

Amari, M., *Storia dei Musulmani in Sicilia*, 3 vols. in 4, Florence, 1886.

Amarotta, A. R., "Real Valle, badia gotica sul Sarno," *Atti dell' Accademia Pontaniana*, n.s., XXII (1974), pp. 163–82.

Ambrasi, D., "Il cristianesimo e la chiesa napoletana dei primi secoli," *Storia di Napoli*, I, ed. E. Pontieri, Naples, 1967, pp. 623–760.

——, "La vita religiosa," *Storia di Napoli*, III, ed. E. Pontieri, Naples, 1969, pp. 439–573.

Ambrosi, A., *Architettura dei crociati in Puglia: Il Santo Sepolcro di Barletta*, Bari, 1976.

Amirante, G., *Aversa. Dalle origini al settecento*, Naples, 1998.

Ammirati, L., *Il francescanesimo a Nola e altri saggi*, Nola, 1989.

Ammirato, S., *Delle famiglie nobili napoletane*, 2 vols., Florence, 1580.

Amodio, P., *Ricerche e studi sui monumenti gotici napoletani*, Pompeii, 1941.

Anderson, D., "'Dominus Ludovicus' in the Sermons of Jacobus of Viterbo (Arch. S. Pietro D. 213)," *Literature and Religion in the Later Middle Ages: Philological Studies in Honor of Siegfried Wenzel*, ed. R. G. Newhouser and J. A. Alford, Binghamton, NY, 1995, pp. 275–95.

Angelillis, C., "Il campanile della basilica di S. Michele in Monte S. Angelo," *Archivio storico pugliese*, III–IV (1949), pp. 248–63.

Angeluzzi, G., *Lettere due sulla chiesa dell'Incoronata e sulla sepoltura di Giovanna I*, Naples, 1846.

Anonymous, *El convento y las monjas de Santa Clara de Palma por una religiosa del mismo*, Palma, 1959.

Antonini, G., *La Lucania: discorsi*, Naples, 1745.

Armstrong, R., ed. and trans., *Clare of Assisi: Early Documents*, New York, 1988.

L'Art au temps des rois maudits: Philippe le Bel et ses fils, 1285–1328 (exh. cat.), Paris, Grand Palais, 1998.

Aubert, M., with the Marquise de Maillé, *L'Architecture cistercienne en France*, 2 vols., Paris, 1947.

Auw, L. von, *Angelo Clareno et les spirituels italiens*, Rome, 1979.

Avril, F., "Un atelier 'Picard' à la cour des Angevins de Naples," *Zeitschrift für schweizerische Archäeologie und Kunstgeschichte*, XLIII (1986), pp. 76–85.

Babelon, J.-P., "La Tête de Béatrice de Provence au Musée Granet d'Aix-en-Provence," *Bulletin monumental*, CXXVIII (1970), pp. 119–25.

Baddeley, W. St. Clair, *Robert the Wise and his Heirs, 1278–1352*, London, 1897.

Barbero, A., *Il mito angioino nella cultura italiana e provenzale fra Duecento e Trecento (Deputazione Subalpina di Storia Patria, vol. 201)*, Turin, 1983.

——, "Letteratura e politica fra Provenza e Napoli," *L'Etat Angevin: pouvoir, culture et société entre XIII et XIV siècle* (Collection de l'Ecole Française de Rome, 245), Rome, 1998, pp. 159–72.

Barbiero, G., "L'Origine delle confraternite del Ss.mo. Sacramento in Italia," *Studia Eucharistica: DCC anni a condito festo santissimi corporis Christi: 1246–1946*, Antwerp, 1946, 187-215.

Baron, F., "La partie orientale détruite du tour du chœur de Notre Dame de Paris," *Revue de l'art*, 128 (2000), pp. 11–29.

Barone, G., "Federico II di Svevia e gli ordini mendicanti," *Mélanges de l'Ecole Française de Rome: Moyen Age Temps Modernes*, XC (1978), pp. 607–26.

Barone, N., *La Ratio Thesauriorum della cancelleria angioina*, Naples, 1885.

Batti, R., and N. Barone, eds., *Repertorio delle Pergamene delle università o commune di Barletta*, Naples, 1904.

Beaumont-Maillet, L., *Le Grand Couvent des Cordeliers de Paris. Etude historique et archéologique*, Paris, 1975.

Belli D'Elia, P., *Alle sorgenti del Romanico: Puglia: XI secolo*, Bari, 1975.

——, *La Puglia tra Bisanzio e l'Occidente*, Milan, 1980.

——, "Barletta," *Enciclopedia dell'Arte Medievale*, III, 1992, pp. 102–09.

——, *La cattedrale di Acerenza: mille anni di storia*, Venosa, 1999.

Benoit, F., "Saint-Jean de Malte," *Congrès archéologique de France*, LXXXXV (1932), pp. 35–41.

Bentley, J., *Politics and Culture in Renaissance Naples*, Princeton, 1987.

Berger-Dittscheid, C., "S. Lorenzo Maggiore in Neapel: Das gotische 'Ideal'-Projekt Karls I. und seine 'franziskanischen' Modifikationen," *Festschrift für Hartmut Bierman* (Acta Humanoria), ed. C. Andreas, M. Bückling, and R. Dorn, Weinheim, 1990, pp. 41–64.

Bernich, E., "L'arte in Puglia: il campanile della basilica di S. Michele sul Monte Gargano," *Napoli nobilissima*, VII (1898), pp. 20–22.

——, "La chiesa dell'Incoronata," *Napoli nobilissima*, XIII (1904), pp. 100–02.

Bertaux, E., "Les Arts de l'Orient musulman dans l'Italie méridionale," *Mélanges d'Archéologie et d'Histoire. Ecole Française de Rome*, XV (1895), pp. 119–53.

——, "Magistri Johannes et Pacius de Florentia marmorarii frates," *Napoli nobilissima*, IV (1895), pp. 147–52.

——, "Sant'Agostino alla Zecca. Architettura angioina e scultura sveva," *Napoli nobillissima*, V (1896), pp. 24–26.

——, "S. Chiara de Naples: l'église et le monastère," *Mélanges d'archéologie et d'histoire de l'Ecole Française de Rome*, XVIII (1898), pp. 165–98.

——, *Santa Maria di Donna Regina e l'arte senese a Napoli nel secolo XIV*, Naples, 1899.

—— *L'Art dans l'Italie méridionale de la fin de l'Empire romain à la conquête de Charles d'Anjou*, 5 vols. in 2, Paris, 1903–04.

——, "Les Artistes français au service des rois de Naples," *Gazette des beaux-arts*, XXXIII (1905), pp. 265–81; XXXIV (1905), pp. 89–115; XXXIV (1905), pp. 313–25.

——, "Gli affreschi di S. Maria Donnaregina: nuovi appunti," *Napoli nobilissima*, XV (1906), pp. 129–33.

Bialoskorska, K., "La fabrique du maître Siman et son activité en Pologne dans la première moitié du XIII siècle: un cas isolé ou un témoignage de la évolution de la pratique de construire chez les cisterciens?," *Arte medievale*, II ser., VIII (1994), pp. 57–85.

Biget, B. L., "Autour de Bernard Délicieux: Franciscanisme et societé en Languedoc entre 1295 et 1330," *Mouvements franciasains et societé française, XIIe-XXe*, ed., A Vauchez, Paris, 1984.

Binski, P., "The Cosmati at Westminster and the English Court Style," *Art Bulletin*, LII (1990), pp. 6–33.

——, *Westminster Abbey and the Plantagenets: Kingship and the Representation of Power, 1200–1400*, New Haven and London, 1995.

Bloomfield, M., "Joachim of Flora: A Critical Survey of his Canon, Teachings, Sources, Biography, and Influence," *Traditio*, XIII (1957), pp. 249–311.

Blume, D., "Andalo di Negro und Giovanni Boccaccio: Astrologie und Mythos am Hof des Robert von Anjou," *Medien der Macht: Kunst zur Zeit der Anjous in Italien*, ed. T. Michalsky, Berlin, 2001, pp. 319–35.

Blunt, A., *Neapolitan Baroque and Rococo Architecture*, London, 1975.

Bock, N., "L'Art à la Cour Angevine: la sculpture et le gothique international," *L'Europe des Anjou: aventure des princes angevins du XIIIe au XVe siècle*, Paris, 2001, pp. 89–101.

——, "I re, i vescovi e la cattedrale: sepolture e costruzione architettonica," *Il duomo di Napoli, dal paleocristiano all'età angioina*, ed. S. Romano and N. Bock, Naples, 2002, pp. 132–47.

——, P. Kurmann, S. Romano, and J.-M. Spieser, eds., *Art, Cérémonial et Liturgie au Moyen Age (Actes du colloque du 3º Cycle Romand de Lettres Lausanne-Fribourg, 24–25 mars, 14–15 avril, 12–13 mai, 2000)*, Rome, 2002.

Bolgia, C., "Il coro medievale della chiesa di S. Maria in Aracoeli a Roma," *Arte d'Occidente: temi e metodi. Studi in onore di Angiola Maria Romanini*, ed. A. Cadei, M. Righetti Tosti-Croce, A. Segnani Malacart, and A. Tomei, 3 vols., Rome, 1999, pp. 233–42.

Bologna, F., *I pittori alla corte angioina di Napoli, 1266–1414* (Saggi e studi di storia dell'arte, 2), Rome, 1969.

——, "Un'aggiunta a Lello da Orvieto," *Studi di storia dell'arte in onore di Raffaello Causa*, ed. P. Leone de Castris, Naples, 1988, pp. 47–51.

Bonaini, F., *Acta Henrici VII Romanorum imperatoris, et monumenta quaedam alia suorum temporum historiam illustrantia a Francisco Bonainio collecta ad in duas partes divisa*, 2 vols., Florence, 1887.

Bonaiuti, E., "L'Apocalissi francescana," *Ricerche religiose*, IX (1933), pp. 32–43.

Bonnelli, R., "Introduzione," *Francesco d'Assisi: Chiese e Conventi*, Milan, 1982.

Bonnot, I., ed., *Marseilles et ses rois de Naples: la diagonale angevine, 1265–1382*, Aix-en-Provence, 1988.

Borrelli, G., "Nota sull'arte del vetro a Napoli nel Medioevo," *Scritti di storia dell'arte per il settantesimo anniversario dell'Associazione Napoletana per i Monumenti ed il Paessaggio*, Naples, 1991, pp. 17–35.

Borroni, C., and G.Vitetti, "La chiesa e il convento di S. Maria della Consolazione in Altomonte," *Rivista storica calabrese*, n.s., IV (1983), pp. 17–33.

Bourdua, L., "The 13th and 14th Century Italian Mendicant Orders and Art," *Economia e Arte, secc. XIII–XVIII Atti della "Trentatreesima Settimana di Studi," 30 aprile–4 maggio 2001*, Florence, 2002, pp. 473–88.

——, "I frati minori al Santo nel Trecento: consulenti, committenti, o artisti," *Il Santo*, XLII (2002), pp. 17–28.

Boyer, J.-P., "La 'Foi monarchique': Royaume de Sicile et Provence (mi-XIII – mi-XIV siècle)," *Le Forme della propaganda politica nel Due e nel Trecento: relazioni tenute al convegno internazionale organizzato dal Comitato di studi storici di Trieste, dall'Ecole française de Rome e dal Dipartimento di storia dell'Università degli studi di Trieste, 1993*, Rome, 1994, pp. 85–110.

——, *Ecce Rex tuus*: le roi et le royaume dans les sermons de Robert de Naples," *Revue Mabillon*, LXVII (1995), pp. 101–36.

——, "Parler du roi et pour le roi. Deux 'sermons' de Barthélemy de Capoue, logothète du royaume de Sicile," *Revue des sciences philosophiques et théologiques*, LXXIX (1995), pp. 193–248.

——, "Sacre et théocratie: le cas des rois de Sicile Charles II (1289) et Robert (1309)," *Revue des sciences philosophiques et théologiques*, LXXXI (1997), pp. 561–608.

——, "Entre soumission au prince et consentement: le rituel d'échange der serments à Marseille (1252–1348)," *120e Congrès nationale des Sociétés historiques et scientifiques: Aix-en-Provence, 1995*, Paris, 1998, pp. 207–19.

——, "Prédication et état napolitain dans la première moitié du XIV siècle," *L'Etat Angevin: pouvoir, culture et société entre XIII et XIV siècle* (Collection de l'Ecole Française de Rome, 245), Rome, 1998, pp. 127–57.

——, "Florence et l'idée monarchique: la prédication de Remigio dei Girolami sur les Angevins de Naples," *La Toscane et les Toscans autour de la Renaissance: mélanges offerts à Charles-M. De la Roncière*, Aix-en-Provence, 1999, pp. 363–75.

——, "Une oraison funèbre pour le roi Robert de Sicile, Comte de Provence (1343)," *Provence historique*, CXCV–CXCVI (1999), pp. 115–31.

——, "Une théologie du droit: les sermons juridiques du roi Robert de Naples et de Barthélemy de Capoue," *Saint-Denis et la royauté: études offertes à Bernard Guenée*, ed. F. Autrand, C. Gauvard, and J.-M. Moeglin, Paris, 1999, pp. 647–59.

——, "La noblesse dans les sermons des Dominicains de Naples (première moitié du XIVe siècle)," *La Noblesse dans les territoires angevins à la fin du Moyen Age. Actes du colloque international organisé par l'Université d'Angers, Angers–Saumur, 3–6 juin 1998*, ed. N. Coulet and J.-M. Matz, Rome, 2000, pp. 567–83.

——, "Vertus privées et bien public. Reines et princesses selon la prédication *De Mortuis* à la cour de Naples," *Reines et princesses au moyen âge: Actes du cinquième colloque international de Montpellier, Université Paul-Valéry, 24–27 novembre 1999*, Montpellier, 2001, pp. 413–35.

Bozzoni, C., *Saggi di architettura medievale: La Trinità di Venosa, Il Duomo di Atri*, Roma, 1979.

——, "L'immagine dell'antico S. Pietro nelle rappresentazioni figurate e nella architettura costruita," *L'Architettura della basilica di San Pietro. Storia e Costruzione* (Atti del convegno internazionale di studi, Roma, Castel S. Angelo, 7–10 novembre, 1995), Rome, 1997,. pp. 63–72.

Bräm, A., "Illuminierte Breviere: Zur Rezeption der Anjou-Monumentalkunst in der Buchmalerei," *Medien der Macht: Kunst zur Zeit der Anjous in Italien*, ed. T. Michalsky, Berlin, 2001, pp. 295–318.

Branner, R., *St. Louis and the Court Style in Gothic Architecture*, London, 1965.

Bresc, H., "1282: classes sociales et révolution nationale," *La società mediterranea all'epoca del Vespro. Atti dell'XIo congresso di storia della Corona d'Aragona*, Palermo, 3 vols., 1983–84, II, pp. 241–58.

——, "La 'mala signoria' ou l'hypothèque sicilienne," *L'Etat angevin: pouvoir, culture et société entre XIII et XIV siècle* (Collection de l'Ecole Française de Rome, 245), Rome, 1998, pp. 577–99.

Bridges, S. F., "Langue d'Oil to Volgare Siciliano: Three Followers of Charles of Anjou," *Papers of the British School of Rome*, XXIII (1955), pp. 169–97.

Brivio, E., *Index of the Gothic Cathedrals*, Milan, 1986.

Brooke, R. B. and N. L. Brooke, "St. Clare," *Studies in Church History. Subsidia* I: *Medieval Women: Dedicated and Presented to Professor Rosalind M. T. Hill on the Occasion of her Seventieth Birthday*, ed., D. Baker, 1978, pp. 275–87.

Brown, E. A. R., "Death and the Human Body in the Later Middle Ages: The Legislation of Boniface VIII on the Division of the Corpse," *Viator*, XII (1981), pp. 221–70.

——, *The Monarchy of Capetian France and Royal Ceremonial*, Brookfield, VT, 1991.

Brownlee, K., "The Practice of Cultural Authority: The Italian Responses to French Cultural Dominance in *Il Tesoretto*, *Il Fiore* and the *Commedia*," *Forum for Modern Language Studies*, XXXIII (1997), pp. 258–69.

Brownrigg, L., "The Taymouth Hours and the Romance of Beves of Hampton," *Manuscript Studies 1100–1700*, ed. P. Beal and J. Griffiths, London, vol. 1 (1989), pp. 222–41.

Brückle, W., "Revision der Hofkunst: Zur Frage historischer Phänomene in der ausgehenden Kapetingerzeit und zum Problem des höfischen Pariser Stils," *Zeitschrift für Kunstgeschichte*, LXIII (2000), pp. 404–34.

Bruzelius, C., "Cistercian High Gothic: The Abbey Church of Longpont and the Architecture of the Cistercians in the Early Thirteenth Century," *Analecta cisterciensia*, XXXV (1979), pp. 2–204.

——, *The Thirteenth-Century Church at St.-Denis*, New Haven and London, 1985.

——, "The Second Campaign at St.-Urbain in Troyes," *Speculum*, LXII (1987), pp. 635–40.

——, "*Ad modum Franciae*: Charles of Anjou and Gothic Architecture in the Kingdom of Sicily," *Journal of the Society of Architectural Historians*, L (1991), pp. 402–20.

——, "Hearing is Believing: Clarissan Architecture, 1212–1340," *Gesta*, XXXI (1992), pp. 83–92.

——, "Il coro di San Lorenzo Maggiore e la ricezione dell'arte gotica," *Il gotico europeo in Italia*, ed. M. Bagnoli and V. Pace, Naples, 1994, pp. 265–77.

——, "Queen Sancia of Mallorca and the Church of Sta. Chiara in Naples," *Memoirs of the American Academy in Rome*, XL (1995), pp. 41–72.

——, "Nuns in Space: Strict Enclosure and the Architecture of the Clarisses in the Thirteenth Century," *Clare of Assisi: A Medieval and Modern Woman* (Clarefest Selected Papers, VIII), ed. Ingrid Peterson, St. Bonaventure, NY, 1996, pp. 41–62.

——, "Charles of Anjou and the French in Italy," *Kunst im Reich Kaiser Friedrichs II. von Hohenstaufen*, Munich and Berlin, 1997, pp. 146–53.

——, "Charles I, Charles II, and the Development of an Angevin Style in the Kingdom of Sicily," *L'Etat angevin: pouvoir, culture et société entre XIII et XIV siècle* (Collection de l'Ecole Française de Rome, 245), Rome, 1998, pp. 99–114.

——, "*Columpnas marmoreas et lapides antiquarum ecclesiarum*: The Use of Spolia in the Churches of Charles II of Anjou," *Arte d'Occidente: temi e metodi. Studi in onore di Angiola Maria Romanini*, Rome, 1999, pp. 187–95.

——, "Giovanni Pipino of Barletta: The Butcher of Lucera as Patron and Builder," *Pierre, lumière, couleur: études d'histoire de l'art du Moyen Age en l'honneur d'Anne Prache*, ed. D. Sandron and F. Joubert, Paris, 1999, pp. 255–67.

——, "'A Torchlight Procession of One:' Le choeur de Santa Maria Maggiore de Barletta," *Revue de l'art*, no. 125 (1999), pp. 9–19.

——, "Charles of Anjou and the Architecture of the French in Italy: Some Issues Pertaining to the Labor Force," *Europa e l'arte italiana: per i cento anni dalla fondazione del Kunsthistorisches Institut in Florenz*, ed. M. Seidel, Florence, 2000, pp. 95–107.

——, "*Il Gran Rifiuto*: French Gothic in Central and Southern Italy," *Architecture and Language: Constructing Identity in European Architecture c. 1000–c. 1650*, ed. P. Crossley and G. Clarke, Cambridge, 2000, pp. 36–45.

——, "Trying to Forget: The Lost Angevin Past of Italy," *International Congress of the History of Art: Amsterdam, 1–6 September 1996*, Amsterdam, 2000, pp. 735–43.

——, "L'Architecture du royaume de Naples pendant le règne de Charles II d'Anjou, 1289–1309," *1300: l'Art au temps de Philippe le Bel*, Rencontres de L'Ecole du Louvre, XVI, Paris, 2001, pp. 253–71.

——, "Les Villes, les fortifications et les églises dans le royaume de Sicile pendant la première phase angevin," *L'Europe des Anjou: aventure des princes angevins du XIIIe au XVe siècle*, Paris, 2001, pp. 49–65.

——, "Ipotesi e proposte sulla costruzione del duomo di Napoli," *Il duomo di Napoli, dal paleocristiano all'età angioina*, ed. S. Romano and N. Bock, Naples, 2002, pp. 119–31.

——, "Una nuova ipotesi sul transetto di San Lorenzo a Napoli: la '*chiesa fantasma*'," *Confronti*, I (2003), pp. 62–66; also published in reduced form as "A Report from Naples: Some New Observations on San Lorenzo Maggiore," *Newsletter of the Italian Art Society*, XV/3 (2002), pp. 4–7.

——, "San Lorenzo Maggiore e lo *Studio* francescano di Napoli: qualche osservazione sul carattere e la cronologia della chiesa medievale," *San Lorenzo e San Domenico a Napoli*, ed. S. Romano and N. Bock, forthcoming.

Buczek, D. S., "Medieval Taxation: The French Crown, the Papacy, and the Cistercian Order," *Analecta cisterciensia*, XXV (1969), pp. 42–106.

Burr, D., *Olivi and Franciscan Poverty: The Origins of the "Usus Pauper" Controversy*, Philadelphia, 1989.

——, *The Spiritual Franciscans: From Protest to Persecution in the Century after Saint Francis*, University Park, PA, 2001.

Bynum, C. W., "Women Mystics and Eucharistic Devotion in the Thirteenth Century," *Women's Studies*, XI (1984), pp. 179–214.

——, *Holy Feast and Holy Fast: The Religious Significance of Food to Medieval Women*, Berkeley, 1987.

——, "The Female Body and Religious Practice in the Later Middle Ages," *Fragments for a History of the Human Body*, ed. M. Feher, I, New York, (1990), pp. 119–150.

Cadei, A., "Cori francescani ad ambulacro e cappelle radiali," *Storia e cultura a Padova nell'età di Sant'Antonio (Fonti e ricerche di storia ecclesiastica padovana)*, XVI (1985), pp. 467–500.

Cadier, L., *Essai sur l'administration du royaume de Sicile sous Charles Ier et Charles II d'Anjou*, Paris, 1891.

Caggese, R., *Roberto d'Angiò e i suoi tempi*, 2 vols., Florence, 1922–30.

——, "Giovanni Pipino conte d'Altamura," *Studi di storia napoletana in onore di M. Schipa*, Naples, 1926, pp. 141–65.

Calò Mariani, M. S., *La chiesa di S. Maria del Casale presso Brindisi*, Brindisi, 1967.

——, *Due cattedrali del Molise. Termoli e Larino*, Rome, 1979.

——, "La scultura in Puglia durante l'età sveva e protoangioina," *La Puglia fra Bisanzio e l'Occidente*, Milan, 1980.

——, *L'arte del Duecento in Puglia*, Turin, 1984.

——, "L'arte medievale e il Gargano," *La montagna Sacra*, ed., G. B. Bronzini, Galatina, 1991, pp. 9-96.

——, *Archeologia, storia, e storia dell'arte medievale in Capitanata*, Bari, 1992.

——, *Foggia medievale*, Foggia, 1997.

——, *Capitanata medievale*, Foggia, 1998.

Camera, M., *Istoria della città e costiera di Amalfi in due parte divise*, Naples, 1836.

——, *Annali delle due Sicilie dall'origine e fondazione della monarchia fino a tutto il regno dell'agosto sovrano Carlo III Borbone*, 3 vols., Naples, 1840–60.

——, *Memorie storico-diplomatiche dell'antica città e ducato di Amalfi cronologicamente ordinate e continuate al secolo XVIII*, 2 vols., Salerno, 1875.

Campanile, F., *L'armi; o, vero Insegne de' nobili*, Naples, 1610.

Candida Gonzaga, B., *Memorie delle famiglie nobili delle province meridionale d'Italia*, 3 vols., Naples, 1875–76.

Canivez, J. M., ed., *Statuta capitulorum generalium ordines Cistercienses ab anno 1116 ad annum 1786* (Bibliothèque de la Revue d'Histoire Ecclésiastique, 10), 8 vols., Louvain, 1933–41.

Cannon, J., "Pietro Lorenzetti and the History of the Carmelite Order," *Journal of the Warburg and Courtauld Institutes*, L (1987), pp. 18–28.

Cantèra, B., *Documenti riguardanti il B. Giacomo da Viterbo*, Naples, 1888.

——, *L'edificazione del duomo di Napoli al tempo degli angioini*, Valle di Pompeii, 1890.

——, *Due documenti angioini*, Naples, 1892.

——, *Ricordi di fatti storici avvenuti nella cattedrale di Napoli fino all'anno 1500*, Naples, 1894.

Capasso, B., "Napoli descritta nei principi del secolo XVII da Giulio Cesare Capaccio," *Archivio storico per le province napolitane*, VI (1882), pp. 68–113, 531–35, 776–85.

——, *Napoli Greco-Romana*, 2nd edn., Naples, 1978, reprint of 1905 edition.

——, *Topografia della Città di Napoli nell'XI secolo*, Naples, 2nd ed.,Sala Bolognese, 1984.

Capo, L., "Da Andrea Ungaro a Guillaume de Nangis: un'ipotesi sui rapporti tra Carlo I d'Angiò e il regno di Francia," *Mélanges de l'Ecole française de Rome*, LXXXIX (1977), pp. 811–88.

Capocci, E., *Catalogo dei terremoti nella parte continentale delle Due Sicilie*, Naples, 1858.

Capone, D., *La chiesa di S. Maria la Nova: il soffito*, Naples, 1978.

Capone, G., "Documenti sull'area di S. Lorenzo Maggiore a Napoli nei secoli XV e XVI," *Napoli nobilissima*, XXXII (1993), pp. 69–75.

——, "Per la storia della regione 'Augustale' di Napoli: corti e portici nel XIII secolo," *Napoli nobilissima*, XXXIV (1995), pp. 117–22.

——, "Documenti sull'area di S. Lorenzo Maggiore tra Quattro e Cinquecento," *Ricerche sul Medioevo napoletano*, ed., A Leone (Testi e ricerche, IX), Naples, 1996, pp. 87–97.

Carabellese, F., "Spigolature storico-artistico Robertine," *Napoli nobilissima*, VIII (1899), pp. 191–92.

Caracciolo, A., *De sacris ecclesiae neapolitanae monumentis*, Naples, 1645.

Carelli, E., and S. Casiello, *S. Maria Donna Regina in Napoli*, Naples, 1975.

Carlucci, C., "Le operazioni militari in Calabria nella guerra del Vespro Siciliano," *Archivio storico per la Calabria e la Lucania*, I (1932), pp. 1–17.

Carozzi, C., "Saba Malapina et la légitimité de Charles Ier," *L'Etat angevin: pouvoir, culture et société entre XIII et XIV siècle* (Collection de l'Ecole Française de Rome, 245), Rome, 1998, pp. 81–97.

Carraz, D., "Une commanderie templière et sa chapelle en Avignon: du temple aux chevaliers de Malte," *Bulletin monumental*, CLIV (1966), pp. 7–24.

Carrera, P., *Saggio topografico, politico, economico di tutto il distretto allodiale di Città Ducale*, 2nd ed., L'Aquila, 1984.

Carucci, C., *Codice diplomatico salernitano del secolo XIII*, I: *1201–1281*, Subiaco, 1931.

——, *La guerra del Vespro Siciliano nella frontiera del Principato: storia diplomatica*, 2 vols., Subiaco, 1934.

Caruso, C., "Santa Maria della Consolazione di Altomonte e Filippo Sangineto," *Archivio storico per la Calabria e la Lucania*, XII (1842), pp. 95–107.

Caserta, A., *Archivi ecclesiastici di Napoli*, Naples, 1961.

Casiello, S., "Restauri a Napoli nei primi decenni del '900," *Restauro*, LXVIII (1983), pp. 68-9 and LXIX (1984), pp. 1-143.

Caskey, J., *Art and Patronage in the Medieval Mediterranean: Merchant Culture in the Region of Amalfi*, NY, 2004.

Castellano, A., "Protomastri Ciprioti in Puglia in età sveva e protoangioina," *Cultura e società in Puglia in età sveva e angioina. Atti del Convegno di Studi: Bitonto, 11–13 dicembre 1987*, ed. F. Moretti, Bitonto, 1989, pp. 263–82.

Catalioto, L., *Terre, baroni e città in Sicilia nell'età di Carlo I d'Angiò*, Messina, 1995.

Cattana, V., "Celestiniani," *Dizionario degli Istituti di Perfezioni*, II, 1975, pp. 731–34.

Cavaglieri, M., *Il pellegrino al Gargano*, Macerata, 1680; reprinted Foggia, 1987.

Cecchetti, I., "S. Brigida," *Bibliotheca Sanctorum*, Rome, 1963, III, 439–534.

Celano, C., *Notizie del bello dell'antico e del curioso della città di Napoli*, 3 vols., Naples, 1692.

Chierici, G., "Il restauro della chiesa dell'Incoronata a Napoli," *Bollettino d'arte*, XXIII (1929–30), pp. 410–23.

——, "Il restauro della chiesa di San Lorenzo a Napoli," *Bolletino d'arte*, XXIII (1929–30), pp. 24–39.

——, "L'elemento romano nell'architettura paleocristiana della Campania," *Roma*, XII (1934), pp. 531–38.

——, *Il restauro della chiesa di S. Maria di Donnaregina a Napoli*, Naples, 1934.

Chioccarello, B., *Antistum praeclarissimae neapolitanae ecclesiae catalogus ab apostolorum temporibus ad hanc usque nostre aetatem ed ad annum MDCXLIII*, Naples, 1643.

Cilento, N., "La chiesa di Napoli nell'alto medioevo," *Storia di Napoli*, II (1967), pp. 623–742.

Civita, M., *Stagioni di una Cattedrale*, Fasano, 1993.

Clarck, A., "The Clericalization of the Friars Minor," *The Jurist*, XXIX (1969), pp. 295–304.

Clementi, A., and E. Piroddi, *L'Aquila*, Rome, 1986.

Codice Diplomatico Barese: Le Pergamene di Barletta. Archivio Capitolare (897–1205), ed. F. Nitti de Vito, Bari, 1914.

Colletta, T., *Napoli: la cartografia pre-castale*, Naples, 1985.

Colvin, H. M., "The 'Court Style' in Medieval English Architecture," *English Court Culture in the Later Middle Ages*, ed. V. J. Scattergood and J. W. Sherborne, London, 1983, pp. 129–40.

Corrado, R., "Il giglio e la pietra serena: il cantiere del castello di Melfi in epoca angioina, 1269–1284," *Tarsia*, XX (1997), pp. 33–48.

——, "Pierre d'Angicourt," *Enciclopedia del'arte medievale*, IX (1998), pp. 390–91.

Corsi, P., "Note per la storia di Monte S. Angelo in età normanna," *Culto e insediamenti micaelici nell'Italia meridionale fra tarda antichità e medioevo. Atti del convegno internazionale: Monte Sant'Angelo, 18–21 Novembre 1992*, Bari, 1994, pp. 405-25.

Cosenza, G., "La chiesa e il convento di San Pietro Martire," *Napoli nobilissima*, VIII (1899), pp. 135–38, 154–57, 171–73, 187–91; IX (1900), pp. 22–27, 58–62, 88–93, 104–09, 136–39.

Coulet, N., "Un couvent royal: les dominicaines de Notre-Dame de Nazareth d'Aix au XIIIe siècle," *Cahiers de Fanjeux*, VIII (1973), pp. 233–62.

——, and J.-M. Matz, eds., *La Noblesse dans les territoires angevins à la fin du Moyen Age. Actes du colloque international organisé par l'Université d'Angers, Angers–Saumur, 3–6 juin 1998*, Rome, 2000.

Coulter, C. C., "The Library of the Angevin Kings," *Transactions and Proceedings of the American Philological Association*, LXXV (1944), pp. 141–55.

Croce, B., *Storia del Regno di Napoli*, Bari, 1931.

——, "I seggi di Napoli," *Aneddoti varia: letteratura*, I, Naples, 1942, pp. 239–46.

Cronica di Notar Giacomo, ed. P. Garzilli, Naples, 1845.

Crossley, P., "Medieval Architecture and Meaning: The Limits of Iconography," *Burlington Magazine*, CXXX (1988), pp. 116–21.

Crozet, R., "Fontevrault," *Congrès archéologique*, CXXII (1964), pp. 426–77.

Cuozzo, E., "I Cistercensi nella Campania medioevale," *I Cistercensi nel Mezzogiorno medioevale* (Atti del convegno internazionale di studio in occasione del IX centenario della nascita di Bernardo di Clairvaux, 25–27 febbraio 1991, ed. H. Houben and B. Vetere, Galatina, 1994, pp. 243–84.

——, "Modelli di gestione del potere nel regno di Sicilia: la 'restaurazione' della prima età antioina," *L'Etat Angevin: pouvoir, culture et société entre XIII et XIV siècle* (Collection de l'Ecole Française de Rome, 245), Rome, 1998, pp. 519–34.

Cutolo, A. *Il Regno di Sicilia negli ultimi anni di vita di Carlo d'Angiò*, Mainz, Rome, and Naples, 1924.

D'Addosio, G., *Origine, vicende storiche e progressi della Real S. Casa dell'Annunziata di Napoli (Ospizio de trovatelli)*, Naples, 1883.

D'Aloe, S., *Storia della chiesa di Napoli provata con documenti*, Naples, 1861.

——, "Catalogo di tutti gli edifici sacri della città di Napoli," *Archivio storico per le province napolitane*, VIII (1883), pp. 111-52, 287-315, 499-546 and 670-737.

Da Napoli, G. R., *Il convento e la chiesa di S. M. La Nova di Napoli*, Naples, 1927.

D'Andrea, G. F., "Il Monastero Napoletano di S. Chiara in regime di soppressione," *Archivum Franciscanum Historicum*, LXIX (1976), pp. 227–39.

——, "Ciò che resta dell'Archivio di S. Chiara di Napoli," *Archivum Franciscanum Historicum*, LXX (1977), pp. 128–46.

——, "Il Monastero Napoletano di Santa Chiara, secondo i registri dell'Archivio di Stato di Napoli," *Archivum Franciscanum Historicum*, LXXX (1987), pp. 39–78.

——, "Chiese francescane nella città di Napoli (MS. Sec. XVII)," *Archivium Franciscanum Historicum*, LXXXVII (1994), pp. 447–76.

Davis, M. T., "On the Threshold of the Flamboyant: The Second Campaign of Construction of Saint-Urbain, Troyes," *Speculum*, LIX (1984), pp. 847–84.

——, "Splendor and Peril: The Cathedral of Paris, 1290–1350," *Art Bulletin*, LXXX (1998), pp. 34–66.

——, "Les Visages du roi: les projets d'architecture de Philippe le Bel," *1300: l'art au temps de Philippe le Bel*, Rencontres de L'Ecole du Louvre, XVI, Paris, 2001, pp. 185–202.

——, "Angevin Architecture in the Kingdom of Naples: A Review of Recent Studies," *Avista*, XIII (2003), pp. 18–21.

D'Avray, D., *Death and the Prince: Memorial Preaching before 1350*, Oxford, 1994.

Dean, Trevor, "The Sovereign as Pirate: Charles II of Anjou and the Marriage of his Daughter, 1304," *English Historical Review*, CXI (1996), pp. 350–56.

De Blasiis, G., "Le case dei Principi Angioini nella Piazza del Castelnuovo," *Archivio storico per le provnce napolitane*, XI (1886), pp. 442–81; XII (1887), pp. 289–435.

——, "Napoli nella prima metà del secolo XIV," *Archivio storico per le provnce napolitane*, XL (1915), pp. 253–60.

De Boüard, A., "Gli antichi marmi di Roma nel Medio Evo," *Archivio storico della Regia Società Romana di Storia Patria*, XXXIV (1911), pp. 239–45.

——, *Actes et Lettres de Charles Ier roi de Sicile concernant la France (1257–1284)*, Paris, 1926.

——, and P. Durrieu, *Documents en français des archives angevines de Naples (règne Charles Ier)*. 2 vols., Paris, 1933–35.

——, "L'abbazia di Santa Maria di Realvalle," *Memoria presentata dal socio ordinario Levi e letta nella tornata dell II maggio*, Rome, XV (1937), pp. 147–53.

De Calvi, "*Vita Innocentii Papae IV*" ed. F. Pagnotti, *Archivio della società Romana di Storia Patria*, XXI (1898), pp. 76–120.

Declino svevo, ascesa angioina e l'arte venuta di Francia (Atti del Convegno a cura dell'Associazione culturale "Giornate Corradiniane"), ed. L. Gatto, M. Sanfilippo, and M. Righetti Tosti-Croce, Tagliacozzo, 1994.

De Cunzo, M., and V. De Martini, *La Certosa di Padula*, Florence, 1985.

De Dominici, B., *Vite de' pittori, scultori ed architetti napoletani*, Naples, 1742-43, 2nd ed. 1840-46.

De Falco, B., *Descrittione dei luoghi antichi di Napoli, e del suo amenissimo distretto*, Naples, 1549.

De Frede, C., "Da Carlo I d'Angiò a Giovanna I, 1263–1382," *Storia di Napoli*, III, ed., E. Pontieri, Naples, 1969, pp. 1–333.

De La Roncère, C. M., "L'Etat angevin, 1265–1340: pouvoirs et sociétés dans le Royaume et le comté: bilan d'un colloque," *L'Etat angevin: pouvoir, culture et société entre XIII et XIV siècle* (Collection de l'Ecole Française de Rome, 245), Rome, 1998, pp. 649–64.

De la Ville sur-Yllon, L., "La costruzione del Duomo di Napoli," *Napoli nobilissima*, IV (1894), pp. 177–79.

——, "L'abside della chiesa di S. Lorenzo Maggiore," *Napoli nobilissima*, IV (1895), pp. 37–41.

——, "La cappella dei Minutolo nel duomo di Napoli," *Napoli nobilissima*, IV (1895), pp. 113–16.

——, "La chiesa ed il convento di San Lorenzo Maggiore," *Napoli nobilissima*, IV (1895), pp. 68-72.

——, "Tombe reali nel duomo di Napoli, *Napoli nobilissima*, IV (1895), pp. 166–68.

——, "La Cappella Espiatoria di Corradino al Mercato," *Napoli nobilissima*, V (1896), pp. 150–53.

——, "La grande navata e la crociera del Duomo," *Napoli nobilissima*, V (1896), pp. 37–41.

——, "Le navate minori del duomo," *Napoli nobilissima*, V (1896), pp. 81–85.

——, "La basilica di S. Restituta," *Napoli nobilissima*, VI (1897), p. 38.

——, "La chiesa di S. Pietro a Maiella," *Napoli nobilissima*, XI (1902), pp. 22–28.

De Lellis, C., *Parte seconda, o' vero Supplimento a Napoli Sacra di D. Cesare d'Engenio Caracciolo*, Naples, 1654.

——, *Discorsi delle famiglie nobili del regno di Napoli*, I–II, Naples, 1654–63.

——, *Gli atti perduti della Cancelleria angioina transuntati da Carlo de Lellis* (Regesta chartarum Italiae, 25), Rome, 1939–42.

Delfino, A., "Il monumento dell'arcivescovo Ayglerio scomparso dal duomo di Napoli," *Scritti di storia dell'arte per il settantesimo dell'Associazione napoletana per i monumenti e il paesaggio*, Naples, 1991, pp. 37–41.

Del Giudice, G., *Codice diplomatico del regno di Carlo I e II d'Angio, ossia collezione di leggi, statuti, e privilegi . . . .*, 3 vols. in 1, Naples, 1863–1908.

Dell'Aja, G., *Il restauro della basilica di S. Chiara in Napoli*, Naples, 1980.

——, *Per la storia del monastero di Santa Chiara in Napoli*, Naples, 1992.

Della Marra, F., *Discorsi delle famiglie estinte, forastiere, o non comprese ne' seggi di Napoli*, Naples, 1641.

——, *La famiglia di re Manfredi: narrazione storica*, Naples, 1880.

Del Treppo, "Aiglerio," *Dizionario biografico degli italiani*, I (1960), p. 520.

——, and A., Leone, *Amalfi medioevale*, Naples, 1977.

D'Engenio Caracciolo, C., *Napoli sacra*, Naples, 1624.

De Rinaldis, A., *Santa Chiara*, Naples, 1920.

——, *Naples angevine*, Paris, 1927.

De Sanctis, M. L., "L'abbazia di Santa Maria di Realvalle: una fondazione cistercense di Carlo I d'Angiò," *Arte medievale*, II serie, VII (1993), pp. 153–96.

De Santis, T., *Historia del tumulto di Napoli*, Leiden, 1652.

De Seta, C., *Cartografia della città di Napoli: lineamenti dell'evoluzione urbana*, Naples, 1969.

——, *Storia della città di Napoli dalle origini al settecento*, Rome, 1973.

——, *Napoli*, Bari, 1981.

De Simone, A., "S. Lorenzo Maggiore in Napoli: il monumento e l'area," *Neapolis. Atti del venticinquesimo convegno di studi su Magna Grecia: Taranto, 3–7 October 1985*, Naples, 1986, pp. 233–53.

Desmulliez, J., "Le Dossier du groupe épiscopal de Naples: état actuel des recherches," *Antiquité tardive*, VI (1998), pp. 345–54.

De Stefano, P., *Descrizione dei luoghi sacri della città di Napoli con li fondatori di essi*, Naples, 1560.

Di Dario Guida, M. P., "Formazione e consistenza del patrimonio artistico delle chiese di Calabria," *Atti del Convegno su i beni culturali e le chiese di Calabria*, Reggio Calabria, 1981, pp. 250–89.

——, "Calabria angioina," *Itinerari per la Calabria*, Vicenza, 1983, pp. 167–95.

——, *Il Museo di Santa Maria della Consolazione ad Altomonte*, Cosenza, 1986.

Didier, A., *Teggiano medievale*, Salerno, 1965.

Di Flaco, B., *Descrittione dei luoghi antichi di Napoli, e del suo amenissimo distretto*, Naples, 1549.

Di Fonzo, L., "Lo studium-Collegio Teologico del Convento di Napoli (*ca.* 1240–1848)," *Miscellanea Francescana*, VC (1995), pp. 174–88.

Di Giacomo, S., "Le chiese di Napoli: S. Eligio al Mercato," *Napoli nobilissima*, I (1892), pp. 151–54.

——, "Santa Maria del Carmine Maggiore," *Napoli nobilissima*, I (1892), pp. 18–23, 56–60, 97–99.

Di Majo, I., "Episodi di 'fortuna dei primitivi' a Napoli nel Cinquecento (intorno al 'San Ludovico di Tolosa' di Simone Martini)," *Prospettiva*, CIII–CIV (2001), pp. 133–50.

Di Mauro, L., "L'architettura dal IV al XV secolo," *Storia del Mezzogiorno*, ed., G. Galasso and R. Romeo, XI, Naples, 1991, pp. 243-96.

Di Meglio, R., *Il convento francescano di S. Lorenzo di Napoli. Regesti dei documenti dei secoli XIII-XV* (Documenti per la storia degli ordini mendicandi nel Mezzogiorno), Salerno, 2003.

——, "Ordini mendicanti e città: L'esempio di S. Lorenzo Maggiore di Napoli," *San Lorenzo e San Domenico a Napoli*, ed. S. Romano and N. Bock, forthcoming.

Dimier, A., *Recueil de plans d'églises cisterciennes*, 2 vols, Grignan, 1949.

Di Montemayor, G., "Santa Chiara. La fondazione e la chiesa primitiva," *Napoli nobilissima*, IV (1895), pp. 65–67 and 84–87.

Di Nicola, A., "Il più antico documento di Cittaducale. Contributo per datare la fondazione della città," *Bullettino della Deputazione Abruzzese di Storia Patria*, LXXI (1981), pp. 91-103.

Di Resta, I., "Il Palazzo Fieramosca a Capua," *Napoli nobilissima*, IX (1970), pp. 53–60.

Di Stefano, R., *La cattedrale di Napoli: Storia, restauro, scoperte, ritrovamenti*, Naples, 1975.

Divenuto, F., "La torre campanaria di San Lorenzo Maggiore in Napoli," *Napoli nobilissima*, XIV (1975), pp. 129–42.

Doberer, E., "Der Lettner: seine Bedeutung und Geschichte," *Mitteilungen der Gesellschaft für vergleichende Kunstforschung in Wien*, IX (1956), pp. 117–22.

D'Onofrio, M. *La cattedrale di Caserta Vecchia*, Rome, 1974.

——, and V. Pace, *La Campania (Italia romanica, IV)*, Milan, 1981.

Douie, D., *The Nature and the Effect of the Heresy of the Fraticelli*, Manchester, 1932.

Dovere, U., *Il Duomo di Napoli*, Naples, 1996.

Duby, G., "Situation de la solitude XIe-XIIIe siècle," *Histoire de la vie privé*, ed. P. Ariès and G. Duby, 5 vols., 2nd ed., 1999, vol. 2, pp. 505–28.

Dunbabin, J., *Charles I of Anjou: Power, Kingship, and State-Making in Thirteenth-Century Europe*, London, 1998.

Durrieu, P., "Etudes sur la dynastie angevine de Naples: le *liber donationum Caroli Primi*," *Mélanges d'archéologie et d'histoire, Ecole Française de Rome*, VI, Rome, 1886, pp. 189–228.

——, *Les Archives angevines de Naples: étude sur les registres de Charles Ier (1265–1285): Bibliothèque des écoles françaises d'Athènes et de Rome*. 2 vols., Paris and Turin, 1933–35.

Dyggve, H. Petersen, "Charles, Comte d'Anjou," *Neuphilologische Mitteilungen*, L (1949), pp. 144–74.

Egidi, P., "Carlo I d'Angiò e l'abbazia di S. Maria della Vittoria presso Scurcola," *Archivio storico per le province napolitane*, XXXIV (1909), pp. 252–91, 732–67; XXXV (1910), pp. 125–75.

——, "La colonia saracena di Lucera e la sua distruzione," *Archivio storico per le province napolitane*, XXXVI (1911), pp. 587–694; XXXVII (1912), pp. 71–89, 664–96; XXXVIII (1913), pp. 115–44, 681–707; XXXIX (1914), pp. 132–71, 697–766.

Ehrle, F., "Olivis Schreiben an die Sohne Karls II von Neapel aus dem Jahr 1295," *Archiv für litteratur und Kirchengeschichte*, III (1888), pp. 64–95.

Elias, N., *The Court Society*, trans. E. Jephcott, New York, 1983.

Elliott, J., "The Judgement of the Commune: The Frescoes of the Magdalen Chapel in Florence," *Zeitschrift für Kunstgeschichte*, LXI/4 (1998), pp. 509-15.

——, "The Last Judgement Scene in Central Italian Painting, *c.* 1266–1343: The Impact of Guelf Politics, Papal Power and Angevin Iconography," Ph.D. dissertation, University of Warwick, 2000.

Emery, R., "The Second Council of Lyons," *Catholic Historical Review*, XXXIV (1953), pp. 257-71.

Emminghaus, J. H., *The Eucharist, Essence, Form, Celebration*, trans. M. J. O'Connell, Collegeville, MN, 1978.

Enderlein, L., "Zur Enstehung der Ludwigstafel des Simone Martini," *Römisches Jarhbuch für Kunstgeschicte*, XXXIII (1995), pp. 136–49.

——, *Die Grablegen des Hauses Anjou in Unteritalien: Totenkult und Monumente, 1266–1343* (Römische Studien der Bibliotheca Hertziana, 12), Worms, 1997.

——, "Die Künstler und der Hof im angiovinischen Neapel," *Medien der Macht: Kunst zur Zeit der Anjous in Italien*, ed. T. Michalsky, Berlin, 2001, pp. 61–78.

Enlart, C., *Origines françaises de l'architecture gothique en Italie*, Paris, 1894.

Erickson, C., "The Fourteenth-Century Franciscans and their Critics," *Franciscan Studies*, XXXV (1975), pp. 107–35; XXXVI (1976), pp. 108–47.

Erlande-Brandenburg, A., "La priorale Saint-Louis de Poissy," *Bulletin monumental*, CXXIX (1971), pp. 85–112.

——, *Le Roi est mort*, Paris and Geneva, 1975.

Esch, A., and A. Kiesewetter, "Süditalien unter den ersten Angiovinen: Abschriften aus den verlorenen Anjou-Registern im Nachlass Eduard Sthamer," *Quellen und*

Forschungen aus italienischen Archiven und Bibliotheken, LXXIV (1994), pp. 646–63.

Esquieu, Y., "L'Eglise des Hospitaliers de Saint-Jean-de-Malte à Aix," *Congrès archéologique de France*, CXLIII (1988), pp. 103–19.

L'Etat angevin: pouvoir, culture et société entre XIII et XIV siècle (Collection de l'Ecole Française de Rome, 245), Rome, 1998.

Eubel, C., ed., *Bullarium Franciscanum Romanorum Pontificum: constitutiones, epistolas ac diplomata continens: tribus ordinibus Minorum, Clarissarum et Poenitentium a seraphico patriarcha Sancto Francisco institutis concessa . . .*, V-VII, Rome 1898-1904.

L'Europe des Anjou: aventure des princes angevins du XIIIe au XVe siècle, Paris, 2001.

Faraglia, N. F., "Le memorie degli artisti napoletani pubblicate da B. De Dominici: studio critico," *Archivio storico per le province napolitane*, VII (1882), pp. 329–64; VIII (1883), pp. 259–86.

——, "Il largo di Palazzo," *Napoli nobilissima*, II (1893), pp. 2-6, 33-35, 61-63, 134-37, 156–59.

Farioli, R., "Gli scavi nell'insula episcopalis de Napoli paleocristiana: tentativo di lettura," *Atti del IX Congresso di archeologia cristiana, 21–27 Septembre 1975*, II, Vatican City, 1978, pp. 278-88.

Fasola, U. M., "Le tombe privilegiate dei vescovi e dei duchi di Napoli nelle catacombe di S. Gennaro," *L'Inhumation privilegiée du V au VIIIe siècle en Occident. Actes du Colloque à Creteil, 1984*, ed. Y. Duval and J. C. Picard, Paris, 1986, pp. 205–10.

Fastidio, (Don), "Per la costruzione del convento di S. Chiara," *Napoli nobilissima*, IX (1990), p. 140.

Feniello, A., ed., *Napoli. Notai diversi 1322–1541*, Naples, 1998.

Fentress, L., C. Goodson, M. Laird and S. Leone, eds., *Walls and Memory: The Abbey of San Sebastiano at Alatri between the Fifth and the Twentieth Century*, Louvain, forthcoming.

Fergusson, P., *The Architecture of Solitude: Cistercian Abbeys in Twelfth-Century England*, Princeton, 1984.

Filangeri, A., "Le Castel Nuovo de Naples," *L'Europe des Anjou: aventure des princes angevins du XIIIe au XVe siècle*, Paris, 2001, pp. 67–71.

Filangieri, G., *Documenti per la storia, le arti, e le industrie delle province napoletane*, 6 vols., Naples, 1883–91.

——, *Chiesa e convento di S. Lorenzo Maggiore in Napoli: descrizione storica ed artistica (Documenti per la storia, le arti, e le industrie delle province napoletane, 2)*, Naples, 1884, pp. 7-231.

——, *Chiesa e convento di S. Pietro a Maiella in Napoli: descrizione storica ed artistica (Documenti per la storia, le arti, e le industrie delle province napoletane, 2)*, Naples, 1884, pp. 233-42.

——, *Chiesa e convento del Carmine Maggiore in Napoli: descrizione storica ed artistica (Documenti per la storia, le arti, e les industrie delle province napoletane, 3)*, Naples, 1885, pp. 249-565.

Filangieri, R., "Castel Nuovo e i suoi restauri," *Bollettino del Comune di Napoli*, V (1927), pp. 1–11.

——, *Rassegna critica delle fonti per la storia di Castel Nuovo*, 4 vols., Naples, 1936–40.

——, *I registri della cancelleria angioina ricostruiti da Riccardo Filangieri con la collaborazione degli archivisti napoletani (Testi e documenti di storia napoletana pubblicati dall'Accademia Pontaniana)*, Naples, 1950ff.

——, *Castel Nuovo, reggia angioina ed aragonese di Napoli*, Naples, 1964.

Filangieri di Candida, A., "La chiesa di S. Lorenzo Maggiore in Napoli ed i lavori di ripristino del coro," *Neapolis*, I (1913), pp. 219–38.

——, ed., *Pergamene di Barletta del Regio Archivio di Napoli, 1075–1309*, Bari, 1927.

Filipiak, M. A., "The Plans of the Poor Clares' Convents in Central Italy from the Thirteenth through the Fifteenth Century," Ph.D. dissertation, University of Michigan, 1957.

Fino, L., *Arte e storia di Napoli in S. Lorenzo Maggiore*, Naples, 1987.

Fiocca, L., "La chiesa di Santa Maria della Vittoria presso Scurcola e gli scavi eseguiti per cura del Ministero della Pubblica Istruzione," *L'Arte*, VI (1903), pp. 201–05.

Fobelli, M, L., "Aquila," *Enciclopedia dell'arte medievale*, II (1991), pp. 196–202.

Folda, J., "Problems in the Iconography of the Art of the Crusaders in the Holy Land, 1098–1291/1917–1997," *Image and Belief: Studies in Celebration of the Eightieth Anniversary of the Index of Christian Art*, Princeton, 1999, pp. 11-18.

Fonseca, C. D., "'Congregationes Clericorum et Sacerdotum' a Napoli nei secoli XI e XII," *La vita comune del clero nei secoli XI e XII*, II (1960), pp. 265–83.

——, ed., "Vescovi, capitoli cattedrali e canoniche regolari (sec. XIV–XVI)," *Vescovi e diocesi in Italia dal XIV alla metà del XVI secolo. (Atti del VII convegno di storia della chiesa in Italia sacra: studi e documenti di storia ecclesiastica)*, 1990, pp. 83–138.

——, *Cattedrali di Puglia: una storia lunga duemila anni*, Bari, 2001.

Fontette, M. De., *Les Religieuses à l'âge classique du droit canon*, Paris, 1967.

Foucault, M., *The Order of Things: An Archaeology of the Human Sciences*, trans. R. D. Laing, New York, 1970.

Fraccaro de' Longhi, L., *L'architettura delle chiese cistercensi italiane con particolare riferimento ad un gruppo omogeneo dell'Italia settentrionale*, Milan, 1958.

Francabandera, O., *L'abbazia di S. Maria di Realvalle presso Scafati*, Bari, 1932.

Fraschetti, S., "I sarcofagi dei reali angioini in Santa Chiara di Napoli," *L'Arte*, I (1898), pp. 385–438.

——, "Il monumento di Arrigo Minutolo," *Napoli nobilissima*, XI (1902), pp. 49–52.

Freigang, C., *Imitare Ecclesias Nobiles: Die Kathedralen von Narbonne, Toulouse und Rodez und die nordfranzössische Rayonnantgotik im Languedoc*, Worms, 1992.

——, "La cathédrale gothique septentionale dans le Midi,

symbole royaliste ou formule ambitieuse?" *Les grandes églises gothiques du Midi, sources d'inspiration et construction* (Actes du 3e colloque d'histoire de l'art méridional au Moyen-Age. Narbonne, 4 et 5 décembre, 1992, Narbonne, 1994, pp. 15–26.

——, "Les Rois, les évêques et les cathédrales de Narbonne, de Toulouse, et de Rodez," *Cahiers de Fanjeaux*, XXX (1995), pp. 145–83.

——, "Kathedralen als Mendikantenkirchen: Zur politischen Ikonographie der Sakralarchitektur unter Karl I., Karl II. und Robert dem Weisen," *Medien der Macht: Kunst zur Zeit der Anjous in Italien*, ed. T. Michalsky, Berlin, 2001, pp. 33–60.

——, "Chapelles latérales privées. Origines, fonctions, financement: le cas de Notre-Dame de Paris," *Art, Cérémonial et Liturgie au Moyen Age (Actes du colloque du 3° Cycle Romand de Lettres Lausanne-Fribourg, 24–25 mars, 14–15 avril, 12–13 mai, 2000)*, ed. N. Bock, P. Kurmann, S. Romano, and J.-M. Spieser, Rome, 2002, pp. 525–44.

Friedman, D., *Florentine New Towns: Urban Design in the Late Middle Ages*, Cambridge, MA, and London, 1988.

Frugoni, A., "Da *'pauperes eremiti domini celestini'* ai *'fraticelli de paupere vita',"* *Celestiniana*, (Nuovi Studi Storici XVI) Rome, 1991, pp. 125–67.

Fusco, A., *Note storiche ed artistiche sul monastero di S. Chiara in Nola*, Nola, 1997.

Gaglione, M., *Sculture minori del Trecento conservate in Santa Chiara a Napoli ed altri studi*, Naples, 1995.

——, *Manomissioni settecentesche dei sepolcri angioini in Santa Chiara a Napoli ed altri studi*, Naples, 1996.

——, *Nuovi studi sulla Basilica di Santa Chiara in Napoli*, Naples, 1996.

——, "Il campanile di S. Chiara in Napoli," *Quaderni di antichità napoletane*, I (1998), pp. 5–23.

——, "Due fondazioni angioine a Napoli: S. Chiara e S. Croce di Palazzo," *Campania Sacra*, XXXIII (2003), pp. 63-110.

Galante, G. A., *Guida sacra della città di Napoli*, Naples, 1872; new edn., ed. N. Spinosa, Naples, 1985.

——, *La tribuna del duomo di Napoli*, Naples, 1874.

——, "Memorie della vita e del culto del beato Nicolò eremita di S. Maria a Circolo in Napoli," extract from *La scienza e la fede*, 1875–77, pp. 5- 90.

Galasso, G., "Gli angioini di Napoli nella storia del Mediterraneo e dell'Europa," *Marseilles et ses rois de Naples: le diagonale angevine, 1265–1382*, Aix-en-Provence, 1988, pp. 31-40.

——, *Il Regno di Napoli: Il Mezzogiorno angioino e aragonese (1266–1494)*, Turin, 1992.

——, "Carlo I d'Angiò e la scelta di Napoli come capitale," *L'Etat Angevin: pouvoir, culture et société entre XIII et XIV siècle* (Collection de l'Ecole Française de Rome, 245), Rome, 1998, pp. 339–60.

Gallino, T. M., *Il complesso monumentale di Santa Chiara di Napoli*, Naples, 1963.

Gandolfo, F., *La scultura normanno-sveva in Campania*, Bari, 1999.

Gardner, J., "The Tomb of Cardinal Annibaldi by Arnolfo di Cambio," *Burlington Magazine*, CXIV (1972), pp. 136–41.

——, "Pope Nicholas IV and the Decoration of Santa Maria Maggiore," *Zeitschrift für Kunstgeschichte*, XXXVI (1973), pp. 1–50.

——, "Saint Louis of Toulouse, Robert of Anjou, and Simone Martini, *Zeitschrift für Kunstgeschichte*, XCIII (1976), pp. 12–23.

——, "Some Franciscan Altars of the 13th and 14th Centuries," *The Vanishing Past: Studies of Medieval Art, Liturgy and Metrology presented to Christopher Hohler*, ed. A. Martindale and A. Borg, Oxford, 1981, pp. 29–38.

——, "A Princess among Prelates: A Fourteenth-Century Neapolitan Tomb and some Northern Relations," *Römisches Jahrbuch für Kunstgeschichte*, XXIII–XXIV (1988), pp. 31–60.

——, "Il patrocinio curiale e l'introduzione del gotico, 1260–1305," *Il gotico europeo in Italia*, ed. M. Bagnoli and V. Pace, Naples, 1994, pp. 85–88.

——, "Cardinal Ancher and the Piscina in Saint Urban at Troyes," *Architectural Studies in Memory of Richard Krautheimer*, Mainz, 1996, pp. 79–82.

——, "Seated Kings, Sea-Faring Saints and Heraldry: Some Themes in Angevin Iconography," *L'Etat angevin: pouvoir, culture et société entre XIII et XIV siècle* (Collection de l'Ecole Française de Rome, 245), Rome, 1998, pp. 115–26.

——, "The family chapel: artistic patronage and architectural transformation in Italy circa 1275–1325," *Art, Cérémonial et Liturgie au Moyen Age (Actes du colloque du 3° Cycle Roman de Lettres Lausanne-Fribourg, 24–25 mars, 14–15 avril, 12–13 mai 2000)*, ed. N. Bock, P. Kurmann, S. Romano, and J.-M. Spieser, Rome, 2002, pp. 545–64.

Gavini, I. C., "I terremoti d'Abruzzo e suoi monumenti," *Rivista abruzzese*, XXX (1915), pp. 235–40.

——, *Storia dell'architettura in Abruzzo*, 2 vols., Milan-Rome, 1927–28.

Genovese, R. A. *La chiesa trecentesca di Donnaregina*, Naples, 1993.

Gilli, P., "L'intégration manquée des Angevins en Italie: le témoignange des historiens," *L'Etat angevin: pouvoir, culture et société entre XIII et XIV siècle* (Collection de l'Ecole Française de Rome, 245), Rome, 1998, pp. 11–33.

Giuduce, G. del, *Codice diplomatico del regno di Carlo I e II d'Angiò*, 3 vols., Naples, 1863–1902.

Giusti, P., "I resti di una sepoltura reale angioina," *Scritti di storia dell'arte in memoria di Raffaele Causa*, ed. S. Cassani and D. Campanelli, Naples, 1988, pp. 39–45.

Glass, D. *Romanesque Sculpture in Campania: Patrons, Painters, and Style*, University Park, PA, 1991.

Glorieux, P., *Répertoire des maîtres en théologie de Paris au XIIIe siècle*, 2 vols. Paris, 1933.

Goetz, W., *König Robert von Neapel (1309–1343): seine Persön-*

lichkeit und sein Verhältnis zum Humanismus, Tübingen, 1910.

Il gotico europeo in Italia, ed. M. Bagnoli and V. Pace, Naples, 1994.

Gradara, C., "L'isolamento del sepolcro di re Roberto d'Angiò, scoperta di affreschi e restauri nella chiesa di S. Chiara di Napoli," *Bollettino d'arte*, XI (1917), pp. 97–104.

Gratien, P., *Histoire de la fondation et de l'évolution de l'Ordre des Frères Mineurs*, Paris, 1928.

Grisotti, M., *Barletta, il castello, la storia, il restauro*, Bari, 1995.

Guadagni, C., *Nola Sagra illustrata*, n.p., n.d.

Guidoni, E., "Città e ordini mendicanti: il ruolo dei conventi nella crescita e nella progettazione urbana nei secoli XIII e XIV," *Quaderni medievali*, IV (1977), pp. 69–106.

——, *Storia dell'urbanistica, Il Duecento*, Rome-Bari, 1992.

Guillaume de Saint-Pathus, *Vie de Saint Louis*, ed. H.-F. Delaborde, Paris, 1899.

Hall, M., "The *Tramezzo* in Sta. Croce, Reconstructed," *Art Bulletin*, 56 (1974), pp. 38–41.

——, *Renovations and Counter Reformation: Vasari and Duke Cosimo in Sta. Maria Novella and Sta. Croce, 1565–1577*, Oxford, 1979.

Hallam, E. M., "Royal Burial and the Cult of Kingship in France and England, 1060–1330," *Journal of Medieval History*, VIII (1982), pp. 359–80.

Hartmann-Virnisch, A., "Bouches-du-Rhone: Aix-en-Provence, église Saint-Jean-de-Malte: approches d'un premier chantier du gothique rayonnant en Provence," *Bulletin monumental*, CLIV (1996), pp. 345–50.

Haseloff, A., *Die Bauten der Hohenstaufen in Unteritalien*, Leipzig, 1920.

——, *Architettura sveva nell'Italia meridionale*, Bari, 1992.

Henriet, J., "La Chapelle de la Vierge de Saint-Mathurin de Larchant: une oeuvre de Pierre de Chelles?," *Bulletin monumental*, CXXXVI (1978), pp. 35–48.

Herde, P., "Die Schlacht bei Tagliacozzo," *Zeitschrift für bayerische Landesgeschichte*, XXV (1962), pp. 679–744.

——, "Carlo I d'Angiò," *Dizionario biografico degli Italiani*, XX, Rome, (1977), pp. 199–226.

——, "Celestino V, papa," *Dizionario biografico degli Italiani*, XXIII (1979), pp. 402–15.

——, *Karl I. von Anjou*. Cologne, 1979.

——, "La battaglia di Tagliacozzo," VII *centenario della battaglia di Taglicozzo*, Pescara, 1980, pp. 7–66.

——, "Carlo I d'Angiò nella storia del mezzogiorno," *Unità politica e differenze regionali nel Regno di Sicilia. Atti del Convegno internazionale di studio in occasione dell'VIII centenario della morte di Guglielmo II, re di Sicilia: Lecce–Potenza, 19–22 Aprile 1989*, Potenza, 1992, pp. 181–204.

Heullant-Donat, I., "Quelques réflexions autour de la cour angevine comme milieu culturel au XIVe siècle," *L'Etat angevin: pouvoir, culture et société entre XIII et XIV siècle* (Collection de l'Ecole Française de Rome, 245), Rome, 1998, pp. 173–91.

Hills, H., "Cities and Virgins: Female Aristocratic Convents in Early Modern Naples and Palermo," *Oxford Art Journal*, XXII (1999), pp. 29–54.

"Hirpinus" (pseud. G. Recupido), "San Lorenzo Maggiore a Napoli: ritrovamenti paleocristiani e altomedioevali," *Napoli nobilissima*, n. s., I (1961), pp. 13–21.

Hobsbawm, E., and T. Ranger, *The Invention of Tradition*, Cambridge, 1983.

Hoch, A., "Beata Stirps, Royal Patronage and the Identification of the Sainted Rulers in the St. Elizabeth Chapel at Assisi," *Art History*, XV (1992), pp. 279–95.

——, "The Franciscan Provenance of Simone Martini's Angevin St. Louis in Naples," *Zeitschrift für Kunstgeschichte*, LVIII (1995), pp. 22–37.

——, "A Proposal for the 'Lost' Clarissite Church of San Giovanni a Nido in Naples," *Arte cristiana*, LXXXIV (1996), pp. 353–60.

——, "Sovereignty and Closure in Trecento Naples: Images of Queen Sancia, alias Sister Clare," *Arte medievale*, ser. 2, X (1996), pp. 121–39.

——, "Pictures of Penitence from a Trecento Neapolitan Nunnery," *Zeitschrift für Kunstgeschichte*, LXI (1998), pp. 206–26.

Houben, H., "La presenza dell'Ordine Teutonico a Barletta (secc. XII-XV)," *Barletta crocevia degli Ordini religioso-cavallereschi medioevali (Seminario di Studio, Barletta 16 Giugno, 1996)*, Taranto, 1997, pp. 25–50.

——, and B. Vetere, eds., *I Cistercensi nel Mezzogiorno medioevale* (Atti del Convegno internazionale di studio in occasione del IX centenario della nascita di Bernardo di Clairvaux, 25–27 febbraio, 1991), Galatina, 1994.

Housley, N., "Angevin Naples and the Defence of the Latin East: Robert the Wise and the Naval League of 1334," *Byzantion*, LI (1981), pp. 548–56.

——, *The Italian Crusades: The Papal Angevin Alliance and the Crusades against Christian Lay Powers*, Oxford, 1982.

——, "Charles II of Naples and the Kingdom of Jerusalem," *Byzantion*, LIV (1984), pp. 527–35.

——, *The Avignon Papacy and the Crusades, 1305–1378*, Oxford, 1986.

——, *The Later Crusades, 1274–1580: from Lyons to Alcazar*, Oxford, 1992.

Hueck, I., "Stifter und Patronatsrecht: Documente zu zwei Kapellen der Bardi," *Mitteilungen des Kunsthistorischen Institutes in Florenz*, XX (1976), pp. 263–70.

——, "Die Kapellen der Basilika S. Francesco in Assisi: die Auftraggeber und die Franziskaner," *Patronage and Public in the Trecento. Proceedings of the St. Lambrecht Symposium: Abtei St. Lambrecht, Styria, 16–19 July 1984*, Florence, 1986, pp. 81–104.

Huyghe, R., *La clôture des moniales des origines à la fin du XIIIeme siècle. Etude historique et juridique*, Rouaix, 1944.

Iannelli, Pio, *Lo studio teologico OFMConv. nel San Lorenzo Maggiore di Napoli (Miscellanea Francescana)*, Rome, 1994.

Iorio, R., *Profilo urbanistico di Barletta medievale*, Barletta, 1988.

——, "Uomini e sedi a Baretta: gli Ospedalieri e Templari come soggetti di organizzazione storica," *Barletta crocevia degli Ordini religioso-cavallereschi medioevali (Seminario di Studio, Barletta, 16 Giugno, 1996),* Taranto, 1997, pp. 71–120.

Jamison, E. M., "Documents from the Angevin Registers of Naples: Charles I," *Papers of the British School at Rome,* XVII (1949), pp. 87-173.

Jansen, K., *The Making of the Magdalen: Preaching and Popular Devotion in the Later Middle Ages,* Princeton, 2000.

Johannowsky, W., "Recenti scoperte archeologiche in San Lorenzo Maggiore a Napoli," *Napoli nobilissima,* n.s., I (1961), pp. 8–12.

Jordan, E., *Les Origines de la domination angevine en Italie,* Paris, 1909.

——, *L'Allemagne et l'Italie aux XIIe et XIIIe siècles,* Paris, 1939.

Jung, J., "Beyond the Barrier: The Unifying Role of the Choir Screen in Gothic Churches," *Art Bulletin,* LXXXII (2000), pp. 622–57.

Jungmann, J., *The Mass of the Holy Rite: Its Origins and Development,* trans. F. A. Brunner, Westminster (MD), 1986.

Kamp, N., *Kirche und Monarchie im Staufischen Königreich Sizilien,* 3 vols., Munich, 1973–82.

Kappel, K., *S. Nicola in Bari und seine architektonische Nachfolge: ein Bautypus des 11.–17. Jahrhunderts in Unteritalien und Dalmatien.* Worms, 1996.

Kelly, S., "King Robert of Naples (1309–1343) and the Spiritual Franciscans," *Cristianesimo nella storia,* XX (1999), pp. 41–80.

——, "Noblesse de robe et noblesse d'esprit dans la cour de Robert de Naples: la question de l'*italianisation*," *La noblesse dans les territoires angevins à la fin du Moyen Âge. Actes du colloque international organisé par l'Université d'Angers, Angers–Saumur, 3–6 juin 1998,* ed. N. Coulet and J.-M. Matz, Rome, 2000, pp. 347–61.

Kiesewetter, A., "Karl II von Anjou, Marseille und Neapel," *Marseille et ses rois de Naples: la diagonale angevine, 1265–1382,* ed. I. Bonnot, Aix-en-Provence, (1988), pp. 61–75.

——, "Das sizilianische Zweistaatsproblem, 1282–1302," *Unità politica e differenze regionali nel regno di Sicilia. Atti del convegno internazionale di studio in occasione dell'VIII centenario della morte di Guglielmo II re di Sicilia,* ed. C. Fonseca, H. Houben, and B. Vetere, Lavello, 1992, pp. 247–95.

——, "Le strutture castellane tarantine nell'età angioina," *Cenacolo (Società di storia patria per la Puglia: sezione di Taranto),* n.s., VII (XIX) (1995), pp. 21–51.

——, "Dar Itinerar Königs Karls II. von Anjou (1271–1309)," *Archiv für Diplomatik, Schriftgeschichte, Siegel- und Wappenkunde,* XLIII (1997), pp. 85–283.

——, "La cancelleria angioina," *L'Etat angevin: pouvoir, culture et société entre XIII et XIV siècle* (Collection de l'Ecole Française de Rome, 245), Rome, 1998, pp. 361–415.

——, *Der Anfänge der Regierung König Karls II. von Anjou (1278–1295),* Husum, 1999.

Klaniczay, G., "Le culte des saints dynastiques en Europe Centrale," *Collection de l'Ecole Française de Rome,* CXXVIII (1986), pp. 221–47.

——, "La Noblesse et le culte des saints dynastiques sous les rois angevins," *La Noblesse dans les territoires angevins à la fin du Moyen Age. Actes du colloque international organisé par l'Université d'Angers, Angers–Saumur, 3–6 juin 1998,* ed. N. Coulet and J.-M. Matz, Rome, 2000, pp. 511–26.

Knoop, D., and G. P. Jones, *The Medieval Mason,* Manchester, 1933.

Knowles, Dom D., *The Religious Orders in England,* Cambridge, 1948.

Knox, L., "Audacious Nuns: Institutionalizing the Franciscan Order of Saint Clare," *Church History: Studies in Christianity and Culture,* LXIX (2000), pp. 41–62.

Kosegarten, A., "*Ecclesia spiritualis:* Joachimismus und Kaiserprophetie in der Pisaner Domkanzel von Giovanni Pisano," *Medien der Macht: Kunst zur Zeit der Anjous in Italien,* ed. T. Michalsky, Berlin, 2001, pp. 149–90.

Krautheimer, R., *Early Christian and Byzantine Architecture,* 4th edition revised with S. Curcic, New Haven and London, 1986.

Kreytenberg, G., "Ein doppelseitiges Triptychon in Marmor von Tino di Camaino aus der Zeit um 1334," *Medien der Macht: Kunst zur Zeit der Anjous in Italien,* ed. T. Michalsky, Berlin, 2001, pp. 261–74.

Krüger, Jürgen, *San Lorenzo Maggiore in Neapel: eine Franziskanerkirche zwischen Ordensideal und Herrschaftsarchitektur: Studien und Materialen zur Baukunst der ersten Anjou-Zeit* (Franziskanische Forschungen, XXXI), Werl and Westfalen, 1986.

Krüger, K., "*A deo solo et a te regnum teneo,* Simone Martinis 'Ludwig von Toulouse' in Neapel," *Medien der Macht: Kunst zur Zeit der Anjous in Italien,* ed. T. Michalsky, Berlin, 2001, pp. 79–121.

Kurmann, P., "Spätgotische Tendenze in der europäischen Architektur um 1300," *Europäische Kunst um 1300. Internationaler Kongress für Kunstgeschichte,* VI, (1983), pp. 11–18.

Kurmann-Schwarz, B., "Les vitraux du chœur du l'ancienne abbatiale de Königsfelden," *Revue de l'art,* 121 (1998), pp. 29–43.

——, *Glasmalerei im Kanton Aargau: Königsfelden, Zofingen, Staufberg,* Aargau, 2002.

Kuthan, J., "Die mitteleuropaischen abwandlungen der Klosterkirche mit geradem Chorschluss," *Arte medievale,* ser. II, VIII (1994), pp. 45–56.

Lainati, C. A., "La clôture de sainte Claire et des premières Clarisses dans la législation canonique et dans la pratique," *Laurentianum,* XIV (1973), pp. 223–50.

Lambert, M. D., *Franciscan Poverty: The Doctrine of the Absolute Poverty of Christ and the Apostles in the Franciscan Order, 1210–1323,* London, 1961.

——, "The Franciscan Crisis under John XXII," *Franciscan Studies,* XXXII (1972), pp. 123–43.

Lavagnino, E., *Cinquanta monumenti italiani danneggiati dalla guerra*, Rome, 1947.

Leff, G., *Heresy in the Later Middle Ages: The Relations of Heterodoxy to Dissent, c. 1250–c. 1450*, Manchester, 1967.

Léonard, E., *Les Angevins de Naples*, Paris, 1954.

Leone, A., *Nola*, trans. and ed. P. Barbati, Naples, 1934.

Leone, A., "Il convento di S. Chiara e le trasformazioni urbanistiche di Napoli nel secolo XV," *Napoli nobilissima*, XXXII (1993), pp. 11–16.

——, "Il convento di S. Chiara e le trasformazioni urbanistiche nel secolo XIV," *Richerche sul Medioevo napoletano*, IX, Naples, 1996, pp. 164-70.

——, ed., *Ricerche sul Medioevo napoletano: aspetti e momenti della vita economica e sociale a Napoli tra decimo e quindicesimo secolo*, Naples, 1996.

Leone de Castris, P., *Arte di corte nella Napoli angioina*, Florence, 1986.

——, "Napoli 'capitale' del gotico europeo: il referto dei documenti e quello delle opere sotto il regno di Carlo I e Carlo II d'Angiò," *Il gotico europeo in Italia*, ed. M. Bagnoli and V. Pace, Naples, 1994, pp. 239–52.

——, "La peinture à Naples, de Charles Ier à Robert D'Anjou," *L'Europe des Anjou: aventure des princes angevins du XIIIe au XVe siècle*, Paris, 2001, pp. 105–21.

Lewis, S., "The Apocalypse of Isabella of France: Paris Bibl. Nat. MS. Fra. 13096," *Art Bulletin*, LXXII (1990), pp. 224–60.

Licinio, R., "Carestie e crisi in Italia meridionale nell'età sveva e primoangioina," *Cultura e società in Puglia in età sveva e angioina*, Bitonto, 1989, pp. 37–60.

Little, L. K., "Saint Louis' Involvement with the Friars," *Church History*, XXXIII (1964), pp. 1–24.

——, *Religious Poverty and the Profit Economy in Medieval Europe*, Ithaca, 1978.

Loffredo, S., *Storia della città di Barletta con corredo di documenti*, 2 vols., 1893.

Lognon, J., "Les Angevins de Naples," (review of Emile Léonard, *Les Angevins de Naples), Journal des Savants*, Oct.–Dec. (1957), pp. 173–86.

Lorenzetti, C., "La cappella Loffredo nella chiesa di Donnaregina," *Bollettino del Commune di Napoli*, LX (1936), pp. XLV–XLVIII.

Loreto, L., *Memorie storiche de'vescovi ed arcivescovi della S. Chiesa Napoletana*, Naples, 1839.

Makowski, E., *Canon Law and Cloistered Women: Periculoso and its Commentators, 1298–1545*, Washington, 1997.

Manselli, R., "La religiosità di Arnaldo da Villanova," *Bulletino dell'Istituto Storico Italiano per il Medio Evo*, LXIII (1951), pp. 1–100.

——, "Espansione mediterranea e politica orientale dei primi angioini di Napoli," *Gli angioini di Napoli e di Ungheria. Colloquio Italo-Ungherese: Accademia Nazionale dei Lincei*, Rome, 1974, pp. 175–86.

Marc-Bonnet, H., "Le Saint-Siège et Charles d'Anjou sous Innocent IV et Alexandre IV," *Revue historique*, CC (1948), pp. 38–65.

Maresca di Serracapriola, A., "Battenti e decorazione marmorea di antiche porte: medioevo," *Le Bussole*, II (November 1992), pp. 1–23; reprinted from *Napoli nobilissima*, IX (1900), pp. 1–9.

Marin, A. M., "L'intervento di Dionisio Lazzari in San Lorenzo e aggiunte documentarie sull'attività ivi del Fanzago," *Napoli nobilissima*, XXXV (1996), pp. 13–22.

Martelli, G., "Il monumento funerario della regina Isabella nella cattedrale di Cosenza," *Calabria nobilissima*, IV (1950), pp. 9–22.

——, "Architetture angioine in Calabria," *Calabria nobilissima*, IX (1955), pp. 157–75.

Martin, J.-M., "Fiscalité et économie étatique dans le royaume angevin de Sicile à la fin du XIIIe siècle," *L'Etat angevin: pouvoir, culture et société entre XIII et XIV siècle* (Collection de l'Ecole Française de Rome, 245), Rome, 1998, pp. 601–48.

Martinelli Marin, A., "L'intervento di Dionisio Lazzari in San Lorenzo e aggiunte documentarie sull'attivita ivi del Fanzago," *Napoli nobilissima,* XXXV (1996), pp. 13–22.

Massa, C., "La distruzione di Gallipoli," *Rivista storica salentina*, III (1907), pp. 133-49.

Mastellone, S., *Pensiero politico e vita culturale a Napoli nella seconda metà del seicento*, Messina and Florence, 1965.

Mazzocchi, A. S., *Dissertatio historica de cathedralis Ecclesiae Neapolitanae*, Naples, 1751.

Mazzoleni, J., *Storia della ricostruzione della Cancelleria Angioina*, Accademia Pontaniana, Naples, 1987.

McGinn, B., *Visions of the End: Apocalyptic Traditions in the Middle Ages*, New York, 1979.

Meier, H.-R., "Santa Chiara in Assisi. Architektur und Funktion im Schatten von San Francesco," *Arte medievale,* IV (1990), pp. 151–78.

——, "Integration und Distinktion in der herrscherlichen Kunst im vorangiovinischen Königreich," *Medien der Macht: Kunst zur Zeit der Anjous in Italien*, ed. T. Michalsky, Berlin, 2001, pp. 13–32.

Melillo, M., "Le apparizioni dell'Arcangelo nella versione dell'Alcuino," *Siponto e Manfredonia nella Daunia*, Siponto, 1989, pp. 71-75.

Merckel, Carlo. "L'opinione dei contemporanei sulla impresa italiana di Carlo I d'Angio," *Atti della R. Academia dei Lincei, classe di scienze morali storiche e filologiche*, ser. IV, V, Rome, 1888, pp. 277–435.

Mérindol, C. de, "Les Monuments funéraires des deux maisons d'Anjou, Naples et Provence," *La Mort et l'au-delà en France méridional (XIIe–XVe siècles)*, Toulouse, 1998.

Miccio, G., "Sant'Eligio Maggiore," *Manuale del recupero delle antiche techniche costruttive napoletane dal Trecento all'Ottocento*, Naples, (1996), pp. 25–33.

Michalsky, T., "Die Repräsentation einer *Beata Stirps*:

Darstellung und Ausdruck an der Grabmonumenten der Anjous," *Die Repräsentation der Gruppen: Texte–Bilder–Objekte*, ed. O. G. Oexle and A. von Hülsen-Esch, Göttingen, 1998, pp. 187–224.

——, *Memoria und Repräsentation: die Grabmäler des Königshauses Anjou in Italien*, Göttingen, 2000.

——, ed., *Medien der Macht: Kunst zur Zeit der Anjous in Italien*, Berlin, 2001.

——, "Sponsoren der Armut. Bildkonzepte franziskanisch orientierter Herrschaft," *Medien der Macht: Kunst zur Zeit der Anjous in Italien*, Berlin, 2001, pp. 121–48.

Middione, R., "San Lorenzo Maggiore," *Napoli Sacra*, VIII (1994), pp. 469–92.

Miller, M., *The Bishop's Palace: Architecture and Authority in Medieval Italy*, Ithaca, 2000.

Minervini, M., "Bartolomeo Picchiatti e la chiesa di S. Agostino alla Zecca a Napoli (I)," *Napoli nobilissima*, XXXII (1993), pp. 17–33.

Minieri-Riccio, *Genealogia di Carlo I di Angiò: prima generazione*, Naples, 1857.

——, *Brevi notizie intorno all'Archivio Angioino di Napoli*, Naples, 1862.

——, *Studi storici su' fascicoli angioini dell'Archivio della Regia Zecca di Napoli*, Naples, 1863.

——, *I notamenti di Matteo Spinelli da Giovenazzo difesi ed illustrati*, Naples, 1870.

——, *Nuovi studi riguardanti la dominazione angioina nel regno di Sicilia*, Naples, 1871.

——, *Cenni storici intorno i grandi uffizii del Regno di Sicilia durante il regno di Carlo I d'Angiò*, Naples, 1872.

——, *Itinerario di Carlo I d'Angiò ed altre notizie storiche tratte da' registri angioini del grande Archivio di Napoli*, Naples, 1872.

——, *Diario angioino dal 4 gennaio 1284 al 7 gennaio 1285*, Naples, 1873.

——, *Alcuni fatti riguardanti Carlo I d'Angio, dal 6 di agosto 1252 al 30 di dicembre, 1270 tratti dall'Archivio Angioino di Napoli*, Naples, 1874.

——, "Il regno di Carlo I d'Angiò," *Archivio storico italiano*, ser. III, XXII (1875), pp. 3–36, 235–63; XXIII (1876), pp. 34–60, 223–41, and 423–40; XXIV (1876), pp. 226–42 and 373–406; XXV (1877), pp. 19–42, 181–94 and 404–16; XXVI (1877), pp. 3–25, 204–24 and 417–26; ser. IV, I (1878), 1–13, 225–47 and 421–44; II (1878), pp. 193–205 and 353–64; III (1879), pp. 3–22 and 161–79; IV (1879), pp. 3–18, 173–83 and 349–60; V (1880), pp. 177–86 and 353–66; VII (1881), pp. 3–24 and 304–12.

——, *Il regno di Carlo I di Angiò negli anni 1271 e 1272*, Naples, 1875.

——, *Nuovi studii riguardanti la dominazione angioina nel regno di Sicilia*, Naples, 1876.

——, *Studi storici estratti*, Naples 1876.

——, *Studi storici fatti sopra 84 registri angioini dell'Archivio di Stato di Napoli*, Naples, 1876.

——, *Notizie storiche tratte da 62 registri angioini dell'Archivio di Stato di Napoli*, Naples, 1877.

——, *Della dominazione angioina nel reame di Sicilia*, Naples, 1876.

——, *Saggio di codice diplomatico formato sulle antiche scritture dell'Archivio di Stato di Napoli*, 3 vols. and 2 supplements, Naples, 1878–80.

——, *Il Regno di Carlo I d'Angiò dal 4 gennaio 1284 al 7 dicembre, 1285*, Florence, 1881.

——, "Genealogia di Carlo II d'Angiò, re di Napoli," *Archivio storico per le province napolitane*, VII (1882), pp. 5–67, 201–62, 465–96, 653–84; VIII (1883), pp. 5–33, 197–226, 381–96, 587–600.

Monaco, G., *S. Maria del Carmine detta "La Bruna*," Naples, 1975.

Mongellli, G., *L'abbazia di Montevergine: regesto delle pergamene*, 4 vols., Rome, 1956–62.

——, *Storia di Montevergine e della congregazione verginiana*, 2 vols., Avellino, 1965.

Monti, G. M., *La dominazione angioina in Piemonte*, Turin, 1930.

——, "La 'Cronaca di Partenope' (Premessa all'edizione critica)," *Annali del Seminario giuridico economico della R. Università di Bari*, V (1931), pp. 72–119.

——, "Da Carlo I a Roberto d'Angiò," *Archivio storico per le province napolitane*, LVI (1931), pp. 135–209; LVIII (1933), pp. 67–98; LIX (1934), pp. 137–223.

——, "Carlo I e i debiti verso la S. Sede," *Archivio storico per le province napolitane*, XVIII (1932), pp. 101–17.

——, "Il cosidetto 'Chronicon di S. Maria del Principio,' fonte della 'Cronaca di Partenope,'" *Annali del Seminario giuridico-economico della R. Università di Bari*, VII (1935), pp. 3–31.

——, *Nuovi studi angioini*, Naples, 1937.

——, "La dottrina anti-imperiale degli Angioini di Napoli," *Studi di storia e diritto in onore di Arrigo Salmi*, I, Mainz, 1941, pp. 11–54.

Moorman, J., *A History of the Franciscan Order*, Oxford, 1968.

Moretti, M., *L'architettura medievale in Abruzzo (dal VI secolo al XVI secolo)*, L'Aquila, 1971.

Morisani, O., "L'arte di Napoli nell'età angioina," *Storia di Napoli*, ed. E. Pontierei, III, Naples, 1969, pp. 575–644.

——, "Monumenti trecenteschi dei Angioini a Napoli," *Gli Angioini di Napoli e Ungheria. Atti del colloquio italo-ungherese*, Rome, 1974, pp. 159–73.

Mormone, R., "Il rifacimento settecentesco nella chiesa di Santa Chiara a Napoli," *Studi in onore di Riccardo Filangieri*, 3 vols., Naples, 1959, III, pp. 85–103.

——, *Sculture trecentesche in San Lorenzo Maggiore a Napoli*, Naples, 1973.

——, *La chiesa trecentesca di Donnaregina*, Naples, 1977.

Musto, R. G., "Queen Sancia of Naples (1286–1345) and the Spiritual Franciscans," *Women of the Medieval World: Essays in Honor of John Hine Mundy*, ed. J. Kirshner and S. F. Wemple, Oxford, 1985, pp. 179–214.

——, "Franciscan Joachimism at the Court of Naples 1309–1345: A New Appraisal," *Archivum franciscanum historicum*, XC (1997), pp. 419–86.

Napoli, M., *Napoli Greco-Romana*, Naples, 1996.

Negri Arnoldi, F., "Pietro d'Oderisio, Nicola da Monteforte e la scultura campana del primo Trecento," *Commentari*, XXIII (1972), pp. 12–30.

——, "Scultura trecentesca in Calabria: il Maestro di Mileto," *Bollettino d'arte*, ser. 6, LVII (1972), pp. 20–32.

——, "Scultura trecentesca in Calabria: apporti esterni e attività locale," *Bollettino d'arte*, LVIII (1983), pp. 1–48.

Nimmo, D., *Reform and Division in the Franciscan Order*, Rome, 1987.

Nitschke, A., "Die Reden des Logotheten Bartholomäus von Capua," *Quellen und Forschungen aus italienischen Archiven und Bibliotheken*, XXXV (1955), pp. 226–74.

——, "Karl II als Fürst von Salerno," *Quellen und Forschungen aus italienischen Archiven und Bibliotheken*, XXXVI (1956), pp. 188–204.

——, "Der sizilianische Adel unter Karl von Anjou und Peter von Aragon," *Quellen und Forschungen aus italienischen Archiven und Bibliotheken*, XLV (1965), pp. 241–73.

——, "Carlo II d'Angiò," *Dizionario biografico degli Italiani*, XX (1970), pp. 227–35.

Nitti de Vito, F., *Codice diplomatico Barese: le pergamene di Barletta, Archivio Capitolare (897–1285)*, Bari, 1914.

Nitto de Rossi, G., "Una risposta ad Emilio Bertaux intorno alla pretesa influenza dell'arte francese nella Puglia ai tempi di Federico II," *Napoli nobilissima*, VII (1898), pp. 129–50, and VIII (1899), 40–45.

Oberman, H., "Fourteenth-Century Religious Thought: A Premature Profile," *Speculum*, LIII (1978), pp. 80–93.

Occhipinti, E., "Clausura a Milano alla fine del XIII secolo: il caso del monastero di S. Margherita," *Felix olim Lombardia: Studi di storia padana dedicati dagli allievi a Giuseppe Martini*, Milan, 1978, pp. 197–212.

Oliver, A., and A. Linage Conde, "Espirituales y 'Fraticellos' en Catalunya, Mallorca, y Castilla," *Historia de la Iglesia en Espana*, 5 vols., Madrid, 1979–82, vol. 2, part 2, (1982), pp. 160–79.

Orlando, G., *Storia di Nocera de' Pagani*, 3 vols., Naples, 1886.

Otranto G., and C. Carletti, *Il Santuario di San Michele Arcangelo sul Gargano dalle origini al X secolo*, Bari, 1990.

Pace, V., "Ancora sulla tutela del patrimonio artistico. Restauri ai monumenti dell'Abruzzo," *Paragone*, XXII (1971), pp. 71–82.

——, Review of J. Krüger, *S. Lorenzo Maggiore in Neapel*, in *Bollettino d'arte*, LII (1988), pp. 104–05.

——, "Morte a Napoli: sepolture nobiliari del trecento," *Regionale Aspekte der Grabmalforschung*, ed. W. Schmid, Trier, 2000, pp. 41–62.

——, "Arte di età angioina nel regno: vicinanza e distanza dalla corte," *Medien der Macht: Kunst zur Zeit der Anjous in Italien*, ed. T. Michalsky, Berlin, 2001, pp. 241–60.

Paciocco, R., "I monasteri cistercensi in Abruzzo: le linee generali di uno sviluppo (fine sec. XII– inizi sec. XIV)," *I cistercensi nel mezzogiorno medievale. Atti del Convegno internazionale di studio in occasione del IX centenario della nascita di Bernardo di Clairvaux, 25–27 febraio 1991*, ed. H. Houben and B. Vetere, Galatina, 1994, pp. 205–42.

——, "Angioini e 'spirituali': i differenti piani cronologici e tematici di un problema," *L'Etat angevin: pouvoir, culture et société entre XIII et XIV siècle* (Collection de l'Ecole Française de Rome, 245), Rome, 1998, pp. 253–86.

Pagnotti, F., ed., "Vita Innocentii IV scripta a fr. Nicolao de Carbio," *Archivio della Archivio della Società Romana di Storia Patria*, XXI (1898), pp. 76-120.

Palmieri, S., "La ricostruzione dei registri della cancelleria angioina," *Atti della Accademia Pontaniana*, n.s., XLVI (1997), pp. 447–56.

——, "L'archivio della Regia Zecca: formazione, perdite documentarie e ricostruzione," *L'Etat angevin: pouvoir, culture et société entre XIII et XIV siècle* (Collection de l'Ecole Française de Rome, 245), Rome, 1998, pp. 417–45.

——, "Il Castelnuovo di Napoli, reggia e fortezza angioina," *Atti della Accademia Pontaniana*, n.s., XLVII (1999), pp. 501–19.

——, "De l'Anjou à la Sicile," *L'Europe des Anjou: aventure des princes angevins du XIIIe au XVe siècle*, Paris, (2001), pp. 23–35.

Palumbo, P. F., *Contributi alla storia dell'età di Manfredi*, (Biblioteca storica, IV), Rome, 1959.

——, "La ribellione antiangioina nel Regno," *Città, terre e famiglie dall'età sveva alla angioina*, Rome, 1989, pp. 325-445.

Parascandolo, L., *Memorie storiche-critiche-diplomatiche della Chiesa di Napoli*, 4 vols., Naples, 1847–51.

Parente, G., *Origini e vicende ecclesiastiche della città di Aversa. Frammenti storici*, 2 vols., Naples, 1857–58.

Pásztor, E., "Per la storia di S. Ludovico d'Angiò, 1274–1297," *Studi storici dell'Istituto Storico Italiano per il Medio Evo*, 10, Rome, 1955.

——, "Il processo di Andrea da Gagliano," *Archivum franciscanum historicum*, XLVIII (1955), pp. 252–97.

——, "La chiesa alla fine del Duecento ed il pontificato di Celestino Quinto," *Celestino V Papa Angelico*, L'Aquila, 1987, pp. 13–32.

Patronage and Public in the Trecento. Proceedings of the St. Lambrecht Symposium: St. Lambrecht, 1984, ed. V. Moleta, Florence, 1984.

Paul, J., "Angevins, frères prêcheurs, et papauté," *L'Etat Angevin: pouvoir, culture et société entre XIII et XIV siècle* (Collection de l'Ecole Française de Rome, 245), Rome, 1998, pp. 221–51.

Percy, W. A., "The Revenues of the Kingdom of Sicily under Charles I of Anjou, 1266–1285, and their Relationship to the Vespers," Ph.D. dissertation, Princeton University, 1964.

Perrotta, V. M., *Descrizione storica della chiesa e del monastero di S. Domenico Maggiore a Napoli*, Naples, 1830.

Pesce, M. I., "Carlo I d'Angiò e i cistercensi: la fondazione dell'abbazia di S. Maria della Vittoria," *Declino svevo, ascesa angioina e l'arte venuta di Francia*, Tagliacozzo, 1994, pp. 47-80.

Pessolano, M. R., "Il convento e la chiesa di Monteverginella," *Napoli nobilissima*, XIV (1975), pp.17-29.

Peters, E., *Heresy and Authority in Medieval Europe*, Philadelphia, 1980.

Petito, L., *Guida del Duomo di Napoli*, Naples, 1988.

Picone, R., "Nuove acquisizioni per la storia del complesso di San Domenico Maggiore in Napoli (I), *Napoli nobilissima*, XXXII (1993), pp. 34-55.

Piemontese, G. S., *Michele e il suo Santuario*, Foggia, 1997.

Pitz, E., "Das Aufkommen der Berufe des Architekten und Bauningenieurs," *Quellen und Forschungen aus italienische Archiven und Bibliotheken*, LXVI (1986), pp. 40-74.

Pollastri, S., "Les Burson d'Anjou, barons de Nocera, puis comtes de Satriano (1268-1400)," *La Noblesse dans les territoires angevins à la fin du Moyen Age. Actes du colloque international organisé par l'Université d'Angers, Angers–Saumur, 3–6 juin 1998*, ed. N. Coulet and J.-M. Matz, Rome, 2000, pp. 89-114.

Pontieri, E., *Ricerche sulla crisi della monarchia siciliana nel secolo XIII*, Collezione Storica, 2nd edn., Naples, 1950.

——, "Lucera sveva-angioina: riflessioni intorno a un momento della sua storia," *Atti della Accademia Pontaniana*, n.s., XVII (1968), pp. 5-26.

Pou y Marti, J. M., *Visionarios, beguinos, y fraticellos catalanes (siglos XIII–XV)*, Vich, 1930.

Prandi, A., ed., *Aggiornamento dell'opera di Emile Bertaux*, 4 vols., Ecole Française de Rome, 1978.

Prawer, J., *Crusader Institutions*, Oxford, 1951.

Prehn, E. T., "Una decorazione murale del duecento Toscano in un monastero Laziale," *Antichità viva*, X (1971), pp. 3-9.

Pryds, D., "*Rex Praedicans*: Robert d'Anjou and the Politics of Teaching," *De l'homélie au sermon: histoire de la prédication médiévale*, Louvain-la-Neuve, 1993, pp. 239-62.

——, "Court as *Studium*: Royal Venues for Academic Preaching," *Medieval Sermons and Society: Cloister, City, University*, Louvain-la-Neuve, 1998, pp. 343-56.

Pryor, John H., "The Galleys of Charles I of Anjou," *Studies in Medieval and Renaissance History*, XIV (1993), pp. 33-103.

Purcell, M., *Papal Crusading Policy: The Chief Instruments of Papal Crusading Policy and the Crusade to the Holy Land from the Final Loss of Jerusalem to the Fall of Acre*, Leiden, 1975.

Quagliarella, P. T., *Guida storica artistica del Carmine Maggiore di Napoli*, Taranto, 1932.

——, "Uno stemma del secolo XV," *Archivio storico per le province napolitane*, 3rd ser., XLI (1961), pp. 244-50.

Quicherat, J. E. J., "Inscription de l'église de St.-Eloi de Naples," *Bulletin de la Société nationale des antiquaires de France*, XXI (1877), pp. 143-45.

Radke, G., *Viterbo: Profile of a Thirteenth-Century Papal Palace*, Cambridge, 1996.

Radogna, M., *Monografia di S. Giovanni a Mare, baliaggio del Sacro Ordine Gerolosomitano in Napoli*, Naples, 1873.

Rashdall, H., *The Universities of Europe in the Middle Ages*, 2 vols., ed. F. M. Powicke and A. B. Emden, Oxford, 1958.

Raspi Serra, J., "L'architettura degli ordini mendicanti nel Principato Salernitano," *Mélanges de l'Ecole Française de Rome, Moyen Age/Temps Modernes*, XCIII (1981), pp. 605-81.

——, and M. Bignardi, "The Abbey of Real Valle in Campania (Italy)," *Studies in Cistercian Art and Architecture*, ed. M. P. Lillich, vol. 2, Kalamazoo, 1984, pp. 223-28.

Recht, R., "Le goût de l'ornament vers 1300," *1300: l'art au temps de Philippe le Bel*, Rencontres de L'Ecole du Louvre, XVI, Paris, 2001, pp. 149-62.

Recupido, Giovanni, "S. Lorenzo Maggiore: centro di studi a Napoli," *Luce Serafica*, XV (1939), pp. 20-28.

——, "L'area di San Lorenzo Maggiore: dalla basilica paleocristiana alla basilica medievale," *La ceramica medievale di San Lorenzo Maggiore in Napoli. Atti del Convegno*, Naples, 1980, Naples, 1984, pp. 7-26.

Reeves, M., *Joachim of Fiore and the Prophetic Future*, London, 1976.

——, and M. Bloomfield, "The Penetration of Joachism into Northern Europe," *Speculum*, XXIX (1954), pp. 772-93.

——, and B. Hirsch-Reich, eds., *The Figurae of Joachim of Fiore*, Oxford, 1972.

Remondini, G., *Della Nolana Ecclesiastica storia*, Naples, 1747. 3 vols.

Reynolds, S., *Kingdoms and Communities in Western Europe, 900–1300*, 2nd edn., Oxford, 1997.

Rhigetti Tosti-Croce, M., "Regno di Sicilia (di Napoli dal 1372)," *Enciclopedia dell'arte medievale*, I, (1991), pp. 665-75.

——, "La chiesa di Santa Chiara ad Assisi: architettura," *Santa Chiara in Assisi: architettura e decorazione*, ed. A. Tomei, Milan, 2002, pp. 21-41.

Riant, P.E. de, "Déposition de Charles d'Anjou pour la canonisation de Saint Louis," *Notices et documents puliés pour la Société de l'Histoire de France*, Paris, 1884, pp. 155-76.

Riccetti, L., ed., *Il duomo di Orvieto*, Rome and Bari, 1988.

——, "Le origini dell'Opera, Lorenzo Maitani e l'architettura del Duomo di Orvieto," *Opera: carattere e ruolo delle fabbriche cittadine fino all'inizio dell'età moderna: Atti della tavola rotonda, Villa I Tatti, Florence, 1991*, Florence, 1996, pp. 157-265.

Ricciardi, E., "Una pianta del convento di S. Lorenzo Maggiore in Napoli," *Napoli nobilissima*, XXXVIII (1999), pp. 195-202.

Rigaux, D., *A la table du Seigneur: L'Eucharistie chez les Primitifs Italiens, 1250–1497*, Paris, 1989.

Romanini, A. M., "Architettura monastica occidentale," *Dizionario degli Istituti di Perfezione*, I, Rome, 1974, pp. 790-827.

——, "L'architettura degli ordini mendicanti: nuove prospettive d'interpretazione," *Storia della città*, IX (1978), pp. 5–15.

——, and M. Righetti, eds., *Enciclopedia dell'arte medievale*, 12 vols, Rome, 1991-2002.

Romano, S., "L'Aracoeli, il Campidoglio e le famiglie romane nel Duecento," *Roma medievale: aggiornamenti*, ed. P. Delogu, Rome, 1998, pp. 193–210.

——, "Die Bischöfe von Neapel als Auftraggeber: Zum Bild des Humber d'Ormont," *Medien der Macht: Kunst zur Zeit der Anjous in Italien*, ed. T. Michalsky, Berlin, 2001, pp. 191–224.

——, "Introduzione: la cattedrale di Napoli, i vescovi e l'immagine," *Il Duomo di Napoli, dal paleocristiano all'età angioina*, ed. S. Romano and N. Bock, Naples, 2002, pp. 7–20.

——, and N. Bock, eds., *Il Duomo di Napoli, dal paleocristiano all'età angioina*, Naples, 2002.

Rossellò LLiteras, J., "Documentes franciscanos del Archivio Diocesano de Mallorca, Monasterio de Santa Clara de Mallorca," *Boletìn de Historia de la Tercera Orden Franciscana*, III (1989–90), pp. 17-63.

Rossetti, G., and G. Vitolo, *Medioevo mezzogiorno mediterraneo: studi in onore di Mario del Treppo*, I, Naples, 2000.

Rossi, P., "Il recupero dell'edilizia ecclesiastica nell'area di Piazza del Mercato a Napoli," *Campania sacra*, XXVIII (1997), pp. 165-74.

Rotili, M., *L'Arte a Napoli dal VI al XIII secolo*, Naples, 1978.

Runciman, S., *The Sicilian Vespers*, Cambridge, 1958.

Ruocco, J., "Regestum Chartarum Trium Ordinum Sancti Francisci in Regno Neapolis," *Miscellanea Francescana*, XXXV (1935), pp. 144–57, 208–19, and XXVI (1936) pp. 313–21.

——., "Regesto angioino-francescano del regno di Napoli," *Miscellanea Francescana*, XXXVII (1937), pp. 125–40; XXXVIII (1938), pp. 223–46.

Rusconi, A., "La basilica paleocristiana di S. Lorenzo," *Atti del VI Congresso internazionale di archeologia cristiana, 1962*, Vatican City, 1965, pp. 709–31.

Russo, F., "La guerra del Vespro in Calabria nei documenti Vaticani," *Archivio storico per le province napolitane*, ser. 3, 1 (1961), pp. 193–219.

Sabatini, F., *La cultura a Napoli nell'età angioina*, Naples, 1974 (extract from *Storia di Napoli*, vol. IV, part 2, pp. 1–314).

——, *Napoli angioina: cultura e società*, Naples, 1975.

Salimbene da Parma, *The Chronicle of Salimbene de Adam*, ed. J. L. Baird, G. Baglivi, and J. R. Kane, Binghamton, NY, 1986.

Salzman, L. F., *Building in England down to 1540*, Oxford, 1952.

Santamaria, P., *Historia collegii patrum canonicorum metrop. Ecclesiae Neapolitanae*, Naples, 1900.

Santeramo, S., *Il simbolismo della cattedrale di Barletta*, Bari, 1917.

——, ed., *Codice diplomatico barlettano*, 3 vols., Barletta, 1924.

Santi, F., "Gli '*scripta spiritualia*' di Arnau de Vilanova," *Studi medievale*, ser. 3, XXVI (1985), pp. 977–1014.

Santoro, L., *Castelli angioini e aragonesi nel regno di Napoli*, Milan, 1982.

Sarnelli, P., *La vera guide de' forestieri, curiosi di vedere e d'intendere le cose più notabili della regal città di Napoli e del suo amenissimo distretto*, Naples, 1685.

Sauerländer, W., "Dal gotico europeo in Italia al gotico italiano in Europa," *Il gotico europeo in Italia*, ed. M. Bagnoli and V. Pace, Naples, 1994, pp. 8–22.

Savarese, S., "Il portale trecentesco della chiesa di S. Domenico in Napoli," *Scritti in onore di Ottavio Morisani*, Catania, 1981, pp. 131–45.

Saxer, V., *Le culte de Marie Madeleine en Occident des origines à la fin du Moyen Age*, Paris, 1959.

Sbaraglia, G. G., *Bullarium Franciscanum Romanorum Pontificum: constitutiones, epistolas, ac diplomata continens: tribus ordinibus Minorum, Clarissarum, et Poenitentium a seraphico patriarcha Sancto Francisco institutis concessa . . .*, 4 vols., Rome, 1759–1804, anastatic reprint, Santa Maria degli Angeli, 1983.

Scaccia Scarafoni, C., "Memorie storiche della badia di S. Sebastiano nel territorio Alatrino," *Archivio della Società Romana di Storia Patria*, XXXIX (1916), pp. 5–52, and XLI (1918), pp. 222–62.

Schäfer-Schuchardt, H., *Die figürliche Steinplastik des 11.–13. Jahrhunderts in Apulien*, 2 vols, Bari, 1987.

Schenkluhn, W., *Ordines studentes: Aspekte zur Kirchenarchitektur der Dominikaner und Franziskaner im 13. Jahrhundert*, Berlin, 1985.

Schipa, M, *Un principe napoletano amico di Dante*, Naples, 1890.

——, *Carlomartello angioino*, Naples, 1926.

Schmitt, A., "Die Apokalypse des Robert von Anjou," *Pantheon*, XXVIII (1970), pp. 475–503.

Schulz, H. W., and A. von Quast, *Denkmäler der Kunst des Mittelalters in Unteritalien*, 4 vols., Dresden, 1860.

Seroux D'Agincourt, J. B. L. G., *Histoire de l'art par les monuments depuis sa décadence au IV siècle jusqu'à son renouvellement au XVIe*, 6 vols., Paris, 1823.

Sersale, B., *Discorso istorico della cappella de' signori Minutolo*, Naples, 1745.

Shatzmiller, J., "Les Angevins et les juifs de leurs états: Anjou, Naples, et Provence," *L'Etat angevin: pouvoir, culture et société entre XIII et XIV siècle* (Collection de l'Ecole Française de Rome, 245), Rome, 1998, pp. 289–300.

Siragusa, G. B., *L'ingenio, il sapere e gli intendimenti di Roberto d'Angiò*, Palermo, 1891.

Small, C. M., "The Crown as an Employer of Wage Labour in Angevin Basilicata," *Social History*, XIV (1989), pp. 323–41.

Sorrentino, A., "La basilica di S. Restituta in Napoli," *Bollettino d'Arte*, III (1909), pp. 217–35.

Spanò, A., "Francescani e Angioini in Calabria: la chiesa di San Francesco e l'insediamento dei Frati Minori a Gerace," *Daidalos*, II (2002), pp. 72–81.

Sparano, G., *Memorie istoriche per illustrare gli atti della S. Napoletana chiesa*, Naples, 1768.

Spila da Subiaco, B., *Un monumento di Sancia in Napoli: opera illustrata con rilievi e disegni originali der Bernich*, Naples, 1901.

Stefano, R. di, *La cattedrale di Napoli: storia, restauro, scoperte, ritrovamenti*, Naples, 1974.

Sthamer, E., *Die Verwaltung der Kastelle im Königreich Sizilien unter Kaiser Friedrich II und Karls I von Anjou*, 2 vols., Leipzig, 1912–14.

——, *Dokumente zur Geschichte der Kastellbauten Kaiser Friedrichs II. und Karls I. von Anjou*, 2 vols. (Königlich Preussisches Historisches Institut in Rom), Leipzig, 1912–26, 2nd ed. 1997.

——, "Die Reste des Archivs Karls I von Sizilien im Staatsarchiv zu Neapel," *Quellen und Forschungen aus italienischen Archiven und Bibliotheken*, XIV (1914), pp. 68-139.

——, "Die verlorenen Register Karls I von Anjou," *Sitzungsberichten der preussischen Akademie der Wissenschaften*, 1923, XXIII, pp. 4-29.

——, "Aus der Vorgeschichte der sizilianische Vesper," *Quellen und Forschungen aus italienischen Archiven und Bibliotheken*, XIX (1927), pp. 262–372.

——, "Der Sturz der Familie Rufolo und della Marra nach der sizilianische Vesper," *Abhandlungen der Preussischen Akademie der Wissenschaften*, III, Berlin, 1937, pp. 1-68.

Strazzullo, F., "Le vicende dell'abside del Duomo di Napoli," *Studi in onore di Domenico Mallardo*, Naples, 1957, pp. 147–82.

——, *Saggi storici sul Duomo di Napoli*, Naples, 1959.

——, "Le piaghe della cattedrale di Napoli," *Napoli nobilissima*, n.s., III (1963–64), pp. 83–84.

——, *Il Duomo di Napoli nel Cinquecento*, Naples, 1965.

——, *Edilizia e urbanistica a Napoli dal '500 al '700*, Naples, 1968.

——, "Edifici sacri dell'antica insula del Duomo di Napoli," *Scritti in onore di Roberto Pane*, Naples, 1969–71, pp. 73–84.

——, "Le due antiche cattedrali di Napoli," *Campania Sacra*, IV (1973), pp. 177–241.

——, *Restauri del Duomo di Napoli tra '400 e '500*, Naples, 1991.

——, "Interventi nel Duomo di Napoli durante il governo del Card. Decio Carafa," *Napoli nobilissima*, XXXIV (1995), pp. 209–26.

——, *Neapolitanae ecclesiae cathedralis inscriptionum thesaurus*, Naples, 2000.

——, *Neapolitanae basilicae S. Restitutae monumenta epigraphica*, Naples, 2001.

Strehlke, C. B., "A Celibate Marriage and Franciscan Poverty Reflected in a Neapolitan Trecento Diptych," *J. Paul Getty Museum Journal*, XV (1987), pp. 79–96.

Suckale, R., "Réflections sur la sculpture parisienne à l'époque de Saint Louis et de Philippe le Bel, *Revue d'art*, **128**, (2000), pp. 33-48.

Summonte, G. A., *Historia della città e regno di Napoli*, 4 vols., Naples, 1601–43.

Tarallo, E., "Avanzi monumentali obliati di tempio cristiano nell'edificio del Palazzo arcivescovile di Napoli," *Rivista di scienze e lettere, organo dell'Accademia ecclesiastica di Napoli*, n.s., II (1931), pp. 182–88, 298–315, 374–90.

Taylor, A. J., *The King's Works in Wales, 1277-1330*, London, 1974.

Tescione, G., *Caserta medievale e i suoi conti e signori*, Marcianise, 1965.

Testini, P., G. Cantino Wataghin, and L. Pani Ermini, "La cattedrale in Italia," *Actes du XI Congrès international d'archéologie chrétienne, 21–28 Septembre 1986*, I, Rome, 1989, pp. 95–96.

Tirelli, V., "Un feudatario nella crisi della monarchia angioina alla metà del secolo XIV: Giovanni Pipino, palatino di Altamura, conte di Minervino," *Archivio storico pugliese*, XI (1958), pp. 108–55.

Tomaiuoli, N., "Il Palatium di Lucera," *Federico II, immagine e potere* (exh. cat.), Bari, 1995, pp. 239–44.

Tomei, A., ed., *Santa Chiara in Assisi: architettura e decorazione*, Milan, 2002.

Tondelli, L., M. Reeves, and B. Hirsch-Reich, eds., *Il Libro delle Figure dell'Abate Gioachino da Fiore*, 2nd ed., 2 vols., Turin, 1954.

Toscano, G., "Sculture del Quattro e Cinquecento a Nola: la Committenza Orsini," *Quaderno dell'istituto nazionale di studi sul rinascimento meridionale*, VI (1989), pp. 117–21.

Toynbee, M. R., *St. Louis of Toulouse and the Process of Canonisation in the Fourteenth Century*, Manchester, 1929.

Trachtenberg, M., "Gothic/Italian 'Gothic?': Toward a Redefinition," *Journal of the Society of Architectural Historians*, L 1991, pp. 22–37.

Traviani, L., "La monetazione nell'Italia del Duecento e la sua trasformazione gotica," *Il gotico europeo in Italia*, ed. M. Bagnoli and V. Pace, Naples, (1994), pp. 343–450.

Tropeano, P. M., *Montevergine nella storia e nell'arte*, Naples. 1973.

Ughello, F., *Italia sacra*, Emended and ed. N. Coletti. 10 vols., Venice, 1717–22. Reprint, Sala Bolognese, 1973–87.

Vadalà, M. E., "Santa Maria della Consolazione in Altomonte: una citadella angioina in Calabria," *Antichità viva*, XIX (1980), pp. 24–31.

Vale, M., *The Princely Court: Medieval Courts and Culture in North-West Europe*, Oxford, 2001.

Valentiner, W. R., "La madre di Corradino," *Art Quarterly*, XV (1952), pp. 242–51.

Valle, R., and B. Minichini, *Descrizione storica artistica letteraria della chiesa di S. Domenico Maggiore*, Naples, 1854.

Varese, S., "Il portale trecentesco della chiesa di San Domenico Maggiore in Napoli," *Miscellanea in memoria di Ottavio Morisani*, Catania, 1981, pp. 5–22.

Vasari, G., *Le vite dei più eccellenti pittori, scultori e architetti*, Milan, 1997.

Vauchez, A., "Beata stirps: sainteté e lignage en Occident aux XIIIe e XIVe siècles," *Famille et parenté dans l'Occident médiéval*, ed. G. Duby and J. Le Goff, Paris, (1977), pp. 396–407.

——, *La Sainteté en Occident aux derniers siècles du Moyen Age (1198–1431): recherches sur les mentalitées médiévales*, Rome, 1981.

——, *Les laïcs au moyen age. Pratiques et expériences religieuses*, Paris, 1987.

Venditti, A., *Architettura bizantina nell'Italia meridionale*, Naples, 1967.

——, "Urbanistica e architettura angioina," *Storia di Napoli*, ed. E. Pontieri, III, Naples, 1969, pp. 665–888.

——, "Problemi di lettura e di interpretazione dell'architettura paleocristiana di Napoli," *Napoli nobilissima*, n.s., XII (1973), pp. 177–88.

Verlinden, C., *The Beginnings of Modern Colonialization: Eleven Essays with an Introduction*, trans. Y. Freccero, Ithaca, NY, and London, 1970.

Verrengia, G., *Tesori artistici in San Lorenzo Maggiore*, Naples, 1995.

Vetere, Benedetto, "Un modelo di sviluppo urbano nel Salento alla fine del Medioevo," *Napoli nobilissima*, XXXV (1996), pp. 121–57.

Vian, P., "'Predicare populo in habitu heremitico': Ascesi e contatto col mondo negli atti del processo di canonizzazione di Pietro da Morrone," *Celestino V Papa Angelico*, L'Aquila, 1987, pp. 167–71.

Vidal, J.-M., "Un ascète de sang royal: Philippe de Majorque," *Revue des questions historiques*, XL (1910), pp. 361–403.

Vidal, P., *Histoire de la ville de Perpignan*, Paris, 1897.

Villari, R., *La rivolta antispagnola a Napoli: le origini (1585–1647)*, Bari, 1967.

Villetti, G., "Legislazione e prassi edilizia degli ordini mendicanti nei secoli XIII e XIV," *Francesco d'Assisi: chiese e conventi*, Milan, 1982, pp. 23–31.

Vitale, G., "Case ed abitanti della regio Nilensis in età ducale: osservazioni," *Palazzo Corigliano: tra archeologia e storia*, Naples, 1985, pp. 12–18.

——, "I Minutolo," *Ricerche sul medioevo napoletano: Aspetti e momenti della vita economica e sociale a Napoli tra decimo e quindicesimo secolo*, ed. A. Leone, Naples, 1996, pp. 208–13.

——, "Nobiltà napoletana della prima età angioina: élite burocratica e famiglia," *Ricerche sul medioevo napoletano: Aspetti e momenti della vita economica e sociale a Napoli tra decimo e quindicesimo secolo*, ed. A. Leone. Naples, 1996, pp. 187–203.

Vitolo, G., "Il Regno Angioino," *Storia del Mezzogiorno*, ed. G. Galasso and R. Romeo, IV, part 1, Rome and Naples 1986, pp. 9–86.

——, "Il monachesimo benedittino nel Mezzogiorno angioino: tra crisi e nuove esperienze religiose," *L'Etat angevin: pouvoir, culture et société entre XIII et XIV siècle* (Collection de l'Ecole Française de Rome, 245), Rome, 1998, pp. 205–20.

——, "Culto della croce e identità cittadina," *Napoli nobilissima*, III–IV (2000), pp. 81–96.

——, "Esperienze religiose nella Napoli dei secoli XII–XIV,"

Medioevo mezzogiorno mediterraneo: studi in onore di Mario del Treppo, ed. G. Rossetti and G. Vitolo, I, Naples, 2000, pp. 3–34.

——, "La Noblesse, les ordres mendiants et les mouvements de réforme dans le royaume de Sicile," *La Noblesse dans les territoires angevins à la fin du Moyen Age. Actes du colloque international organisé par l'Université d'Angers, Angers–Saumur, 3–6 juin 1998*, ed. N. Coulet and J.-M. Matz, Rome, 2000, pp. 553–66.

——, "Aspetti e problemi della storia delle certose nel mezzogiorno medievale: gli esempi di Napoli e Padula," *Napoli nobilissima*, ser. 5, II (2001), pp. 5–14.

——, *Tra Napoli e Salerno: la costruzione dell'identità cittadina nel mezzogiorno medievale*, Salerno, 2001.

——, and R. Di Meglio, "La piazza del mercato e l'ospedale di Sant'Eligio," *Ospedali, confraternite e dinamiche politico-sociali nella Napoli angioino-aragonese*, Salerno, forthcoming 2003.

Voci, A. M., "La cappella di corte dei primi sovrani angioini di Napoli," *L'Etat angevin: pouvoir, culture et société entre XIII et XIV siècle* (Collection de l'Ecole Française de Rome, 245), Rome, (1998), pp. 447–74.

Von Auw, L., *Angelo Clareno et les spirituels italiens*, Rome, 1979.

Wadding, L., *Annales minorum seu trium ordinum a S. Francisco institutorum*, 32 vols., Quarachi, 1931–64.

Wagner-Rieger, R., *Die italienische Baukunst zu Beginn der Gotik*, 2 vols., Graz and Cologne, 1956–57.

——, "Der Chor von S. Lorenzo Maggiore in Neapel," *Actes du XIXe Congrès d'Histoire de l'Art*, Paris, 1958, pp. 139–44.

——, "San Lorenzo Maggiore: il coro," *Napoli nobilissima*, n.s., I (1961), pp. 1–17.

——, "S. Lorenzo Maggiore in Neapel und die süditalienische Architektur unter den ersten Königen aus dem Hause Anjou," *Miscellanea Bibliothecae Hertzianae, Römische Forschungen der Bibliotheca Hertziana*, XVI (1961), pp. 131–43.

Waley, D. P., *The Papal State in the Thirteenth Century*, London, 1961.

Walter, I, and M. Piccialuti, "Bartolomeo da Capua," *Dizionario biografico degli italiani*, VI, Rome, 1964, pp. 697–704.

Warnke, M., *The Court Artist: On the Ancestry of the Modern Artist*, tr. D. McLintock, Cambridge and Paris, 1993.

White, J., *Art and Architecture in Italy 1250 to 1400*, Harmondsworth, 1966.

Widemann, F., "Le Triptyque disparu de la Madonna della Bruna de la cathédrale de Ravello," *Apollo: Bollettino dei Musei Provinciali del Salernitano*, VII (1991), pp. 61–69.

——, "Les Rufolo, les voies de l'anoblissement d'une famille de Marchands en Italie Méridionale," *La Noblesse dans les territoires angevins à la fin du Moyen Age. Actes du colloque international organisé par l'Université d'Angers, Angers–Saumur, 3–6 juin 1998*, ed. N. Coulet and J.-M. Matz, Rome, 2000, pp. 115–130.

——, and P. Peduto, *L'Ambiente culturale a Ravello nel Medio-*

evo: il caso della famiglia Rufolo (Centro Universitario Europeo per i Beni Culturali, Ravello, I), Bari, 2000.

Wieruszowski, H., "Art and the Commune in the Time of Dante," *Speculum*, XIX (1944), pp. 13–33.

Willemsen, K. A., *I castelli di Federico II nell'Italia meridionale*, Naples, 1978.

Wille, F., "*Quod sumus hoc eritis:* Die Begegnung von Lebenden und Toten im Regnum der Anjou," *Medien der Macht: Kunst zur Zeit der Anjous in Italien*, ed. T. Michalsky, Berlin, 2001, pp. 225–40.

Wolohojian, S., "Closed Encounters: Female Piety, Art and Visual Experience in the Church of Santa Maria Donna Regina in Naples," Ph.D. Dissertation, Harvard University, 1964.

Zampino, M., "La chiesa vecchia di S. Chiara in Nola," *Atti del V convegno nazionale di storia dell'architettura: Perugia, 23 settembre 1948*, Florence, 1957, pp. 437–50.

———, "Relazione sui restauri," *Il complesso monumentale di Santa Chiara in Napoli*, ed. T. M. Gallino, Naples, 1963, pp. 82–107.

Zeller, G., "Les Rois français candidats à l'Empire," *Revue historique*, CLXXIII (1934), pp. 273–311 and 497–534.

Zigarelli, D. M., *Biografie dei vescovi e arcivescovi della chiesa di Napoli con una descrizione del clero, della cattedrale, della basilica di S. Restituta e della cappella del tesoro di S. Gennaro*, Naples, 1861.

Zigarelli, G., *Viaggio storico artistico al reale santuario di Montevergine*, Naples, 1860.

Index

Page numbers in *italics* refer to illustrations